GRIMM LEGACIES

GRIMM LEGACIES

The Magic Spell of the Grimms' Folk and Fairy Tales

Jack Zipes

Princeton University Press
Princeton and Oxford

Copyright © 2015 by Princeton University Press
Published by Princeton University Press, 41 William Street, Princeton, New Jersey 08540
In the United Kingdom: Princeton University Press, 6 Oxford Street, Woodstock, Oxfordshire OX20 1TW

press.princeton.edu

Jacket images: Photograph of Wilhelm and Jacob Grimm by Hermann Biow, 1847. Detail of illustration from "The Frog Prince" by Charles Folkard, orginally published in *Grimm's Fairy Tales*, 1911.

Library of Congress Cataloging-in-Publication Data

Zipes, Jack, 1937–
   Grimm Legacies : the Magic Spell of the Grimms' Folk and Fairy Tales / Jack Zipes.
      pages   cm
   Includes bibliographical references and index.
   ISBN 978-0-691-16058-0 (hardback)
   1. Grimm, Jacob, 1785-1863—Influence. 2. Grimm, Wilhelm, 1786-1859—Influence. 3. Fairy
tales—Germany—History and criticism. 4. Tales—Germany—History and criticism. 5. Folklorists—
Germany. I. Title.
   GR166.Z57 2014
   398.20943—dc23
   2014005508

British Library Cataloging-in-Publication Data is available
This book has been composed in 10.5/13 Minion Pro
Printed on acid-free paper. ∞
Printed in the United States of America
10 9 8 7 6 5 4 3 2 1

For Heinz Rölleke
With great admiration and respect

CONTENTS

LIST OF FIGURES

Legacies and Cultural Heritage

In 2012, the bicentenary year of Jacob and Wilhelm Grimm's first edition of *Kinder- und Hausmärchen* (*Children and Household Tales*), published 1812 and 1815 in two volumes, numerous conferences and individual lectures in Europe and North America were held that commemorated and celebrated the achievement of the Brothers Grimm. Moreover, their tales continued to be honored in 2013 and 2014. Almost all the conferences that I attended produced new insights into the significance of the Grimms' tales from different critical perspectives. Yet, from my own standpoint, it was clear to me that many scholars and critics were not fully aware of the cultural heritage of the Grimms' folk and fairy tales and their impact throughout the world. Therefore, in the talks that I delivered, I concentrated on the different legacies of the Grimms' tales. In my opinion, there are many legacies to consider, not just one. My goal was to test my ideas at the conferences, learn from the critical reception, and then revise my talks after a year to address the question of the legacies of the *Kinder- und Hausmärchen* in greater depth.

Central to my efforts was the question: Did the Grimms consciously begin collecting folk and fairy tales with the intention of bequeathing a legacy that would be cultivated in German-speaking principalities? Related to this question are others such as: What exactly is a legacy? How have the Grimms' tales as legacy been received and honored in Germany up to the present? How have the tales been received as legacies in other countries and regions of the world? As I have stated, it is quite clear that there is more than one legacy. Moreover, it is also clear that the Grimms' intentions were different from the reception and impact that the tales have had, not only in Germany, but also in other parts of the world. And this difference is indeed great.

To give one example: It is impossible in the twenty-first century to think of all the Walt Disney adaptations of fairy tales and their worldwide popularity without the legacy of the Brothers Grimm. In fact, it is, in part thanks to the Disney corporation, impossible to think about the dissemination of fairy tales throughout the world without taking into account the Grimms' collection of tales, even though most of the Grimms' stories were not strictly speaking fairy tales, nor were they intended for children. Through Disney, the Grimms' name has become a household name, a trademark, and a designator in general for fairy tales that are allegedly "appropriate" for children. More than any author or collector of fairy tales, including Charles Perrault and Hans Christian Andersen, the Grimms are totally associated with the fairy-tale genre, and their tales, which have been translated into 150 languages, have seeped into the conscious and subconscious popular memory of people throughout the world.

Some of the ramifications of the Grimms' worldwide influence have been carefully analyzed in a recent book, *Grimms' Tales around the Globe: The Dynamics of Their International Reception* (2014) edited by Vanessa Joosen and Gillian Lathey. However, it is, of course, impossible to study the impact of the Grimms' tales in the cultural heritage of all the countries in which they have had an important reception. Therefore, my present study focuses primarily on the role that the Grimms' tales have played in German-speaking and English-speaking countries. My hope is that my work might pave the way for similar studies about the reception of the Grimms' tales as a legacy in other countries.

Most of the essays in my book were first composed as talks that I held at various conferences and universities in 2012 and 2013. The introduction, "The Vibrant Body of the Grimms' Folk and Fairy Tales, Which Do Not Belong to the Grimms," discusses how the Grimms began developing the corpus of their tales at the beginning of the nineteenth century with the purpose of preserving an ancient tradition of storytelling. The Brothers were among the first scholars to recall and establish the historical tradition of "authentic" folk tales that stemmed from oral storytelling. In the course of their research from 1806 until their deaths, Wilhelm in 1859, and Jacob in 1863, they published seven large editions and ten small editions of folk and fairy tales along with separate volumes of notes that were constantly changed and edited. These are the books that form the body of their work on folk and fairy tales, but it is a live and vibrant body that consists of other books of legends and tales that they collected, edited, and published. In addition, one must take into consideration the 150 or more translations and the Grimms' manuscripts such as the Ölenberg manuscript of 1810 and their posthumous papers. What then, I ask, is the corpus that they left behind them? How are we to appraise the neverending and seemingly eternal reproduction of their tales?

In chapter one, "*German Popular Stories* as Revolutionary Book," I propose that the Grimms' legacy was already undergoing a change during their lifetime, and this change was brought about directly by the influence of a young British lawyer. One of the fascinating aspects of their legacy in English-speaking countries is that the first so-called translation, *German Popular Stories*, by Edgar Taylor, published in 1823 and 1826 in two volumes, generated three major "myths": (1) that the tales were primarily intended for children (which they weren't); (2) that the Grimms themselves collected the tales from peasants, represented by the image of an ideal peasant woman, whom Taylor called Gammer Grethel;

(3) that the tales were German (which they aren't). The great success of Taylor's books with illustrations by the famous caricaturist, George Cruikshank, stimulated the Brothers, especially Wilhelm, to change the format of their tales so that they might find a greater resonance among young readers primarily from middle-class families in German-speaking principalities.

Chapter two, "Hyping the Grimms' Fairy Tales," explores Taylor's influence in greater depth to examine how, without realizing it, the Brothers began embellishing and marketing their tales to seek a greater reading public. There was an overt change in policy that was initiated in 1825, when they decided to publish their Small Edition of fifty tales with illustrations by their brother Ludwig Grimm. It was not a question of money and profit, but the Grimms created more hyperbolic paratexts to their editions with the hope that German folk culture would gain the respect that it deserved. At the same time, they also maintained their scholarly philological approach. However, in the twentieth and twenty-first centuries this marketing strategy also led to a trivialization if not banalization of the tales. So in this chapter, I discuss the ramifications of hyping the Grimms' tales in today's hyperglobalized cultures.

One of the results of the hyping is explored in chapter three, "Americanization of the Grimms' Fairy Tales: Twists and Turns of History," in which I demonstrate that the Grimms' tales have been so thoroughly Americanized that Americans (and people in other countries) are more liable to think that Disney created the Grimms' tales. There is very little information in the United States about the Grimms' lives and their scholarly project of salvaging relics from the past. Their image and their tales have been distorted in the popular memory of Americans, and yet there have been some interesting Americanized innovations and appropriations of their tales that lend them new meanings in the twenty-first century.

Although Germans respond to the Grimms' tales much differently from Americans, there is still a noticeable similarity in the manner in which they have received the tales since 1945. Chapter four, "Two Hundred Years after Once Upon a Time: The Legacy of the Brothers Grimm and Their Tales in Germany," reveals that, even in Germany, there is a tendency either to transform the Grimms' tales into kitsch or to lionize them. While there was a stronger sense of nationalism among the readers of and listeners to the Grimms' tales in the nineteenth and early part of the twentieth century, a sense that the Grimms had contributed to a German national identity, World War II, and the Nazi appropriation of German culture have led to a more nuanced appreciation of the Grimms' tales. German scholars have carefully analyzed this reception history, and therefore, I focus primarily on literary and filmic adaptations of the tales in the twenty-first century and also discuss a few recent scholarly studies that shed new light on the Grimms' legacy.

In chapter five, "How Superheroes Made Their Way into the World of Fairy Tales: The Appeal of Cooperation and Collective Action from the Greek Myths to the Grimms' Tales and Beyond," I deal with an aspect of the tales that has made them memetically relevant in countries throughout the world from the Greco-Roman period to the present. I trace different variants of a particular tale type, "The Extraordinary Companions" (ATU 513), to understand how and why collective action forms the basis of hundreds if not thousands of stories. Greek gods, Japanese samurai, folk heroes, and superheroes share a basic purpose that connects them in remarkable international relationships and networks. I argue that if a particular international tale type such as the Grimms' "How Six Made Their Way in the World" sticks in people's memories throughout the world, there should be an evolutionary explanation for this relevance, and here I endeavor to connect the tale to our innate human disposition for cooperation.

Chapter six, "The Grimmness of Contemporary Fairy Tales: Exploring the Legacy of the Brothers Grimm in the Twenty-First Century," is a critique of the manner in which numerous contemporary English-speaking writers and artists have adapted the Grimms' tales. There is, of course, no right way to rewrite the Grimm's tales, but I maintain that one can discern whether the Grimms' legacy is abused by writers, artists, and filmmakers. Basically I ask the questions: What is an authentic adaptation? Who does and who doesn't take the Grimms' tales seriously? Have the Grimms' tales become merchandise? Is it possible to cultivate a genuine legacy when the Grimms made their legacy somewhat ambivalent?

The epilogue, "A Curious Legacy: Ernst Bloch's Enlightened View of the Fairy Tale and Utopian Longing," concludes this book with a philosophical discussion about the utopian quality of the Grimms' tales and what role utopian longing plays in the legacy and tradition of the Grimms' tales, and is an essential element in the magic appeal of fairy tales in general. Here I recount an interview about fairy tales that Bloch, the great German philosopher of hope, had with Theodor Adorno, the most astute member of the Frankfurt School of critical theory. Both were familiar with the Grimms' tales, and ironically, though they were often at odds with one another in their writing about aesthetics and politics, they come to more or less the same conclusion in this conversation and reinforce some of the underlying notions that the Grimms had as they began to collect their tales some two hundred years ago.

As I have stated earlier, the essays in this book were first delivered in different versions as talks at Harvard University, Lisbon University, the University of Ghent, Kingston University, the University of Chichester, the Folklore Society (London), the Goethe Institute (Chicago), Miami University (Ohio), Göttingen University, the University of Winnipeg, and Homerton College (Cambridge University). Thanks to the invitations by colleagues from these institutions, I was able to share and discuss my ideas with different audiences of students, professors, and people interested in the Grimms, and thanks to their suggestions and critical responses, I altered and modified the talks as I began to transform them later into essays. At times I have been compelled to repeat information that I present in one chapter in another. I have endeavored to keep this repetition to a minimum, but sometimes it is unavoidable because the theses of the original talks depended on some of the same basic material.

Numerous friends and scholars have made suggestions that have helped me reevaluate my ideas, and they have also provided me with important information and materials. I should therefore like to express my gratitude to Maria Tatar, Francisco Vaz da Silva, Vanessa Joosen, Stijn Praet, Caroline Oates, Bill Gray, Andrew Teverson, Marina Warner, Irmi Maunu-Kocian, Wolfgang Mieder, Todd Cesaratto, Ulrich Marzolph, Pauline Greenhill, Karin Kukkonen, Morag Styles, and Maria Nikolajeva. In addition, I have benefited greatly from conversations and correspondence with Cristina Bacchilega, Sadhana Naithani, Don Haase, Pat Ryan, Mike Wilson, Mick Gowar, and David Hopkin. At the beginning of this project I was given wise counsel and encouragement by Alison MacKeen, and when Alison left Princeton, Anne Savarese graciously and seamlessly stepped in to become my editor and has been an enormous help to me. Sara Lerner has waved her magic wand as usual to make sure the production of the book went as smoothly as possible, while Jennifer Harris has provided careful and insightful copy-editing. Last but not least, I want to thank my wife, Carol Dines, who has been a great inspiration throughout the past thirty years.

GRIMM LEGACIES

INTRODUCTION

The Vibrant Body of the Grimms' Folk and Fairy Tales, Which Do Not Belong to the Grimms

The example of the Brothers Grimm had its imitators even in Russia, including the person of the first editor of Russian Folk Tales, *A. N. Afanasyev. From the viewpoint of contemporary folkloristics, even a cautious reworking and stylization of the texts, written down from their performers, is considered absolutely inadmissible in scientific editions. But in the era of the Brothers Grimm, in the world of romantic ideas and principles, this was altogether permissible. To the credit of the Brothers Grimm, it must be added that they were almost the first to establish the principle of publication of the authentic, popular oral poetic productions.*

—Y. M. Sokolov, *Russian Folklore* (1966)[1]

It is the brothers Jacob and Wilhelm Grimm who illustrate the connection between folklore and textual criticism most powerfully, just as they demonstrate the continuing influence of Herder on thought. Nationalist politics and folkloric endeavours intertwine throughout all the Grimm brothers' projects, but the Europe-wide significance of the Kinder- und Hausmärchen *(first edition 1812) was the inspiration it provided to proto-folklorists to go out and collect "vom Volksmund," that is from the mouth of the people (whether or not this was the Grimms' own practice).*

—Timothy Baycroft and David Hopkin, *Folklore and Nationalism in Europe During the Long Nineteenth Century* (2012)[2]

Just what is a legacy, and what was the corpus of folk and fairy tales that the Brothers Grimm passed on to the German people—a corpus that grew, expanded, and eventually spread itself throughout the world? What do we mean when we talk about cultural legacy and memory? Why have the Grimms' so-called German tales spread throughout the world and become so universally international? Have the Grimms' original intentions been betrayed? Did they betray them? If we fail to address these questions, the cultural legacy of the Grimms' tales and their relevance cannot be grasped. This does not mean that there are right and wrong answers. Rather, the questions set a framework for inquiry that will lead to greater insight into the Grimms' legacies, for there is more than just one that they bequeathed to the German people.

There are several definitions of legacy in the *Oxford Universal Dictionary*, and the most pertinent one for my purposes concerns legacy as a bequest: "what one bequeaths . . . anything handed down by an ancestor or a predecessor."[3] But legacy also carries with it a notion of binding or connecting something to someone as in the Italian verb *legare*—to bind, to connect, to attach. And I want to suggest that the Grimms bound themselves to a German popular tradition of storytelling through the collecting of tales that belonged to the German people. Whether these tales actually belonged to the German people is irrelevant here because the Grimms assumed that these tales, largely gathered on Hessian and Westphalian soil, emanated from the lips of German people, primarily from the lower classes but also from the upper classes. What counts is their assumption, and what counts is their firm belief in the ancient origins of storytelling. What counts is that they wanted to discover and forge a German heritage that had greater cultural value than they realized. The Grimms wanted to save the folk and fairy tales from extinction and to bequeath this *Naturpoesie* as a gift to the German people of all social classes. Here is what they state in the first volume of the first edition of 1812:

> We have tried to grasp and interpret these tales as purely as possible. In many of them one will find that the narrative is interrupted by rhymes and verses that even possess clear alliteration at times but are never sung during the telling of a tale, and these are precisely the oldest and best tales. No incident has been added or embellished and changed, for we would have shied away from expanding tales already so rich in and of themselves with their own analogies and similarities. They cannot be invented. In this regard no collection like this one has yet to appear in Germany. The tales have almost always been used as stuff to create longer stories which have been arbitrarily expanded and changed depending on their value. They have always been ripped from the hands of children even though they belonged to them, and nothing was given back to them in return. Even those people who thought about the children could not restrain themselves from mixing in mannerisms

of contemporary writing. Diligence in collecting has almost always been lacking. Just a few, noted by chance, were immediately published. Had we been so fortunate to be able to tell the tales in a very particular dialect they would have undoubtedly gained a great deal. Here we have a case where all the accomplishments of education, refinement, and artistic command of language ruin everything, and where one feels that a purified literary language as elegant as it may be for everything else, brighter and more transparent, has here, however, become more tasteless and cannot get to the heart of the matter.

We offer this book to well-meaning hands and thereby think chiefly of the blessed power that lies in these hands. We wish they will not allow these tiny morsels of poetry to be kept entirely hidden from poor and modest readers.[4]

And in the preface to the second volume of the first edition published in 1815, they state:

Our collection was not merely intended to serve the history of poetry but also to bring out the poetry itself that lives in it and make it effective: enabling it to bring pleasure wherever it can and also therefore, enabling it to become an actual educational primer. Objections have been raised against this last point because this or that might be embarrassing and would be unsuitable for children or offensive (when the tales might touch on certain situations and relations—even the mentioning of the bad things that the devil does) and that parents might not want to put the book into the hands of children. That concern might be legitimate in certain cases, and then one can easily make selections. On the whole it is certainly not necessary. Nature itself provides our best evidence, for it has allowed these and those flowers and leaves to grow in their own colors and shapes. If they are not beneficial for any person or personal needs, something that the flowers and leaves are unaware of, then that person can walk right by them, but the individual cannot demand that they be colored and cut according to his or her needs. Or, in other words, rain and dew provide a benefit for everything on earth. Whoever is afraid to put plants outside because they might be too delicate and could be harmed and would rather water them inside cannot demand to put an end to the rain and the dew. Everything that is natural can also become beneficial. And that is what our aim should be. Incidentally, we are not aware of a single salutary and powerful book that has edified the people, in which such dubious matters don't appear to a great extent, even if we place the Bible at the top of the list. Making the right use of a book doesn't result in finding evil, rather, as an appealing saying puts it: evidence of our hearts. Children read the stars without fear, while others, according to folk belief, insult angels by doing this.[5]

I have quoted extensively from the two prefaces of the first edition because they significantly embody the early intentions of the Grimms' legacy of tales that they bequeathed to the German people. What is striking, I believe, about their language is their inclination to use metaphors of nature, religion, and education. This is also the language of German romanticism—idealistic and somewhat mystical. For the Grimms the folk and fairy tales were divinely inspired and pure. They evolved organically, encapsulating human experience and behavior, and it was through the common people if not people of all social classes that their "essential" messages were remembered and articulated. These messages contained information and truths about human experience, but they were not didactic commandments or lessons. As I have stated in the introduction to my translation of the first edition of *Kinder- und Hausmärchen* (*Children's and Household Tales*):[6] Though mindful of the educational value of their collection, the Grimms shied away from making the tales in their collection moralistic or overly didactic. They viewed the morality in the tales as naïve and organic, and readers, young and old, could intuit lessons from them spontaneously because of their "pure" poetry.

In his book, *Einfache Formen* (*Simple Forms*, 1930) André Jolles claims that the Grimms saw a paradoxical morality in the miraculous events of folk and fairy tales alike. Jolles writes that the basic foundation of these tales derives from the paradox that the miraculous is not miraculous in the fairy tale; rather it is natural, self-evident, a matter of course. "The miraculous is here the only possible guarantee that the immorality of reality has stopped."[7] The readers' interpretations of folk and fairy tales are natural because of the profound if not divine nature of the tales, and in this sense, the Grimms envisioned themselves as moral cultivators of a particular cultural heritage and their collection as an educational primer of ethics, values, and customs that would grow on readers who would grow by reading these living relics of the past and also by retelling them. In collecting and publishing the tales and all their other philological works, the Grimms were actually returning "gifts" of the people through writing and print that would safeguard folk culture. In addition, their work on the German language and medieval literature contributed to nation building, not through politics but through a profound interdisciplinary and cultural approach to words that tied different Germanic peoples together. Not only did the tales become a great source of cultural memory, but their unusual romantic approach to philology and literature played a great role in forging a new discipline at German universities. As Jeffrey Peck has remarked:

> Any critical history of *Germanistik* that wants to unearth its origins, especially in struggles for national identity, seems always to begin with the Grimm Brothers. The Grimms represent in their work what [Hans Ulrich] Gumbrecht typifies for Romanticism: "National identity—as a representation of collective identity— seems to depend—at least for the early 19th century—on the existence of socially distant folktales and historically distant medieval cultural forms, which can be identified as the objectivations of one's own people." Merely the titles of the Grimms' publications reflect their preoccupation with "the German" and the German past: *German Legends* (2 vols., 1816–18) and their periodical *Old German Woods* (1813–16); Jacob's own projects, *Old German Song* (1811), *German Grammar* (1819–37), *German Monuments of Law* (1828), *German Mythology* (1835), *History of the German language* (2 vols., 1848); and, of course, their well-known *Fairy Tales* and the *German Dictionary*.[8]

The Corpus of the Tales

Here it should be pointed out that the Grimms' tales are not strictly speaking "fairy tales," and they never used that term, which, in German, would be *Feenmärchen*. Their collection is much more diverse and includes animal tales, legends, tall tales, nonsense stories, fables, anecdotes, religious legends, and, of course, magic tales (*Zaubermärchen*), which are clearly related to the great European tradition of fairy tales that can be traced back to ancient Greece and Rome and beyond. It is because their collection had such deep roots and a broad European heritage that the Grimms asserted that reading these tales would serve as an education for young and old alike. In some ways their collection was intended to be part of the European civilizing process, not just a national legacy. It was never intended for children even if it became children's reading matter, something I shall address in chapter one.

In this regard, the corpus of their collected tales was formed to change constantly and to remain alive forever as vital talking points in oral and literary traditions. Collecting was an act of resuscitation. Editing and translating were artistic methods that guaranteed the conservation and communication of the indelible nature of the tales. Incredibly, the pulse of their tales can still be felt today. The magic spell of their tales binds us. Here it is important to note that the legacy of the tales is not the only legacy that the Grimms bequeathed to the German people. One could also study their other legacies with regard to legends (*Deutsche Sagen*, 1816–18), myths (*Deutsche Mythologie*, 1835), linguistics (*Deutsche Grammatik*, 1819–37, and *Deutsches Wörterbuch*, 1854–63), and jurisprudence (*Deutsche Rechtsaltertümer*, 1828). For some scholars, the Grimms' greatest achievement was the creation of the first great *German Dictionary*, but it would be foolish to try to single out the Grimms' most important contribution to the German cultural heritage. Overall their philological, aesthetic, legal, and ethical concerns coalesced in the *Kinder- und Hausmärchen* that absorbed them from 1806 until their deaths in 1859 and 1863.

In Jens Sennewald's highly significant study, *Das Buch das wir sind* ("The Book That We Are"), he explores and explains the intentions and concepts developed by the Grimms as romantic writers and philologists just as Jacob had sought over two hundred years ago to clarify their beliefs and methods to the writer Achim von Arnim,[9] their friend, who provided the contact to Georg August Reimer, the publisher of the first edition of *Kinder- und Hausmärchen* in 1812. Sennewald emphasizes that we must bear in mind that there was not just one edition of their large collection of tales, but seven, and that the narratives, consisting of fairy tales, animal tales, legends, religious stories, fables, tall tales, and anecdotes, were constantly edited and changed over the course of forty-seven years. These seven large editions were part of the Grimms' other linguistic and philological works. Given the Grimms' great erudition and aesthetic concerns, Sennewald maintains that the tales in all the editions need to be considered as a collective whole because these stories, according to the Grimms, originated in antiquity and continued to be formed and reformed in a flowing process of retelling and remaking that enabled words to come alive and remain alive as part of the popular cultural memory. Indeed, the Grimms wanted to resuscitate relics and muted words of the past so that they could speak for themselves. As part of the process, the Grimms saw themselves as excavators and cultivators, who sought to make the past livable for German people of all social classes and enable them to become at one with the words of the tales. This task that the Grimms set for themselves demanded great artistry and philological knowledge. Sennewald remarks:

> The *poetry* of the *Kinder- und Hausmärchen* is the result of their authorship of a "romantic book." Their poetics is stamped by philological poetry: at each turn of speech the "prevailing mark" of the philologists is at work who produced highly poetical texts and

permanently concealed this singular achievement. . . . The *Kinder- und Hausmärchen*, collected by the Brothers Grimm became a "book that we are" through their poetics. The "we" of this book is one of brotherhood, of the "collaterals," as Jacob Grimm wrote. The figures of the *Kinder- und Hausmärchen*, the *female informant* and the *collector* represent a "folk widely speaking," and it seems as if the closed collection, read as ethnographical record, reaches way beyond the borders of the book. Whoever turns to the tales of the "folk" after reading the *Kinder- und Hausmärchen* will find what let him turn to the tales: the structures and regularity of a "romantic book." A research of folk tales that connects itself to the *Kinder- und Hausmärchen* and dedicates itself to finding "original" folk tales that correspond to the "instinctual doings of nature" follows the *prescribed* tracks of the *Kinder- und Hausmärchen*.[10]

The binding element and memetic appeal of the Grimms' legacy is, in my opinion, as strong and as necessary as Sennewald states, and research must account for the widespread reception of their collected tales throughout the world. Legacies are not just bequeathed but require an active chain reaction from generation to generation. They demand accountability of reception. They require that one knows and appreciates the value of the offering or gift, who gave it, and why. Consequently, research into the corpus of the Grimms' legacy must include some basic acknowledgment of the tales' history and how they contributed to the tradition of European folklore and to the study of world folklore. In my opinion, some of the following fundamental aspects of their work and lives are helpful in appreciating their legacy of tales and how this legacy spread beyond German borders:

1. Although the Grimms collected folk songs, poems, and tales before 1807, they became more focused on prose tales at this time and expanded this focus up through 1810 to assist Clemens Brentano, a talented romantic writer and poet, who wanted to adapt oral tales for a book of literary fairy tales that he was planning to publish. The Grimms dutifully sent him fifty-four tales. However, Brentano did not like the Grimms' stories and left behind their manuscript in the Ölenberg Monastery in Alsace. By chance the tales, now called the Ölenberg manuscript, were discovered in 1920. Ever since this discovery researchers have been able to study the manner in which the Grimms began editing and honing the tales.[11] Moreover, as Vanessa Joosen has demonstrated,[12] the Ölenberg manuscript provides the basis not only for understanding the Grimms' process of retelling tales but also serves as a case study of intertexuality and how contemporary writers have followed

in the Grimms' footsteps, so to speak, and developed a dynamic process of retelling fairy tales that enriches the Grimms' legacy.

2. In 1812 Achim von Arnim—another significant romantic writer and friend of Brentano—advised the Grimms to publish the tales they had sent to Brentano along with many new ones that they had collected. Although Arnim had differences with the Grimms when it came to judging modern literature, he had great faith in their project and was a strong proponent of collecting folk material. As a result, the Grimms not only produced one edition of their tales but also published seven different editions of their large collection (called the *große Ausgabe*) from 1812 to 1857, including different prefaces, essays, and scholarly notes, which were first published together with the tales of the first edition and later in separate volumes of 1822 and 1856. There were many unusual variants of the tales in the notes that reveal the Grimms' extraordinary knowledge of different genres of orality and literature throughout the world. Some of the tales in the notes were replaced by other versions in the final edition or published elsewhere. By the final publication of the 1856 edition of the notes, there were many new tales as well as numerous variants and rough drafts in their posthumous papers.

3. In addition to the Large Edition there were ten different printings of their Small Edition (called the *kleine Ausgabe*) published from 1825 to 1858. The tales in the Small Edition were carefully selected by Wilhelm Grimm to appeal to bourgeois children and their families and included six illustrations by their brother Ludwig Grimm, a painter. There were no prefaces, notes, or long essays in the ten printings of the Small Edition. The intention here was to popularize their tales and to appeal to a growing reading public of children and their families.

4. The posthumous papers of the Grimms contain a large quantity of tales that the Brothers received from friends and colleagues or collected themselves. For some reason or other, they did not want to use these tales in the published corpus of their collections. Heinz Rölleke has reproduced many of these interesting tales in *Märchen aus dem Nachlaß der Brüder Grimm*,[13] and there have been several other books of omitted or deleted tales published from the Grimms' posthumous papers that are worth examining as part of the Grimms' legacy, including an English translation and tales that appeared in journals and magazines but are not the same as those published in the large editions of the collection.[14]

5. Although the Grimms maintained that they did not alter the words of the tales that they collected from the lips of their informants, and that all their

tales stemmed from the oral tradition, none of this is true. A simple comparison of the tales in the Ölenberg manuscript of 1810 with the tales in the first edition of 1812/15 reveals that the Grimms made or had to make substantial changes because it was difficult for them and their contributors to copy down on paper the exact words of the tales that they heard. Moreover, the Grimms also began adapting tales from books published from the fifteenth through the eighteenth century. In short, none of their tales could ever be designated as "pure," "authentic," or "original." The Grimms actually knew this, and yet they used those terms because they believed their tales bore the traces of a profound oral tradition. They felt justified to proclaim that their tales were "genuine" and "pure" because the changes that they made were based on their understanding of the "natural" poetics of oral storytelling, and the more they did research about the oral tradition, the more they felt confident in their skills as writers to re-present the unique elements of traditional stories. Incidentally, most collectors worked this way in the eighteenth and nineteenth centuries.

6. During the first phase of their collecting tales from 1806 up to approximately 1817, Jacob Grimm was the dominant figure and more or less established the principles of their collecting and recording of tales. For instance, more than 60 percent of the tales in the Ölenberg manuscript are in his handwriting, and it is apparent from letters, prefaces, and essays that his ideological thinking set the tone for their project that he developed collectively with his brother, other interested scholars, and friends. Both Brentano and Arnim were enthusiastic about the Grimms' desire to collect oral folk tales and publish them either in a journal or book dedicated to old German literature. In a long letter to Brentano, written on January 22, 1811, Jacob composed an appeal, "Aufforderung an die gesammten Freunde altdeutscher Poesie und Geschichte erlassen" ("Appeal to All Friends of Old German Poetry and History"),[15] which spelled out the initial premises of the Brothers' project and their intense engagement to foster a greater understanding of popular German culture. Here are some of the emphatic romantic ideas from this letter that were to underlie all their work on folk and fairy tales:

> We are going to start by collecting all the oral tales from the entire German fatherland and only wish that we do not misconstrue the general and extensive sense of the matter by the manner in which we are approaching it. We are thus going to collect each and every tradition and tale of the common man whether the contents be sad or humorous, didactic or amusing, no matter what the time

period is, whether they have been composed in the simplest prose or set in rhyme. . . .

Isn't folk poetry (*Volkspoesie*) the vital lifeblood that is drawn from all the deeds [of the German people] and continues to exist for itself? And mustn't it do so because otherwise no history would reach the folk and no other kind of history would be used by the folk? . . .

We especially mean here the fairy tales, the evening conversations, and the stories from the spinning rooms, and we know two kinds of things very well. Names held in contempt and things that have been ignored until now continue to stick in each and every human mind from childhood to death. Consequently, we think that even in the locked-up energy of the special social classes, like beneath the cool shadow of the tree, that the source of tales cannot vanish, while whatever lies in the middle, where the general heat of the sun flows, has long since been dried out. Certainly, among old craftsmen, silently working miners, and the green free foresters and soldiers many peculiarities and particular ways of conversing and telling stories, customs and manners have continued to be maintained, and it is high time that they are collected before they are completely extinguished or new forms of those traditions have their meaning torn away from them. . . .

Now we want to record all this as faithfully and literally as possible, with all the so-called nonsense that is easy to find but always even easier to cast off than the artificial reproduction which one would want to try instead of keeping the nonsense.[16]

The ideas in this private letter to Brentano, read and approved by Wilhelm, were more fully developed later in the *Circular wegen der Aufsammlung der Volkspoesie* (*Circular-Letter Concerned with Collecting of Folk Poetry*) printed and distributed in 1815. It is worth citing this circular-letter, once again conceived by Jacob, because it outlines the basic principles and intentions of the Grimms:

Most Honored Sir!

A society has been founded that is intended to spread throughout all of Germany and has as its goal to save and collect all the existing songs and tales that can be found among the common German peasantry (*Landvolk*). Our fatherland is still filled with this wealth of material all over the country that our honest ancestors planted for us, and that, despite the mockery and derision heaped upon it, continues to live, unaware of its own hidden beauty and carries within it its own unquenchable source. Our literature, history, and language cannot seriously be understood in their old and true origins without doing more exact research on this material. Consequently, it is our intention to track down as diligently as possible all the following items and to write them down as faithfully as possible:

1. Folk songs and rhymes, that are performed at different occasions throughout the year, at celebrations, in spinning parlors, on the dance floors, and during work in the fields; first of all, those songs and rhymes that have epic contents, that is, in which there is an event; wherever possible with their very words, ways, and tones.

2. Tales in prose that are told and known, in particular the numerous nursery and children's fairy tales about giants, dwarfs, monsters, enchanted and rescued royal children, devils, treasures, and magic instruments as well as local legends that help explain certain places (like mountains, rivers, lakes, swamps, ruined castles, towers, stones, and monuments of ancient times). It is important to pay special attention to animal fables, in which fox and wolf, chicken, dog, cat, frog, mouse, crow, sparrow, etc. appear for the most part.

3. Funny tales about tricks played by rogues and anecdotes; puppet plays from old times with Hanswurst and the devil.

4. Folk festivals, mores, customs, and games; celebrations at births, weddings, and funerals; old legal customs, special taxes, duties, jobs, border regulations, etc.

5. Superstitions about spirits, ghosts, witches, good and bad omens; phenomena and dreams.

6. Proverbs, unusual dialects, parables, word composition.

It is extremely important that these items are to be recorded faithfully and truly, without embellishment and additions, whenever possible from the mouths of the tellers in and with their very own words in the most exact and detailed way. It would be of double value if everything could be obtained in the local live dialect. On the other hand, even fragments with gaps are not to be rejected. Indeed, all the derivations, repetitions, and copies of the same tale can be individually important. Here we advise that you not be misled by the deceptive opinion that something has already been collected and recorded, and therefore that you discard a story. Many things that appear to be modern have often only been modernized and have their undamaged source beneath it. As soon as one has a great familiarity with the contents of this folk literature (*Volkspoesie*), one will gradually be able to evaluate the alleged simplistic, crude and even repulsive aspects more discreetly. In general the following should still be noted: although actually every area should be completely searched and explored, there are preferential places more deserving than the large cities and the towns, than the villages, and these are the places in the quiet and untouched woods and mountains that are fruitful and blessed. The same is the case with certain classes of people such as the shepherds, fishermen, miners—they have a stronger attachment to these tales, and these people are to be preferred and asked as are in general old people, women, and children, who keep the tales fresh in their memories.

You have been selected to become a member of this society, my honored Sir, and to lend a helping hand in the firm conviction that you will be moved by the usefulness and emergency of our purpose, that today cannot be postponed without great harm in view of the increasing and damaging decline and closure of folk customs. We hope that you will be in a position to explore the region of _____ according to our intention.[17]

From the very beginning of their project, the Grimms worked collectively. They had already collaborated with Brentano and Arnim on their important collection of folk songs, *Des Knaben Wunderhorn* (1805–8), and they had formed a pact never to separate and share their ideas. They spent their entire lives in constant contact with colleagues who were developing the field of folklore and literature at universities, schools, and other institutions. Their correspondence is immense. As the corpus of the *Kinder- und Hausmärchen* expanded and grew in stature, they were very much dependent on friends and colleagues who often had more intimate contacts with lower-class people, considered by the Grimms to be the primary source of folk and fairy tales. This dependence raises some questions: Were the Grimms bestowing a legacy on the German people that was not theirs to give? Did they pay due homage to the people who told them or sent them tales? Did they appropriate the tales to transform them into entertaining stories for a middle-class reading audience that would include children?

Collecting is never a neutral endeavor, and over a period of approximately fifty years, the Grimms were socially and personally "involved" in the tales that they selected for editing and publishing in their different editions. In other words, what Pierre Bourdieu has termed a *habitus* played a major role in the orientation of the Grimms' tales that they made their own but were originally not their own and that they returned to the German people to share as a common heritage. Bourdieu has explained that a person's comportment depends on his or her habitus, which is a set of acquired dispositions determined at first by the social class, ethnicity, nationality, and religion of the family into which one is born. A child will internalize the dispositions at the same time that he or she is structuring the dispositions (gestures; tastes of dress, music, literature; speech and accents; and so on) to form his/her identity under the conditions of a particular civilizing process.[18] In the case of the Grimms it is important to know that they were born into a solid middle-class family in the small town of Hanau in Hessia. They could speak and read the Hessian dialect, which colored their own high German accents and use of language, and were raised with the expectation that they would attend a university and become lawyers like their father. They were honest and diligent Calvinists, extremely loyal to their family, especially after their father's early death in 1796. His death caused a traumatic fall in social class, and the Grimms became dependent on friends and relatives. The Brothers realized that only through hard work would they be able to reclaim their social position, so to speak. The region of Kassel played a role in the formation of their habitus. Like most principalities, Kassel was a monarchy and remained patriarchal and hierarchical during their youth. The Napoleonic Wars affected the people of Kassel, and at one time the city was occupied by the French. The Brothers attended the University of Marburg from 1802 and 1806, and the family lived under severe pecuniary conditions. Despite hardships, they became known as assiduous and ambitious scholars and formed important friendships, especially with one of their professors, Friedrich Carl von Savigny. After their mother's death in 1808, Jacob became the virtual head of the family at twenty-three, and for both Wilhelm and Jacob, it became extremely important to support all their siblings and to provide a cooperative home atmosphere. Fidelity, piety, cooperation, faithfulness, industry, purity, naturalness, dedication, patriarchy marked their characters. I do not want to create an image of them as good boy scouts. On the other hand, it is important to emphasize that the Brothers were honorable men with an idealistic bent and a clear compassion for common German people struggling to find their places when Germany was divided into numerous principalities, wars were fought, and promises of freedom by the ruling aristocracies, not kept. I mention all these factors that contributed to the formation of the Grimms' habitus because they chose the tales and began sorting the tales that they wanted to publish from an orientation strongly influenced by the Protestant ethic and patriarchal viewpoint that shaped their sense of social justice. They infused their chosen tales with their own beliefs, styles, and ideological preferences. At the same time, it was through their selected tales that voices of "other" people managed to speak.

In a very insightful essay about the significance of the rise of the Grimms from an impoverished middle-class family and from a status as genial amateur antiquarians to eminent professors of philology, Joep Leerrssen makes the point that

> The amateur antiquary of the eighteenth century now begins to fulfil a public role in connecting the nation with its cultural roots; thus the professionalization of the historical and philological sciences goes tightly in hand with the national instrumentalization of ancient vernacular culture. The career of Jacob Grimm is exemplary in this process. [And the same could be said for Wilhelm.] He owes his special status to the fact that his name became linked to the regular sets of consonantal shifts now known as "Grimm's laws." As such he is the standard-bearer of the new climate of scientific philology. His influence spread far and wide from the fairytale- and folksong-collecting of Lönnrot, La Villemarqué, Karadžić, Afanas'ev, and Croker to the troubadour studies of Diez, and from the Slavic philology of Dobrovský and Kopitar to the great national dictionary projects of the *Oxford English Dictionary* and the *Woordenboek der Nederlandsche Taal*. If any individual man of letters was responsible for the idea, general all over Europe from the late nineteenth century onwards, that language, culture, and identity amounted to the same thing, it was he.[19]

The majority of the other people who contributed tales to the Grimms' early collection was relatively small and located either in or nearby Kassel or in Bökendorf near Münster in Westphalia. Two of the exceptional storytellers from the lower classes were Johann Friedrich Krause, a poor retired soldier, who lived in the nearby village of Hoof, and Dorothea Viehmann, married to a village tailor in Zwehren outside Kassel. Krause contributed seven texts, of which only four were published, that frequently focused on discharged and badly treated soldiers and animals in need.[20] The Grimms deleted some of his tales or combined them with others because they were a bit raw and radical in tone. Dorothea Viehmann differed from most of the informants, who were young women from educated middle-class or aristocratic families.[21] She was considered the exemplary peasant storyteller, and her image, based on a drawing by Ludwig Grimm, was published

Figure 1. Dorothea Viehmann, the ideal peasant storyteller. Drawing by Ludwig Grimm.

as the frontispiece to the second volume of the second edition of 1819 (figure 1). She was called the "Märchenfrau" (representative of the typical fairy-tale story-teller similar to mother goose), and the Brothers Grimm sought to validate the genuine nature of their folk tales with her picture as a "mythic" peasant woman.[22] Indeed, she was from the lower classes and poor, but she was not typical of the storytellers who contributed tales to the first edition. On the other hand, she was perhaps the most gifted storyteller the Grimms had ever met, and they described her in full in the preface to the second volume of the *Kinder- und Hausmärchen*:

> One of our lucky coincidences involved making the acquaintance with a peasant woman from the village of Zwehrn near Kassel. It was through her that we received a considerable number of the tales published here that can be called genuinely Hessian and are also supplements to the first volume. This woman, still active and not much over fifty years old, is called Viehmann, and she has a firmly set and pleasant face with bright, clear eyes and had probably been beautiful in her youth. She has retained these old stories firmly in her memory, a gift which she says is not granted to everyone. Indeed, many people can't even retain any tales, while she narrates in a manner that is thoughtful, steady, and unusually lively. Moreover, she takes great pleasure in it.[23]

Viehmann, who contributed forty tales from her repertoire to the Grimms' collection, was raised in an inn, and some of her ancestors stemmed from French Huguenot and Dutch families. Born in 1755, she worked in her father's inn, where she undoubtedly heard many of her tales, and she lived with her family until she married in 1795. She had six children with her husband, Nikolaus Viehmann, and when the Grimms met her, she was very poor and sold vegetables at a market in Kassel to help her family. Her tales can be considered a blend of stories marked by oral traditions in France, the Netherlands, and Hessia. What is striking about her tales such as "The Lazy Spinner," "The Goose Maid," and "The Clever Farmer's Daughter" is her the depiction of courageous, if not feisty, young women. In addition, many of her tales such as "Clever Else," "The Young Giant," "Doctor-Know-It-All," and "The Devil's Sooty Brother" are parodies and humorous portrayals of peasant life.

In contrast to Viehmann, the middle-class young ladies in Kassel told tales that stemmed either from a French literary tradition, from tales they heard from their nannies, or from stories they had read on some occasion. Among the storytellers in Rudolf Wild's family—he was a well-to-do pharmacist—were Lisette, Johanna, Gretchen, Mimi, and Dortchen, mainly in their teens or early twenties; they lived in Kassel, and Wilhelm eventually married Dortchen, the most prolific of the storytellers. Interestingly, they generally spoke in the local Hessian dialect, and together they produced about forty tales for the Grimms, who did not publish all of them. As for preferences, Dortchen often favored tales that reflected sibling rivalry between sisters such as "The Three Little Men in the Forest" and "Mother Holle," and the Wild family as a whole had a strong sense of social justice.

The group of young women in the Hassenpflug family, whose father, Johannes Hassenpflug, was the governmental president of Kassel, consisted of Marie, Jeanette, and Amalie. They spoke French at home and were clearly influenced by reading or hearing French fairy tales. They contributed over thirty stories and may have heard some from an elderly housekeeper by the name of Marie Müller. They generally spoke in a Hessian dialect and mixed German with French stories. The most gifted of the Hassenpflug sisters was Marie,[24] who was responsible for tales that reflected a preference for happy ends in which a female protagonist weds a prince after many difficulties such as "Little Brother and Little Sister," "Snow White," "Briar Rose," and "The Maiden without Hands." In most of her tales such as "The Robber Bridegroom" and "The Carnation," the female protagonist survives ordeals thanks to her courage.

The von Haxthausen family lived on an estate in Westphalia called Bökendorf. Wilhelm met Werner von Haxthausen in 1808 during a cure in Halle, where they developed a warm friendship despite major class differences. Later Wilhelm was invited to Bökendorf, and it was there that the Grimms collected over eighty tales either verbally or through letters. The contributors were Marianne, Ludowine, Anna, and August and their cousin Jenny von Droste-Hülshoff. Many of the tales were told to the young ladies and August by servants, farmers, and craftsmen, and they recorded them for the Grimms, several in a low German dialect (*plattdeutsch*). The entire family was very interested in folk literature and culture and helped Jacob in his compilation of German legends. Aside from the social circles in Kassel and Bökendorf, there were other significant informants such as Friederike Mannel, a minister's daughter in nearby Allendorf, who sent eight beautifully written tales to Wilhelm, and Friedrich Siebert, a teacher, rector of a school in Treysa, and friend of the Grimms, who provided ten tales.

As Heinz Rölleke has amply demonstrated in two books that deal with the informants and sources of the Grimms' tales,[25] it is extremely difficult to determine the provenance of a Grimms' tale because most of the informants obtained them from some other source through either oral or written transmission. What appears to be clear is that there is a strong "underdog" perspective in the first edition of the tales, in which most of the protagonists are peasant women and men, shoemakers, tailors, soldiers, shepherds, carpenters, smiths, spinners, servants, millers, country bumpkins, hunchbacks, and so on. Even the animals are mostly "underdogs" or threatened with extinction. In addition, there is an abundant number of tales with kings, queens, princes, princesses, wicked stepmothers, giants, dwarfs, and nixies in which princes and princesses are unjustly treated or oppressed. A good many of the tales deal with persecuted young women such as "Maiden without Hands" or third sons called simpletons who prove that they are clever and can overcome obstacles to survive and become happy. In short, we have a situation in which the Grimms "appropriate" tales that do not really belong to the people who tell them but who share the "underdog" perspective. The Grimms, too, shared this viewpoint, but they did make changes connected to their habitus so that their perspective could be added to the hypothetical social class view of the narrator. This constant change of perspective is typical of storytelling in general and is even the case with the two major lower-class storytellers, Dorothea Viehmann and Johann Friedrich Krause, as well with the painter Philipp Otto Runge, who provided the Grimms with two tales in a Hamburg and Pomeranian dialect, "The Juniper Tree" and "The Fisherman's Wife." It is well-known that Runge stylized the tales that he sent to the Grimms, and the Grimms also touched up the tales. Interestingly, both tales concern the plight of lower-class families in which a woman seeks to become as powerful as God, and a boy is transformed into a bird after his murder and then takes revenge on his wicked stepmother. The fisherman's wife must return to a pisspot at the end of her tale because she is too arrogant, while the boy is miraculously reunited with his father who had unknowingly eaten him.

These tales that were not the Grimms' tales—that is, all the tales in their corpus were not theirs and were not even the property of the informants—fascinated the Brothers, and they felt that the unique qualities of the tales ultimately came from some divine source. They also believed that the common people were the carriers of these narratives. This is the reason why they insisted on their purity while rewriting or even censoring them so that the stories would illuminate and enlighten readers. Moreover, to their credit, the Grimms brought diverse tales in dialogue with one another and let them "speak" different views within the corpus of their editions. That the Grimms' habitus had to play a role in their preferences and embellishments is to be expected. What could not have been anticipated was the growing popularity of their collection. After the second Small Edition was published in 1836 and the third Large Edition was published in 1837, the *Kinder- und Hausmärchen* gradually became a bestseller in German-speaking principalities and remains a bestseller today.

Ironically, if it were not for the remarkable artistic talent of Wilhelm Grimm, it is conceivable that the *Kinder- und Hausmärchen* might never have become a household favorite in Germany. Just compare the three different beginnings of "The Frog King" in the Ölenberg manuscript of 1810, in the first edition of 1815, and in the seventh edition of 1857:

The Frog King (1810)

The king's youngest daughter went outside into the forest and sat down on the edge of a cool well. Then she took a golden ball and played with it. Suddenly it rolled down into the well. She watched as it sank into the deep water and stood at the well and was very sad. All at once a frog stuck its head out of the water and said, "Why are you moaning so much?"[26]

The Frog King (1812)

Once upon a time there was a princess who went out into the forest and sat down at the edge of a cool well. She had a golden ball that was her most favorite plaything. She threw it up high and caught it in the air and was delighted by all this. One time the ball flew quite high, and as she stretched out her hand and bent her fingers to catch it again, the ball hit the ground near her and rolled and rolled until it fell right into the water.

The princess was horrified as she watched it, but the well was so deep that she couldn't see the bottom. Then she began to weep miserably and to moan: "Oh, if only I had my ball again! I'd give anything—my clothes, my jewels, my pearls and anything else in the world—to get my ball back!"

As she sat there grieving, a frog stuck its head out of the water and said: "Why are you weeping so miserably?"[27]

The Frog King (1857)

In olden times, when wishing still helped, there lived a king whose daughters were all beautiful, but the youngest was so beautiful that the sun itself, which had seen so many things, was always filled with amazement each time it cast its rays upon her face. Now, there was a great dark forest near the king's castle, and in this forest, beneath an old linden tree, was a well. Whenever the days were very hot, the king's daughter would go into this forest and sit down by the edge of the cool well. If she became bored, she would take her golden ball, throw it into the air, and catch it. More than anything else she loved playing with this ball.

One day it so happened that the ball did not fall back into the princess's little hand as she reached out to catch it. Instead, it bounced right by her and rolled straight into the water. The princess followed it with her eyes, but the ball disappeared, and the well was deep, so very deep that she couldn't see the bottom. She began to cry, and she cried louder and louder, for there was nothing that could comfort her. As she sat there grieving over her loss, a voice called out to her, "What's the matter, Princess? Your tears could move even a stone to pity."[28]

The ornate descriptive changes made by Wilhelm transform the tale, originally told by one of the Wild sisters, into an elegant, somewhat sentimental tale that celebrates the reincarnation of a cursed prince, the strange reward of a princess, who does not totally obey her father, and the faithfulness of a servant. The driving force of the narrative consists of the frog, desperate to be released from a magic spell, and the authoritarian king/father, who insists that the princess behave correctly and keep her word. The basic plot of the tale follows a pattern deeply ingrained in the European storytelling tradition of the beast/bridegroom type, generally categorized by folklorists as ATU 425 or 440.[29] It is not clear how old this tale type is, but it is clearly related to ancient beast/bridegroom stories and initiation rituals that involve a young maiden overcoming her fear of sexual intercourse. One of the first written versions in Latin appeared in Berthold von Regensburg's thirteenth-century *Rusticanus de sanctis*. The Grimms thought that this tale type was one of the oldest and most beautiful in the world, and it was therefore placed as number one in their collection from the first edition of 1812 to the seventh and final edition of 1857. Their interest in the tale was so great that they published a second variant in 1815 in the second volume of their first edition.

The original draft for the Grimms' versions of the "Frog King" tales was probably provided by a member of the Wild family in 1810. By 1810 the Grimms were well aware of other late medieval versions, especially the Scottish one published in John Bellenden's *The Complaynt of Scotlande* (1548), as well as tales contributed by Marie Hassenpflug and the family von Haxthausen. The editing changes made by Wilhelm Grimm from 1819 to 1857 indicate that he was anxious to de-eroticize the tale and to emphasize the moral of listening to the father and keeping one's promises.

From approximately 1815 to 1857 Wilhelm took charge of the changing corpus of the tales that the Brothers collected. Remarking on how Wilhelm edited "The Frog King," Siegfried Neumann states: "The Grimm fairy-tale style is fully developed here. But what also clearly emerges is Wilhelm's manner and art of narration, which seek—in this case to the extreme—to plumb the fairy-tale events down to their very details. One can respond to the result in two ways—by lamenting the loss of the folktale's simplicity, or by welcoming the poetic enrichment. In any case, these examples clearly demonstrate the growth of an aesthetically oriented attitude."[30]

It is well-known that Wilhelm went so far as to include his version of a literary tale, "Snow White and Rose Red," taken from a book by Karoline Stahl,[31] in the *Kinder- und Hausmärchen* in 1837. He had first published it in Wilhelm Hauff's journal, *Mährchen-Almanach*, in 1827, and it, too, represents the charming Biedermeier style and perspective that Wilhelm brought to both oral and literary stories that the Grimms gathered. The Biedermeier period (1815–48) in the German principalities was marked by a petty bourgeois taste for coziness and hominess, and in literature the Biedermeier style manifested itself by a charming, sometimes elegant simplicity that aroused and pacified heartfelt emotions. Biedemeier writing was comforting and comfortable. It would be perhaps an exaggeration to associate Wilhelm's style completely with Biedermeier characteristics that one can find throughout Ludwig Bechstein's saccharine fairy tales in *Deutsches Märchenbuch* (1845), *Ludwig Bechsteins Märchenbuch* (1853), and *Neues Deutsches Märchenbuch* (1856). Once more popular than the Grimms, Bechstein is practically forgotten today. Wilhelm differs from Bechstein in that he endeavored to capture the quaint folk "undertones" of the tales and to respect the orality of the tales. But he certainly shied away from provocative subjects and vulgarity in editing the tales and added a good deal of Christian sentiment to them along with more than 400 pleasant proverbs and sayings from the German language. The result in the final edition of 1857 is a corpus of mixed tales with voices from unknown people, voices and styles of specific friends and colleagues, and the voices of Wilhelm and Jacob, who initially sought to re-create oral tales with sincere fidelity and model them on the dialect tales, "The Juniper Tree" and "The Fisherman's Wife." Neumann concludes his essay on their collecting by stating:

> With a remarkable feel for the nature of folk literature, the Brothers Grimm collected as much of the oral narrative tradition and documented it as "faithfully" and as comprehensively as was possible for them under the existing conditions. The *Kinder- und Hausmärchen* became a worldwide success "because here for the first time significant national and international traditions of the intellectual culture from the broadest spectrum of the folk appeared elevated to the level and clothed in the language of 'belle lettres,' without their content or message having been altered" (*Geschichte der deutschen Volksdichtung*, 90).[32]

Tradition, Nationalism, and Legacy

The Brothers were aware from the very beginning that they were bequeathing their collected tales to a growing literate Germanic public; they endeavored to make these people more aware of popular culture in the German principalities. By doing this—bequeathing a legacy that was not really theirs to bequeath—they helped to create a new tradition of folklore that had a nationalist tinge to it. They often used the term "Vaterland" when talking about the German principalities as a whole, supported the movement to unite German principalities, and wanted to create more respect for human rights in all the German principalities. They were loyal to their monarch in Kassel, but left their jobs as librarians in 1828 when they felt they were not appreciated by the king and his councilors. Fortunately, they were offered excellent positions at the University of Göttingen, but after teaching nine years as professors, they defended their constitutional rights by refusing to sign an arbitrary oath to the King of Hannover and were consequently banished in 1837 from the University of Göttingen. Later, when they were in Berlin in the 1840s, they expressed their sympathies for the 1848 revolutionaries, and Jacob had a place of honor in Frankfurt am Main at a meeting of the revolutionary delegates. But the Grimms were never radical. They believed more in a constitutional monarchy than in a republican government. They believed more in words and in an ideal concept of the German *Volk*, which, in reality, did not exist. What did exist in reality, however, were Germans living in different regions of central Europe, people who lived and worked under oppressive regimes, and to a certain extent, the Grimms' work in folklore was an endeavor to bring these different Germans together by enabling them to recognize the cultural value of their tales and customs. In this respect, the collecting of tales embodied a romantic wish-fulfillment dream that would unite the German people and bind them to a culture that they could honor. Their collecting had nothing to do with children or children's literature or simply "entertaining" adult readers. It had everything to do with "artistically" creating a German popular culture rooted in the belief systems and customs of the German people.

The Grimms made it clear in public statements such as the *Circular Letter* and in correspondence with friends, especially Achim von Arnim, and colleagues that their collection was *not* intended for children. The word *Kinder* (children) in the title of *Kinder- und Hausmärchen* did not mean that their tales were for or about children or domestic, rather it signified that the stories were innocent, naïve, and pure, to be appreciated and cared for like children. In their opinion, these tales were produced by common people and needed to be preserved to give the German people a sense of moral German values. These tales were designated to provide narratives of self-education largely for adult readers. If the tales were read by children, all the better. But they were not the Grimms' intended readership. In the second volume of the second edition of 1819, they wrote a very long academic essay about children's beliefs and customs that no child would have ever wanted to read but that serious scholars would have wanted to study. In general the format of the first two editions of *Kinder- und Hausmärchen* was exclusively shaped for adult readers, who might pass on the tales through oral storytelling. It was not until 1825, when they decided to select fifty tales with seven illustrations to form the Small Edition that they specifically included children as part of their audience. In short, their initial purpose was to contribute to a broad German tradition of *Naturpoesie* (ancient folk and oral literature) as against *Kunstpoesie* (artificial literature that emanated from creative writers). As their meticulous philological work on German and Nordic ancient literature reveals, they never abandoned this project. However, they made compromises by mixing oral and literary tales and by editing all the tales they received so that the oral tradition would gain the respect of the educated classes in Germany. At the same time, they began dividing their legacy with the creation of their Small Edition in 1825 that was directed at young readers and their families. More than the Large Edition, the small one was intended to attract a larger reading audience. It did not include prefaces or notes, rather illustrations, and the tales were "doctored" to fit the tastes of bourgeois children and their parents, with the result that the Small Edition gradually led readers to believe that the collected tales were part of the growing field of children's literature. Given these two different editions of their tales, we can and should speak about the double legacy of the Grimms' tales—and we should also remember that the Grimms left behind other legacies in fields that pertain to etymology, anthropology, linguistics, and philology.

Here I want to focus on how the Grimms' bequeathed a legacy of the tales to adults, primarily folklorists and educated people, and how they became pioneers of German folklore and influenced numerous folklorists in the nineteenth century, not only in Germany but also in Europe. In the next chapter I shall deal more fully with their legacy to children's literature, which they never intended, and yet, they were gratified that children became fond of their tales.

Two good examples of the breadth and depth of the Grimms' influence on German folklorists in the nineteenth century are found in the work of Johann Wilhelm Wolf (1817–55), founder of the *Zeitschrift für Deutsche Mythologie und Sittenkunde* (Journal for German Mythology and Customs),[33] and Heinrich Pröhle (1822–95),[34] a student of Jacob Grimm in Berlin, who went on to become a notable folklorist and teacher. When and how Wolf discovered the Grimms' collections of folk tales and their philological writings on epics, folk tales, mythology, and legends is unclear. As a young boy in Cologne, he had gathered all kinds of ancient artifacts and tales. Sometime during his teenage years, he fled his family due to their rigid Catholicism and went to Belgium, where he dedicated himself to the causes of oppressed peoples and to salvaging Germanic myths and legends that stemmed from pagan rituals. His model for collecting and transcribing oral tales as a means to preserve community was the work of the Grimms, especially Jacob's studies of mythology and legends, and it was obvious that by the time he became a folklorist and teacher in his early thirties, he had consumed almost every word and tale that that they had written. In fact, he came to embody what the Grimms had projected as the exemplary collector of tales: Wolf became the ideal fieldworker and collected tales, sayings, proverbs, superstitions, and artifacts directly from the mouths of the folk as well as writing erudite and theoretical commentaries.

Wolf's first major work, *Niederländische Sagen* (1843), was a collection of Dutch legends and tales that he had gathered while in Brussels and Ghent; it represented his endeavor to give voice to the minority Flemish people, who, he maintained, were suffering due to French domination. After his return to Germany he settled first in Cologne and then Darmstadt, where he systematically collected tales from soldiers, blacksmiths, carpenters, and farmers, and published the tales in *Deutsche Märchen und Sagen* (1845) and *Deutsche Hausmärchen* (1851). Endorsing the Grimms' philosophy and approach, he believed that his collections were "educational primers" and that the tales naturally carried within themselves moral lessons that were derived from the customs and belief systems of the common people. He was clearly a "republican" German, who supported the revolutions of 1848, and took great pleasure in meeting Jacob Grimm in Frankfurt during this period. One of his books, *Die deutsche Götterlehre. Ein Hand- und Lesebuch für Schule und Haus* (The German Teaching of the Gods: A Handbook and Reader for the School and Home, 1852) was intended to explain and elaborate Jacob Grimm's theories in *Deutsche Mythologie* (1835). But more important than this study was Wolf's founding of the journal, *Zeitschrift für Deutsche Mythologie und Sittenkunde* in 1853. Though it lasted only four years and Wolf died after the second issue was published, this journal served briefly as one of the most central contact points for the very best German-speaking scholars in Central Europe: Karl Weigand, Ignaz and Joseph Zingerle, Adalbert Kuhn, Ernst Meier, Heinrich Pröhle, Nikolaus Hocker, Wilhelm Creccelius, R. O. Waldburg, August Stöber, Karl Sinnrock, Franz Josef Vonbun, Reinhold Köhler, Wilhelm Mannhardt, Karl Ernst Hermann Krause, E. J. Reimann, Wilhelm von Ploennies, Friedrich Wöste, Heinrich Runge, and many other of the leading folklorists of this time. They contributed and commented on legends, puzzles, superstitions, nursery rhymes, children's games, folk tales, animal stories, proverbs, and myths that they had discovered in countries from France to Russia and in every region of Germany and the Hapsburg Empire including Switzerland. The majority of these men did original fieldwork. Most transcribed their tales from different dialects, although some published dialect versions. They were all familiar with and influenced by the Brothers Grimm. Wilhelm himself contributed commentary and tales to the *Zeitschrift für Mythologie und Sittenkunde* and corresponded with Wolf.

Among the more notable young folklorists who was in contact with Wolf was Heinrich Pröhle, born in 1822 in the town of Satuelle not far from Magdeburg in northern Germany. His father was a pastor in various churches in the Harz region. When Pröhle turned thirteen, he was sent to study at the Dome School of Halberstadt and then completed his studies at a gymnasium in Merseburg. In 1843 he enrolled at the University of Halle, but because of his radical political activities, he was forced to leave the university. So in 1845 he transferred to the Humboldt University in Berlin, where he spent a year studying under the tutelage of Jacob Grimm and also made the acquaintance of Wilhelm Grimm. However, he interrupted his studies after a year to wander by foot in southern Germany, Hungary, and Austria. During the revolutionary year of 1848, he became a political correspondent for the *Augsburgische Allgemeine Zeitung* based in Vienna and sent reports to this newspaper about the turbulent times in Austria. When he returned to Germany, he continued working as a journalist and wrote a book about life in Vienna. At the same time be began hiking in the Harz Mountains and gathering tales and legends from the lips of peasants and artisans. He eventually made his home in Wenigerode in the Harz region from 1853 to 1857, where he continued gathering and translating the tales from the local dialects into high German and published several important collections: *Kinder- und Volksmärchen* (1853), *Märchen für die Jugend* (1854), *Harzsagen* (1853), *Harzbilder: Sitten und Gebräuche aus dem Harzgebirge* (1855), and *Unterharzische Sagen* (1856).

Like Wolf and unlike the Grimms, Pröhle did an enormous amount of fieldwork and wrote down the tales from the dialect spoken by his informants. However, like Wilhelm Grimm, he felt free to stylize the tales in high German so that they became poetically effective. Rarely did he change substantive matters or the plots of the tales. However, he was very concerned about their moral impact on young readers. For instance, in *Märchen für die Jugend* ("Tales for Young People"), he wrote about the importance of folk and fairy tales for the creation of a national literature and stated: "More and more these tales are also being recognized as essential nourishment that are not to be kept from young minds in any way."[35] Indeed, he even included instructions for teachers and educators on how to bring out the ethical nature of the tales in their work with children. Pröhle, who dedicated two of his books to the Grimms and corresponded with them, was clearly a loyal disciple, who became a prominent writer and teacher at a high school in Berlin from 1857 to 1890 while publishing other collections such as *Rheinlands schönste Sagen und Geschichten* (1886) in the Grimms' spirit and searching for authentic tales from the oral tradition that contributed to a national literature. What is fascinating in Pröhle's relationship with the Grimms is that he was an important link in the chain reaction of their legacy. As Ines Köhler-Zülch has remarked,

> We can point to the impact of Pröhle's Grimm reception on the Grimms themselves. Not only did Pröhle thoroughly know the

Kinder- und Hausmärchen and *Deutsche Sagen* and use them for comparative purposes—in the fifty-five notes to his *Kinder- und Volksmärchen*, for example, he refers to approximately thirty parallels in the Grimms' collection—but Wilhelm Grimm also knew Pröhle's collection very well and included in the final edition of his fairy tales forty references to both the *Kinder- und Volksmärchen* and *Märchen für die Jugend*. So, as in the closing of a circle or perhaps the turning point of a spiral, Pröhle's reception of the Grimms' methodological legacy is reciprocated and compounded in Wilhlem Grimm's reception of Pröhle's work.[36]

What is also significant about Pröhle's and Wolf's reception of the Grimms' methodology, in particular, the cultivation of dialect tales in high German and their endeavor to be faithful to oral transmission, is their fieldwork in particular regions of Germany. For Pröhle it was Harz, and for Wolf it was Rhineland. Other German folklorists of their generation took great care in designating the regions in which they collected their tales. That is, their focus was on a particular region, not on a nation or nation-state. Most of them also produced books and collections of stories, often with subtitles, "gathered orally from the folk" or with dedications to the Grimms.

In general the typical collection of tales in mid-nineteenth-century Europe was usually published in the standard or "high" language of the country. Therefore, any story collected orally would be transcribed or translated into a "literary" language or the dominant vernacular, and though most of the folklorists tried not to add phrases or hone their tales, they all more or less touched up the "raw" language in which they had heard the tale. Many of the tales were recited or read in one language and then written down in another. For instance, this type of transcription/translation can be seen in the collecting practices throughout Europe during the nineteenth century. In *Sicilianische Marchen* (*Sicilian Folk Tales*, 1870), Laura Gonzenbach's tales were told in a Sicilian dialect by rural women and then written down in high German; Rachel Busk translated Roman dialect tales into English in *The Folk-Lore of Rome. Collected by Word of Mouth from the People* (1874); in *Russian Fairy Tales: From the Skazki of Polevoi* (1893), Robert Nisbet Bain translated Russian into English; as did W.R.S. Ralston in *Russian Folk-Tales* (1873). Two important scholars, Johann von Hahn and Bernhard Schmidt, translated Greek tales into German in *Griechische und albanesische Märchen* (*Greek and Albanese Folk Tales*, 1864) and *Griechische Märchen, Sagen und Volkslieder* (*Greek Folk Tales, Legends, and Folk Songs*, 1877). In *Basque Legends* (1877), Wentworth Webster, a British minister, was the first to translate Basque tales into English, while Albert Henry Wratislaw (*Sixty Folk-Tales from*

Exclusively Slavonic Sources, 1890) and Jeremiah Curtin (*Myths and Folk Tales of the Russians, Western Slavs, and Magyars*, 1890) published important anthologies of Slavic tales in English the same year. It was not until the latter part of the nineteenth century that folklorists began publishing dialect tales. Here the work of Giuseppe Pitrè, Vittorio Imbriani, François-Marie Luzel, Emmanuel Cosquin, Achille Millien, Angelo Gubernatis, and Carolina Coronedi-Berti is important.[37] And of course, the founding and remarkable growth of folklore journals enabled folklorists to provide all kinds of source materials and essays on customs and beliefs as well as historical articles that traced the origins of the tales and their motifs. Aside from Wolf's *Zeitschrift für Deutsche Mythologie und Sittenkunde*, some of the other important journals that were founded in the latter half of the nineteenth century are *Revue Celtique* (1870), *Alemannia* (1873), *Romania* (1872), *The Folk-Lore Record* (1878), *Mélusine* (1877), *Archivo per lo Studio delle Tradizioni popolari* (1882), *El Folklore Andaluz* (1882), *Revue des Traditions Populaires* (1886), *Ethnologische Mitteilungen aus Ungarn* (1887), *Journal of American Folklore* (1888), and *Schweizerisches Archiv für Volkskunde* (1897).

Thanks to the journals, private correspondence, and books, almost all the leading folklorists in nineteenth-century Europe and North America were in touch with each other's works and were all familiar with the Grimms' *Kinder- und Hausmärchen* and the Brothers' scholarly work in philology and linguistics. What is significant, however, is that most folklorists after 1850 became more precise and more thorough than the Grimms in collecting and publishing their tales; they paid more attention and respect to the tellers of the tales, the regional relevance of each tale, the linguistic peculiarities, and the significance of the tales within the sociocultural and historical context. It is here that the tales must be understood as part of the nationalist trends and the formation of new nation states in the latter half of the nineteenth and early part of twentieth centuries. The Grimms' legacies became part of a German cultural heritage.

Collecting folk tales was a social and political act of some kind. Not only did educated middle-class collectors give voice to the lower classes, but they also spoke out in defense of their native languages and in the interests of national and regional movements that sought more autonomy for groups with very particular interests.[38] For instance, Norway separated from Denmark in 1814 and became an independent state with its own language and dialects. There was a tendency, therefore, to shake off the Danish yoke. Moe and Asbjørnsen regarded themselves in the 1830s and 1840s as defenders of the Norwegian language and customs by collecting diverse types of folk songs, legends, and tales in dialect and transcribed them.[39] In contrast to the Grimms, Moe and Asbjørnsen traveled to different regions of Norway and stimulated other collectors to write down local tales. Indeed, the collecting throughout Scandinavia had strong nationalist and regional aspects.[40] Denmark, too, manifested signs of romantic nationalism. As Reimund Kvideland points out: "The struggle against German influences in the southern boundary region created a nationalistic atmosphere in Denmark which promoted interest in folklore. Svend Grundtvig, who was working on a major publication of Danish ballads, made a public appeal for the collection of folktales."[41] His disciple, Evald Tang Christensen took his appeal very seriously and became one of the most prolific collectors of folklore in Europe. Altogether he collected Danish ballads, folk tales (2,700), humorous anecdotes, proverbs, rhymes, riddles, and approximately 25,000 legends.[42] In Russia, the great scholar Alexander Afanas'ev was also interested in the deep traditions of storytelling and realized that his large collections of tales in the 1850s and 1860s might assist the numerous ethnic groups in Russia to become more aware of the virtues of their different languages and customs.[43] He was also censored when he sought to publish anti-clerical tales. Many French collectors such as Luzel, Sébillot, Cosquin, and others took pride in the regional traditions that they sought to keep alive, and of course, after the defeat of the French by the Prussians in 1871, there was a strong element of regionalism and nationalism that animated their collecting, whether they were liberals or conservatives.[44]

All this is not to say that European folklorists were political activists, but there was a certain mutual spirit of *romantic nationalism* that can be traced in almost every effort to collect tales from the common people in the nineteenth century. Perhaps "nationalism" is the wrong word, for the tales, the storytellers, and the collectors were more linked to regions of Europe and the peculiarities within localities. What is striking is that there are strong ties and similar goals in the work of all the European folklorists that continually hark back to the Brothers Grimm, who provided the inspiration for their collecting tales and efforts to interpret them as the foundational relics of different cultural traditions.

Although one might speak of a Grimm or romantic tradition within folklore and the work of folklorists, I prefer to use the term "legacy," or to discuss the different Grimm legacies within diverse cultural traditions. In the past thirty years the term "tradition" or the concept of tradition has undergone numerous stimulating revisions. One of the best standard definitions of tradition from a folkloristic viewpoint has been provided by Randal Allison, who states that

> Tradition [is] a repeated pattern of behaviors, beliefs, or enactment passed down from one generation to the next. Traditions are culturally recognized and sustained; in general, folklorists have maintained a particular interest in those that are orally transmitted. Within the discipline of folklore, the historicity of tradition has been subjected to a variety of interpretations—for example,

a set of cultural ideals regarded as a coherent unit in which past ideals influence the present patterns of behavior in the group, a recognized set of present practices with origins in the past, or a set of practices created in the past that are purposefully maintained by the group in the present.[45]

One of the more significant divergent approaches to this concept of tradition has been taken by Eric Hobsbawm and Terrence Ranger, who coined the term "invented tradition." In the introduction to their edited book, *The Invention of Tradition*, they assert: "'Invented tradition' is taken to mean a set of practices, normally governed by overtly or tacitly accepted rules and of a ritual or symbolic nature, which seek to inculcate certain values and norms of behaviour by repetition, which automatically implies continuity with the past. In fact, where possible, they normally attempt to establish continuity with a suitable historic past."[46] In other words, many so-called authentic traditions have been artificially created and established to maintain control over or manipulate people in favor of ideas in the interests of elite groups within a nation-state. Written in 1983, Hobsbawm and Ranger's book addressed historians and other scholars from other disciplines and insisted they must question whether there is such a thing as organic or authentic tradition. They focused on tradition as a process in flux that constantly undergoes innovation or transformation. Accordingly, they argued that there are three overlapping types of invented traditions since the industrial revolution: "a) those establishing or symbolizing social cohesion or the membership of groups, real or artificial communities, b) those establishing or legitimizing institutions, status or relations of authority, and c) those whose main purpose was socialization, the inculcation of beliefs, value systems and conventions of behaviour."[47]

Their notions of invented traditions have had a great impact on scholars in a variety of ways, and more recently Trevor Blank and Robert Glenn Howard have edited a relevant collection of essays, *Tradition in the Twenty-First Century: Locating the Role of the Past in the Present* (2013), that explores manifold approaches to understanding the function that tradition plays in folklore studies. For instance, in "Thinking through Tradition," Elliott Oring makes the important point that "the process of tradition . . . is the process of *cultural reproduction*. Cultural reproduction refers to the means by which culture is reproduced in transmission and repetition. It depends on the assimilation of cultural ideas and the reenactment of cultural practices."[48] In this regard, he argues that both genuine and invented traditions depend on whether they are "handed down" from generation to generation. Thus, more attention, he contends, must be paid to those forces that sustain and generate traditions and must be studied and problematized in greater depth by folklorists.

Along the same lines but with a different emphasis, Simon Bronner argues in his highly original essay "The 'Handiness' of Tradition": "As a body of material, tradition is literally and figuratively associated with being hand-wrought—that is, personally rendered, manipulated or conveyed, whether a basket or a well-delivered story. As a process of transmission and generation, folklore may be referred to as being handed (passed) down, handed over, and more recently with digital culture, handed up to draw attention to social interaction, even with electronic mediation, out of which framed expression or practices emerge."[49] Like Oring and some of the other contributors to *Tradition in the Twenty-First Century*, Bronner has a sophisticated interest in understanding the implicit and explicit forces and agencies that constitute the process of tradition. For my purposes, Bronner's notion of "handiness" is most valuable for explaining the Grimms' different legacies and how they handed tales, legends, words, sayings, proverbs, linguistic laws, philological principles, and much more to contribute to German traditions and thought of a nation that actually did not exist in their time.

Bronner remarks,

> The hand is important to tradition because of its capacity to grasp objects physically and intellectually and attach meaning to them. Being "in hand" suggests that the tradition's value of being possessed for human purposes. "Handing it over" as the basis of tradition implies a social connection, made with deliberateness, much like the transporting of a valued possession. Giver and recipient come together at that moment and become familiar as a consequence. The image of the hand gives the transaction a "personal touch," the ability to "reach out and touch someone" rather than being thought about in solitude. Being "handed down" brings elders or predecessors into the scene but in a way that implies a familial tie from one generation to another. In other words, a social bond or identity goes "hand in hand" with tradition.[50]

If we look at how the Grimms worked with pens in their hands, inscribing the words of friends and acquaintances, reproducing words that they believed emanated from ancient sources, reaching out with their finished books to celebrate a cultural memory in solidarity with the German people, I think we can gain a clearer idea of what their legacies are. In fact, the Grimms deliberately sought to reinforce and reinvigorate the cultural memory and heritage of the German people through collecting and editing their tales. When I speak of cultural memory, I am referring specifically to the work of Jan and Aleida Assmann.[51] In *Cultural Memory and Early Civilization*, Jan Assmann explains the basic principles that constitute cultural memory:

This book deals with the connection between these three themes
of memory (or reference to the past), identity (or political imagination), and cultural continuity (or the formation of tradition). Every culture formulates something that might be called
a connective structure. It has a binding effect that works on two
levels—social and temporal. It binds people together by providing
a "symbolic universe" . . .—a common area of experience, expectation, and action whose connecting force provides them with trust
and with orientation. Early texts refer to this aspect of culture as
justice. However, it also links yesterday with today by giving form
and presence to influential experiences and memories, incorpo-
rating images and tales from another time into the background of
the onward moving present, and bring with it hope and continuity. This connective structure is the aspect of culture that under-
lies myths and histories. Both the normative and the narrative
elements of these—mixing instruction with storytelling—create a
basis of belonging, of identity, so that the individual can then talk
of "we." What binds him to this plural is the connective structure
of common knowledge and characteristics—first through adher-
ence to the same laws and values, and second through the memory of a shared past.[52]

Assmann stresses that repetition is the basic principle behind all the connective structures, and in the case of folk and fairy tales, I would contend that
there are also elements in the narratives that are transcultural that account for
the wide dissemination of similar tale types throughout the world. In some of
my previous books, I have argued that certain tales become memes or meme-like
because of their relevance to common human struggles and issues related to adaptation to the environment. These tales are repeated, imitated, and transformed
so frequently that they play a major role both within a particular culture and in
other cultures as well. In today's globalized world the connections are such that
the Grimms' "German" legacies have had a binding effect in other cultures. The
bonds created by the Grimms' tales that entail an understanding of the "we" in
cultural memory, tales that did not belong to the Grimms, are highly unusual
and account for the their remarkable popularity because they touch us in profound ways that break down national barriers.

As Johannes Bolte (1858–1937), a German folklorist and philologist, and
Georg Polívka (1858–1933), a Czech folklorist and professor of Slavic literature, demonstrated in the five volumes of their meticulous reference book to
the Grimms' tales, *Anmerkungen zu den Kinder- und Hausmärchen der Brüder
Grimm* (1913–32), the Grimms' "Germanic" tales were not to be defined,

studied, and interpreted solely within a particular cultural heritage. Indeed, the tales that sprouted and were picked and cultivated on "German" soil could be found throughout Europe and may have come from other regions of the world. In fact, the Grimms recognized very early on in their collecting of stories that their tale types could be found in many other European countries and might not derive from Nordic myths, customs, and rituals, as much as they wanted to believe this. In fact, this awareness was one of the reasons that they never used the title "German" in the title of their book to describe their *Kinder- und Hausmärchen*, as did some other collectors and writers such as Wolf, Bechstein, and Meier. Undoubtedly, the tales revealed more about the particular conditions experienced by the storytellers and more about particular cultural traditions in specific regions of Europe than anything about their "national" identity. At the same time, they also reflected and continued to reflect that humans throughout the world invent and use stories in very similar ways to expose and articulate common problems and struggles as well as their wishes to overcome them. This human urge to tell and to share experiences so that listeners might find ways to adapt to the world and improve their situation accounts for the utopian tendency in folk and fairy tales that can be considered a longing for a better and happier world. We tell and retell tales that become relevant in our lives, and the tales themselves form types that we use in our telling or reading to address various issues such as child abandonment, the search for immortality, sibling rivalry, incest, rape, exploitation, and so on. No tale is ever told for the first time, but every tale has the potential to be memetically disseminated and retained in our memory to enable us to navigate our way through the tons of messages and tales that bombard our lives from the day we are born. The Grimms discovered how tale types evolve and change, and they put their imprint on the tales that came their way. They were not alone in their endeavors in the nineteenth century as other collectors and folklorists reached out to preserve told tales before they changed and might evaporate. Yet the strange thing is—as the Grimms noted—people always evaporate before tales do, and certain tales have assumed different shapes and hues in the course of history that can be considered a substantial part our cultural legacies and memories.

CHAPTER ONE

German Popular Stories as Revolutionary Book

We have recently been translated into English, that is, part of the children's tales. Everything neatly printed, and it seems to me, very readable (except the selection is not remarkable). Yes, except for the rhymes, more readable and smoother at times than the German text. The succinct, nice English in itself suits the storytelling children's tone much more than the somewhat stiff high German. We had not taken necessary care of the style for reasons that I would now abandon or modify.

—Jacob Grimm, letter to Karl Lachmann, May 12, 1823[1]

With all its faults, Taylor's translation has achieved a sort of classic status of its own. If modern readers were aware that it is a period piece, that would not much matter, but most do not realize how skewed a picture of the Grimms' collection they get through reading Taylor. Not that Taylor attempted to camouflage what he was doing in adapting, combining and expurgating his originals—on the contrary, he signalled his changes very frankly in the notes he appended to the tales. But what he presents is not what a modern reader would be entitled to expect.

David Blamires, "The Early Reception of the Grimms'
Kinder- und Hausmärchen in England"[2]

Cruikshank's etchings here have long been recognized as one of his greatest achievements; what is less frequently noticed is the aptness of their setting. The coherence of Taylor's text, the typography, the mis-en-page all combine with the illustrations to make German Popular Stories *one of the most attractive books of its time, and one entirely suited to its humble but revolutionary contents.*

—Brian Alderson, "The Spoken and the Read: *German Popular Stories* and English Popular Diction"[3]

It may seem strange if not startling to refer to Edgar Taylor's (1793–1839) translation of the Grimms' *Kinder- und Hausmärchen* as a revolutionary book, but his *German Popular Stories*, including the two volumes of 1823 and 1826 and George Cruikshank's (1792–1878) unusual and delightful illustrations, radically changed the destiny of what we today call the "fairy tales" of the Brothers Grimm. Moreover, Taylor altered the legacy in English-speaking countries by shaping his books so that they would appeal to young readers and their families. And, indeed, they had a great appeal.

Ironically, the reason for the success of *German Popular Stories* is that Taylor did not translate the tales. Rather, he *adapted* them, initially with the help of his friend David Jardine in 1823, and later, alone in 1826 and in 1839. He rewrote and reconceived them in such a careful and innovative way that they were transformed into amusing stories that emphasized the importance of freeing the imagination of children while catering at the same time to the puritanical tastes and expectations of young middle-class readers and their families. Not only did Taylor change and sanitize a small amount of tales selected from the second edition of the Grimms' 1819 collection, deleting anything that smacked of obscenity, irreverence, and violence, but he also rearranged the plots, combined stories, and changed the tone of the language,[4] often making the tales illogical and unrecognizable from their original German stories. In short, he appropriated the tales, turning them upside down, and this anglicized transformation laid the basis for a misunderstanding of the German tales in Great Britain and America for the next sixty-odd years or more until Margaret Hunt's more faithful rendition of the stories appeared in 1884. And even later, Taylor's adaptations have continued to be disseminated in the twentieth-first century and mistaken as "genuine" translations of the Grimms' tales.[5] As late as 2012, Puffin published a children's edition titled *Fairy Tales from the Brothers Grimm* without any mention of Edgar Taylor, but with Taylor's tales, George Cruikshank's illustrations, and a trivial and misleading introduction by Cornelia Funke, the German popular writer of fantasy books similar to J. R. Rowling's *Harry Potter* series. After plugging one of her new novels based on the lives of the Brothers Grimm, she exclaims enthusiastically:

> For me, Grimms' fairy tales know every secret of the human heart. They know about our fear and greed, but also about true friendship and unquestioning love. They know about the darkness of the world and about its endless treasures. They are whispers from the past, where children could starve in the woods and where forests were dangerous places, but also filled with treasure and magic. Where animals could talk and people shift their shape whenever

they wanted because they knew they were part of nature . . . something we easily forget these days.[6]

What we really should forget are these insincere trite compliments that have nothing to do with the Grimms' tales. Not only does this Puffin "celebrity" introduction and publication do a disservice to the Grimms' legacy but also to Taylor's mission.

As pioneer—that is, the first English "translator" of the Grimms' tales—Taylor benefited from the numerous illustrations that spruced up his book. Charles Baldwyn, his publisher, recruited George Cruikshank to provide etchings, and Taylor welcomed this decision (figure 2). As a consequence, the tales were enriched by images before the Grimms did anything like this in Germany. Indeed, Baldwyn and Taylor were fortunate to have hired the gifted and well-known caricaturist, for Cruikshank's illustrations were in keeping with Taylor's adaptations, which he depicted with levity and made Taylor's texts appear even more humorous than they actually were. (Cruikshank could not read German and based his illustrations on Taylor's adaptations.) In this regard, the diverse and serious implications of the German texts were discarded in favor of droll satire to foster amusement. The tales were visually homogenized to emphasize quaintness and community.[7] Cruikshank's illustrations provoke laughter, not reflection and moral education, two goals that the Grimms had sought to achieve, something that the sentimental illustrations of their brother Ludwig were to show later in the German editions.

As a consequence of all the changes, *German Popular Stories* is revolutionary and extraordinary, for the book prompted the Brothers Grimm to revise their publishing strategy and seek a broader readership for their collected stories in Germany. Initially, when they published their first edition in two volumes with scholarly notes in 1812 and 1815, they did not have children in mind as their primary audience. It is also the case with their second edition of 1819, two volumes containing 170 tales (along with a third volume filled with comprehensive notes, published separately in 1822). It is true that, in the second edition, the Grimms modified many of the tales to please potential young readers or auditors and their parents. New tales were added; some that were overly violent were eliminated. However, the Grimms were still more inclined to favor the philological and historical qualities of the tales, and it was this scholarly 1819 edition on which Taylor, along with Jardine, based his so-called translation of 31 tales in 1823, and 24 in 1826.

Thanks to the success of Taylor's work *more directed at children* in England, the Grimms decided in 1825 to create a smaller edition of fifty tales taken from their large collection of 1819, and they intended this Small Edition to appeal

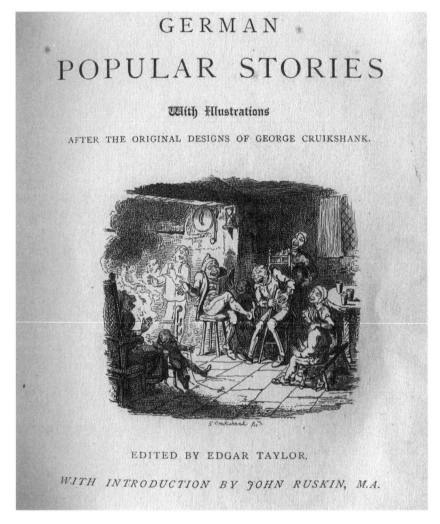

GERMAN

POPULAR STORIES

𝔚𝔦𝔱𝔥 𝔉𝔩𝔲𝔰𝔱𝔯𝔞𝔱𝔦𝔬𝔫𝔰

AFTER THE ORIGINAL DESIGNS OF GEORGE CRUIKSHANK.

EDITED BY EDGAR TAYLOR,

WITH INTRODUCTION BY JOHN RUSKIN, M.A.

Figure 2. Title page of *German Popular Stories* (volume 1, 1812). Drawing by George Cruikshank.

more to family audiences. Referred to as the *Kleine Ausgabe*, it was issued periodically along with the Large Edition (*Grosse Ausgabe*) until 1858.[8] So, it was under Taylor's influence that Wilhelm, who was fully in charge of both the small and large editions after 1819, began editing the German tales for the benefit of children, keenly aware that parents of solid bourgeois families might object to scatological topics, irreverent language, and provocative inferences. The Grimms did not believe this kind of editing compromised their goal of recovering "pure" folk tales. Therefore, Wilhelm shaped the tales in all editions according to an idealistic concept of the Protestant ethic and folk poetry. He reinforced what the Grimms considered to be the natural virtues of the stories that were to serve as exemplary lessons without didactic morals. Together, the Brothers, who had already begun to "revolutionize" the study of ancient and medieval literature and to lay the groundwork for the study of folklore in Europe and North America, were stimulated by Taylor to make changes that resulted in the transformation of their collection into one of the *great classics of children's literature* worldwide.[9]

To understand the revolutionary and extraordinary qualities of Edgar Taylor's *German Popular Tales*, its broad international and intercultural impact, and the ironies and coincidences of history that contributed to the success of his books as well as the reputation of the Grimms' original collection in German, I want to recount and analyze the Grimms' intentions in collecting and publishing the two volumes of the first edition of their tales in 1812 and 1815 as well as the second edition of 1819. Then I want to review the history of how Taylor came upon their tales in the early 1820s and why he decided to "translate" them into English. Finally, I want to conclude this chapter by discussing how Taylor participated in the romantic antiquarian movement, what we would today call folklore, to recapture neglected relics of the past, and to defend the imagination against rationalism. Taylor belonged to a group of British writers and intellectuals who confronted a general trend among English educators, religious groups, writers, and publishers who questioned whether fairy tales were appropriate literature for children. In some respects, it was through Taylor that the Grimms made the fairy tale more respectable and paved the way for the translation of Hans Christian Andersen's stories and the remarkable rise of experimental literary fairy and folk tales in Victorian England in the latter half of the nineteenth century.[10]

The Daring Quest of the Brothers Grimm

Interestingly, Jacob and Wilhelm Grimm did not demonstrate a particular interest in folk tales during their youth in the small towns of Hanau and Steinau where they were raised. Both of them were precocious students, and when they were sent to study at the Lyzeum in Kassel after their father had died in 1797, they made every effort to succeed in a classical curriculum at school, to prepare themselves to study law at the University of Marburg, and to find employment as civil servants to help support their family. Folklore was not on their minds. Their father, Philip Wilhelm Grimm, a prominent district magistrate in Steinau, had died suddenly and had left the large family in difficult circumstances. Jacob and Wilhelm had three younger brothers and a sister, and their mother had to depend on financial support from her father and relatives to keep the family together. Socially disadvantaged, the Grimms sought to compensate by achieving recognition in their studies at school and at the university. They wanted to follow diligently in their father's footsteps. However, neither became a lawyer or magistrate.

While studying at the University of Marburg from 1802 to 1806, the Grimms were inspired and mentored by Friedrich Carl von Savigny, a young professor of jurisprudence, who opened their eyes to the historical and philosophical aspects of law as well as literature. It was Savigny's historical approach to jurisprudence, his belief in the organic connection of all cultural creations of the *Volk* (understood as an entire ethnic group) to the historical development of this *Volk*, that drew the attention of the Grimms. Furthermore, Savigny stressed that the present could only be fully grasped and appreciated by studying the past. He insisted that the legal system had to be studied through an interdisciplinary method to explore and grasp the mediations between the customs, beliefs, values, and laws of a people. For Savigny—and also for the Grimms—culture was originally the common property of all members of a *Volk*. The Germanic culture had become divided over the years into different realms such as religion, law, literature, and so on, and its cohesion could be restored only through historical investigation. The Brothers felt that language rather than law was the ultimate bond that united the German people and were thus drawn to the study of old German literature—though they were in agreement with Savigny's methods and desire to create a stronger sense of community among the German people.

The Grimms, who had always been voracious readers and had digested popular courtly romances during their teenage years, turned more and more to a serious study of medieval and ancient literature during their university years. Since literature and philology were not recognized fields at German universities, however, they set their sight on becoming librarians and independent scholars of German literature. They began collecting old books, tracts, calendars, newspapers, and manuscripts; wrote about medieval literature; and even debated with formidable professors and researchers of old Germanic and Nordic texts. They had concluded a pact to remain and work together for the rest of their lives, and together they cultivated a passion for recovering what they called the true essence of the German people. Yet, these were difficult times, and their plans were not easily realized.

By 1805 the entire family had moved to Kassel, and as I mentioned in the introduction, the Brothers were constantly plagued by money problems and concerns about their siblings. Their situation was further aggravated by the rampant Napoleonic Wars. Jacob interrupted his studies to serve the Hessian War Commission in 1806. Meanwhile, Wilhelm passed his law exams, enabling him to become a civil servant and to find work as a librarian in the royal library with a meager salary. In 1807 Jacob lost his position with the War Commission, when the French occupied Kassel, but he was later hired as a librarian for the new King

Jérome, Napoleon's brother, who now ruled Westphalia. Amid all the upheavals, their mother died in 1808, and Jacob and Wilhelm became fully responsible for their brothers and sister. None of the brothers attended the university. Ludwig studied painting and received financial assistance from friends of the family. Carl became a bank manager. Ferdinand was unable to hold a job for a long time and caused strife within the family. Lotte took care of the household duties until she married in 1822. Despite the loss of their mother and difficult personal and financial circumstances from 1805 to 1812, the Brothers managed to prove themselves to be innovative scholars in the new field of German philology and literature— and it should be noted that Jacob and Wilhelm were still in their early twenties.

Thanks to Savigny, who remained a good friend and mentor for the rest of their lives, the Grimms made the acquaintance of Clemens Brentano, one of the most gifted if not most eccentric German romantic poets, in 1803, and three years later, Achim von Arnim, one of the foremost German romantic novelists. These encounters had a profound impact on their lives, for Brentano and Arnim had already begun collecting old songs, tales, and manuscripts and shared the Grimms' interest in reviving ancient and medieval German literature. In the fall of 1805 Arnim and Brentano published the first volume of *Des Knaben Wunderhorn* (*The Boy's Wonder Horn*), a collection of old German folk songs, and they wanted to continue publishing more songs and folk tales in additional volumes. Since they were aware of the Grimms' remarkable talents as scholars of old German literature, they requested help from them in 1807, and the Brothers made a major contribution to the final two volumes of *The Boy's Wonder Horn*, published in 1808. At the same time, Brentano enlisted them to collect folk tales, fables, and other stories for a new project. The Grimms responded by gathering tales from old books and recruiting friends and acquaintances in and around Kassel to tell them tales or to gather them from whatever source they might find. In this initial phase, the Grimms were unable to devote all their energies to their research and did not have a clear idea about the significance of collecting folk tales. However, they were totally devoted to uncovering the "natural poetry" (*Naturpoesie*) of the German people, and all of their research was geared toward exploring the epics, sagas, and tales that contained what they thought were essential truths about the German cultural heritage. Underlying their work was a pronounced "patriotic" urge to excavate and preserve German cultural contributions made by the common people before they became extinct. In this respect their collecting "Germanic" tales was a gesture of protest against French occupation and a gesture of solidarity with those people who wanted to forge a unified German nation. In short, they wanted to contribute to the German cultural memory by excavating neglected works that they thought stemmed from oral traditions.

What fascinated or compelled the Grimms to concentrate on old German literature was a belief that the most natural and pure forms of culture—those that held the community together—were linguistic and were to be located in the past. Moreover, modern literature, even though it might be remarkably rich, was artificial and thus could not express the genuine essence of *Volk* culture that emanated naturally from people's experiences and bound the people together. In their letters between 1807 and 1812 and in such early essays as Jacob's "Von Übereinstimmung der alten Sagen" ("About the Correspondences between the Old Legends," 1807) and "Gedanken wie sich die Sagen zur Poesie und Geschichte verhalten" ("Thoughts about the Relationship between the Legends and Poetry," 1808) and Wilhelm's "Über die Entstehung der deutschen Poesie und ihr Verhältnis zu der nordeutschen" ("About the Origins of German Poetry and Its Relationship to Nordic Poetry," 1809), they began to formulate similar views about the origins of literature based on tales and legends or what was once oral art. The purpose of their collecting folk songs, tales, proverbs, legends, and documents was to write a history of old German *Poesie* and to demonstrate how *Kunstpoesie* (cultivated literature) evolved out of traditional folk material and how *Kunstpoesie* had gradually forced *Naturpoesie* (natural literature such as tales, legends, and so on) to recede during the Renaissance and take refuge among the folk in an oral tradition.

By 1809 the Grimms had amassed a large amount of tales, legends, and other documents, and they sent Brentano fifty-four texts that he intended to adapt. Since the Grimms had a different intention, Brentano told them that they could make use of the tales as they wished. This is the reason why they made a second copy of the manuscript before they sent him these tales. As I have already remarked, Brentano never did make use of them and fortunately left them in the Ölenberg Monastery in Alsace. I say "fortunately" because the Grimms destroyed the texts after using them in their first edition of *Kinder- und Hausmärchen* in 1812. The handwritten texts that the Grimms had sent to Brentano, now referred to as the Ölenberg manuscript, were only discovered in 1920 and have provided researchers with important information about the Grimms' editing process.[11] All fifty-four tales of the Ölenberg manuscript, most of them collected by Jacob, were transformed in their first edition of 1812 by the Brothers into carefully formed stories that corresponded to the Grimms' philological and poetical concept of a folk tale.

In 1812, Arnim, perhaps Brentano's closest friend at that time, visited the Grimms in Kassel. Aware that Brentano might not do anything with their texts, he encouraged the Grimms to publish their own collection, which would represent their ideal of "natural poetry." Thanks to Arnim's advice and intervention, the Brothers spent the rest of the year organizing and preparing eighty-six tales for publication that formed volume one of the first edition of 1812 published by Georg Reimer in Berlin and dedicated to Anrim's wife, Bettina von Arnim, who became a major support to them when they were later expelled from Göttingen in 1837.

As I have already noted in the previous chapter, the German scholar Jens Sennewald stresses that the Grimms intended from the very beginning to recover folk tales so that they could breathe new life into the German cultural heritage. According to Sennewald the frame of the *Kinder- und Hausmärchen* includes the complete body of their philological and poetlogical works, including frontispieces, prefaces, tales, illustrations, and notes from 1810 until the last large edition of 1857. The frame/body provides the space in which they felt they could "heal" people's lives and salvage the essence of the tales. It is through the corpus of the tales that the Grimms wanted to provide "authentic transmission" of original stories.[12] Sennewald demonstrates that the Grimms dealt with their collected and selected tales according to two premises: (1) the collected fragments of the relics (stories) had to be part of a meaningful whole; and (2) the entire collection of written words had to be grouped around an internal middle, which was *not* script. This internal essence, which is not present in script, was to provide the words with a voice.[13] Sennewald maintains that that the motivation for the Grimms' philological project consisted in showing that the internal voice could be heard in each individual "relic" and that the relics were dynamic. To do this they continued to edit and enlarge one collection of tales after another because it was only through the collection that the relics received their voice, and that cultural memory could be reinvigorated. According to the Grimms, the wholeness of the original German language had been lost and thus the collecting of relics became necessary. Such deliberate collecting, they felt, was what first made the origins of language thinkable.

Although the Grimms had not entirely formalized their concept while they worked on the publication of the first edition, the principles outlined by Sennewald could already be seen in their previous works. Unfortunately, the first volume of the *Kinder- und Hausmärchen* of 1812 was not well-received by friends and critics, who thought that the stories were too crude, were not shaped enough to appeal to children, and were weighed down by the scholarly notes. Nevertheless, the Brothers were not deterred from following their original philological and poetical concepts. Even though there were some differences between Jacob and Wilhelm, they basically held to their original principles to salvage relics from the past and reinforce cultural memory. Just how important these principles were can be seen in their correspondence with Arnim between 1810, as the Grimms were making plans to publish the tales they had collected, and 1815, when the second volume of the first edition appeared. In a very long letter of October 29, 1810, Jacob wrote to Arnim:

Contrary to your viewpoint, I am completely convinced that all the tales in our collection without exception had already been told with all their particulars centuries ago. Many beautiful things were only gradually left out. In this sense all the tales have long since been fixed, while they continue to move around in endless variations. That is, they do not fix themselves. Such variations are similar to the manifold dialects that should not suffer any violation either.[14]

And in another letter, written on January 28, 1813, Jacob wrote in support of Wilhelm's views:

The difference between children's and household tales and the reproach we have received for using this combination in our title is more hairsplitting than true. Otherwise one would literally have to bring the children out of the house where they have belonged forever and confine them in a room. Have children's tales really been conceived and invented for children? I don't believe this at all just as I don't affirm the general question, whether we must set up something specific at all for them. What we possess in publicized and traditional teachings and precepts is accepted by old and young, and what children do not grasp about them, all that glides away from their minds, they will do so when they are ready to learn it. This is the case with all true teachings that ignite and illuminate everything that was already present and known, not teaching that brings both wood and fire with it.[15]

In the same letter Jacob also wrote:

My old saying, which I have already defended earlier, is still valid: one should write according to one's ability and desires and not adapt to outside forces and comply with them. Therefore, I don't consider the book of tales (*Märchenbuch*) as being written for children, but it does suit them very well, and I am very happy about that. However, I would not have worked on it with pleasure if I hadn't believed in its importance for the most serious and adult people as well as for poesy, mythology, and history. These tales only live for children and adults 1) because children are receptive to the epic; thus, we are thankful for their minds that have retained these records. 2) Because the badly educated people disdain them.[16]

Though the Grimms made it clear in the second volume of the first edition of *Kinder- und Hausmärchen*, published in 1815, that they would follow the agenda of their first volume, they also explained the important difference they made between a book for children and an educational primer (*Erziehungsbuch*) in their preface:

> In creating our collection we wanted to do more than just perform a service for the history of poesy. It was our intention at the same time to enable poesy itself, which is alive in the collection, to have an effect: it was to give pleasure to anyone who could take pleasure in it, and therefore, our collection was also to become an intrinsic educational primer. There have been some complaints about this latter intention because there are things here and there [in our collection] that cause embarrassment and complaints that the collection is unsuitable for children or indecent (such as the references to certain incidents and conditions, also children should not hear about the devil and anything evil). Accordingly, parents should not offer the collection to children. In individual cases this concern may be correct, and thus one can easily choose which tales are to be read. On the whole it is certainly not necessary. Nothing can better defend us than nature itself, which has let certain flowers and leaves grow in a particular color and shape. Whoever does not find them wholesome, suitable for their special needs, which nobody knows, can easily walk right by them. But he cannot demand that they should be colored and cut in another way. . . . Everything that is natural can become beneficial, and we should try to strive to grasp this. Incidentally we know of no other healthy and powerful book that has edified the folk other than the Bible, which we place above all, and here, too, people would have some misgivings. The right usage, however, will not draw out evil things, rather, as some beautiful words say: [they draw out] testimonies from our heart. Children point to the stars without fear, while, according to the folk belief, others insult angels.[17]

In referring to the work as an educational primer, the Grimms emphasized that the morals and other lessons flowed from the tales organically. They were never didactic, and many other German folklorists such as Johann Wilhelm Wolf and Heinrich Pröhle picked up on this notion of an educational primer in their collections. There are, indeed, numerous issues of social justice and moral behavior that are at the heart of the folk and fairy tales in *Kinder- und Hausmärchen*.

After the publication of the second volume in 1815, however, the Grimms were once again disappointed by the critical reception. Despite the changes they had made, the Grimms continued to place great emphasis on the philological significance of the collection that was to make a major contribution toward understanding the origins and evolution of language and storytelling. The layout and contents of the two volumes of 1819 make it abundantly clear that the Grimms were still dedicating the tales to the perusal of adults. The preface in the first volume is long and academic and is followed by another long introduction, "About the Essence of Tales" ("Über das Wesen der Märchen"); the second volume begins with Ludwig Grimm's portrait of Dorothea Viehmann as the exemplary genuine peasant storyteller, and is followed by a very scholarly essay, "The Essence of Children and Their Customs" ("Kinderwesen und Kindersitten"). The 1822 third volume of notes, which completes the second edition, is only for scholars. In short, although many changes were made in the second edition, including the addition of religious legends, and although the Grimms now wanted to include children more directly as part of their audience, they remained philologically faithful to their principles. Their book, *Kinder- und Hausmärchen*, was not a book for children. Not yet. That is, the tales that were not their tales had not been fully appropriated by the Grimms and had not been fully fleshed out to meet Wilhelm's poetical standards.

It was only after they received a letter and a copy of *German Popular Stories* in 1823 from the young Englishman Edgar Taylor that they clearly began to alter the tendency of future editions of the *Kinder- und Hausmärchen* by creating the Small Edition and taking greater pains to address a general bourgeois reading public. In this respect, Taylor's sudden appearance in their lives—his letter and book came out of the blue—represented a momentous occasion that caused the Grimms to rethink their "marketing" strategy and how they might better guarantee the reception of the tales.

Edgar Taylor's Revolutionary and Extraordinary Intervention

Just who was this Edgar Taylor, and how did he come to translate the *Kinder- und Hausmärchen*? More precisely, why did a young successful lawyer—ironically, a man who joined the very profession that the Grimms had abandoned during their studies—take an interest in German literature and take the time to translate German folk tales primarily for young and old British readers?

Taylor was born 1793 into a wealthy, prominent family in Norfolk.[18] There were ministers, merchants, and industrialists among his forefathers. His own father was a landlord interested in new modes of agriculture; his mother died when Taylor was two. As a young boy he was sent to Palgrave in Suffolk to attend a private boarding school, where he studied the classics and also learned Italian, Spanish, German, and French. By 1809, when he was only sixteen, he left school to enter an apprenticeship as law clerk in his uncle Meadow Taylor's firm in Diss, a small city close to Norwich, the county town of Norfolk. At that time Norwich was one of the leading cultural cities in England, and Taylor had numerous opportunities to mix with the intelligentsia of the region, where there was a strong interest in German literature. Some of Taylor's acquaintances had translated important German authors and had personal ties to them. Given Taylor's knowledge of European languages and literature, the groundwork for his future scholarly work was laid in Norwich, which was experiencing a cultural boom. But first came law.

In 1814, after he finished his apprenticeship, he moved to London to practice law, and there he met Robert Roscoe, the son of a famous historian; together they founded their own law firm in 1817. Both young men had similar interests in literature and used their spare time to cultivate them. They also developed friendships among intellectuals and writers interested in English romantic literature as well as German culture. One of Taylor's acquaintances was Sir Francis Cohen (1788–1861), also a lawyer and scholar, who had already been corresponding with the Grimms and wrote some complimentary remarks about *Kinder- und Hausmärchen* in the May 1819 issue of the *Quarterly Review*. It was Cohen who first referred to the Grimms' collection as "German Popular Stories," which he considered the most important addition to what he called nursery literature; he did not use the term "fairy tales" or "tales for children". What is striking about this article by an early British folklorist is his great erudition and scholarly perspective on popular tales that was very similar to that of the Grimms. For instance, he argued:

> The man of letters should not disdain the chap book, or the nursery story. Humble as these efforts of the human intellect may appear, they shew its secret workings, its mode and progress, and human nature be studied in all its productions. . . . Hence, we may yet trace no small proportion of mystic and romantic lore in the tales which gladden the cottage fireside, or, century after century, soothe the infant to its slumbers.[19]

More than likely, it was Cohen who first stirred Taylor's interest in the Grimms' tales.[20] In addition, during 1819 and 1821, the time that Taylor may have made Cohen's acquaintance, he began publishing a series of articles titled

"German Popular and Traditionary Literature" in the *New Monthly Magazine and Literary Journal*[21] that cited Cohen and corresponded to Cohen's thinking about the importance of preserving folk culture. For example, Taylor, who also demonstrated a comprehensive knowledge of folklore and ancient literature, wrote:

> Our scholars busy themselves in tracing out the genealogy and mythological connexions of Tom Thumb and Jack the Giant Killer; and surely if the grave and learned embark in these speculations, we are justified in expecting to be able to welcome the æra when our children shall be allowed once more to regale themselves with that mild food which will enliven their imaginations, and tempt them on through the thorny paths of education;—when the gay dreams of fairy innocence shall again hover around them, and scientific compendiums, lisping botanies, and leading-string mechanics, shall be postponed to the Delights of Valentine and Orson, the beautiful Magalona, or Fair Rosamond.[22]

Clearly Cohen and Taylor were on the same page in their writings about the Grimms' tales. But it was not only Cohen who may have influenced Taylor to adapt *Kinder- und Hausmärchen*. It may have also been his friend David Jardine, who led him to translate them. He had been a student of theology at the University of Göttingen, and Taylor acknowledged that Jardine assisted him in translating the Grimms' tales in the 1823 volume of *German Popular Tales*, which contained thirty-one stories, but Jardine evidently had nothing to do with Taylor's second new 1826 volume of *German Popular Tales*, which contained twenty-four additional stories. Not all the tales in the second volume were selected from the Grimms' collection. Taylor, who had a vast knowledge of German literature, chose two from Johann Gustav Büsching's *Volks-Sagen, Märchen und Legenden* (1812), one from Otmar's *Volks-Sagen* (1800), and one called "Die Elfen" from Ludwig Tieck's *Phantasus* (1812–16). Altogether, Taylor's two volumes of *German Popular Stories* (1823/1826) contain fifty-five titles. With the exception of the four taken from other books mentioned earlier, Taylor actually created amalgamations of other stories and used sixty-one of the Grimms' tales taken from their 1819 edition, and one from the 1812 edition. Taylor's first volume contained two tales in Pomeranian and Hamburg dialect, "The Fisherman and His Wife" and "The Juniper Tree," and since Taylor had not spent any time in Germany to become familiar with dialects, he would have needed the assistance of some one like Jardine, who was more fluent in German, to have translated those tales. Aside from Jardine, Taylor had the help of George Cruikshank, who contributed a total of twenty-two illustrations to the editions of 1823 and 1826.

As Robert Patten points out in his informative essay, "George Cruikshank's Grimm Humor," the motives of Baldwyn, Taylor, and Cruikshank in producing *German Popular Stories* in 1823 and 1826 were very different. Baldwyn was trying to avoid bankruptcy and needed a "bestseller" to stabilize the fragile financial condition of his publishing house. Taylor sought to transform unusual folk tales from Germany and make them accessible to the scholarly interests of antiquarians and to provide amusement for middle-class families and their children. In doing this he emphasized the moral qualities of the tales without being didactic. Cruikshank had no great expectations in accepting the commission but used the occasion to demonstrate his unique imaginative capacity to capture the playful and humorous aspects of the tales as they had been adapted by Taylor and Jardine. He wanted to breathe life and movement into the pictures to help tell the stories. In fact, his motives jelled with those of Baldwyn and Taylor, and as Patten comments, "the resulting publication, *German Popular Stories* (Volume I, 1823; Volume II, 1826), was one of the most influential of the nineteenth century. It established precedents in the literature and visualization of fairy tales that profoundly affected Hans Christian Andersen, John Ruskin, and legions of artists from Richard Doyle to Walt Disney."[23]

The first volume was an immediate success and led to a second printing that very same year and two other printings in 1824 and 1825 before the second volume appeared in 1826. Taylor was also gratified by a letter in 1823 from Sir Walter Scott, who wrote, "I have to return my best thanks for the very acceptable present your goodness has made me in your interesting volume of German tales and traditions. I have often wished to see such a work under-taken by a gentleman of taste sufficient to adapt the simplicity of the German narrative to our own, which you have done so successfully."[24]

And it was this success that evidently prompted Taylor to expand the first volume, just as the Grimms continued to do so with their edition. But it was not just success that motivated Taylor. He had always had a serious scholarly interest in medieval literature and the history of law, as his essays and correspondence with the Grimms reveal. While working on his second volume of *German Popular Stories*, he published *Lays of the Minnesingers* in 1825. Unfortunately, he was handicapped by an incurable disease in 1827, which was to plague him until his death in 1839. Though the illness prevented him from pursuing his legal work, Taylor continued to publish important scholarly books such as *The Book of Rights: or Constitutional Acts and Parliamentary Proceedings Affecting Civil and Religious Liberty in England from Magna Charter to the Present Time* (1833) and *Master Wace's Chronicle of the Norman Conquest, from the Roman de Rou* (1837).[25] In the year of his death he produced a revised edition of *German Popular Stories* under a new title, *Gammer Grethel or German Fairy Tales, and Popular*

Stories, which included forty-two revised Grimms' tales, Cruikshank's engravings converted to woodcuts by John Byfield, and Ludwig Emil Grimm's wood-engraved portrait of the so-called peasant storyteller, Dorothea Viehmann, at the beginning of the book. This was a gesture of thanks to the Grimms, who had extolled the virtues of Viehmann as the ideal peasant storyteller, and she is pictured as a type of Mother Goose or Mother Bunch, who tells tales to sooth children and to impart the verities of life.

Curiously, from this point on, two different editions of Taylor's adaptations were published throughout the nineteenth century in England and America and competed with one another: *German Popular Stories*, which combined the 1823 and 1826 editions into one volume, and *Gammer Grethel*, which provided a totally different framework for a smaller selection of tales once again heavily revised by Taylor. The numerous publications were due to the lack of copyright and the popularity of the tales. Publishers could easily obtain rights or publish pirated editions. Some of the titles were vastly changed. For instance, Taylor's translations were often labeled *German Popular Tales and Household Stories* or *Grimms' Fairy Tales*. One of the more exotic titles is *Grimm's Goblins. Grimm's Household Stories, Translated from the Kinder und Haus Marchen by E. Taylor* in 1876. Robert Meek, the enthusiastic publisher of this latter edition, wrote an introduction that reflects the popular reception of the Grimms' tales as *children's literature* that was largely brought about by Taylor during the Victorian period:

> The Brothers Grimm, with an imagination as rich and fanciful as any writers of Fairy Tales, leave most kindred writers far behind in the especial adaptability of their tales to the tastes of children. In many, animals represent the leading characters and with inimitable drollery retain their animal traits with a fidelity that teaches as much natural History as a study of Buffon would to some minds. In the finer ideal embodiments of men and things, birds and butterflies, beasts and fishes; they rival Hans Andersen, that prince of fairy writers; wonderful word pictures have they revealed to the fresh pure minds of millions of little ones, in the magic mirror of Fairyland—creations in words, that all artists in colour falls short of their intrinsic merit to be called the princes of Fairy Tale writers, is pre-eminent in the bewitchery of the style and grace of these stories. . . . The Brothers Grimm are entitled to the augmented blessings of every fresh reader, who, we trust, will be added to the innumerable company that have gone before the publication of this Edition. May this present Edition increase their number by fresh thousands; and may every reader (big or little)

swell the paean of praise and blessing we now raise to the immortal Brothers Grimm for this work of theirs, which is the paradise of our nurseries and the heaven of our infancy.[26]

Though there was some competition from Hans Christian Andersen's stories, as Meek notes, the Grimms' tales were considered classical fairy tales by the end of the nineteenth century and established a model for what a fairy tale should be in Great Britain and North America as well, even though there are hardly any fairies in their tales. Indeed, it was Taylor who reintroduced several, but his major accomplishment was to *adapt* the tales so they would be acceptable for a rising bourgeois class and a general population that was becoming more and more literate. His English renditions also appealed to adults and were reinforced by the general positive reception of Perrault's tales. Yet from the beginning there was a certain ambivalence on the part of Taylor, who also regarded the tales as unusual folk tales that could liberate the imagination of children and adults, not restrain them with didactic and moralistic stories. In this regard he was attuned to the German and English romantic movements that sought to break with the stringent rationalist and religious ideologies of the late eighteenth and early nineteenth centuries.

Ironies of Taylor's Revolutionary Work

Taylor's adaptations of the Grimms' tales are exceptional because his ideological and poetical premises were based on ideals and myths about the origins and dissemination of the folk tales that the Grimms themselves perpetuated. Indeed, he fulfilled them to such an extreme that he subverted the Grimms' intentions, even though he thought he was following them. In no way, despite the Grimms' creation of the Small Edition in 1826, did they want their German tales to be treated as tales for children. In no way did they want, nor did Taylor for that matter, the philological and historical attributes of *Kinder- und Hausmärchen* to be neglected. Yet, this was exactly what happened throughout the nineteenth century: the Grimms' different kinds of folk tales, derived allegedly from ancient German sources, became English "fairy tales" for the entertainment of children. And it was not until the latter part of the twentieth century that the mis-reception and misunderstanding of the Grimms' tales were somewhat rectified in English-speaking countries. Of course, the "rectification" has been limited due to the Disneyfication, trivialization, infantilization, and commercial exploitation of the tales, processes that became dominant in the twentieth century and continue into the twenty-first.

Taylor's adaptation of the tales is, of course, partially to blame for the "degeneration" of the tales from the highest model of the Grimms' *Naturpoesie* to amusing popular reading matter for children. But some of the blame for this ironic turn in history must be placed on the Grimms themselves, who created certain exaggerated "myths" about the sanctity of the tales that led Taylor to adapt them the way he did. And, of course, the tales in Taylor's hands did not lose their historical and intrinsically cultural value, for they have always provided more than mere entertainment. As Jacob Grimm commented, Taylor's appropriated tales read well. In fact, they are out-of-the-ordinary nursery tales because he favored the oral tradition and cleverly edited the tales as reading matter for children while endeavoring to maintain their "antiquarian" quality. In reaching out to family-reading audiences, both the Grimms and Taylor ironically created the conditions for a mixed reception of the tales favoring bourgeois households that has become part of their legacy in Europe and North America.

In Martin Sutton's superb book *The Sin-Complex: A Critical Study of English Versions of the Grimms' Kinder- und Hausmärchen in the Nineteenth Century*, he quotes an important passage from F. J. Harvey Darton's *Children's Books in England* to explain what he means by "sin-complex," and Darton's remarks are worth repeating here:

> The fear or dislike [in England] of fairy-tales, in fact, was not and is not dependent to a marked extent on the feeling of any one period. It is a habit of the mind which has often been dominant in the history of children's books without much aid from contemporary circumstances. It is a manifestation, in England, of a deep-rooted sin-complex. It involves the belief that anything fantastic on the one hand, or anything primitive on the other, is inherently noxious, or at least so void of good as to be actively dangerous.[27]

During Taylor's youth in England, the general attitude toward fairy tales among literate people was more disparaging than positive, and he was well aware of this. This does not mean that fairy tales and folk tales did not circulate and were not accepted by readers. The times were changing. As Sutton, Alderson, Jennifer Schacker, and more recently Matthew Grenby have pointed out from different perspectives,[28] books of fairy and folk tales for middle-class children and adults remained popular from the seventeenth century up through the nineteenth century. Their reception was more ambivalent than black and white because these tales of fantasy and magic were questioned by conservative religious groups but not totally rejected. The debates always centered around their moral qualities and how they might be used and printed to elevate the behavior of

young readers. They were somehow tainted by the sin-complex. What was somewhat different during Taylor's formative years is that that the tales were gradually
treated by intellectuals and antiquarians as historical and cultural relics that revealed cultural and national values and international commonalities. By emphasizing how historically significant the tales were and how pure and refreshing
they were for children, Taylor, following the Grimms, wanted to appeal to the
scholarly interests of adults and the curious, "innocent" minds of young readers.
He could point to the uniqueness of the Grimms' tales because they were much
different from the French fairy tales of Mme d'Aulnoy and Charles Perrault and
the stories of *The Arabian Nights* that had been prevalent in England up through
the 1820s. Not all of the Grimms' stories were *fairy* tales but comic anecdotes,
animal stories, fables, wonder tales, and religious legends—closer to the soil of
the common people.

It is interesting to note that Taylor changed the order of the Grimms' tales
in the 1819 edition and began with "Hans in Luck" (an anecdote), followed by
"The Traveling Musicians" (animal story), "The Golden Bird" (wonder tale), and
"The Fisherman and His Wife" (a dialect tall tale). Three of these four tales are
comical. In contrast, the Grimms always began with more serious and somewhat
horrific tales: "The Frog King, or Iron Henry," "The Companionship of the Cat
and Mouse," "The Virgin Mary's Child," and "A Tale about the Boy Who Went
Forth to Learn What Fear Was." In these tales a princess lies to a helpful frog and
throws him against the wall; a cat eats a mouse; a young woman is almost burned
at the stake for disobeying the Virgin Mary; and a young boy learns what fear
means. In the seven Large Editions published by the Grimms, they always ended
their collections with a short tale, "The Golden Key," which was intended to keep
the dynamic flow of folk tales alive and keep readers curious. It is about a poor
boy who discovers a golden key and iron casket in the snow. He searches for a
keyhole to see if the casket contains a treasure, and readers are kept in suspense
about his discovery. In contrast, Taylor ended his combined two volumes with
"The Juniper Tree," a ghastly tale about a woman who murders her stepson and
feeds him in a stew to his father. Yet, all's well that ends well when the stepson returns in the form of a bird to kill the woman and is retransformed into a human
to live happily ever after with his stepsister and father. Taylor's framework for the
tales contains the storytelling that begins with a comic tale and concludes with
a happy end to a gruesome tale, whereas the Grimms' framework allows for an
open end and more tales to be told.

But it was not simply the order and choice of tales that made Taylor's
German Popular Tales different from the Grimms' collection and more suitable for children, it was an editing process that was geared to propriety, something to which the Grimms also paid attention, but Taylor was much more the

consummate censor: he artfully made the tales more succinct, changed titles, characters, and incidents, mistranslated rhymes, deleted references to God and Christianity, downplayed brutality, and eliminated sexual innuendoes. For example, in the first two tales, the titles "Hans in Luck" and "The Traveling Musicians" depart from the German and should be designated "Lucky Hans" and "The Bremen Town Musicians." Throughout these tales there are all sorts of errors. Hans carries gold not silver; two references to God are changed, the rhymed verse that the scissor-grinder sings makes no sense; the word *Sonntagskind* should be "fortune's child"; "horsepond" should be "a dark hole." In "The Traveling Musicians," the dog's master does not want to knock him on the head, he wants to kill him; the cat is not a "good lady"; the role of the captain of the robbers is changed; a judge is turned into a devil; and there are numerous other misleading translations.

Two of the most egregious adaptations are "Hansel and Grethel" and "The Frog King." Taylor's tale, "Hansel and Grettel" is actually the Grimms' "Brother and Sister," and his "Roland and May-Bird" is an amalgamation of "Foundling," "Sweetheart Roland," and "Hansel and Grethel." In the Grimms' original "Brother and Sister," a stepmother, who is a witch, beats a brother and sister, who run away. In the woods, the brother drinks from a brook, contaminated by the stepmother, and is turned into a fawn. His sister takes care of him in a cottage in the woods until a king discovers the fawn while out hunting. He follows the fawn to a hut and is so taken by the sister's beauty that he weds her and takes her and the fawn/brother to his castle. Later, after the young queen gives birth, her stepmother the witch learns about her happiness and seeks to destroy her. The stepmother goes to the castle, kills the young queen, and replaces her with her own nasty daughter. However, thanks to God, the queen had not really died and visits her infant son at midnight. A nanny informs the king what has been transpiring, and on the third night, he interrupts her visitation. The "true" queen tells him what has happened, and the king has his false bride and the witch mother executed. The fawn is then transformed into a human, and they all live happily ever after.

In Taylor's "Hansel and Grettel," the stepmother is an evil fairy. All references to God are deleted. The tale is cut in half and ends with the king taking Grettel and the fawn Hansel to his castle, where they inform the king about the wicked fairy. Instead of having the fairy killed, the king compels the fairy to change Hansel back into his human form. Once she does that, she is mildly punished and disappears, while the king lives happily ever after with Hansel and Grettel.

Whereas Taylor's "Hansel and Grettel" is a sweet and simple version of the Grimms' "Brother and Sister," devoid of any tension and sadism, his "Roland and May-Bird" is a convoluted tale that borders on being a nonsensical version of the Grimms' "Hansel and Grethel." In this tale, the baby May-Bird is kidnapped and carried off to a tree by a vulture. A poor woodcutter finds her and raises her with his son, Roland. They are like brother and sister and happy to be together. However, the woodcutter is so poor that his wife convinces him to abandon the children in a forest. Lost, the youngsters find the sweetmeat house of a spiteful fairy, who wants to eat Roland. However, May-Bird steals the fairy's wand, and she runs off with Roland, pursued by the fairy, who wears seven-league boots. Yet they manage to trick the fairy with her own wand until she becomes entangled in thorns. Freed of the fairy, Roland wants to rush home for help, but May-Bird is too tired to accompany him. So he leaves her in the woods and promises that he will return and marry her. However, he meets another maiden and falls in love. May-Bird is desolate and wants to commit suicide. Instead, she changes herself into a flower. A shepherd picks her off a field and wants to wed her, but she wants to remain true to Roland. Therefore, she tells the shepherd about her plight, and he lets her stay and clean house for him. In the meantime, she discovers that Roland is going to marry the maiden he found. Compelled to attend the wedding, May-Bird sings in front of the guests before Roland marries the maiden, and her singing makes him realize who his true love is, and he marries May-Bird.

It is clear that Taylor let his imagination run away with him in this tale. The patchwork does not work. The motives of the characters and the fairy-tale motifs do not blend. None of the original German tales are done justice in this weird adaptation, and the invented story's only saving grace is in the amusing hodge-podge conflation of the three tales. Taylor was less adventurous in his adaptation of the Grimms' "Frog King." However, he did change the title, did not allow the frog to sleep with the princess, introduced yet another wicked fairy who had turned the prince into a frog, and reduced the role played by faithful Heinrich, the prince's servant. In Taylor's chaste version the spell cast on the prince is broken because the princess allows the frog to sleep on her pillow for three nights. There is no slamming the frog against a wall or indications of possible sexual intercourse. In the end the prince takes the princess to his father's castle, where they will be married.

In almost all the tales that Taylor adapted, he made key changes that basically "cleansed" the tales of dubious allusions to religion and sex and minimized horror and brutality. Sutton does a thorough line-by-line comparison of the Grimms' "Snow White" and Taylor's "Snow-drop" to demonstrate how radically Taylor changed the tone and tenor of the original German.[29] His notion of harmony and happiness was much different from that of the Grimms, and he takes pains not to offend any potential ethically minded reader. Very rarely does Taylor allow anyone to be tortured or punished severely. So, instead of having the wicked queen dance to her death in red-hot shoes, he has her simply choke with passion, fall ill, and die.

There are other notable changes that Taylor made. For instance, Rumpel-stiltskin is not allowed to stamp his foot into the ground and tear himself in half when the queen announces his name in the German text. Instead, he pulls out his leg from the ground and runs off. A devil is turned into a giant in "The Devil with the Three Golden Hairs." "Chanticleer and Partlet" is another fascinating amalgamation of "Riffraff," "Herr Korbes," and "The Death of the Hen." Ludwig Tieck's powerful tale, "The Elves," is bowdlerized. One can find numerous errors of translation in almost every tale, but these errors do not necessarily diminish the quality of Taylor's stories, and we must remember that there were different standards of translation in the early part of the nineteenth century from what exist in the twenty-first century. The emphasis was not placed on literal translation or exact fidelity to the original text. Taylor explained how and why he changed the stories, and he even felt impelled to change his own adaptations.

His final revolutionary contribution to transforming the Grimms' folk tales into a classic of children's literature was *Gammer Grethel, or German Fairy Tales, and Popular Stories*, published in 1839, the year of his death. What is significant about the title is the addition of the character "Gammer Grethel" and the term "fairy tales" to give the impression that the tales were ancient and taken straight from the mouths of peasants. In fact, the entire book is shaped around the figure of a storyteller, based on a fictitious representation of Dorothea Viehmann by the Brothers Grimm, as an authentic peasant storyteller. In addition, emphasis is now placed on *fairy tales* thanks in part to Taylor's introducing fairies into the Grimms' tales. Altogether there were forty-two tales selected for this edition organized in a different sequence from *German Popular Stories*. There are twelve evenings with three or four tales told each evening. The anonymous collector and translator of the tales informs readers that he had gathered the tales in Germany from Gammer Grethel, an honest farmer's wife, and asked her permission to write them down for the benefit of young friends in England. The very first tale is *not* a comic anecdote as in *German Popular Stories*, but rather a moralistic fairy tale, "The Golden Goose," which Taylor greatly revised. For instance, in *German Popular Stories*, his adaptation of the Grimms' tale begins as follows:

> There was a man who had three sons. The youngest was called Dummling, and was on all occasions despised and ill-treated by the whole family.[30]

In *Gammer Grethel*, we read:

> There was a man who had three sons. The youngest was called Dummling—which is much the same as Dunderhead, for all

thought he was more than half a fool—and he was at all times mocked and ill-treated by the whole household.[31]

In the end of both versions it is the virtuous Dummling, not his selfish brothers, who triumphs. After he helps an old man, who is maltreated by his brothers, he is given a golden goose, and people who want to steal its feathers become attached to it. As Dummling drags the people with him, he arrives in a city where the king has promised to reward anyone with his daughter if he can make the solemn princess laugh. Dummling easily accomplishes this with the goose and the helpless people attached to it. (Cruikshank's illustration is delightful [figure 3].) Then he is rewarded by a king who allows him to marry his daughter and become his heir.

Of course, both adaptations are very different from the 1819 German text, which is much longer and complicated, for the haughty king of the German tale refuses to give his daughter to Dummling after he makes her laugh, and the young man must complete three tasks, helped by the mysterious old man, before the king relents and they all live happily ever after. Taylor's "new" book, *Gammer Grethel*, did not want to offer complication but simplicity. It is the simple small heroes, the "Tom Thumbs" of the world, who are to be rewarded for their virtuous childlike behavior.

In *Gammer Grethel*, Taylor made his ideological approach to folk tales much more explicit than in any of his previous adaptations. Aside from shortening and stylizing the tales from *German Popular Stories* and focusing on children, he changed the titles of some of the tales and added names to the characters. For instance "Peter the Goatherd" became "Karl Katz," and animals were given names in "The Grateful Beasts," which was now called "Fritz and His Friends." There was only one new German tale, "Das Schrätel und der Wasserbär," translated under the title "The Bear and the Skrattel." In the note to this tale, Taylor stated that he took it from the Grimms' preface to Thomas Crofton Croker's *Fairy Legends and Traditions of the South of Island*, which Wilhelm had translated into German as *Irische Elfenmärchen* in 1826. It was a medieval German text in verse that Taylor translated because of its "authentic antiquity." By including it in *Gammer Grethel* in 1839, the connection to the Grimm Brothers was completed. However, the Taylor revolutionary touch continued to make itself felt throughout the rest of the nineteenth century in England and America in numerous reprints and new editions.

For instance in 1843 the publisher James Burns included some of Taylor's texts, slightly changed, in *Popular Tales and Legends* and followed this publication in 1845 with *Household Tales and Traditions of England, Germany, France, Scotland, etc.*, in which he stole and adapted more of Taylor's translations

Figure 3. "The Golden Goose." Illustration by George Cruikshank.

without giving credit. Gradually, Taylor's adaptations were regarded as fairy tales not popular stories. Indeed, his cousin John Edward Taylor, a London printer, published another selection of the Grimms' tales in 1846 under the title *The Fairy Ring: A New Collection of Popular Tales, Collected from the German of Jacob and Wilhelm Grimm*. This volume, which contained thirty-six Grimms' tales never

translated before, was illustrated by Richard Doyle, one of the great Victorian illustrators, and it added to the popularity of the Grimms' collection as a children's
book. But the fact is that Edgar Taylor's revolution had already been successful
by the time this new adaptation had appeared and had set the tone for what
were to be considered "authentic" fairy tales from Germany. Interestingly, the
very first so-called genuine translation of the Grimms' "German tales" in France,
Vieux Contes pour l'Amusement des Grands et des Petits enfans (1824), published
by Antoine Boulland, was actually based totally on Taylor's English adaptations
with Cruikshank's illustrations. However, the greatest irony in the history of the
Grimms' tales in England is that Taylor had already turned the Grimms' stories into *classical* folk and fairy tales for children with a British flavor while the
Brothers were still alive and struggling to preserve the role of authentic folk tales
in the German cultural heritage.

CHAPTER TWO

Hyping the Grimms' Fairy Tales

*If paratexts exist, as Genette notes, in a zone of "transaction: a privi-
leged place of a pragmatics and a strategy, of an influence on the public,
an influence that . . . is at the service of a better reception for the text and
a more pertinent reading of it," then paratextual devices in fairy-tale
translations and editions may be more important in the tales' reception
than the märchen themselves. And because they have a public impact
on how readers understand, respond to, and evaluate written cultural
artifacts, authorial and editorial paratexts have a social, cultural, and
political role. Engaged in a continuing debate about the identity and
hierarchy of cultures, the paratexts that present Grimms' stories seek
to direct and capture the reader's allegiance in a struggle over the tales'
authority, control, and ownership, and—most fundamentally—in a
struggle over the stories that we tell each other about them.*

—Donald Haase, "Framing the Brothers Grimm"[1]

Perhaps the Brothers Grimm, wherever they may be, are happy about all the
conferences, books, and papers that have honored them and their tales in the
bicentenary celebrations from 2012 to 2015. More than likely, however, they
have turned over in their graves because of the mass-mediated hype of fairy tales
too often transformed into trivial pulp by the globalized culture industry. Then
again, if that is the case, the Grimms are partially to blame for the hype.

There is a fascinating, deeply ironic tale that needs to be told here. As we
have seen, the Grimms, inspired by their first English translator Edgar Taylor,
helped pave the way for the modern hyping of fairy tales and the classification
of fairy tales as a staple of children's literature. And it all began with the Grimms'
sincere commitment to salvaging the genuine essence of folk tales, their oral
authenticity and historical significance, if you will. But before I discuss how the
Grimms became involved in hyping their own tales to change their reception
at the beginning of the nineteenth century, I want first to discuss some of the
theoretical aspects of hyping and the particular role hyping plays in the media
paratexts of the culture industry. Then I should like to review again how the
Brothers Grimm changed the format and scope of their tales, primarily under

the influence of Taylor's 1823 translation, *German Popular Stories*, to make their tales more accessible to the general reading public in Germany. Finally, I want to examine some recent filmic adaptations of fairy tales and consider whether the hyping of these films detracts from the value of the fairy-tale genre and storytelling in general. Underlying my endeavor to understand the hyping of fairy tales is the question whether the historical integrity of any genre or any project such as the preservation of folk tales promoted by the Brothers Grimm can be appreciated and understood as part of our western cultural heritage. Or what happens to the meaning and value of a legacy in societies where hype is accepted if not celebrated as the norm?

Hyping and Paratexts

In his highly significant book, *Show Sold Separately: Promos, Spoilers, and Other Media Paratexts*, Jonathan Gray defines "hype" as "advertising that goes 'over' and 'beyond' an accepted norm, establishing heightened presence, often for a brief, unsustainable period of time: like the hyperventilating individual or the spaceship in hyperdrive, the hyped product will need to slow down at some point. Its heightened presence is made all the more possible with film and television due to those industries' placement—at least in their Hollywood varieties—within networks of synergy."[2] He then notes that within the entertainment industry, "synergy refers to a strategy of multimedia platforming, linking a media product to related media on other 'platforms,' such as toys, DVDs, and/or videogames, so that each product advertises and enriches the experience of the other. And whereas hype is often regarded solely as advertising and as PR, synergistic merchandise, products, and games—also called *peripherals*—are often intended as other platforms for profit generation."[3]

Although hype is associated with hyperbole, embellishment, and extravagance, Gray argues that, as a paratext, it has become part of business as usual, and what formerly appeared to be uncommon and on the periphery of culture today is actually at its center and more decisive in creating meaning than source texts. Whether talking about a book or a film, Gray maintains that the meanings of primary texts or source texts are now determined by paratexts—that is, by all the peripheral products and things that surround or are connected to the texts. Here he is building upon the work of Gérard Genette, who created the term and indicated that paratexts prepare us for the source text; they are gateways to assessing a product or artifact. Paratexts are both the inside of a book (turned toward the text) and the outside of a book (the fringe turned toward the world). They are intended to manage a person's reading of the text. Genette states: "The paratext, then, is empirically made up of a heterogeneous group of practices and discourses of all kinds and dating from periods which I federate under the term 'paratext' in the name of a common interest, or a convergence of effects, that seems to me more important than their diversity of aspect."[4]

In the case of literature or a book, the paratexts consist of the cover, the frontispiece, the title page, the preface, the introduction, the dedication, the inscription, the epigraph, the notes, the format, the type, the bibliography, the index, the blurbs on the back page, the prepublication advertising, the webpages on the Internet, reviews, blogs, interviews, talks delivered by the author on tour, and so on. Gray maintains that "paratexts are not simply add-ons, spinoffs, and also-rans: they create texts, they manage them, and they fill them with many of the meanings that we associate with them. Just as we ask *para*medics to save lives rather than leave the job to others, and just as a *para*site feeds off, lives in, and can affect the running of its host's body, a paratext constructs, lives in, and can affect the running of the text."[5]

Though Gray often alludes to the paratextual strategy of hyping as a nuisance, he never explores how pervasive and deleterious it is to the quality of the product that it allegedly promotes. He fails to critique how hyping can actually deplete the meaning of a product—just as a parasite can weaken if not kill its host—and conceal its lack of quality through exaggerations and lies. (This is the unintended consequence of paratexts that generally want to guarantee and validate its message. A hyped paratext is invented to disguise the fact that the message is meaningless or does not have the quality that it purports to have.)

In some respects almost all hypes and much of publicity rely on fairy-tale motifs because they promise us magical transformation if we imbibe it, wear it, touch it, smell it, breathe it, smoke it, drink it, steal it, live in it, or aspire to it. Hypes delude us into believing that the impossible can be realized by some kind of miracle—that is, through the product we are to consume. Hypes are tantalizing and frustrating because they keep us trying and wanting to fulfill the impossible. They distract to prevent critical reflection. In effect, hypes celebrate meaningless and wanton consumption. They stimulate longing. Yet Gray wants hyping and other peripherals to become more artistic and lend themselves to the quality of the source text. This wish is impossible because the basis of hyping is artful exploitation through untruth; the purpose of hype is to discard and undermine the substance of an artwork, to transform it into a desirable commodity, and to make it profitable not necessarily for the author/creator of a work but for the corporation that assumes property rights to the text. Indeed, copyrighting is also a paratext because it gives a publisher, for example, the right to create and add as many meanings as he or she wants to the text. Since there is no such thing as a neutral paratext—that is, since every paratext no matter how slight has an ideological purpose—criticism cannot just accept the necessity of paratexting. Gray's study is valuable, not because it is a critique, but because he explains just how peripherals work while failing to examine the ideological consequences of hyping.

Let us examine how the meaning of a literary work is created in contemporary western societies using Gray's description of how hyped peripherals operate. As Gray explains, citing Genette, paratexts prepare readers for an approach to the text and an ongoing discourse after the text has been published. Depending on the author of a book, famous or young and recently discovered, the publisher of the book might announce the signing of a contract with a succinct and glowing description of the book even before it is in print or even written, as in the case of Harry Potter sequels by J. K. Rowling. Depending on the genre, readers will already be prepared to read the work in a certain way. An indicated genre will already predispose a reader. Fans of science fiction, mysteries, true romances, fantasy, nonfiction, and so on are already conditioned to read in a certain way, and publishers will alert target and guide groups that a certain type of book will soon appear. After the announcement, all sorts of mass media (newspapers, magazines, radio, television, websites, blogs) will be approached with the publisher's publicity releases and promos that describe the book along with blurbs. Readers will begin to discuss the forthcoming book and even begin to debate its contents before they have read the book. Its meaning is well under way to becoming created by reading audiences and promoters. Glossy posters and pictures will reveal the cover of the book. Interviews and readings will be held. Once the book is produced, publishers will seek to have it placed in the windows of bookstores or in prominent places, and ads will be featured on the Internet and through various venues; reviews will appear on Amazon and other booksellers' websites. The book's front and back covers will have a lavish design, and the title is carefully chosen to intrigue readers. Blurbs by famous people and authorities certify that the book is unique and that readers have never read anything like it. Once the book is actually accessible, reviews begin and discussions by readers in informal groups, on phones, through texting, at schools, and universities, on the Internet, and through e-mail; they will contest or agree with all the previous hyped promotions and meanings that have circulated. Hundreds if not thousands of new meanings will be produced. There will be follow-ups such as additional interviews, tours, and readings by the author. In fact, the author might be moved to retract or question the meaning that he or she sees in the literary work. The author might be encouraged to write a sequel, prequel, or a similar work. Whatever the case may be, the author loses control and touch with his or her work, which circulates in a world of hype.

Lost in the circulation of commodified peripherals is the author-intended "substantial meaning" of the literary work—what I call its "integrity." Of course, one could argue, as many French critics such as Roland Barthes and Michel Foucault have done, that there is no such thing as an essential meaning or an author.[6]

Meaning is produced through diverse readings of the text, signs, and even the author, and meaning will be subjectively and relatively produced. Yet, there is always something intrinsic to a work of art even if we consider it *bricolage*. The signs of an artwork are humanly and skillfully assembled by a particular individual within a literary or cultural tradition. A material cultural heritage has its basis in what humans memetically consider relevant; these relevant signs and objects enable readers to adapt to their environment and fit together as societies evolve. Hype is not relevant, and it is only by critically "deflating" hype that we come close to understanding intrinsic relevant relics and new cultural products. To truly read a literary work or film, we must first learn to deflate.

Why and How the Grimms Hyped Their Tales

As we have seen, the Brothers Grimm revered all types of tales told by the folk, not just fairy stories or wonder tales. They thought that the stories they collected were innocent expressions and representations of the divine nature of the world. For them, the simplicity of pristine spoken tales was culturally and historically profound, and the Grimms viewed themselves as cultivators of lost relics whose essence had to be conserved and disseminated before the tales vanished. In particular, they firmly believed that these wondrous tales enabled people to get in touch with their inner selves and the outside world. They fostered hope. This was because "genuine" folk and fairy tales served as moral correctives to an unjust world and revealed truths about human experience through exquisite metaphor. As I have explained in previous chapters, there is no indication in the *initial* paratexts pertinent to the collecting of folk and fairy tales that the Grimms considered their tales as part of children's literature or intended the tales for children. Their work was a scholarly endeavor from the very beginning.

After the publication of the second volume of the first edition in 1815, however, the Grimms were once again disappointed by the critical reception. They were convinced that their project was being misunderstood. Although they did not abandon their basic notions about the origins and significance of folk tales in the second edition of 1819, they began shaping their collection with new paratexts and materials to make it more accessible for a larger bourgeois reading public than just scholars and educated readers. Donald Haase points out that

> as authors—or at least authorial agents—the Grimms carefully
> framed their collection with a variety of significant paratexts that
> sought to contextualize their fairy tales and explain to the reader
> a multitude of relevant and often complex issues. The title, desig-
> nation of the compilers, dedication, preface, and annotations were

all intended to help the recipient understand the place, nature, and function of the tales in historical, political, cultural, ethnic, mythological, scholarly, and pedagogical terms. Without these paratexts legitimizing and contextualizing them, the tales would likely have been an unremarkable assemblage of disdained stories. They became texts worthy of attention and serious reception only in light of the Grimms' larger—and enormously successful—cultural project that sought to give the stories legitimacy as primary cultural documents from oral translation.[7]

All this is very true, but Haase also adds that "one measure of how translators of Grimms' stories deal with cultural issues important to the Grimms is the extent to which their translations make use (or no use) of the Grimms' paratexts."[8]

For Taylor, who used the second edition of 1819 for his translation, the Grimms' paratexts had changed somewhat so that he was led to believe that all the tales were from oral traditions, that there were many storytellers like Dorothea Viehmann, and that the target audience for the tales consisted of young people.

Indeed, there were clear signs that the Grimms wanted to attract younger readers and their families to their stories and convince them of their great value. Two important paratexts indicate that the Grimms were leaning in fact toward hyping their collection of tales: the first is the preface; the second is the use of Dorothea Viehmann's portrait. In the preface to the 1819 edition, they state that

these stories are suffused with the same purity that makes children appear so wondrous and blessed to us; they have the same bluish-white, flawless, shining eyes, which are as big as they will ever get, even as other body parts remain delicate, weak and awkward for use on earth. That is the reason that we wanted, through our collection, first of all to serve the cause of the history of poetry and mythology, but it was also our intention that the poetry living in it be effective and bring pleasure wherever it could, and also that the book serve as an educational primer [*Erziehungsbuch*]. To that end we are not aiming at the kind of innocence achieved by timidly excising whatever refers to certain situations and relations that take place every day and that simply cannot be kept hidden. In doing that you can fool yourself into thinking that what can be removed from a book can also be removed from real life. We are looking for innocence in truth of a straightforward narrative that does not conceal anything wrong by holding back on it. Nonetheless, in this new edition, we have carefully eliminated every phrase not appropriate for children.[9]

This statement repeats many points that the Grimms wrote in their correspondence with Achim von Arnim, but it is more striking for its hyperbole, especially the flowery language, and apparent concession to critics who wanted them to include children as readers or listeners. Moreover, it is clear that they are trying to exaggerate and persuade readers about the profound authenticity of the tales. To do this more effectively, they introduced Dorothea Viehmann as the type of ideal storyteller that one could find among German peasants.

What is fascinating about the peripherals of the 1819 edition, especially the preface and the portrait of Viehmann, is that they convinced Taylor to take a few steps further in hyping the first English edition, *German Popular Stories* (1823). As I have pointed out, Taylor's adaptations of the Grimms' tales are exceptional and had ironical consequences because his ideological and poetical premises were based on the ideals and myths about the origins and dissemination of the folk tales that the Grimms perpetuated. Indeed, he fulfilled them in a way that transformed their collection into a book of children's literature. In chapter one I demonstrated how Taylor *adapted* the Grimms' tales of the second German 1819 edition and changed them into a collection of delightful moralistic English stories for children. Aside from freely adapting the tales, he celebrated their genuine antiquarian quality and eventually included Viehmann as the major character in the second revised edition of his tales, *Gammer Grethel or German Fairy Tales, and Popular Stories* (1839). Moreover, Cruikshank's illustrations imparted a comic tone to the tales that they did not possess in the German editions. From 1839 onward, two different editions of Taylor's adaptations were published throughout the nineteenth century and competed with one another: *German Popular Stories*, generally produced in one or two volumes, and *Gammer Grethel or German Fairy Tales, and Popular Stories*, which provided a totally different framework for a smaller selection of tales once again heavily revised by Taylor.

What is significant about the 1839 title is the paratextual addition of the character "Gammer Grethel" and the term "fairy tales" to give the impression that the stories were ancient and magical and had been taken straight from the lips of peasants. In fact, the entire book is shaped around the figure of a fictitious storyteller, based on a fictitious representation of Dorothea Viehmann by the Brothers Grimm, as an authentic peasant storyteller. In addition, emphasis was now placed on *fairy tales* thanks in part to Taylor's introducing fairies into the Grimms' tales which did not have them.

Altogether there were forty-two tales in the *Gammer Grethel* book selected from the 1823/1826 editions for this book, and they were organized in a different sequence within a frame. There are twelve evenings with three or four tales told each evening. The anonymous collector and translator of the tales informs his readers that he had gathered the tales in Germany from Gammer Grethel, an honest farmer's wife, and asked her permission to write them down for the benefit of young friends in England. With this dramatic paratextual change, Taylor obviously hoped to gain and influence more young readers. Indeed, all his different editions gained in popularity, especially since his works were the only collections of putative Grimms' tales on the market that began using the latest forms of advertising to sell them. Success came in different forms of reprints and advertising.

In 1869, thirty years after Taylor's death, Taylor's widow granted the publisher John Camden Hotten permission to combine the first two editions of *German Popular Stories* into one book with the original prefaces by Taylor, an introduction by the famous critic John Ruskin, a letter endorsing the book by the even more famous author Sir Walter Scott, and a new advertisement. (Incidentally, this was the first edition in which Taylor's name as translator appeared on the title page.) All these peripherals added to the meaning of Taylor's adaptations, not to the integrity of the Grimms' collections. By this time the paratextuals were all geared to present the Grimms' tales as morally appropriate literature for children.

In another example of how the Grimms' tales were hyped in strange intertextual and intracultural ways, Taylor's distant cousin, John Edward Taylor, published his own free translation called *The Fairy Ring: A New Collection of Popular Tales* in 1846 with illustrations by the gifted Richard Doyle. This volume contained fifty-five newly translated tales from *Children's and Household Tales*, and they were just as bowdlerized as the tales in Edgar Taylor's collections. What is astounding is that the different Taylor editions and publications, many of them pirated, disseminated false impressions of the Grimms' tales in English-speaking countries throughout the nineteenth century because these selected adaptations were the only versions available until the translations by Mrs. H. B. Paull in 1882, Lucy Crane in 1882, and Margaret Hunt in 1884. Nevertheless, Taylor's versions were the ones that that held sway even up through the late twentieth century, when Puffin Classics reprinted *German Popular Stories* in 1948 without mentioning Edgar Taylor anywhere in the book but making full use of the Cruikshank illustrations.

All the changes that Taylor made in his 1823 and 1826 editions of *German Popular Stories* along with *Gammer Grethel* and later editions of his so-called translations had powerful cultural consequences not only in the United Kingdom and North America but also in Germany. As I have previously demonstrated, the Brothers Grimm were so impressed by the format of Taylor's book that they decided to publish a shorter version of their Large Edition (*Große Ausgabe*) in 1825, which contained fifty of their most popular tales[10] and six charming illustrations such as "The Goose Girl" by Ludwig Grimm (figure 4), much more serious than those by George Cruikshank.

Figure 4. "The Goose Girl." Illustration by Ludwig Grimm.

Yet, in no way, despite the Grimms' creation of the Small Edition in 1825, did they want their German tales to be treated as tales for children. In no way did they, or Taylor for that matter, want the philological and historical attributes of *Kinder- und Hausmärchen* to be neglected. Yet this was exactly what happened throughout the nineteenth century in Germany and in English-speaking countries.

Contemporary Hyping of Fairy Tales

The Grimms promoted the collecting of all sorts of folk tales throughout the nineteenth century, and they were certain that if other educated men and women began gathering tales from the common people, these stories, especially the fairy tales, would resonate among young and old from all social classes. Indeed, to a great extent, they were right. The nineteenth century, especially in Europe and North America, became the golden age of fairy-tale collecting that led to the foundation of folklore societies. By the twentieth century, the fairy tale and other simple folk genres began to thrive not only by word of mouth and through print as they had for centuries, but they were also transformed, adapted, and disseminated through picture books of single tales, radio, postcards, greeting cards, comics, cinema, fine arts, performing arts, wedding ceremonies, television, dolls, toys, games, theme parks, clothes, the Internet, university courses, and numerous other media and objects. Among the modes of hyped advertising were posters, billboards, interviews, window dressings, department store shows, radio, TV, parades, theme parks, and Internet interviews, ads in newspapers, magazines, and journals, and all the other kinds of paratexts that accompany a cultural product. As I have argued in my book *Why Fairy Tales Stick: The Evolution and Relevance of a Genre*, the classical fairy tales have become memes, cultural bits of relevant information, and the paratexts of fairy tales have formed memeplexes—that is, groups of variants that add to the meaning of the meme. In correspondence with Michael Drout, who has written a significant book about memes, *How Tradition Works: A Meme-Based Cultural Poetics of the AngloSaxon Tenth Century*, he suggested:

> In memetic terms, I think a para-text is a meme-plex that forms around a text, and the para-textual material can provide extra data about how to interpret what's inside the text. That material, because it stays in its own form, can become separated from its original cultural context, which evolves more quickly than something in a fixed form can. The para-text, then, provides meta-data

about how ambiguities in the main text should be interpreted. The most obvious place where this happens is when we get a particular image of an actor or actress (or animation) of a traditional tale, and that image is thereafter fixed in place even when some of the written descriptions might be more ambiguous, but I'm thinking that material like toys, posters, etc., also works to form around the text in this way (I have a box in the basement filled with my daughter's Disney princesses; these dolls lock into place a particular look for fairy tale characters whose descriptions are not quite as fixed as the icon designed to sell merchandise to little girls).[11]

Today we are inundated by fairy tales that are not only present in the home but are also taught from preschool through the university in the United Kingdom and North America. They are in all walks of life, and to some degree, we even try to transform our lives into fairy tales. They have become second nature, or as Roland Barthes might say, fairy tales have become "mythic." They appear to be universal and natural stories of the way life should be while concealing their artistic constellations and their basic history and ideology. In my book *Fairy Tale as Myth/Myth as Fairy Tale*, I remarked that it is impossible to grasp the history of the fairy tale and the relationship of the fairy tale to myth without taking into consideration the manner in which tales have been revised, duplicated, adapted, and manipulated to reinforce dominant ideologies and often to subvert them. To be more precise, the evolution of the fairy tale as a cultural genre is marked by a process of dialectical appropriation involving imitation, memorization, and revision that set the cultural conditions for its mythicization, institutionalization, and expansion as a mass-mediated genre through radio, film, television, and the Internet. For the most part, the history of this memetic process that is connected to cultural memory is obscured if not negated today by hyping newly produced fairy-tale films, books, musicals, and other products as extraordinary achievements that actually cheapen the meaning of fairy tales that the Brothers Grimm and other nineteenth-century collectors sought to preserve. Hyping is the exact opposite of preservation and involves, as I have argued, conning consumers and selling products that have meager cultural value and will not last.

Some recent fairy-tale films produced by the mainstream culture industry in America reveal how filmmakers and producers hype to sell shallow products geared primarily to make money. They use the mass media to exploit the widespread and constant interest in fairy tales that has actually deepened since the nineteenth century. For instance, in December of 2010, the Disney corporation dubbed the Grimms' "Rapunzel," called it *Tangled*, and announced: "Disney presents a new twist on one of the most hilarious and hair-raising tales ever told."[12] Actually, the Disney promoters should have called the film "Mangled" because of the way it slaughtered and emptied the meaning of the Grimms' and other "Rapunzel" folk tales. When viewed closely, *Tangled* is yet another inane remake of Disney's *Snow White*. The major conflict is between a pouting adolescent princess and a witch. The Disney films repeatedly tend to demonize older women and infantilize young women. Gone are any hints that "Rapunzel" might reflect a deeper initiation ritual in which wise old women keep young girls in isolation to protect them.

Gone, too, are any hints in Catherine Hardwicke's 2011 film *Red Riding Hood* that "Little Red Riding Hood" is a serious and complicated tale about rape. Let us recall the serious nature of this story that is made into a mockery by Hardwicke's film. The history of the tale type "Little Red Riding Hood" reflects the remarkable ways in which the oral and literary traditions have interacted to produce conflicting versions of the same incident. The incident is the violation or rape of a young girl who goes into the forest on an errand or to undertake some kind of initiation test. Of course, the motif of rape can be found in many Greco-Roman myths and most pagan cultures, and it is not clear when all the other significant motifs were brought together to form the basic structure of the "Red Riding Hood" tale that was disseminated in Europe. Jan Ziolkowski and Yvonne Verdier have maintained that fragments of this tale, without the red cap, can be found in late-medieval oral tales.[13] In particular, Verdier, along with the great French folklorist, Paul Delarue, have argued that the tale was probably circulating among women during the early part of the seventeenth century in southern France and northern Italy and was told among women in sewing societies. These tales were never titled, and so the red cap (*chaperon*) does not play a role in them.

Delarue published a composite tale made up of several nineteenth-century versions that he called "The Grandmother": Here a young peasant woman takes some bread and milk to her grandmother. At a crossroads in the woods, she meets a werewolf, who asks her whether she is going to take the path of the pins or the path of the needles. She generally chooses the path of the needles. He rushes off to the grandmother's house and eats the grandmother, but he also puts some of her flesh in a bowl and some of her blood in a bottle before getting into the grandmother's bed. When the girl arrives, the werewolf tells her to refresh herself and eat some meat in the bowl and drink some wine. A cat or some creature at the fireplace condemns her for eating the flesh of her grandmother and drinking her blood. Sometimes there is a warning. All at once the werewolf asks her to take off her clothes and get into bed with him. She complies, and each time she takes off a piece of her clothing, she asks what she should do with it. The werewolf replies that she should throw it into the fireplace because she won't be needing it anymore. When the girl finally gets into bed, she asks several questions such as "my, how hairy you are, granny," until the customary "my what a big mouth you have, granny." When the wolf announces, "all the better to eat you, my dear," she declares that she has to relieve herself. He tells her to do it in bed. But she indicates that she has to have a bowel movement, and so he ties a rope around her leg and sends her into the courtyard through a window. Once there the smart girl unties the rope and ties it around a plum tree and then runs off toward home. The werewolf becomes impatient and yells, "What are you doing out there, making a load?" Then he runs to the window and realizes that the girl has escaped. He runs after her, but it is too late, and she makes it safely to her home.[14]

It is unclear whether Charles Perrault knew a definite oral tale like this when he published the first literary version in 1697. But it is clear that he must have known some version like this and transformed it into a tale in which a naïve bourgeois girl pays for her stupidity and is violated in the end. Both Perrault's tale and the oral folk version became popular in the eighteenth century, and more than likely they began influencing oral and literary stories that gradually became widespread throughout Europe. In Gustav Doré's fascinating nineteenth-century illustration (figure 5), there is already an indication that artists and readers also saw the possibility that Little Red might have wanted to seduce the wolf. Today the "Red Riding Hood" tale type (ATU 333) is considered one of the most famous fairy tales in the world. Perrault's tale was translated into English, German, and Russian during the eighteenth century. In 1800 Ludwig Tieck published *Leben und Tod des kleinen Rothkäppchens* (*Life and Death of Little Red Cap*), and he was the first to introduce a hunter, who saves Red Cap's life. The Grimms also felt sympathy for Little Red Cap and followed Tieck's example in their versions. In addition, they added a second didactic part to show that the grandmother and Little Red Cap learned their lesson. Their tale includes two intact segments that were sent to them by two sisters, Jeanette and Marie Hassenpflug, who were familiar with the Perrault version. The first segment includes the hunter who saves granny and Little Red Riding Hood; the second is similar to a moralistic coda in which Little Red Riding Hood and her granny demonstrate that they have learned their lesson and can defeat the wolf by themselves.

Following the publication of the Grimms' more optimistic "Little Red Cap," storytellers and writers have chosen either their version or Perrault's tale to adapt in hundreds if not thousands of different ways, and these two tales have also entered into the oral tradition. Indeed, the best writers, artists, and filmmakers have interpreted the basic plot in unique ways and have either consciously or unconsciously entered into a discourse about the civilizing process that involves rape, pedophilia, and manners. Not Hardwicke, however. She is attracted to hype and the spectacle.

Figure 5. "Little Red Riding Hood." Illustration by Gustav Doré.

Here much of the hype, which cost millions of dollars, began long before Hardwicke's film was even shown. For instance, the *Los Angeles Times* proclaimed: "Catherine Hardwicke understands impetuous teen heroines the way George Lucas reverse-engineers robot sidekicks. In March, the director of 'Twilight' and 'Thirteen' will unleash her newest troublemaker upon the world with a dark, sensuous spin on 'Red Riding Hood.'"[15] However, the only thing that this film demonstrated is that Hardwicke understands neither teens nor fairy tales, and her theme-park sets, stereotyped characters, and father-turned-werewolf gave rise to a ridiculous, convoluted plot that bored audiences. Her film was basically about hype and selling all the products connected with the film. Writing on March 8, 2011, in the *Los Angeles Times*, Susan Carpenter reported about the novel and e-book, which were issued before the film:

> The book debuted at No. 1 on the New York Times children's paperback bestseller list when it was released in late January, serving as a sort of multimedia prequel and pump-primer for the film, directed by Catherine Hardwicke. As an e-book, "Red Riding Hood" includes video interviews with Hardwicke and her many collaborators, an animated short film, audio discussion about the set design and props, costume sketches and Hardwicke's hand-drawn maps of the world where "Red Riding Hood" takes place, among other things. . . . To novelize "Red Riding Hood," Hardwicke got the OK from her publisher, Little Brown. She just needed an author to write it. For that, she turned to a 21-year-old graduate of Barnard's creative writing program named Sarah Blakely-Cartwright.[16]

Neither the print novel nor the e-book are worth the paper or screen on which they are printed or beamed. Somehow, however, Hardwicke and her producers had to keep trying to make money, and of course, there was a DVD issued in June with special features including an alternative ending to the film, which depicts Valerie alias Red Riding Hood with a newborn child in her arms at her grandmother's house, where her lover unites with her. If this were not enough, there was a sequel book to the film and prequel to the DVD, *Red Riding Hood from Script to Screen*, written by Hardwicke and David Leslie Johnson and published on April 12, 2011. It contains an introduction, notes, and sketches by Hardwicke; the screenplay by Johnson; ninety-six pages of color concept art, storyboards, and costume evolution and illustrations; and behind-the-scenes photographs. The synergy was completed later in June by the DVD. Profits for a planned blockbuster that was a critical flop and commercial fiasco have to be obtained several weeks after the premiere. But nothing could save Hardwicke's film, not even her vapid comments about the tale nor the ridiculous hyperbole to foster consumerism.

As for other ridiculously hyped films, there is *Hoodwinked Too! Hood vs. Evil*, touted on one of the official websites on October 28, 2009, a year and a half before the film was even released: "This is a film that all children should watch! A fun, exciting movie with a lesson to be learned by the end. The animation is quite exceptional, and the actors as well as actresses do a great job in displaying their roles within the film. The story is a must have for those who enjoy good happy endings. Not to reveal too much but the story of Hood vs. Evil is a very attractive one. Keep your eye on this film because it could be something to talk about for some time."[17] Yet, this computer-animated film is nothing less than an uninspired sequel to the 2005 *Hoodwinked*, which features Red Riding Hood and the wolf as sleuths, called upon to work together to rescue Hansel and Gretel from a witch. As the AP reporter Jake Coyle has written, "Such mash-ups of fairy tales have become commonplace since 'Shrek' and children's books like David Wiesner's 'The Three Pigs.'"[18]

What has also become commonplace, of course, is hype that currently forms the core of the production and distribution of Hollywood fairy-tale films. In the past three years several mass-mediated, spectacular fairy-tale films, often called "blockbusters,"[19] have appeared: *Mirror, Mirror* (2012), *Snow White and the Huntsman* (2012), *Hansel & Gretel: Witch Hunters* (2013), *Oz the Great and Powerful* (2013), *Jack the Giant Slayer* (2013), *Frozen* (2014), and *Maleficent* (2014), to name but a few. What these films have in common is not only hype but also a tendency to disregard the binding responsibility that the legacy of traditional storytelling needs to develop the cultural value of the Grimms' tales. These films "thrive" parasitically by draining meaning and from warping memetic stories. Not all these films are based on the well-known classical Grimms' tales, but all these fairy-tale films tend to distort source stories to such a degree that the narratives basically celebrate the massive technological power of Hollywood corporations through spectacle. The story is trivialized while the paratexts assume the center of attention, shifting the focus to the glossy aspects of special effects, actors, and discussions of the film. In his remarkable analysis of the spectacle in contemporary society, Guy Debord noted that

> by means of the spectacle the ruling order discourses endlessly upon itself in an uninterrupted monologue of self-praise. The spectacle is the self-portrait of power in the age of power's totalitarian rule over conditions of existence. . . . But the spectacle is by no means the inevitable outcome of a technical development perceived as *natural*; on the contrary, the society of the spectacle is a form that chooses its own technical content. If the spectacle—understood in the limited sense of those "mass media" that are in its most stultifying superficial manifestation—seems at times to be invading society in the shape of a mere *apparatus*, it should be remembered that this apparatus has nothing neutral about it, and that it answers precisely to the needs of the spectacle's internal dynamics.[20]

In the case of the recent "Snow White" films, the spectacular techniques of the two films *Mirror, Mirror* and *Snow White and the Huntsman* depend on special effects that conceal their ideologies and make it seem natural that rich princesses should by virtue of their bloodline regain their rightful place to rule over the people in their kingdom. Of course, to do this successfully, the young princesses must learn that true womanhood demands that they become warriors and killers like men. From a feminist perspective, we can see what Debord means when he asserts that the ruling classes just enjoy speaking to themselves and receiving accolades when power is at stake. More and more fairy-tale films and TV series such as *Once Upon a Time* portray the women as finally having their say in the manner in which power will be adjudicated just as long as they play by men's rules and just as long as evil is represented by "vicious" and neurotic women threatening to dominate a society. Almost all the recent Hollywood fairy-tale films, unless they have been made in other countries or by independent filmmakers, trivialize the plots of the Grimms' fairy tales and make it appear that women are demented witches and are threatening to corrupt the world.

Despite the fact that Tommy Wirkola's ludicrous *Hansel & Gretel: Witch Hunters*, filled with gratuitous violence, stereotypical characters, and banal black humor, had bad ratings by major film critics, this film not only gained over $200 million dollars and was a huge success in Germany, Russia, Brazil, and Mexico, it has also spawned plans for a sequel and other grade B horror films such as *Witchslayer Gretl* (2012), *Hansel & Gretel* (2013), and *Hansel & Gretel: Warriors of Witchcraft* (2013). It is difficult to say whether the commercial success of this very stupid film that condones all kinds of violence and depicts the hunting of female witches as an infantile game much like the violent video games that are sold throughout the world is due to all the paratexts that surround it. But it is clear that the pathetic storyline and screenplay are an insult to the Grimms' fairy tale and that the film would not have attained its success without the hyped reception and the "fun" that the director, producers, and actors sought to provide audiences.

Wirkola constantly uses the word "fun" in interviews in discussing his intention in making the film. For instance, he has stated:

> I have a strong memory from my childhood of just how dark and gruesome their tale was and I wondered what would have happened to the two of them [Hansel and Gretel] when they grew up? They had this dark past and this intense hatred of witches. So as I thought about it, it made sense to me that of course they would be fated to become great witch hunters. We wanted to feel like this could be happening 300 years ago but at the same time, there is a modern spin on all the action, characters and weaponry. It was a fun way to make a classical world feel fresh.[21]

And in another interview, he explained:

> We wanted the movie to feel timeless and for the movie to feel
> like a fairy tale, but still grounded. It was a lot of fun coming up
> with the different weapon designs and ways of killing witches. We
> mixed old and new elements. But no matter how modern some of
> the weapons are, they all have an old-fashioned feel and look like
> they could fit into this world.[22]

But is it really "fun" to watch handsome Hansel and beautiful Gretel murder one person after another with weird weapons? Are we supposed to enjoy
violence? Should we indulge the puerile fun the actors, crew, and director have,
all who show no sign of comprehending what the Grimms' legacy is? Wirkola's
imaginative projection of Hansel and Gretel in adulthood is purely an infantile fantasy that detracts from all the nineteenth-century serious versions about
child abandonment and famine. According to Wirkola, Hansel and Gretel become professional mercenaries seeking revenge after they discover that their
mother and father had been killed unjustly by townspeople who thought they
were witches. There is not the slightest hint in the film that the Grimms' various
versions illuminated the harsh conditions under which the poor peasants lived
and how they starved and were compelled to make desperate choices. Instead,
Wirkola takes delight in weaponry, monstrous images of women as witches, constant killing, and all kinds of magical special effects. As Claudia Puig wrote in
USA Today: "This convoluted hybrid of fairy tale and fantasy/action/comedy/
horror aims for campy fun, but comes off tedious and blood spattered."[23]

Yet despite numerous negative reviews of the film, announcements by Paramount Studios have revealed that a sequel to *Hansel & Gretel: Witch Hunters* is
in the making,[24] and paratextual discussions on the Internet and in the media
have begun to feed the public with hype that will inevitably turn into millions
of dollars. Even if the Grimms may have contributed somewhat to the hyping of
their tales, they would never have approved how filmmakers have exploited their
stories for shallow purposes.

Ever since the end of World War II, advertising and publicity have exaggerated and distorted the value of all products. We live in a world of hype, but
it is also a world that manages to produce works of art that take fairy tales and
the Brothers Grimm seriously—and not only the Grimms but also many of
the writers of classical fairy tales such as Charles Perrault, Madame d'Aulnoy,
Hans Christian Andersen, Carlo Collodi, and Lewis Carroll. Their works continue to resonate with us not because of hype, but because of their integrity:
they have tapped into our utopian need for the "corrective" worlds of fairy tales.

In respecting the integrity of past fairy-tale artworks, numerous contemporary filmmakers such as Michel Ocelot and Catherine Breillat in France, Hayao Miyazaki in Japan, Jan Svankmajer in the Czech Republic, Christoph Hochhäusler in Germany, Yim Phil-Sung in South Korea, Garri Bardin in Russia, Guillermo del Toro and Tim Burton in the United States, and Pablo Berger in Spain have re-created fairy tales with such verve and imagination that, though they need advertisement, they do not depend on hype to appeal to audiences. They depend on our hope for changing the world in a meaningful way. The same can be said for some of the remarkable fairy tales written by such talented authors as Angela Carter, Salman Rushdie, A. S. Byatt, Marina Warner, Tanith Lee, Philip Pullman, and Helen Oyeyemi in the United Kingdom; Margaret Atwood in Canada; Margo Lanagan and Kate Forsyth in Australia; Robert Coover, Jane Yolen, Donna Jo Napoli, John Barth, Francesca Lia Block, Catherynne Valente, and Kelly Link in the United States. They do not need hype to be recognized as storytellers who are keeping the profound tradition of the fairy tale alive. Thanks to them the Grimms can rest peacefully in their graves, for hype can never destroy the substantial quality of meaningful fairy tales.

Ramifications of Hyping

Initially, the text, the book, the oral tale, the play, the vaudeville show, the film, the church ceremony, and so on did not depend on paratexts and hyping to circulate and become known. Or, if they did, the advertisement and promotion were minimal and certainly not central to the reading or viewing of the primary source and the creation of meaning by recipients. With the rapid technological development of paratexts and peripherals by the end of the twentieth century that were once marginal, we are witnessing a most unusual transformation of the way meaning becomes established in the public spheres of the West. What was marginal has now, through hyping, become central and has practically effaced the source text, artwork, or event in the cultural field of production. Moreover, the peripherals have driven what I call the more complex and quality texts to the margins of conflicts within cultural field of production. The result is that critics are compelled—and paid—for the most part to discuss and review schlock, whether it is a book, film, play, television show, or some kind of product to be celebrated, just as celebrities lend themselves to schlock, which is waste without any redeeming value. But it is not just the profession of critics that is driven to dwell in schlock. We are all defined by and define ourselves by peripherals that is, the surroundings that have become central to our lives. Not all of it is schlock, for relevance and value continue to be produced on the margins of society.

Unfortunately, much of what is relevant and valuable is transformed into schlock when it is moved to the center.

The major product of consumerist societies is waste, and most socio-economic systems today do not know what to do with waste that engenders taste and determines choice. Therefore, corporate culture is in the business of obscuring how and why schlock is produced and of hyping it as a miracle cure to the sociopolitical crises affecting our lives that we cannot cure. To a great degree, the fairy tale as flexible and expansive genre becomes a metaphorical mode of communication in which invested hopes, wishes, ideas, and information are exchanged to hype and question the dominant production of waste. The goal of hype is the uncritical acclamation of con and medicine men, witch doctors, and waste and the celebration of hegemonic rule, while marginal questioning seeks to expose the contradictions in society and expose the hype that dominates our lives. Given cultural flux, there is no clear-cut dichotomy between hype and real value. What is at the center of culture—namely, waste—vanishes rapidly, and the paratextual center must rapidly replace what wastes away.

CHAPTER THREE

Americanization of the Grimms' Folk and Fairy Tales: Twists and Turns of History

In public discourse, the Grimms' tales became an issue of values, both ethical and commercial, and folklorists devoted to the search for the authentic and "natural" use in culture appeared to avoid discussion of both. Increasingly, the Grimms' tales in America became a children's genre, a visual medium and form of entertainment. The discourse over their use heatedly engaged parents and teachers because of the image of children's innocence altered by vivid romance, violence, and prejudice— depending on the moral position taken. The tales became the center of a tension between the unity, the hope, of Western tradition in American social reality. They became simultaneously a sign of Eurocentrism and commercial Americanization. The tales in their various consumed forms were part and parcel of mass culture, and drew attention to the Hollywood recontextualization from America to a global audience.

—Simon Bronner, "The Americanization of the Brothers Grimm,"
Following Tradition (1998)[1]

Hey Folks!

Welcome to Grimmer Tales, *a collection that takes you to a dark and magical place near and dear to my heart. Back in the old (old with an e, actually) days, fairy tales were scary, full of blood and trickery. They taught you something—don't trust strangers, never tell a lie! But nowadays, fairy tales are gentle and fluffy. There's simply no room for screaming or sobbing anymore. And nobody learns anything except that being a spoiled princess will still get you your way. I'd bet the Brothers Grimm are rolling in their graves.*

—Erik Bergstrom, *Grimmer Tales: A Wicked Collection of Happily Never After Stories* (2010)[2]

Although it might seem to most Americans that the Grimms' folk and fairy tales have been with us for centuries and that they are part and parcel of true

Americana, thanks to Walt Disney's films, books, merchandise, and theme parks, these notions about the Americanism of the Grimms' tales are far from the truth. The Grimms and their tales have a very distinct history of their own in their own culture. But very few Americans know anything about Jacob and Wilhelm, when they lived, or how they came to write their tales. There are three nonsensical American films[3] about their lives that are so infantile, misleading, and corny that it will take the best of the very best American biographers many years to set the record straight about the Grimms' lives and their project of collecting tales, if they ever do.[4] Very few Americans know anything about the German legacy of the Grimms' tales, which, as we know, were not called fairy tales by the Grimms but *Märchen*, or "little tales," a term indicating all types of folk tales. And very few people in the world realize how Americanized the Grimms' tales have become through the advent of globalization. Though the Grimms' stories are still widely disseminated and revered in Germany as part of the Germans' profound cultural heritage, and though many people regard the tales as the Germans' most significant cultural gift to the world and to classical children's literature, the so-called German narratives have been greatly appropriated by the powerful American culture industry, and the American reception of the tales, primarily as entertaining children's literature and family films, has led to a gross misunderstanding of the Grimms' intentions and the early reception of the tales in Germany. (Incidentally, the same could be said of Charles Perrault's and Hans Christian Andersen's tales.)

Of course, the intentions of authors, composers, inventors, and so on are often incidental in determining the meaning and in influencing the reception of their works. It is also very difficult to know the intentions of an author and to grasp the essence of an artwork. As I have already demonstrated in chapters one and two, however, the Brothers made their intentions very explicit in letters, essays, prefaces and introductions to the different editions of their tales: they intended to salvage ancient German folk stories that stemmed from oral traditions before they disappeared. Their hope—and they initially addressed educated adult readers as their major audience—was that the tales and their publications of Germanic legends, proverbs, epics, sagas, and fables as well as their scholarly studies would contribute toward unifying the Germanic peoples within one nation-state. Little did they realize that the tales they collected would be transformed into classics of worldwide children's literature by the end of the twentieth century and that their "Germanic" essence, if there ever was one, would be almost totally effaced by and associated with American popular culture.

The process of the Americanization[5] of the Grimms' tales, which one could also call globalized Disneyfication, has a long history to it that began in England at the beginning of the nineteenth century, and I want to concentrate on just two key features of Americanization: (1) the English and American translations and adaptations of the Grimms' tales from 1823 to the present; (2) the filmic adaptation of the Grimms' tales in the age of globalization. Before I begin analyzing the literary translations and the cinematic adaptations, however, I want briefly to discuss three significant essays and an anthology of European folk and fairy tales that provide important information and analyses of the Americanization of the Grimms' tales: "The Tales of the Brothers Grimm in the United States" (1963) by Wayland Hand; "The Americanization of the Brothers Grimm" (1998) by Simon Bronner; and *Cinderella in America: A Book of Folk and Fairy Tales* (2007), edited and compiled by William Bernard McCarthy.[6]

Hand's essay deals mainly with the reception of the Grimms by philologists, folklorists, and literary critics. He points out that the Grimms' tales were virtually ignored by most American scholars in the nineteenth century. If the Grimms received any attention, it was by philologists who wrote about the linguistic achievements of the Brothers. Even in the twentieth century, Hand maintains that the Grimms' influence on American folklore and fairy-tale studies had been minimal. It was only after World War II that the tales were fully recognized by leading folklorists such as Stith Thompson and Richard Dorson, but there were no significant studies of the Grimms' tales by folklorists, who tended to neglect them as well as the great tradition of European folklore. The Grimms' tales were generally sequestered in the field of children's literature and pedagogy, where the interest of educators in fairy tales has always been strong. Though Hand cites the popularity of the Grimms' tales in American culture, he does not explore the great diversity and revision of the tales in any depth. As we shall see, the fortunes of the Grimms' tales in America were more varied at the end of the nineteenth and beginning of the twentieth century than Hand indicates, and they changed greatly after 1945, when the United States became a political and cultural superpower dominating the market of fairy tales.

Bronner's superb essay, published thirty-five years after Hand's article, has the advantage of time and more accumulated research on the Grimms so that he can explore the manifold historical and complex reception of the Grimms' tales in much greater depth than Hand. He states at the beginning of his essay that

> the Grimm connection to folklore in American cultural discourse is evident first in the popularity of the fairy tale as a public reference for entertaining fantasy and wish-fulfillment. Second is the idea that folk traditions representing the character of nature provide renewing spiritual or poetic powers for modern existence. Third is the juxtaposition of folklore's international spread with its use for building a romantic sense of nation of peoplehood. Each of

these connections brings up the centrality of tradition taking organic form and drawing on the past in references to the Grimms' influence on American uses of folklore.[7]

Bronner demonstrates that there were three conflicting tendencies in the American reception, production, and appropriation of the Grimms' folk and fairy tales from the nineteenth century to the present. One tendency focused on the Grimms' tales, which were viewed in connection to German romantic nationalism and the notion of cultural unity. The second involved the disparity between folklorists and literary critics in their treatment of the Grimms' tales. Like Hand, Bronner demonstrates that there has been a great neglect of the tales by folklorists, and that the significant critical work on the Grimms' stories has been done by literary critics and theoreticians with a few exceptions. The third tendency has been a transformation of the Grimms' tales into children's literature as well as the commercialization of the tales. Most important for my purposes is his closing statement:

> The Grimms became recast toward the close of the twentieth century as literary artists and inspirations, who presented problems of cultural constructions. If folklorists mused about tales as experienced "narratives," as socially real traditions of the informal and noninstitutional, public rhetoric focused on therapeutic uses of fantasy in institutional settings. That difference in rhetoric reflected the need of a public to commodify the Grimm legacy as products for modern consumption serving different ends of unity and fragmentation, while academic practice called for recovering objective ways of knowing and following tradition.[8]

To complement the work of Bronner and Hand, it is necessary to situate the reception of the Grimms' tales in a larger historical and sociocultural context. As is well known, Germans began to emigrate to America in large groups from the eighteenth century up through the early part of the twentieth century. They spoke German at home and brought with them German books and developed their own communities, schools, and traditions. It is difficult to estimate whether the Grimms' tales played a large role in these German communities, but one can gauge from Henry Pochmann's study, *German Culture in America: Philosophical and Literary Influences, 1600–1900* (1957),[9] that the Grimms' tales were known and told by a fairly large part of the growing American population, In this respect William McCarthy's anthology of "Americanized" European folk tales, *Cinderella in America*, provides concrete evidence of their influence and dissemination. The title of this carefully edited book is misleading and yet accurate. At first glance one might think that the book's focus would be on different versions of the tale type "Cinderella" in America. This is not at all the case. Yet the title is apt, for the book is truly about a neglected and mistreated "Cinderella genre," the European wonder fairy tale in America, in all its diverse oral and literary forms, and about how scholars and educated readers have tended to believe that the European tale types never took root in the early days of the founding of America. Some have even asserted that there is no such thing as an American fairy tale. McCarthy's purpose is to prove them wrong. His goal, he states, is "to demonstrate the scope of the Old World repertoire as it settled into U.S. American culture, changing, developing, and acclimating in much the same way the tales of this repertoire have always settled and acclimated, wherever they have found themselves"[10] Not only does he fulfill his goal, but he does it convincingly and with great thoroughness and originality and with a stunning collection of approximately 200 tales from the eighteenth century to the present.

McCarthy explains that "credit must go to the Grimm brothers, Jacob and Wilhelm, for recognizing the scope of this repertoire and its unity. Their famous collection of 'fairy tales,' the *Kinder-und Hausmärchen*, provided the model for many later national and regional collections. The Grimm collection includes a wide range of genres or types of tales." McCarthy's purpose is to "keep the tales as told, not as reimagined by the editor."[11] Therefore, all the tales taken from print are reproduced as they were unless there were typographical errors. With regard to translations and tales based on recordings, McCarthy has tried to preserve the voice and oral style of the narrator as best he could. His insightful explanations that follow each tale provide important historical information and clarification about the sources and informants.

Since nobody can define and decide what "America" or "American" means, McCarthy takes a historical and "existential" approach to designating what American folk and fairy tales are and in justifying the selection of the tales that he includes in this anthology. All of the tales in the collection are American because they are based on the storytelling of storytellers whose families had been in America for generations, including tales from Native Americans, of course, and from all possible ethnic groups. What fascinates McCarthy, and what is fascinating about the "American" versions of the wonder tales from the Indo-European tradition is how they express the American experience with clear traces of the old world. One need only study the derivation of tale types such as "The Three Stolen Princesses" (ATU 301) or "The Boy Steals the Ogre's Treasure" (ATU 328) in McCarthy's anthology to sense how the British, German, and Irish sensibilities have been altered to address a different audience in another sociocultural context. The tales are roughly hewn, in verse, humorous, and inventive. Their transformations delineate the adaptive practices and transformative experience of the narrators and people who kept them alive. It is to McCarthy's great credit that he has resuscitated the "Cinderella" tradition of folklore in America with a profound understanding of what these tales meant and mean for American culture and with acute insights into the extraordinary diversity of American culture. What is also significant is that the German-American tales in the collection and others as well are not meant specifically for children, nor are they part of children's literature. Though reflecting a clear influence of the Grimms' tales, they have been appropriated by storytellers and writers to speak to the American experience.

From Germany to the World

The most fascinating aspect, I believe, in the history of the Grimms' collecting and editing of so-called pure German tales is how the publication, dissemination, and translation of the tales began on a provincial level and led to globalization. In seeking to uncover the profound meanings and mysteries of German folk tales at the beginning of the nineteenth century, the Grimms, who were assiduous scholars, living and working in the small, provincial city of Kassel, fostered a worldwide movement of research and cultural appropriation that enabled folklorists, historians, philologists, writers, translators, musicians, and artists to demonstrate how and why we are so different and at the same time how we are extraordinarily similar and connected through storytelling, more than we realize. There is something particularly personal and universally relevant that drove the storytelling behind the Grimms' tales and led to the Americanization and globalization of the tales. Though we might celebrate the "universality" of the tales, there is a danger in what I call their "Americanized globalization," and it lies in the trivialization and commercial homogenization of the tales by current cultural forces that respect market conditions more than they respect diversity, particularism, sovereignty, history, and art.

I shall comment in more depth about both the positive and negative aspects of "Americanization" at the end of this chapter. For the moment, a few general remarks about this process are necessary to frame my present analysis. In the case of the Grimms' tales we must be aware that, when we read them in English, we are reading *translations of translations*. That is, one of the roles that the Grimms played as cultural mediators was that of translator. But the Brothers did not translate literally. The Grimms continually adapted and edited the words from the lips of informants and texts that were sent to them from 1810 to 1857. It is important to emphasize this point about translation, for the tales were never "authentic German," nor did they ever belong to the Grimms. Most of the tales they collected were originally told in some kind of German dialect or other European dialects and were translated either by literate informants or by the Grimms themselves into high German. Since more than a third of the tales stemmed from oral traditions, they underwent many changes before they were written down in high German. There are only two dialect tales in the Grimms' final collection of 1857 that were left from the eleven in the first edition, and even these tales were edited by the Grimms to provide an exemplary model for the "perfect" folk tale. In short, the Grimms were not simply collectors but *translators, adapters*, and *mediators* of tales, who endeavored to create poetic stories based on German folklore and based on what they imagined an authentic oral story to be. As Orrin Robinson has pointed out in his meticulous study, *Grimm Language: Grammar, Gender and Genuineness in the Fairy Tales*, "The Grimms wanted their fairy tales to appear authentic. With a few exceptions, they rejected tales in pure dialect, because the audience for this would have been small. As a compromise, the body of the tale itself normally appears in more or less standard, if not antiquated German prose, while occasional bits of verse provide the stamp of regional authenticity."[12] The poeticization of oral art was never far from their minds—that is, from Wilhelm's mind. As Thomas Frederick Crane, one of the first great American folklorists, has claimed: "For all their scientific interest the brothers, especially Wilhelm, could not escape the influence of their literary *milieu*. The result is that the *Kinder- und Hausmärchen* is a great literary work which has had a profound influence upon the language and the literary forms of Germany. The result was not gained at once, but was the consequences of nearly fifty years of patient revision."[13] This is not to say that the tales should be treated only as literary texts. This would be a simplistic and reductionist approach to the tales. What is truly unusual about the Grimms' pioneer collection is the manner in which they wove oral and literary versions together so that the nineteenth-century texture of their tales is like a magic tapestry that represents different aspects of telling, representing, interpreting, and translating ancient tales.

As other European translators began translating the Grimms' "translations," they also used their distinctive "high" languages such as standard English, French, Danish, Dutch, and so forth and sought to appeal largely to the educated classes in their respective languages and cultures. Translation always involves adaptation and appropriation to make a foreign text comprehensible for a native reader who does not know the foreign language or culture. Depending on the purpose of the translator, he/she will either use markers to denote the unique foreign character of the original text or eliminate any indication that the text is foreign so that it appears to have been created and produced in the same language and culture in which it is published. I call this "appropriation," and appropriation can work in manifold ways. In English-speaking countries, the tendency in the nineteenth century was to anglicize the Grimms' tales so that there was very little "Germanness" about them by the end of the nineteenth century. Americans were first introduced to the Grimms through the British translations, and it was only at the end of the nineteenth century and beginning of the twentieth that the American appropriation of the Grimms' tales began in full force. A good example is Horace Elisha Scudder (1832–1902), a prolific man of letters, who was not only a writer of children's books but also editor of the prestigious *Atlantic Monthly* and also *Riverside Magazine*. Among the numerous books he published are three anthologies of tales, *The Book of Folk Stories Rewritten by H. E. Scudder* (1887), *The Book of Legends* (1899), and *The Book of Fables and Folk Stories Told Over Again* (1906). Influential and inventive, Scudder's revisions of the Grimms' tales—and he also revised tales by Perrault, d'Aulnoy, and other European writers—are lively abbreviated versions geared to his notions of how children read, their tastes, and what children read. In his preface to *The Book of Fables and Folk Stories Told Over Again*, he states: "In the case of the folk-stories, I have not departed knowingly from the generally accepted structure. I have tried simply to use words and constructions which present the fewest difficulties. I should like to believe that I have succeeded to some extent in thinking out these stories as a child would think them, and so have used that order and choice of words which would be the natural expression of a child's mind."[14] The fact that Scudder did not work as an educator or a psychologist with children did not prevent him from making false pronouncements about children, children's literature, and how children related to stories. Nor did it matter much that he knew next to nothing about folklore even though he corresponded with Hans Christian Andersen. Scudder set himself up to be a judge of good children's literature, and the Grimms' tales were thus appropriated by Scudder and marked as positive and healthy for children—just as long as they were carefully edited. Indeed, he was not alone in his appropriation of the Grimms' tales, as I will shortly show.

The American appropriation was unlike any other national appropriation of the Grimms' tales because it led to a cultural hegemony of fairy tales. Within America, it was clearly important to translate the tales and appropriate them in some manner so that they would become culturally accessible for readers and viewers of the tales, especially for children. With the rise of the American film and culture industry in the period between 1920 and 1960, the Americanized models of the Grimms' tales were exported to countries throughout the world as books, films, advertisements, and comics so that the notion of fairy tale or a Grimms' fairy tale is generally associated with American standards and norms. American appropriation can thus be tied to cultural imperialism. However, it is misleading to interpret Americanzation of the Grimms' tales as totally one-sided

and without conflict. I shall return to the questionable nature of Americanization. First, it is important to turn to history.

English and American Translations of the Grimms' Tales from 1823 to the Present

There are three factors about *English* translations of the Grimms' tales and how
they were received in America that must be taken into consideration when
studying the process of Americanization. The first is that the Grimms' tales were
often confused with the fairy tales of Charles Perrault, which were first published in 1697 and translated into English by Robert Samber in 1729. All ten of
Perrault's tales, "Cinderella," "Sleeping Beauty," "Little Red Riding Hood," "Bluebeard," "The Fairies," "Tom Thumb," "Donkey Skin," "Puss in Boots," "Riquet
with the Tuft," and "The Foolish Wishes" circulated orally in France, England,
and different European countries and in print in diverse forms such as chapbooks and anthologies before the publication of the first edition of the Grimms'
Kinder- und Hausmärchen (1812/1815) in Germany.[15] Moreover, the French
fairy tales of Perrault, Mme d'Aulnoy, and Mme Leprince de Beaumont along
with "Aladdin and the Wonderful Lamp" from *The Arabian Nights* and English
folk tales such as "Jack and the Beanstalk" were well known in England by the
end of the eighteenth century, thanks to various translations and chapbooks and
in part to the publisher Benjamin Tabart (ca. 1767–1833), who produced a series
of fairy-tale pamphlets called "Tales for the Nursery."[16] All the illustrated pamphlets were collected and published as a four-book set in 1804 under the title
Tabart's Collection of Popular Tales, and they were revised and published in one
volume as *Fairy Tales; or the Lilliputian Library* in 1817 and *Popular Fairy Tales*
in 1820. Tabart's collections and other early books of fairy tales prepared the
way for the very first translation of selected Grimms' tales by Edgar Taylor. As
I have noted in chapter one, he called them *German Popular Stories*, which he
published in two volumes in 1823 and 1826 and in a later book, *Gammer Grethel*,
in 1839. Almost from the beginning they were associated with French fairy tales,
and this led to a confusion that has lasted up through our present day, especially
because many of Perrault's tales can be found in the Grimms' editions, and to
make things even more complicated, many of the Grimms' tales can be found in
French nineteenth-century editions such as *Contes Bleus et Roses* (1865), which
is dedicated to the amusement of big and little children with some of Taylor's
adaptations and Cruikshank's illustrations.[17]

The second important factor to consider about the early English translations of the Grimms' tales is that, as I have already demonstrated, Taylor did not

faithfully translate them. Instead, he adapted them and made immense changes. For example, in "Ashputtel" or "Cinderella," the girl's own father tries to prevent the prince from recognizing Cinderella, and the wicked stepsisters are not punished by having their eyes pecked out. Taylor avoids all extreme and cruel punishments so that even the nasty queen in "Snow White" is *not* forced to dance to death in red-hot shoes. Taylor's "Hansel and Grettel" is actually an abbreviated version of the Grimms' "Brother and Sister," and his "Roland and May-Bird" is a combination of "Foundling," "Sweetheart Roland," and "Hansel and Grethel." Instead of a tale about the abandonment of children, it becomes a romantic and sentimental story about true love in which brother and sister, who are not really brother and sister, marry in the end. Incest is avoided but suggested. In many of the original Grimms' tales, which did not contain fairies, Taylor added them as if they were similar to the tales of the French tradition of Perrault and d'Aulnoy. The changes in the two volumes of *German Popular Stories* and in Taylor's other edition, *Gammer Grethel*, in which he further revised the tales that he had translated, are so great that one must use the term adaptation not translation when reading and citing his tales. And they are *his* tales, for Taylor "appropriated" the Grimms' tales, shaped them primarily for English bourgeois families and their children, and anglicized them through the linguistic references that took into consideration a British sensibility when it came to religion, sex, violence, and ideology.

And this leads us to the third important key factor that determined the early reception of the Grimms' tales in England and America: Taylor's adaptations for young readers, which also began circulating in America right after they were published in London, included twenty-two humorous illustrations by the talented caricaturist George Cruikshank. These drawings heightened the comic and sentimental changes made by Taylor and helped transform the tales into classical fairy tales for children. Altogether Taylor published fifty-five stories from the 1819 Grimms' edition. Remarkably, this collection was reprinted and pirated in all sorts of formats up through the end of the twentieth century in England and America. In short, two different editions of Taylor's adaptations were published throughout the nineteenth century, generally without scholarly notes or long introductions about the Grimms and the German qualities of the tales. The Taylor editions competed with one another: *German Popular Stories* combined the 1823 and 1826 editions into one volume, and *Gammer Grethel* provided a totally different framework for a smaller selection of tales once again heavily revised by Taylor.

Some of the titles of Taylor's tales were vastly changed. For instance, his books were often labeled *German Popular Tales and Household Stories* or *Grimms' Fairy Tales*. One of the more exotic titles is *Grimm's Goblins: Grimm's Household Stories,*

Translated from the Kinder und Haus Marchen by E. Taylor in 1876. Other publishers combined Taylor's tales with well-known European folk and fairy tales. The publisher James Burns published two volumes of tales, *Popular Tales and Legends* (1843) and *Household Tales and Traditions of England, Germany, France, Scotland, etc.* (1846), which included a few new translations and modified Taylor translations. Edgar Taylor's cousin John Edward Taylor, a London printer, published another selection of the Grimms' tales in 1846 under the title *The Fairy Ring: A New Collection of Popular Tales, Collected from the German of Jacob and Wilhelm Grimm*. This volume, which contained thirty-six Grimms' tales never translated before, was illustrated by Richard Doyle, one of the great Victorian illustrators, and it added to the popularity of the Grimms' collection as a children's book. None of these books—and there were several other minor translations—rendered a complete faithful translation of the Grimms' tales, which grew to 210 by the publication of the final German edition in 1857. Almost all of the editions that I have mentioned were also published in America.

As Martin Sutton has demonstrated in his thorough study, *The Sin-Complex: A Critical Study of English Versions of the Grimms'* Kinder- und Hausmärchen *in the Nineteenth Century*, it was not until 1884 that Margaret Hunt produced the first complete translation of all 210 tales of the Grimms' last edition of 1857.[18] For the most part Hunt's edition, which contained all the Grimms' scholarly notes, became the most reliable English translation of the twentieth century until Ralph Manheim's excellent version, *Grimms' Tales for Young and Old: The Complete Stories*, in 1978. It should be noted that the first complete American translation, *The Grimms' German Folk Tales*, by Francis P. Magoun Jr. and Alexander Krappe, was not published until 1960. However, it did not have an introduction or notes. In 1988 I published *The Complete Fairy Tales of the Brothers Grimm*, which was the first American publication of the tales to include all the tales from the 1857 edition and a substantial introduction about the Brothers Grimm along with minimal notes. Successive editions of my work also contained additional tales from the Grimms' notes and posthumous papers. There were also other American books with the complete tales published in the twentieth century that were revisions of the British Hunt translation. In general, the dissemination of the complete Grimms' tales in America up through the end of the twentieth century was dominated by British versions that were at times Americanized through editing and illustrations by Americans.

This does not mean that American readers received the Grimms' tales entirely through a British lens. By the late nineteenth century many of the major classical tales in the Grimms' collection were published individually as illustrated "toy" books or picture books for children in Great Britain and America. Moreover, in the first half of the twentieth century the tales were re-created and revised throughout America as vaudeville acts, plays for children, postcards, poems, parodies, novels, cartoons, radio plays, and feature films. While many of the Grimms' fairy tales were mixed with those by Perrault, Andersen, and other European classics such as Mme Leprince de Beaumont's "Beauty and the Beast," and while they were often addressed to adults as well as children, it was generally assumed that fairy tales belonged in the nursery and were a basic component of children's acculturation.

By 1916 Laura Kready published *A Study of Fairy Tales*, one of the first important educational manuals that argued for the inclusion of fairy tales as part of the literature curriculum in elementary schools. Aside from discussing the high literary standards of the tales and the importance of adaptation, Kready argued:

> The fairy tale is also related to life standards, for it presents to the child a criticism of life. By bringing forward in high light the character of the fairy, the fairy tale furnishes a unique contribution to life. Through repeated impressions of the idea of fairyhood it may implant in the child a desire which may fructify into that pure, generous, disinterested kindness and love of the grown-up, which aims to play fairy to another, with sincere altruism to make appear before his eyes his heart's desire, or in a twinkling to cause what hitherto seemed impossible. Fairy tales are thus harbingers of that helpfulness which would make a new earth, and as such afford a contribution to the religion of life.[19]

While Kready is too idealistic in her approach to fairy tales, her pedagogical and historical book was a comprehensive and useful textbook for teachers at that time and indicated how the fairy tale had become acceptable among educators and a large segment of the American population. Little did she realize just how intricately the Grimms' tales would weave themselves or be woven into the American acculturation process. Some of the notable early American translations and adaptations of the Grimms' tales include the following:

- *Grimm Tales Made Gay* (1902) by Guy Wetmore Carryl. This book contains twenty witty verses such as "How Fair Cinderella Disposed of her Shoe," How Rumplestilz Held Out in Vain for a Bonus," and "How Little Red Riding Hood Came to be Eaten," which had first been published in popular magazines, *The Smart Set*, *The Century*, *Life*, *The Saturday Evening Post*, and *Harper's*.
- *Fairy Tales from Grimm* (1905) in the Christmas Stocking Series. This book contains four sentimentalized Grimms' tales translated by an anonymous

writer with an introduction by L. Frank Baum, whose *Wonderful Wizard of Oz* (1900), an American fairy-tale novel, bears the strong influence of the Brothers Grimm. Unfortunately, Baum's introduction drips with Christian sentimentality, and the Grimms' tales are treated as pious gifts.

- *Grimm's Fairy Tales* (1914) containing the complete 210 stories translated by the British Margaret Hunt, unvarnished and without notes, but with the illustrations by the talented American artist John Gruelle. The brief introduction by P. W. Coussens indicates that the stories and illustrations were totally designed for children: "The child is entitled to pass through the golden door into a Fairyland pictured by Tale and Rhyme. He has not only a right, by reason of his tender years. to a childhood shielded from all possible lack of that which appeals to his imagination (and every normal child is happily well supplied in this respect by an all-wise Providence), but the glorious vista revealed to his immature mind by means of the Fairy and Wonder Tale is a great and primary appeal making for his intellectual and moral development."[20] It should be noted that Gruelle, who also illustrated *My Very Own Fairy Stories* (1928), went on to become the famous illustrator and author of the *Raggedy Ann and Andy Stories*, which included some of the Grimms' tales, such as *Raggedy Ann's Fairy Stories* (1928). There were other important American and immigrant illustrators such as Millicent Sowerby, George Soper, Louis John Rhead, Kay Nielsen, and Fritz Kreidl, who contributed unusual images for editions of the Grimms' tales designed for young readers during the first three decades of the twentieth century.

- *Nize Baby* (1926) by Milt Gross, a well-known New York cartoonist, who retold some of the Grimms' tales in a Yiddish-American dialect with such titles as "Baby Sleeps on Cheecken Fets—Sturry from Rad Rindink Hoot" and "Ferry Tale from Romplesealskin for Nize Baby Wot Ate Opp All de Crembarry Suss." Later, in 1948, Dave Morrah published a similar collection of tales in German-American dialect called *Cinderella Hassenpfeffer and Other Tales Mein Grossfader Told*. In general, Gross's work indicates how cartoonists who worked for magazines and newspapers and illustrated books were also entering the film industry to create fairy-tale films based on the Grimms' tales and the stories of other writers such as Perrault and Andersen.

- The most important American adaptations of the Grimms' tales for children in the 1930s and 1940s were published by Wanda Gag in four books: *Tales from Grimm* (1936), *Snow White and the Seven Dwarfs* (1938), *Three Gay Tales* (1943), and *More Tales from Grimm* (1947). Born in New Ulm, Minnesota, Gag spoke German during her early childhood, and after she became famous as the author/illustrator of *Millions of Cats* (1928), she turned her attention to her beloved Grimms, in part to rectify the "damage" that Disney had done to "Snow White" in his 1937 film and to preserve the Germanness of the tales. Gag had never set foot in Germany, and since she was familiar with Germany only through the Grimms' tales and other books, she could not possibly preserve anything German or European. On the contrary, she was creating something new, and this "novelty" was her imagined conception of what it might be like to be German or European, and how American children should receive something German. All this she sought to do through the American language that she learned to speak in New Ulm, colored by anecdotes and information of the old country, and through her distinctive artwork. In the final analysis, however, she added very little to our understanding of the Grimms' tales, nor did she daringly revise or challenge some of their messages and themes. That is, her interpretations of the tales through her revisions are bland, as is her artwork. Nevertheless, there is a quaint appealing quality to her translations and a sweetness to her illustrations that set the tone for hundreds of illustrated Grimms' tales that were to follow the publication of her books up through the twenty-first century. Incidentally, her work was more in keeping with the sanitization of the Disney films and books than she realized.

Ever since the end of the nineteenth century there has been a tendency to protect the innocence of American children by sweetening and purifying the Grimms' tales. Whether they were cheap, individual fairy-tale books as in the long-running series Golden Books, expensive glossy illustrated books of single tales for upper-class families, or a group of modified, that is, sanitized tales, American publishers have tended to hire writers and illustrators to reflect American values and customs, and their books are primarily designed to amuse children, certainly not to reflect critically about the products that have increasingly become mere merchandise. In contrast, some contemporary illustrators such as Will Eisner, Margot Tomes, Babara Cooney, John Wallner, Trina Shart Hyman, Mercer Mayer, Paul Zelinsky, William Steig, and Maurice Sendak have been creative in their endeavors to interpret the Grimms' tales, but underlying their diverse images is the notion that children should delight in the illustrations and not be exposed to the seriousness of the tales. This is not to say that American illustrators and writers are in agreement with one another, and in fact, there has been a startling change in the rewriting and reimagining of the Grimms' tales, especially for young adults and adults, ever since the publication of Anne Sexton's *Transformations* (1971), which includes twenty-five highly provocative verse renditions of the Grimms' tales that questioned the treatment of women in the stories, and Bruno Bettelheim's *The Uses of Enchantment: The Meaning and*

Importance of Fairy Tales (1976), a controversial pseudo-Freudian book, which argued that the dark side of fairy tales helps children grapple with emotional problems.

In particular it was the feminist and civil rights movement that, among other things, called for a revising of the literary canon in accordance with the "revolutionary" spirit of the 1960s and 1970s, inspiring numerous writers, artists, producers, and critics to re-create and reutilize the Grimms' fairy tales. The more profound transformation and Americanization of the tales occurred largely in the domain of young adult and adult literature. Writers such as Jane Yolen, Robin McKinley, Donna Jo Napoli, Robert Coover, Vivian Vande Velde, Gail Carson Levine, Francesca Lia Block, Gregory Maguire, Catherynne Valente, Carolyn Turgeon, Camille Rose Garcia, and many others have explored problems concerning child abuse, drugs, sexism, violence, and bigotry through their transformation of the traditional fairy-tale motifs and plots. Many of their fairy-tale adaptations can be considered crossover books. At the same time there has been a large number of American short-story writers and novelists who have written complex and unusual fairy-tale works for adults. There are too many to note, but I would like to mention Donald Barthelme, *Snow White* (1967); Robert Coover, *Pricksongs & Descants* (1969) and *Briar Rose* (1996); Jane Yolen, *Briar Rose* (1992); Robin McKinely *Deerskin* (1993) and *Spindle's End* (2000); Nancy Springer, *Fair Peril* (1997); Gregory Maguire, *Confessions of an Ugly Stepsister* (1999); Francesca Lia Block, *The Rose and the Beast: Fairy Tales Retold* (2000); Kate Bernheimer, *The Complete Tales of Ketzia Gold* (2001) and *The Complete Tales of Merry Gold* (2006); Kelly Link, *Stranger Things Happen* (2000) and *Magic for Beginners* (2005); Lauren Slater, *Blue Beyond Blue: Extraordinary Tales for Ordinary Dilemmas* (2005); Catherynne Valente, *The Orphan's Tales: In the Night Garden* (2006) and *Six-Gun Snow White* (2013); Mercedes Lackey, *The Sleeping Beauty* (2010); Erik Bergstrom, *Grimmer Tales: A Wicked Collection of Happily Never After Stories* (2010); and Tom McNeal, *far far away* (2013).

In addition to the novels and stories by individual authors, there have been numerous anthologies such as Martin Greenberg's and John Helfers' *Little Red Riding Hood in the Big Bad City* (2004); Denise Little's *Hags, Sirens, and Other Bad Girls of Fantasy* (2006); and Nancy Madore's *Enchanted: Erotic Bedtime Stories for Women* (2006). Michael Buckley has written *The Sisters Grimm*, a series of nine novels for young readers, beginning with *The Fairy-Tale* Detectives (2005) and ending with *The Council of Mirrors* (2012), while Ellen Datlow and Terri Windling have edited an important series of fairy-tale anthologies for adults with such titles as *Black Thorn, White Rose* (1993) and *Black Heart, Ivory Bones* (2000) containing stories by some of the best fantasy writers in North America. In addition, many talented American and Canadian poets have made extraordinary use of the Grimms' tales in verse as can be seen in the important book *The Poets' Grimm: 20th Century Poems from Grimm Fairy Tales* (2003), edited by Jeanne Marie Beaumont and Claudia Carlson.

More recently, graphic artists and writers have produced important series of graphic novels such as *Scary Godmother* (1997–2006), developed by Jill Thompson, in which an odd fairy-witch befriends a young girl named Hannah and helps her in comic situations in the modern world. Linda Medley's *Castle Waiting* (1996–2006) uses the fantastic to subvert the classical fairy tales. She self-published her graphic novel with black-and-white ink drawings in 1996 and has intermittently produced comic book sequels and graphic novels that focus on different characters who come to inhabit the castle that Sleeping Beauty abandoned after she had been wakened by a prince. Zenescope Entertainment began publishing a horror comic book series, *Grimm Fairy Tales*, in 2005 that is still being produced. It concerns a professor of literature named Dr. Sela Mathers who helps people by showing them gruesome fairy tales that provide lessons about their lives. Another series, *Nightmare and Fairy Tales* (founded in 2002), also introduces the macabre into traditional fairy tales. One of the more interesting series of comic books is *Fables*, which began appearing in 2002. It deals with a besieged community of refugees and now includes over sixty issues of stand-alone comics and composite graphic novels. Conceived by Bill Willingham, the series begins with the premise that numerous characters from fairy tales, legends, myths, and folklore have been compelled to leave the lands of their origins, or Homelands. They do not know their mysterious enemy called the Adversary, except that he has taken over their homelands. So they migrate to New York City and form a clandestine community called Fabletown. However, many of them have difficulty adapting to the contemporary world, and their community is dysfunctional. The first five episodes, gathered in a trade paperback titled *Legends in Exile* and illustrated by Lan Medina, Steve Leialoha, and Craig Hamilton, concern the alleged murder of Rose Red, whose body is missing from her devastated apartment that has a warning written in blood on a wall: "No More Happy Endings." Actually, there will be a happy ending because Bigby Wolf, security officer of Fabletown, discovers that Jack the Beanstalk and Rose Red concocted a scheme to make it appear she had been murdered because they were in need of money. During the investigations we learn that King Cole is the incompetent head of the Fabletown community; Snow White is the intrepid director of operations, trying to hold the fairy-tale and legendary characters together; Prince Charming is a philanderer; Beauty and the Beast are having marital problems; Bluebeard is a wealthy baron and philanthropist; and a talking pig escapes the Farm in upstate New York where nonhuman characters from fables must live. Inversion and subversion of classical fairy tales are characteristic of the more prominent fairy-tale graphic novels, which are at their best when they employ irony so that they are not taken seriously. Some of these graphic novels have inspired new American fairy-tale TV series in the fall of 2011, either directly or indirectly: *Once Upon a Time* (ABC), a TV version of *Fables*, which dumbs down the graphic novels; and *Grimm* (NBC), a bizarre crime drama, which distorts the Grimms' tales beyond recognition and imitates the standard detective films that generally feature buddy cops and a touch of romance. And as if American viewers have not had enough to satisfy their fairy-tale hearts, *Beauty and the Beast* returned to the small screen in 2012 thanks to a series produced by CW that depends very much on the CBS 1987 series. In this trivial stereotypical show Beauty witnesses her mother's murder and is saved from the murderers by an ex-soldier, the beast, whom everyone believes is dead. Later Beauty becomes a policeman, and a romance ensues with guess who?

Of course, well before TV, Broadway had adapted some of the Grimms' fairy tales for the stage; the most significant was Steven Sondheim's and James Lapine's *Into the Woods* (1986), a rare tragic-comedy and musical, which makes use of several fairy tales to explore the meanings of wishes and desires and their consequences. This remarkable musical is now scheduled to be adapted for the cinema, and it will be interesting to see whether the Disney corporation shapes the adapted tales in the play artistically and takes the ideas seriously.

In all the novels, stories, poetry, plays, TV series, and musicals the Grimms' tales have been thoroughly Americanized even when there is a pretense to set the stories in the eighteenth or nineteenth centuries. There are always clear references to the contemporary period and sociocultural concerns of the period in which the adaptations and translations have been made. The idioms, social references, jokes, innuendos, and topics bear the marks of American culture. Perhaps the clearest evidence of the Americanization of the Grimms' tales can be found in the filmic adaptations. In my opinion, the most powerful factor in the process of Americanization was the cinema and the revolutionary technological inventions that allowed the tales to be fleshed out and represented on screen. Thanks to the cinema and the film industry the Grimms' tales are now continually reformed in live-action, cel and digital animation, and other unique collages.

The Filmic Adaptation of the Grimms' Tales in the Age of Globalization

The adaptation of fairy tales, largely French tales and the Arabian Nights, began almost as soon as the cinema industry developed in the 1890s. The first pioneer of this genre was Georges Méliès, the French magician and filmmaker, who made numerous live-action films based on the French cultural tradition. His films were widely distributed and influenced a great number of European and American filmmakers, who largely produced live-action fairy-tale films until the 1920s, when more and more artists began experimenting with fairy-tale animation. A case in point is the work of Walt Disney from 1922–24 in Kansas City, when he produced five fairy-tale films called Laugh O' Grams based on the tales of the Grimms and Perrault. More indicative of the work during the 1920s was the adaptation of American daily comic strips for animated and live-action films. For instance, Bud Fisher, a talented artist and writer, began the first American daily comic strip, *Mutt and Jeff*, on November 15, 1907, in the *San Francisco Chronicle*, that became widely popular in America. By 1911 Nestor Studios of New Jersey bought the rights to the cartoon strip to make short films. However, in 1913 Fisher set up his own film company in 1913 with American Pathé, and together they produced thirty-six short comedies about the rivalry between the tall Mutt and the short Jeff. One of his most innovative films was *A Kick for Cinderella* (1926), which was animated and directed by Raoul Barré and Charles Bowers. The tall Mutt decides to show off his talents at a dance hall, where he wants to perform the Charleston, and he leaves the desolate Jeff at home before a fireplace. As Jeff weeps, a fairy appears and graciously grants him a tuxedo and magic dancing shoes. She then offers him a limousine that drives through the wall of the house to take him to the dance hall. He is warned, however, that he must return home by midnight. Once Jeff appears at the hall, he dances solo and outdoes Mutt, who had made a grand impression on the audience. As Jeff is showing off, however, Mutt throws banana peels on the floor and ties his coat tails to a large plant to interfere with his performance. This does not stop Jeff, but when he sees the clock about to strike twelve, he anxiously tries to stop it by springing in vain onto the clock's hands. As soon as the clock strikes twelve, Jeff loses his clothes, to his embarrassment, and suffers from humiliation. Then, all at once, he is struggling with a pillow in front of the fireplace. He had been dreaming, and Mutt appears to call him a sap!

Not only is the cartoon unusual because the main character is a tiny oppressed male, but also because it ends abruptly with a disappointed "Cinderella man," who does not realize his dreams. And there is certainly no marriage on the horizon. Jeff is a mock Cinderella. Unlike many early cartoons, there are no chase scenes. The adroitly drawn characters dance in a delightful way, and their facial expressions reveal their jealousy and competitive spirits. The competition between Mutt and Jeff is fierce, and the gags are satirical, if not a bit sadistic. All the scenes are set in American locales of the early twentieth century, and the references to either a Grimm or Perrault tale are indirect. Indeed, Jeff is Cinderella as an American loser.

Another one of the most interesting films about "Cinderella," produced the very same year as *A Kick for Cinderella*, was *Ella Cinders* (1926), directed by Alfred Green and starring Colleen Moore and Lloyd Hughes. Here, too, the film was based on a syndicated comic strip written by Bill Conselman and drawn by Charles Plumb that originated in 1925 and ended in 1961. The comic strip featured a wide-eyed pert girl named Ella, with black hair in a dutch-bob haircut, who must carry out all the housework in a dysfunctional family run by the tyrannical Myrtle "Ma" Cinders and her two nasty daughters, Lotta and Prissy Pill. There is a clear Midwest ambience. Though not beautiful, Ella wins a beauty contest, and the prize enables her to leave the small town of Roseville with her kid brother, Blackie, and head for Hollywood, where she discovers that the film company that had sponsored the contest no longer existed. However, during the next thirty-five years of the comic strip she stays in Hollywood and endeavors to make a name for herself in all sorts of adventures in the West and in a marriage to a young man named Patches, who has his own sort of amusing experiences. In the process of producing a comic strip over many years, Conselman and Plumb dropped the core Cinderella story in favor of a series of brief tales depicting a smart young woman who would fall into and out of trouble.

In contrast, Green's filming of *Ella Cinders* retains the core Cinderella plot of both the Grimm and Perrault tales; he transformed it into an exceptional farce that focuses on class differences and reinforces the personality of Ella as a young woman with determination, a great sense of humor, and pride. Again, the provincial ambience of the Midwest is pervasive and clear. Green discards the brother as best friend in favor of Waite Lifter, who is a handsome iceman/fairy godfather and soon to become suitor. Although Ella knows how to fend for herself, she does need some protection and encouragement from Waite to enter the beauty contest. When she must submit a picture to the judges, her photographer submits one in which she makes a funny face. The reason she wins the contest is because the down-to-earth judges value personality and humor above beauty. They are also apparently critical of the pretentious class climbers represented by Ma Cinders and her daughters. There is no love lost between Ella and her stepmother and stepsisters. They do not part on good terms. But it is clear that she and Waite are in love with each other as he drives her to the train station and she departs for Hollywood. Shortly thereafter, we learn that Waite is actually from a very rich family and the star of the Illinois football team. He rebels against his father and follows Ella to Hollywood, where we see her sneaking into a Hollywood film studio, determined to become a star even though she has no connections. In an amusing scene in which she busts through the gates of a studio and interrupts the shooting of a film, Ella shows her acting talent and becomes a "discovered" young star. In another amusing scene, Waite arrives to rescue her from what he thinks is her impoverished existence, and he, too, interrupts the shooting of a scene to propose to her.

There are no miraculous transformations in this very American fairy-tale film. Instead, we have fortunate accidents that enable a young woman from the lower classes to discover her profession and to find a young man who accepts her for what she is: frank, funny, forceful, and talented. It is true that she abandons acting for marriage and a family, but she makes the decision to follow her heart. The "modernization" of Perrault's and the Grimms' tale and the adaptation of the comic strip are effective. Green does not dabble in melodrama. The action combines elements of Méliès's burlesque humor with a touch of Chaplinesque comedy, especially when the gifted actress Colleen Moore makes faces at the camera. Indeed, she brought a new face to Cinderella.

But this film was not exceptional in adapting "Cinderella" to American conditions either in live-action or animated versions. Between 1926 and 1934 there were twelve unusual Americanized adaptations of "Cinderella" with titles such as *Mr. Cinderella* (1926), *A Bowery Cinderella* (1927), *The Patsy* (1928), *The Bush Cinderella* (1928), *The Jazz Cinderella* (1930), *Cinderella Blues* (1931), *A Modern Cinderella* (1932), and *Naughty Cinderella* (1933).[21] To a certain degree, these fairy-tale films and others reflected the changing role of women in the United States. Soon after women attained the right to vote in 1920, there was a marked change in their attitudes in a challenge to traditional notions of womanhood. Aside from sexual liberation, women sought greater educational and economic opportunities, and they began to identify themselves with the modern image of the New Woman, free from patriarchal restraints and discrimination.

One of the most influential cartoon figures who reflected the changing behavior of women was Betty Boop. Created by Max Fleischer in 1930 as a caricature of the popular singer Helen Kane, Betty Boop soon became a sex symbol as a pert and frank young flapper, not afraid to speak her mind. Initially, the Betty Boop cartoons were designed for adult audiences and were filled with all kinds of sexual innuendos that had to be toned down after the 1934 National Production Code brought about censorship. Nevertheless, the Fleischer Brothers, Max and Dave, produced about 110 cartoons starring Betty during the Depression period in America. Autonomous, fearless, smart, and attractive, Betty Boop was more than just sexy, she expressed the force of a feminist movement.

The Fleischers sensed this, and their 1933 version of *Snow White* is a minor masterpiece, which can be interpreted as a generation conflict between older and younger women (figure 6). The film begins immediately with a series of frames that show the common-looking, conceited queen powdering her nose in front of a hand mirror. At one point the mirror actually polishes her nose as if polishing a shoe. When the queen asks who's the fairest in the land, the mirror turns into a

Figure 6. Betty Boop as Snow-White. Max and Dave Fleischer, directors. Fleischer Studios, 1933.

male face singing that she's the fairest in the land. This is the first anthropomorphized depiction of the magic mirror in cinematic history, and the Fleischers add a great deal of personality to it: the mirror is saucy, frank, and rebellious, and the queen spends much of her time trying to tame and control the mirror. She wants absolute control over her representation and the standard for beauty in the world. Once Betty swoops and swaggers into the court, the queen commands the two clown figures Koko and Bimbo, dressed in armor, who appear in many Betty Boop films, to execute her. But they fall down into a strange underworld followed by Betty who slides into the Seven Dwarfs' house on a sled. The queen asks the mirror again whether she's the fairest in the place, and the mirror responds: "If I were you, I'd hide my face." Outside the palace, the witch turns the mirror into a shovel at the grave site of Snow White. Then she steps through the mirror as a witch and descends into the underworld, where she joins a funeral march to the music of Cab Calloway singing "The St. James Infirmary Blues." Once the march is concluded, the queen returns to her original shape and asks the mirror one more time who the fairest in the land is. This time the mirror sticks out its tongue with a duck attached to it and points to Snow White. The queen transforms herself into a snarling dragon and pursues Betty, Koko, and Bimbo in a hilarious chase scene. In the end, she is turned into a skeleton, and the three friends hold hands and dance.

In their radical adaptation of "Snow White," the Fleischers introduced key motifs that would appeal to American audiences: a wacky male mirror that keeps changing his perspective; a vain old-maid stereotype who thinks she is beautiful; a saucy, fresh Betty Boop, no longer the passive virgin, but the New Woman, who struts and shows off her wares; a vaudeville repartee; a frenzied chase scene that parodies the classical fairy tale; jazz music by Cab Calloway; and the elimination of the prince as savior. There is nothing smooth about the early images in the Fleischer cartoons, but the frenzy derives from a resistance to the norm. The Fleischers opposed traditional storytelling, especially sweet and saccharine retellings of fairy tales. If fairy tales were to be sweetened and infantilized, they left this to Walt Disney.

Indeed, by the early 1930s, it was clear that a conflict about the cinematic adaptation of the Grimms' and other classical fairy tales was under way in America. The Fleischers along with many other cartoonists and filmmakers, who created live-action films, wanted free rein to experiment and free expression to critique and reenvision the classical fairy tales. To the extent that they targeted adults as their major audience, they were allowed to be as artistic and liberal as they desired. However, the dominant trend, even for adults, was toward conservatism with an emphasis on stressing the morals and values of the Protestant ethic as well as sentimental love. The major promoter of good family fairy-tale films in accord with so-called American norms, especially with patriarchy and capitalism, was Walt Disney. His "Three-Little-Pig-Trilogy" at the beginning of the 1930s is a good example of how he and his corporation were to Americanize and market classical fairy tales for decades to come.

Disney, who had been somewhat radical in revising fairy tales in the early 1920s, changed his perspective on animation when he began developing his Silly Symphonies, the 1930 cartoons that favored smooth transitions, carefully composed characters and sets, a rational plot, and appropriate gags for family audiences that barely had a trace of sexual innuendo. His conservatism, despite his technological and artistic innovations, are very evident in *The Three Little Pigs* (1933), *The Big Bad Wolf* (1934), and *The Three Little Wolves* (1936). Most significant is *The Big Bad Wolf* because it is Disney's infantilized rendition of "Little Red Riding Hood," with clear references to the depression era and Disney's expectations for little girls and the American work ethic. At the beginning of the cartoon, the oldest pig is, as usual, constructing something with bricks and pictured high above his two brother piglets when Little Red Riding Hood comes skipping along. She is characterized as a sweet simpleton, and when the two piglets want to accompany her to grandma's house, they are warned by the master inventor and builder to beware of the big bad wolf. Their response is typical; they sing the famous song, "Who's Afraid of the Big Bad Wolf?" already made popular by *The Three Little Pigs*, a song that resonated in America because it was a challenge to cruel capitalism, which Disney had originally identified with Jews. So, despite the song, the two younger piglets are scared to death when they meet the wolf in the forest. In truth, however, the wolf, who disguises himself as a transvestite, is ludicrous and somewhat of a klutz. While he chases dainty Red Riding Hood to grandma's house, the piglets run to their fatherly brother, who takes his tools to teach the wolf a lesson, not to kill him. After the eldest pig sends the wolf flying from granny's house, the final scene is set in the pigs' home sweet home with the piglets and Little Red Riding Hood singing "Who's Afraid of the Big Bad Wolf?" Everything is regulated—form and content.

By complying with notions of a well-made suitable film for young audiences, Disney outraged many animators, who still believed that the animated cartoon was the art form that defied harmony and synchronicity and raised provocative questions about social decorum and propriety. Moreover, they preferred off-color jokes and ambivalent acts. In the case of "Little Red Riding Hood," many of the animators objected to making the wolf harmless and to creating a sense that all was well with the world, especially during the years of the Great Depression. Their cinematic versions of "Little Red Riding Hood" differed greatly from Disney's, and though not all of them departed clearly from Disney's fixed characterization of the wolf and the dainty little girl, there was certainly a debate if not a battle over these two characters and how they should be represented with more focus on male desire, guilt, and stupidity.

A good example is Tex Avery's *Swing Shift Cinderella* (1945), loosely based on his *Red Hot Riding Hood* film of 1943 (figure 7). Avery was one of the greatest American animators during the golden age of cartoons, approximately 1930 to 1960, and he constantly tested the limits of conventionality and acceptability. His *Swing Shift Cinderella* begins with the wolf chasing a tiny and bratty Red Riding Hood until the wolf realizes it is the wrong character. (Incidentally, they are both modeled after Disney stereotypes.) So he ditches Little Red Riding Hood, transforms himself into a debonair gentleman, and drives to Cinderella's house. Cinderella is a voluptuous blonde, and he attempts to invade her house. She calls upon an older fairy godmother to protect her. Eventually, Cinderella goes off to perform in a nightclub, and the fairy godmother tames the wolf and brings him to the nightclub where Cinderella, reminiscent of Red Riding Hood in *Red Hot Riding Hood*, struts and sings, "All the little chicks are in love with a groovy wolf. Oh, Wolfie, Oh Wolfie!" In the end, she escapes, returns home, and changes into factory clothes for her swing shift. When she boards a bus, she thinks she is free of the wolf, but the passengers all turn out to be wolves who ogle her.

Figure 7. (a) *Swing Shift Cinderella*. Tex Avery, director. (b) *Red Hot Riding Hood*. Tex Avery, director. Metro-Goldwyn Mayer, 1943.

Avery's Cinderellas and Red Riding Hoods are cunning, strong, and feisty young women. Marriage is far from their minds. Even in cartoons in which Cinderella marries, it is clear that she refuses to be a wimp. *Swing Shift Cinderella* resounds with references to wartime in America and chaotic times. After World War II, the cinematic Americanization of the Grimms' and other classical fairy tales became more stable and were dominated by the Disney mode of production and ideology. Disney had already set a standard for the well-made sexist fairy tale with *Snow White* in 1937, and following 1945, almost all the major Disney feature animated fairy-tale films followed a certain prescription based on Broadway and Hollywood musicals: beautiful young Barbie-doll virgin is persecuted and needs to be rescued by a prince-like Ken doll. From *Cinderella* (1950) and *Sleeping Beauty* (1959) up through the *The Princess and the Frog* (2009) and *Tangled* (2010), the Disney fairy-tale films have followed conventional principles of technical and aesthetic organization to celebrate stereotypical gender and power relations and to foster a world view of harmony consecrated by the wedding of elite celebrity figures.

However, as we have seen in the early cartoons of the 1930s and 1940s, the Disneyfication of the Grimms' fairy tales has never been without opposition, and numerous American film producers have contested the reign of the Disney fairy-tale model in different ways through the markets of movies, television, video, DVDs, and the Internet. As early as 1969, Jim Henson, the founder of *Sesame Street* (1968) and *The Muppet Show* (1976–81), created *Hey, Cinderella!*, using his puppet creations such as Kermit the Frog to parody "Cinderella." He followed this with other unusually provocative adaptations such as *The Muppet Musicians of Bremen* (1972) and *Tales from Muppetland: The Frog Prince* (1972). In many of the animated TV series, *The Muppet Babies* (1984–90), muppet children in a nursery experiment with fairy tales in highly original and post-modernist interpretations of the Grimms' tales. And, of course, Henson's crowning achievement was his TV production of *The Storyteller* (1988), a series of ten short films, in which several Grimms' tales such as "The Youth Who Wanted to Learn What Fear Was," "Hans My Hedgehog," "The Three Ravens," and "The True Bride" were scripted by Anthony Minghella and adapted brilliantly with montage, estrangement effect, and sophisticated artistic techniques.

In 1975, Tom Davenport, an independent filmmaker, assisted by his wife Mimi, began producing eleven live-action fairy-tale films all based on the Grimms' stories and set in the rural South.[22] For instance, his first film was titled *Hansel and Gretel: An Appalachian Version*, which was followed by other Grimms' tales such as *Rapunzel, Rapunzel* (1979), *The Frog King* (1980), *Bearskin, or The Man Who Didn't Wash for Seven years* (1982), *The Goose Girl* (1983), *Ashpet: An American Cinderella* (1990), and *Willa: An American Snow White*

(1996). Davenport is one of the few filmmakers who meticulously researched the background of the Grimms' tales and Appalachian folklore to draw out unusual historical parallels. Produced as antidotes to the Disney versions and for use in schools, his films have never received the recognition and dissemination that they deserve.

In contrast, Shelly Duvall's films have received more attention than they deserve. A popular American actress, Duvall produced twenty-seven live-action adaptations of fairy tales for cable television in her series *Shelly Duvall's Faerie Tale Theatre* (1982–87) that have had a broader reception than Davenport's films. Duvall hired celebrity directors and actors to re-create the tales as they wished, and the lack of a unified concept shows. Among the films Duvall produced, several were taken from the Grimms' collection such as *Rumpelstiltskin* (1982), *The Frog King* (1982), *Hansel and Gretel* (1983), *Sleeping Beauty* (1983), *Rapunzel* (1983), *Little Red Riding Hood* (1983), *Snow White and the Seven Dwarfs* (1984), and *The Boy Who Left Home to Find Out about the Shivers* (1984). These films, still available as DVDs, were made in haste and vary greatly in quality. The overall tendency, however, was to make sweet entertainment for young viewers and to dumb down the stories.

The dumbing down of the Grimms' tales is most apparent in the *Canon Movie Tales*, a series of nine films that included *The Frog Prince* (1986), *Rumpelstiltskin* (1987), *Snow White* (1987), *Sleeping Beauty* (1987), *Hansel and Gretel* (1987), and *Red Riding Hood* (1989). The producers, Menahem Golan and Yoram Globus, intended to compete with the Disney films, but their live-action adaptations, some of them musicals, suffer from shoddy conceptions of the tales and hackneyed acting and sets. The commercial purposes of the Canon group overwhelm any sincere artistic and educational concern to appeal to young viewers.

The *Rugrats* animated television series that ran from 1991 to 2004 is a different story. Similar to Henson's *Muppet Babies*, this Nickelodeon production featured eight babies and a dog who speak in baby language and use their imaginations to make sense out of their environment and actions of their parents. In 2005 a special DVD, *Rugrats Tales from the Crib: Snow White* was produced and questioned the sentimental Disney love story, just as the Muppet film did. Both the Rugrats and Muppet adaptations transform the mirrors into characters who reveal that they are helpless when the queen wants to take over the narrative for her own selfish reasons. The primary conflict is not between the queen and Snow White, but between the queen and the mirror. Even though the mirrors claim they know the truth, they are challenged and dismissed. They have little authority and power. The truth is difficult to uphold in the world of American babies, and both films depict the conflict over narrative authority that is threatened by the powerful will and desire of young American Snow Whites insistent on telling their own stories and gratifying their ambitions. Autonomous voices always cause conventional narratives to crack and fracture.

The trend in Americanized fairy-tale films for young viewers since the 1960s has been to fracture the original Grimms' and classical tales in the tradition of the early cartoon work of the Fleischers, Tex Avery, Fitz Freleng, and many other animators. The most obvious example in America is the *Rocky and Bullwinkle* TV series, when the animators of the show began producing their inimitable four-minute fractured fairy-tale cartoons in 1959. From 1959 to 1961 and from 1961 to 1964, a total of ninety-one fairy-tale cartoons were filmed, all narrated by Edward Everett Horton. All were parodies of the classical and not-so-classical fairy tales, reconceived to provoke audiences with a blend of irony, minimalist techniques, and sophistication. Some of the tales such as "Jack and the Beanstalk," "Beauty and the Beast," "Snow White," and "Little Red Riding Hood" were fractured two or three times. For instance, in *Rumpelstiltskin* (1959) a young woman named Gladys will do anything to become famous. A tiny, weird character suddenly appears and informs her that he is a public relations man. All she must do is sign a contract that has a tiny clause in which she must promise to give him her first-born child. She signs, becomes famous thanks to the PR man's work, marries a prince, and has a child. However, Gladys finds a loophole in the contract and prevents the PR man from taking her son. He moves on, looking for a girl who will make diamonds out of turnips. In *Rumpelstiltskin Returns*, the tiny PR man encounters a young woman who wants to win prize contests and become rich. She, too, signs a contract, and begins winning every contest imaginable, even one that allows her to marry a prince and have a son with him. She calls the boy Blunder. Since the PR man makes his money by recruiting boys for a rich summer camp, he returns to the princess when Blunder, an uncontrollable child, is about seven or eight. In fact, Blunder is so bad and mean that he causes catastrophes at the camp, and Rumpelstiltskin wants to bring him back to the princess, who refuses to have anything to do with her terrible son.

In both these two cartoons, drawn as colorful comic strips, audience expectations are constantly reversed, and the conclusions are ironic morals that pertain to a modern sensibility and changed social relations. Thus, in *Sleeping Beauty* (1959), the princess only pretends to be asleep for twenty years while the prince and the evil fairy godmother make an amusement park out of the princess's castle and earn a good deal of money. Only when there is a great amount of money does the princess decide to awake and take her cut of the profits. In *Leaping Beauty* (1960), a princess jumps about and makes ordinary people happy, but she steps on the toe of an evil fairy godmother, who curses her by having her leap about and bore people to sleep. Eventually, she collides with a prince, kisses him accidentally, and breaks the curse. This is a consummate fractured fairy-tale film.

From the very beginning of the twentieth century the fracturing of the Grimms' fairy tales has been a major *American* characteristic of their appropriation in the United States—tearing them apart so that the original tales become unrecognizable; parodying them so they become ludicrous; turning them upside down and inside out so that they contradict themselves; imbuing them with ironic and complex meanings; resetting the tales in contemporary American society and also in the future; combining and mixing the Grimms' tales with other classical fairy tales as in the case of the four *Shrek* films (*Shrek*, 2001; *Shrek 2*, 2004; *Shrek the Third*, 2007; and *Shrek Forever After*, 2010) and *Hoodwinked* (2005) and *Hoodwinked Too! Hood vs. Evil* (2011). These are just some of the techniques and devices that one can note in the Americanzation of the Grimms' tales for young viewers, and it should be borne in mind that the filmmakers and producers of these "fractured" Grimms tales also have Disney in mind and the conventional format of the Disney fairy-tale films. The Disney model is often mistaken for the Grimm model.

Of course, the filmic adaptations of the Grimms' tales, designed more for adult audiences, have also taken every and any liberty with the Grimms' tales in what could best be described as a free-for-all fight over who can produce the most innovative, if not profound interpretation of the essence of a Grimms' fairy tale or fairy tales in general. The putative adult films, which are often more infantile than adult, cover a wide range of perspectives, approaches and modalities with an eye more on producing profit than on creating art. Some recent examples are Mike Nichols's *Bread Crumbs* (2011), a vapid horror film, in which a group of filmmakers and actors who want to film a porno film in the woods are brutally slaughtered one by one by two zombie-like adolescents representative of sicko Hansel and Gretel; Catherine Hardwicke's *Red Riding Hood* (2011), a pubescent teeny bop film that includes incest, romance, and werewolves and may win awards for the most sensationalist film without meaning in 2011; Joe Wright's *Hanna* (2011), an intriguing thriller in which a sixteen-year-old girl, likened to a super-powered Red Riding Hood, is trained by her father to become an assassin and seek revenge for him in a world out of joint flickering with fairy-tale motifs and symbols. I have already discussed the questionable spectacular features of films like *Mirror, Mirror* (2012), *Snow White and the Huntsman* (2012), and *Hansel & Gretel: Witchhunters* (2013). There are literally hundreds of live-action films with fairy-tale plots, characters, motifs, and references taken from the Grimms' tales that reveal how the Grimms have inundated the American film industry while being transformed in American culture. The question I would like to ask now is how are we to assess the Americanization of the Grimms' tales?

The Consequences of Americanization

In assessing the Americanization of the Grimms' tales, I want to summarize some of the more prominent factors in the appropriation of the stories and then raise questions about the consequences of Americanization:

1. Translated and adapted first by British writers, the Grimms' tales, intended for scholars and adult educated readers, were changed into entertaining and moral tales for children during the course of the nineteenth century. There were no great signs of Americanization. The British influence was strong, and the Grimms' tales were primarily disseminated as children's tales. American folklorists were familiar with the tales, but did not study them or write about them in great depth. About the only American folklorist who had a thorough understanding of the Grimms and their legacy was Thomas Frederick Crane, who wrote extensively about the Grimms in two important essays, "The Diffusion of Popular Tales" and "The External History of the *Kinder- und Hausmärchen* of the Brothers Grimm."[23] Basically, American folklorists paid very little attention to the Grimms' accomplishments, and Americans read and published anglicized Grimms' tales.

2. At the beginning of the twentieth century, American writers, illustrators, playwrights, and filmmakers began to experiment with the tales and radically transform them into *American stories*, whether produced for young or old. The characters of the tales became easily recognizable American types and spoke in an American vernacular using slang, idioms, sayings, and references. The setting of the action in most revisions was clearly in America, and the topics and plots were related to American issues. Any allusion to Germanic qualities or characteristics of the Grimms' tales was minimal, and this approach may have been due in part to the negative reaction to Germany during and after World War I. Essentially, any credit to the Grimms and their original designs and intentions were obliterated. Nevertheless, the Grimms' tales did become a kind of brand in the realm of children's literature that connoted fairy tale, and fairy tale was associated with children's culture.

3. The Grimms were not the only ones who suffered "obliteration" in the twentieth century. Charles Perrault, Hans Christian Andersen, Madame d'Aulnoy, Madame Leprince de Beaumont, and other writers suffered the same fate. Their tales were also fully Americanized, and as I have mentioned before, some of their tales were mixed with the Grimms' tales. What counted

was simply the title as reference. For instance, in the case of "Cinderella," "Little Red Riding Hood," or "Sleeping Beauty," it is often impossible to know whether a writer or filmmaker is drawing upon a Perrault or Grimm tale as source, or both. Just the titles are to serve memetically as recalls of whatever the reader/viewer experiences. It is as though the titles of the tales were second nature and as though all Americans should know something about these tales. The popular diffusion of the tales occurred during the interwar years of 1919–42, and it was as if the Grimms had nothing to do with Germany or transcended Germany, as Walt Disney's *Snow White and the Seven Dwarfs*, produced in 1937, demonstrated. In this sense, the Americanization fostered a kind of universalization of the tales or provided evidence for the universality of the Grimms' tales. In other words, Americanization returned the Grimms' tales to common people. Nobody could be considered their owner. There are no property rights. The tales cannot be copyrighted. Whether in German or any other language, the Grimms' tales are in the public domain. Anyone can tell them, retell them, change them, reinvent them, film them any way she or he wishes.

4. Yet, at the same time, Americanized versions do become property and are copyrighted. Publishers, film companies, corporations make their versions of the Grimms' tales their property. In their view, the tales are commodities— that is, their renditions—and thus the tales in whatever form are expected to make profits. The ideal form is the blockbuster. In order to generate profits and distinguish their tales from other corporate versions, American companies and corporations concentrate on marketing the tales through sensationalist advertising. Art is abandoned for commercialism, or put another way, commercial ads and publicity become artful and more important than a given tale. This does not mean that all adaptations and appropriations of the Grimms' tales are trivial distractions and amusements. But it does mean that millions of dollars are wasted on wasteful projects.

5. Although it is difficult to make comparisons, I would argue that America has become more home to the Brothers Grimm than Germany and that the Americanized Grimms' tales are better known than the German versions, thanks to the massive power of the American culture industry and globalization. Given the immense size difference between America and Germany, and given the vast spread of American English and American popular culture, the Americanized versions of the Grimms' tales dominate all others in the world and have led to various types of homogenization.

In his astute sociological study, *Network Power*, David Grewal claims,

> What we are experiencing now, in "globalization," is the creation
> of an international in-group that welcomes the entire globe on set-
> tled terms: a new world order in which we clamor for connection
> to one another using standards that are offered up for universal
> use. Yet, while we may all come to share these new global stan-
> dards—to the extent, at least, that we desire access to the activities
> that they mediate—we may not all have much influence over their
> establishment.[24]

Grewal views the convergence of values, coordination of production, and cooperation of multinational corporations, governments, and institutions that constitute the major thrust of globalization as part of network power that hinders
free choice and sovereignty. It has already led to the elimination of hundreds of
languages and cultures and created a situation in which we are coerced to accept
what have become standardized ways of thinking and behaving. Grewal does
not believe that we are living in a "Brave New World," but that we are living in
a world in which particular cultural narratives and histories are disappearing
or are being destroyed. There are many forces propelling the intricate power of
network systems, and certainly Americanization has been a dominant force. It
is for this reason that we should try to understand what has happened to the
Grimms and their tales, for in many respects their tales are being used today to
wipe out their memory and their quest to understand the particular essence of
storytelling. When Erik Bergstrom jokes that the Grimms are rolling in their
graves because their tales today have become gentle and fluffy, he may be right,
but the reasons he gives are all wrong. The Grimms are turning in their graves
because they can no longer identify with the tales that they so graciously gave to
the world.

CHAPTER FOUR

Two Hundred Years after Once Upon a Time: The Legacy of the Brothers Grimm and Their Tales in Germany

The thoughts of philosophy, which we had taken to be timeless, are not—and the word should be taken quite literally—"thinkable" without the the new science, which focused on tracing the phases of this long history, "philology," which he [Vico] contrasted with the timeless rationality of "philosophy." Philology is thus the disciplined act of remembering that, by following the thread of language through etymologies, finds its way back to the long buried visual substance of poetic, sensual, primeval imagery. According to Jacob Grimm, a similar journey backward through time can also be effected through the art of etymology, "which acts as a beacon where no written history can lead us."

—Aleida Assmann, *Cultural Memory and Western Civilization* (2011)[1]

Any critical history of Germanistik *that wants to unearth its origins, especially in struggles for national identity, seems always to begin with the Grimm Brothers. The Grimms represent in their work what [Hans Ulrich] Gumbrecht typifies for Romanticism: "National identity—as a representation of collective identity—seems to depend—at least for the early 19th century—on the existence of socially distant folktales and historically distant medieval cultural forms, which can be identified as the objectivations of one's own people." Merely the titles of the Grimms' publications reflect their preoccupation with "the German" and the German past:* German Legends *(2 vols., 1816–18) and their periodical* Old German Woods *(1813–16); Jacob's own projects* Old German Song *(1811),* German Grammar *(1819–37),* German Monuments of Law *(1828),* German Mythology *(1835),* History of the German language *(2 vols., 1848); and, of course, their well-known* Fairy Tales *and the* German Dictionary.

—Jeffrey Peck, "'In the Beginning Was the Word': Germany and the Origins of German Studies"[2]

The first question to ask when discussing the legacy of the Brothers Grimm and their tales in Germany, two hundred years after the publication of *Kinder- und Hausmärchen* in 1812 and 1815, is: Would the Grimms have been happy with the way their legacy of folk and fairy tales have been treated by people in their so-called fatherland? The second important question is: What is their legacy exactly and what are their tales? As we have already seen, the stories in their collection are not strictly speaking all fairy tales or Germanic, for there is hardly a fairy in any of their tales that range from fables, legends, and animal tales to folk anecdotes, trickster stories, tall tales, and religious narratives. On the other hand, there is, of course, a great deal of magical or miraculous transformation and moral counter worlds that constitute prime characteristics of the great tradition of fairy tales. Bearing that in mind, the third question, for there must always be three, is: What has happened to their tales, which are not really their own, in Germany since the 1990 reunification of East and West Germany, and why are they still so relevant? Why is there a contemporary fairy-tale boom in all cultural fields in Germany, not to mention in the United States and other parts of the world?

Since there have been excellent studies about the influence and heritage of the Grimms' tales up to 1990—I am thinking here of Ludwig Denecke and Ina-Maria Greverus's *Brüder Grimm Gedenken: 1963* and Donald Haase's *The Reception of Grimms' Fairy Tales*, two informative collections of essays,[3] among others—I want to set the discussion of the legacy of the Grimms' tales in the German sociocultural context of the last twenty-five years and begin by discussing some of the more recent popular manifestations of their stories. There are literally hundreds if not thousands of Grimm fairy-tale products and productions that have been created in the cultural fields of literature, theater, fine arts, opera, music, dance, film, television, Internet, comics, and so on that it would be impossible to do all of them justice. The same can be said about fairy-tale products in the world of advertising, commerce, and trade. The dissemination of the Grimms' tales is enormous. Therefore, I shall focus mainly on literature, including picture books, and filmic adaptations, and even here I must be very selective due to the large amount of material. Following my discussion of popular manifestations, I shall discuss the concept or notion of a Grimm legacy and conclude with an analysis of scholarly studies that, in contrast to popular culture, have grounded the legacy of the Grimms in substantial ways that, I believe, would have gratified the Grimms. To be sure, I don't believe that the Grimms would have been upset by popular culture and the manner in which the culture industry has bowdlerized their tales, but they certainly would have been shocked and at times, distressed by the massive transformation of the tales that runs the gamut from banal and infantile kitsch to sublime and profound re-creation—something that they had not experienced during their lifetime.

The contemporary kitsch aspect of their tales has been more or less "celebrated" and certainly exposed in the exhibit "Grimmskrams & Märchendising: Die Popularität der Brüder Grimm und ihrer Märchen" (Grimms' Junk and Fairy-Tale Merchandising: The Popularity of the Brothers Grimm and Their Fairy Tales),[4] held from December 2008 to February 2009 in Marburg and organized by the Institute for Ethnology and Cultural Studies of the Philipps-University Marburg. The exhibit was divided into modules consisting of the German fairy-tale road and regional marketing, language and storytelling, psychology, pornography and fairy-tale fetishism, fairy-tale illustrations, fairy-tale films, fairy-tale archaeology, Grimm street art in Marburg, and the poetry of boxes. "The basic idea of the exhibit," according to the organizers was "to comprehend objects as nodal points that to a certain extent dwell within the popularity of the Brothers Grimm as they manifest themselves today and to comprehend where they are stored and preserved. In this regard the theory of the exhibit is based on the notion that things contain an energy that radiates, and they have an effect that harks back to the context of their origins through the network of their forces."[5] Whether this is true—that is, whether the seemingly trivial and everyday objects associated with the Grimms and their tales actually vibrate and effectually resonate with traces of their original sociocultural context—is questionable. But it is certainly important to study and analyze junk and kitsch as part of a "culture of experience" (*Erlebniskultur*) that has always been an intrinsic part of folklore.

While the exhibit in Marburg reveals how seriously German curators and scholars take the slightest popular traces of the Grimms' legacy in the twenty-first century, it is important to note that there have been other exhibits and catalogues that explore fascinating aspects of the Grimm legacy and are just as significant. I am thinking here of five publications in particular that originated either in conferences or in exhibits: Klaus Kaindl and Berthold Friemel, eds., *Die Brüder Grimm in Berlin* (The Brothers Grimm in Berlin, 2004)[6]; Harm-Peer Zimmermann, ed. *Zwischen Identität und Image: Die Popularität der Brüder Grimm in Hessen* (Between Identity and Image: The Popularity of the Brothers Grimm in Hessia, 2009)[7]; Ehrhardt Holger, *Dorothea Viehmann* (2012)[8]; Andreas Hedwig, ed., *Die Brüder Grimm in Marburg* (The Brothers Grimm in Marburg, 2013)[9]; and Thorsten Smidt, ed. *Expedition Grimm* (2013).[10] Taken together all these works provide a broad basis for understanding different facets of the Grimms' lives, the societies in which they worked and moved, their experiences, and the reception of their tales and other philological works. For instance Kaindl's and Friedl's catalogue was derived from the exhibit about the Grimms' work on the *German Dictionary* after they moved to Berlin in 1841 and documents how the Grimms lived and conducted their research during the latter part of their lives. In *Zwischen Identität und Image*, Zimmermann has gathered nineteen essays from international scholars who explore the significance of Hessian culture, past and present, for the Grimms as well as the imprint that the Grimms left on Japanese culture and the general commercialization of the Grimms' legacy. *Die Brüder Grimm in Marburg* is also a collection of essays that stem from an exhibit and conference held at the University of Marburg, where the Grimms studied at the beginning of the nineteenth century. Here the papers are much more specific and deal with such topics as the work ethic of the Brothers Grimm, the places where they lived, the posthumous papers in the Marburg archives, the collection of tales contributed by Dortchen (Wild) Grimm and her talent as storyteller. Of course, the most famous of the Grimms' informants was Dorothea Viehmann, and the book of essays dedicated to her work, *Dorothea Viehmann,* is a superb collection of seven essays which analyze her family background, the French influences in her tales, the cultural importance of the Huguenots and the legends surrounding her as the ideal folk storyteller. Finally, *Expedition Grimm* accompanied the large exhibit held in Kassel in 2013 and includes essays by prominent Grimm scholars such as Steffen Martus, Heinz Rölleke, Bernhard Lauer, and Holger Ehrhardt among others. Their essays focus on topics such as the Grimms as modern traditionalists, the Grimms' studies of animal epics, their work on the *German Dictonary* and legal customs, and the world success of their tales.

While all these studies and catalogues are invaluable for comprehending the complex legacy of the Grimms in Germany, none of them deal with the contemporary literary and cinematic reception. There is a world of difference between the way the Grimms' tales have been received by academics and by writers and filmmakers, but the differences are part of the very same legacy that has profound contradictions.

Literature and Film

In the field of literature, as I have already mentioned, it is well known that the Grimms' tales constitute one of the most widely published and disseminated books in Germany that can be categorized as fiction. Large and small publishing houses such as Insel, Reclam, Rowohlt, Goldmann, Fischer, Diederichs, Beltz & Gelberg, Wissenschaftliche Buchgesellschaft, Heyne, Die bibliophilen Taschenbücher, Zweitausendeins, and Vandenhoeck & Ruprecht have issued various editions of the complete tales during the past thirty years, many of them with illustrations by contemporary artists. The most significant books are the annotated scholarly reprints of different editions that the Grimms published. For instance, Heinz Rölleke has edited the first edition of 1812 and 1815 for Vandenhoeck & Ruprecht, the third edition of 1837 for Deutscher Klassiker Verlag, and the seventh edition of 1857 for Reclam, and Hans-Jörg Uther has edited the second edition of 1819 for Olms-Weidmann and the seventh edition of 1857 for Diederichs.[11] As I have already noted, the body of the tales, including the notes, is a vast and never-ending collection, which keeps appearing in many different versions. For instance, in the latter part of the twentieth century Rölleke edited three significant volumes of tales that were omitted in the final 1857 edition as well as tales from letters, endnotes, and manuscripts.[12]

The never-ending aspect of the Grimms' tales can be seen especially in the variety of the books intended for children and family audiences. There have been well over 500 different types of Grimms' books published in German during the past twenty-two years, including single volumes for pre- and beginning readers, comic books, graphic novels, picture books, selected tales for young readers, pornographic books, adaptations, and fine art books. Here is a tiny sample of the diverse products that have been cast onto the book market:

- Dagmar Kammer as illustrator for *Mein großes Märchenbuch* (My Big Book of Fairy Tales, 2009).[13] Her illustrations are typical of the standard illustrations for children—sweet, cute, literal, nonprovocative. They are basically intended to amuse and divert children, provide brief entertainment, lull them to sleep, or stimulate them to buy similar products. The tendency of most Grimm picture books and small collections for children is to infantilize the texts and to provide illustrations that downplay sensitive but significant social issues. An example of infantilization is Claudia Blei-Hoch's *Das große Märchen Bilderbuch der Brüder Grimm* (The Big Picturebook of the Brothers Grimm, 2006).[14] This expensive book is noteworthy because five young illustrators reveal how imbecilic it is to cater to a false illusion of what children need visually to grasp the supposed benefits of fairy tales à la Bruno Bettelheim. Blei-Hoch's afterword is a travesty of good commentaries that seek to provide information about the Grimms. Her remarks are totally misinformed. A good example of a witty book for children is Rotraut Susanne Berner's work, actually two books, *Märchen-Stunde* (Fairy-Tale Hour, 1998), which she reissued as *Märchen-Comics* (Fairy-Tale Comics) in 2008.[15] Similar to the tradition that George Cruikshank started in 1823, Berner transforms the characters of the tales into funny caricatures that enliven the plots of the tales. This is also the case in another book, *Grimmige Märchen: 13 kurze Märchen aus der Sammlung der Brüder Grimm* (Gruesome Grimm Fairy Tales: 13 Short Fairy Tales from the Collection of the Brothers Grimm, 1999), edited by Berner and Armin Abmeier.[16] This book is highly unusual because thirteen talented artists illustrate some of the more gruesome and dark tales from *Kinder- und Hausmärchen* that are not fairy tales and are not as well known as the classical fairy tales. The illustrations are exceedingly provocative and uncover an aspect of the Grimms' tales that needs more attention.

- As pedagogical complements to the standardized picture books and small collections that tend to trivialize the Grimms' tales, there have been a large number of books that explain how parents and teachers can use the Grimms' tales. Some examples are: Linda Knoch's *Praxisbuch Märchen: Verstehen-Deuten-Umsetzen* (Practice Book for Fairy Tales: Understanding-Interpreting-Transforming, 2001); Cordula and Reinhold Pertler's *Kinder in der Märchenwerkstatt: Kreative Spiel- und Projektideen* (Children in the Fairy-Tale Workshop: Ideas for Creative Play and Projects, 2009); and Ute Hoffmann's *Die kreative Märchen-Werkstatt* (The Creative Fairy-Tale Workshop, 2010).[17]

- In my opinion, the most interesting illustrated books of the Grimms' tales are the experimental works of Nikolaus Heidelbach, Susanne Janssen, Květa Pacovská, and Ulrike Persch. Heidelbach illustrated 110 of the Grimms' fairy tales in 1995[18] and has also published two other important illustrated books, *Hans Christian Andersen's Märchen* (2004) and *Märchen aus aller Welt* (2010).[19] His images are stark, surrealistic and folk interpretations of the tales that tend to bring out both the deep dark side of the stories as well as their blasphemous humor. Susanne Janssen has published two picture books, *Rotkäppchen* (2001) and *Hänsel und Gretel* (2008).[20] Both are extraordinary retellings of the tales that use montage, distorted figures, and modern settings to bring out the horrific aspects of the tales. In her interpretation of "Hansel and Gretel," she focuses on the desperation of the parents and the children and counters the happy ending of the tale through a disturbing collage of boy, duck, and fish that do not leave the reader with the impression that Hansel and Gretel's lives will be saved through a "ferry" to home. In keeping with the innovative ways that Heidelbach and Janssen tend to fracture fairy tales—that is, to challenge the trivialized and standard depictions of the classical tales with complex and tantalizing compositions—the Czech illustrator Pacovská, who works and publishes a great deal in Germany, has used stunning graphics, paper collages, and bizarre figures. Unlike Janssen, however, she emphasizes the free play of the imagination with fairy tales in her versions of *Rotkäppchen* (2007) and *Hänsel und Gretel* (2009)[21] and lends an optimistic aura to her fairy tales. Perhaps the most optimistic and subversive adaptation of "Little Red Riding Hood" is Ulrike Persch's *Rotkäppchens List* (2005),[22] which portrays a tiny Red Riding Hood in a contemporary city that often looms as dangerous. However, she is street-smart and outwits the wolf on her own. Persch uses black-and-white drawings as panels with a striking similarity to graphic novels. Only the little girl is colored, with a red cap, violet t-shirt, and blue jeans, and the feminist implications of the adaptation are made clear through contrasting colors.

- While the subversive illustrations by Heidelbach, Janssen, Pacovská, and Persch are clearly intended to appeal to adults as well as young readers, there are a number of books for adults that are mildly interesting or highly provocative if not outrageous. For instance, Peter Ellinger has edited a book with the title *If the Grimms Had Known That! New Fairy Tales in the Grimms' Year 2012* (*Wenn das die Grimms wüssten! Neue Märchen zum Grimm-Jahr 2012*),[23] which includes eighty-six mildly interesting stories by eighty-six different authors. Although the book contains a few remarkable tales such as Bettina Ferbus's "Die drei roten Haare des Teufels" (The Three Red Hairs of the Devil) and Irene Beddies's" Die singende Prinzessin" (The Singing Princess), the majority of the narratives are formulaic and suffer from being commissioned and not having originated from the authors' own motivations. The Grimms' tales fare no better with the provocative pornographic and erotic adaptations. The Unfug-Verlag published an outlandish sexy version, *Rotkäppchen*, in 2009 that leaves nothing to any reader's sexual imagination.[24] Some other examples of erotic Grimm fairy tales are Theodor Ruf's novel *Die Schöne aus dem Glassarg: Schneewittchens märchenhaftes und wirkliches Leben* (The Beautiful Maiden from the Glass Coffin: Snow White's Fabulous and Real Life, 1995) and Anne Kühne's collection of stories, *Der goldene Mörser* (The Golden Mortar, 2000/2008).[25] Less erotic but very subversive are the fractured tales of murder, sex, and gore in René Hemmerling's *Total versaute Märchen: Die Brüder finden das schlimm* (Totally Messed-Up Fairy Tales: The Brothers Find This Awful, 2006).[26] Hemmerling calls his parodies "trash fairy tales," and they have titles such as "Hansel and Grethel, & Co. Celebrate Halloween," "Rapunzel Among Druggies," and "The Frog King and the Ungrateful Barber's Daughter."

There have, of course, been more serious adaptations of the Grimms' tales such as Cornelia Funke's *Reckless* (2010) and *Fearless* (2012),[27] Karin Duve's *Grrrimm* (2012),[28] and Florian Weber's *Grimms Erben* (2012).[29] It is obvious that these works were timed to appear during the bicentenary celebrations of the first edition of the Grimms' *Kinder- und Hausmärchen*, and all of them have a critical edge to them. Funke's two novels are part of a trilogy, "Mirror World series," in which she depicts the Brothers Grimm as Jacob and Will Reckless in their early twenties. They enter a nineteenth-century fantasy world through a mirror, and in the first novel, *Reckless*, Jacob must rescue his brother, who is transformed into a Goyl, a humanoid race with stone skin. In this fast-paced narrative Jacob encounters dwarfs, wicked and good fairies, and a female shape-shifting fox. Motifs from several Grimms' tales such as "The Frog King," "Rapunzel," "Sleeping Beauty," and "Snow White" are thrown into the brew to enliven the plot. In the end Jacob can save his brother only by sacrificing his own life. He sends Will back to the "real" world and has only a year to live unless he finds a cure for his curse. Of course, this ending leads to a new beginning in *Fearless*, in which Jacob falls in love with the shape-shifter fox, also called Celeste, while seeking to obtain an antidote to the deadly moth implanted in his heart. Again, motifs such as a miraculous apple, water of immortality, and magic blood are employed as possible cures for Jacob's curse. Whether he will ultimately find peace and happiness will be determined in the third novel that is in the process of being written. This process includes a critical revision of the Grimms' tales, which Funke has called somewhat reactionary in a 2010 interview: "Fairy Tales play with many kinds of wishes, sometimes for revenge, sometimes for power. They often appeal to everything other than what is good in us. When one reads a fairy tale, one is astonished by how reactionary they often are. Indeed, often fairy tales merely reinforce existing norms. In addition when one regards what the Grimms did with the female figures, then one is really horrified."[30]

Yet, while the female figures, even the evil fairies, in Funke's novels tend to be more politically correct, her character portrayal of women (and men) is somewhat thin and predictable in her narratives intended for a young adult (YA) audience. In fact, Funke's fantasy works tend to be conventional and stilted. She arbitrarily uses clichés and worn-out fairy tale motifs in absurd and imitative ways so that her characters become more caricatures suited for comic strip than a novel. In contrast Karin Duve's characters in her five unusual tales are highly complex and original. Using different narrative voices that are blunt, colorful, and idiomatic, she retells five of the Grimms' tales ("Snow White," "The Frog King," "Sleeping Beauty," "Brother Lustig," and "Little Red Cap") to explore hidden meanings that add greater social and philosophical depth to the stories. For instance, "Zwergenidyll" (Dwarf Idyll) is told in the first person by a dwarf who is in love with Snow White and tries to seduce her. He makes several unsuccessful and somewhat comic attempts to sleep with her, but she is eventually carried off by a prince, married, and then divorced within a year because the prince considers her beneath him. Consequently, Snow White becomes the mistress of a series of members of the royal court and finally drifts off to nowhere, while the dwarf becomes rich after discovering gold and waits for her in the cottage in which Snow White used to clean and cook. There is nothing idyllic in Duve's version of a Grimm tale that suggests Snow White will live happily ever after. In "Die Froschbraut" ("The Frog's Wife") narrated by the princess, we learn that her tyrannical father is a criminal and maltreats his daughter. Under investigation for his illegal activities by the police, he hides incriminating papers in a golden ball, the princess's favorite plaything. A young policeman, disguised and transformed into a frog, finds the ball and investigates the father's illegal activities. Eventually, he liberates the daughter from her prison-like existence, instead of the typical ending in which the princess breaks the frog's magic spell by throwing him against a wall. Duve clearly undermines expectations of readers of the classical versions of the Grimms' tales to cast light on the seamy side of "real life." In the title story, "Grrrimm," a tour-de-force retelling of "Little Red Cap" combined with "The Boy Who Set Out to Learn about Fear," she sets the tale in a contemporary village in the mountains of some apparently Slavic country, where conditions are very primitive. Told from the alternating perspectives of Elsie (Little Red Cap) and Stepan, Elsie's childhood friend, who has moved to a village farther down the mountain and has become a young man who knows no fear, we learn that Elsie is the one of twelve children in a poor family. Both the mother and father appear to be alcoholics. The village and district are without funds so that garbage is everywhere as are wolves. Elsie's father, Kimi, and his friend Istvan are attacked by a werewolf. The friend dies and the father appears to be dying from a bite. So Elsie, wearing her red cap, is sent to her grandmother, Uchtatka, a feisty witch, for a cure. She accidentally meets Stepan as she walks through the forest, and he helps her to bring the cure to Elsie's father. However, he dies. After the burial and brutal treatment from her mother and siblings, Elsie decides to run off with Stepan and wants to meet him at her grandmother's house. However, when she arrives there, she discovers that her grandmother, herself, is a werewolf but has learned to control her aggressive instincts. As they wait for Stepan, the dead Istvan, who has arisen from his grave as a vampire, arrives and kills the grandmother. Then Stepan appears, and since he doesn't know what fear is, he attacks Istvan and is saved when Elsie uses an ax to cut off Istvan's head. Ironically, the narrative ends with Stepan revealing that Elsie was bitten by her grandmother so that she could defend herself against Istvan. Fortunately, Stepan has no fear about living with Elsie. Duve's narrative harks back to eighteenth- and nineteenth-century European versions of "Little Red Riding Hood," and though it is gruesome, she captures the heroic aspect of two young people born into a barbaric society. Together, despite the depraved conditions of the village and surrounding community, Elsie and Stepan have learned to survive on their own.

Survival also plays a major role in Florian Weber's extraordinary novel, *Grimms Erben* (Grimms' Heirs), which concerns the fate of writers of fairy tales, or storytelling in general, in the post-Holocaust era. The novel, filled with gallows humor and strange coincidences, is divided into three parts that take place in the Warsaw Ghetto in 1943, in the latter part of the twentieth century and early part of the twenty-first century in Lower Bavaria, and then in the contemporary world of the Austrian Alps. The plot is based on an oath that two brothers, Ignaz and Zacharias Buchmann, sons of a shoemaker in a tiny village in Bavaria, make to each other at the beginning of World War II, when they decide to avoid serving in the German army: they intend to live in a hut in the Austrian Alps until the war is terminated and to publish a book of Ignaz's fairy tales under the title "Grimms' Heirs." Before they seek refuge in the mountains, Ignaz wants to publish his book as a sign of resistance to the Nazis and as a gesture for a peaceful world. Zacharias is to be the publisher. However, they become separated in Warsaw, where they had hoped to find a printer for the book. Ignaz is captured by the Nazis and sent to Treblinka as a Jew. Zacharias is recruited into the German army as a truck driver, and unfortunately, he witnesses the execution of his brother when he is sent to pick up supplies in Treblinka. Nevertheless, he is able to save five of his brother's tales, and thereafter, his mission in life is to fulfill the oath that he made to Ignaz. To do this, he changes his identity and becomes Zacharias Locher, and the rest of the novel focuses on how this oath is passed on to his grandson August in postwar Germany, and the difficult conditions under which August, also a writer of tales, must learn, like Job, to suffer and prove himself "worthy" to carry out the oath after his grandfather commits suicide. The final part of the novel includes a fairy tale written by Ignaz that exemplifies the morality behind the oath: Night challenges Day to a duel to determine who will dominate the world for all twenty-four hours instead of sharing each day for twelve hours. As their armies are about to engage in war, the Tides, Ebb and Flow, appear and talk sense to Day and Night so that they realize it would be too much work to control the world for twenty-four hours. So Day and Night settle their conflict in peace. The result is that "Ebb and Flow still continue to ensure there will be chaos in human emotions—because they have not expired."[31]

Aside from the fairy-tale novels of Günter Grass, Weber's work is one of the few narratives that deepen the ethical legacy of the Grimms' tales, and his novel sets out to explore the morality of writing fairy tales as a mission in light of the Nazi past without being overly didactic. Weber's unusual approach shows how entangled the Grimms' heritage is, and this is what makes Weber's novel so significant.

Filmic Adaptations

Whether there is such a strong moral aspect in the adaptation of the Grimms' tales for the cinema remains to be seen. The quantity, quality, and variety of these films, made mainly for television and DVD markets, are vast. First, it should be noted that the reunification of Germany allowed all the East German Deutsche Film-Aktiengesellschaft (DEFA), Czech, and Russian fairy-tale films to be marketed in the former West Germany, and today many of these films have been shown on television and in theaters, and are readily available as DVDs through the small distribution company Icestorm. As Sebastian Heiduschke points out,

> By transforming the films from intangible products into commodity items that could be purchased and owned by individuals, Icestorm established DEFA as a unique German brand name, allowing former GDR citizens to claim them as part of their identities. Initially, the company selected titles for release based on the input from previous customers to determine the most successful DEFA film genres in the GDR and therefore the most promising products for commercialization on home video. Thus the first wave of VHS releases saw fairy tales such as Wolfgang Staudte's *Die Geschichte vom kleinen Muck* (*The Story of Little Mook*, 1953) that had enchanted children and adults alike in the GDR and now targeted parents who wanted their children to grow up with these movies from their childhood.[32]

Most of them are live-action films, although one should not forget that numerous excellent animated fairy-tale films were also created in Eastern Europe from 1945 to 1990.

DEFA produced twenty-three live-action fairy-tale films from 1956 to 1989 based on the Grimms' tales, not to mention other films adapted from the fairy tales of Hans Christian Andersen and Wilhelm Hauff and co-productions with Czech filmmakers.[33] Intended for young viewers, the DEFA fairy-tale films were directed by some of the best filmmakers in East Germany and included many of the country's foremost actors. Moreover, the manner in which the Grimms' tales were transformed to emphasize class struggle, the radical transformation of society, industriousness, and social and political justice makes it clear that the filmmakers and their crews did a thorough study of the ideology of each tale and sought to highlight textual contradictions as well as the contradictions of the East German state and party. For the most part the aesthetic quality of the films is very good, even when the plots and themes may be overly didactic. What is interesting today is that, while DEFA sought to demonstrate how the Grimms' tales were part and parcel of a German socialist heritage, the films as DVDs circulate in a reunified capitalist Germany and must compete with other German series of fairy-tale films that are ideologically more in keeping with patriarchal and capitalist ideas.

For instance, Greenlight Media introduced the animated series *Simsala-Grimm* in 1999 and produced fifty-two episodes up through 2010 based largely on the Grimms' tales and several tales from the works of Hauff, Andersen, and Joseph Jacobs. The format of each 25-minute episode calls for two charming characters, a zany mischief-maker named YoYo and the more serious and studious Doc Cro to become involved in a revised tale geared primarily toward amusing audiences. Their major function is to provide comic relief as they intervene in the action always to help the good characters. For the most part the directors of these skits have simplified the tales in an effort to provide commercially digestible amusement for children between the ages of four and ten without questioning the ideology of the original Grimm texts as the DEFA films always did to address political conflicts. To a great extent the focus tends to be on the two comic characters Yo Yo and Doc Cro rather than on exploring the Grimms' tales in any critical or creative depth. For this reason, despite the good reception of *SimsalaGrimm* by young viewers, two important societies, the Europäische Märchengesellschaft and the Märchen-Stiftung Walter Kahn, along with numerous independent storytellers, educators, and film critics, initiated a controversial debate in 2000 about the denigration of the Grimms' legacy that continues up to the present day. According to Daniel Drascek, the critics of *SimsalaGrimm* (and also other fairy-tale TV series) accuse the producers of falsifying the folklore tradition of the Brothers Grimm, commercializing the tales irresponsibly, and harming the imagination of children by visualizing tales that were created to be told.[34]

Diverse opinions were represented in the book, *Märchen—Kinder—Medien* (Fairy Tales—Children—Media, 2000), edited by Kurt Franz and Walter Kahn,[35] that reveal how critics are seriously concerned about the Grimms' legacy of folk and fairy tales and how differently they assess the filmic adaptation of the tales. Some such as Christoph Schmitt, Joachim Giera, and Lutz Röhrich suggest that the questionable or nonauthentic fairy-tale films keep the Grimms' tradition alive and that it will remain resilient no matter how differently it is interpreted or transformed. Despite or because of the critical reception, the *SimsalaGrimm* series continues to enjoy popular success; it is well-funded and widely disseminated throughout the world, and it is accompanied by toys, puzzles, coloring books, games, and other peripheral products. To a certain extent, the success of this series has spawned two live-action fairy-tale series for television, *Märchenperlen* (Fairy-tale Pearls, 2005) and *Sechs auf einen Streich* (Six with One Blow, 2008). Both series are modernized interpretations of the Grimms' tales and are intended for older children and families. Thus far, there have been over twenty different adaptations that vary greatly in quality and draw large audiences. While the producers of these series tend to draw contemporary meanings from these tales and at the same time preserve their so-called original messages, it is clear that the films are bound by the demands and ideologies of German television codes and prescriptions.

It seems as though the success of these television fairy-tale films has discouraged filmmakers from producing films for the cinema. Aside from various foreign films, there have been relatively few feature-length fairy-tale films produced by German corporations in the last twenty years. Two films are noteworthy for their high kitsch "quality": *7 Zwerge—Männer allein im Wald* (7 Dwarfs—Men Alone in the Woods, 2004) and the sequel *7 Zwerge—Der Wald ist nicht genug* (7 Dwarfs—The Woods Are Not Enough, 2006), live-action films both directed by Sven Unterwaldt and both with great success at the box office. The comedies are loosely based on the Grimms' "Snow White" and depict the absurd adventures of seven men named Brummboss, Sunny, Cloudy, Tschakko, Cookie, Bubi, and Speedy, who have decided to live deep in a forest without women because they have all had mishaps with the female sex. Indeed, they are all misfits, and when Red Riding Hood and Snow White wander into the forest, the blundering men are at first flustered but eventually save Snow White from the evil queen. In the sequel, they rescue her once again, this time from Rumpelstiltskin. Both films are insipid; the gags are infantile and offensive to anyone who has a mind; the slapstick acting is worse than the acting of the Three Stooges; the pandering directors simply want to feed nonthinking audiences accustomed to trivial fun some more junk food to go along with the popcorn they eat.

Two other films, Christoph Hochhäusler's *Milchwald* (*In This Very Moment*, 2003) (figure 8) and Doris Dörrie's *Der Fischer und seine Frau* (*The Fisherman and His Wife*, 2005), are to be taken much more seriously. In a clear reference to the Grimms' "Hansel and Gretel," Hochhäusler's bleak but brilliant film concerns the accidental abandonment of two children, Lea and Constantin, or the incapacity of parents in our post-industrialist world to provide the young with the nurture and care that they need. The plot is simple and straightforward: a young woman named Sylvia has become a stepmother by marrying an older man named Joseph, a widower, who has two children. They are clearly well-to-do and have recently moved into a suburban house still in the midst of renovation in the former East Germany, which itself is in need of renovation. Everything is white, sterile, and unfinished inside the house, and Sylvia has obviously not adjusted to the house and the two stepchildren, who resent her. The house undergoing renovation and the unprepared young wife married to a rich professional can easily be interpreted as a representation of contemporary East Germany after the fall of the wall in 1989. The young stepmother is not up to the task of raising children who do not belong to her. In the film's initial scene, she picks them up from school and drives them to do some shopping in Poland, where prices are cheaper than in Germany. However, she has an argument with Lea and abandons

Figure 8. *Milchwald* (*In This Very Moment*). Christoph Hochhäusler, director. Feiber Film, 2003.

both children temporarily on the road to the shopping center. The abandonment turns out to be permanent when the children wander into a forest and become lost and eventually are taken to a Polish city by a worker who delivers cleaning fluid to different hotels in the region. At first he wants a reward for finding them, but he eventually abandons them on a highway because they cause him so much trouble.

There is no happy ending in this film, for the family has degenerated and cannot hold itself together in an apathetic world. The children are left to their own devices because anxiety and alienation cannot create bonds of support for the young. The film reflects how misunderstanding is the way people communicate, whether it be in the former East Germany or Poland, and certainly the language and cultural misunderstandings contribute to the conflicts concerning the children. Silence, alienation, and repression are also contributing factors to the dilemma of the family. Certainly, the children are not willfully abandoned in this film, but they have been psychologically abandoned, and though they head for home at the end, it is questionable whether they can find home in a world of lies and miscommunication.

Such is Hochhäusler's comment on the Grimms' legacy, while Dörrie is much more optimistic even if she is somewhat simplistic and reactionary. That is, she simplistically argues for a simple anti-capitalist life while she reacts to the feminist movement by displaying how women are weak and more drawn to glamour and money than men. Her film is a comedy based on the Grimms' dialect tale,

"The Fisherman and His Wife," and it begins first in Japan, where a young German fish doctor named Otto accidentally meets a lovely young fashion designer named Ida. They fall in love and decide to have a blitz marriage in Japan. When they return to Germany, they live in a shabby caravan, where Otto makes a living curing and dealing in exotic fish. Ida designs unusual scarves and dresses. As they begin to prosper, Ida insists on moving to more comfortable and luxurious places—an apartment, a condominium, a huge mansion with servants—and she also changes her looks to become more stylish and fashionable. Her ambition leads to marital strife and separation, until Ida and Otto lose all their money and wealth. Most of the blame is placed on Ida, as is the case with the fisherman's wife in the Grimms' tale. Gradually, she realizes how much happier she was with Otto when they were living in a caravan and struggling. Consequently, she returns to Otto in a grand, sentimental gesture of reconciliation.

The film is framed by two talking fish—Otto's pets, so to speak—who comment on the relationship between Otto and Ida. They appear to be humans living under a curse and will be released from the spell if Otto and Ida stay together three years. Ironically, they are then transformed into frogs, supposedly Dörrie's light-hearted joke about the Grimms' tale and fairy-tale expectations. But it is not a joke to depict a young contemporary woman punished because she is too ambitious while her tender young man tries to preserve the integrity of their marriage. While not as banal as the "Snow White" filmic adaptations, Dörrie's film is a superficial interpretation of the Grimms' tale with stereotypical Hollywood touches.

With films such as the *The Fisherman and His Wife*, *7 Zwerge*, and many other kitsch uses of the Grimms' tales in the past twenty-five years, it is a wonder that the Grimms' legacy has survived. However, as I have already suggested, there are always conflicts and disputes over legacies and heritages. There are always valid and invalid claims. Now, I should like to turn to what I believe are the more serious and legitimate claims to the Grimms' legacy in Germany, and I want to begin with another brief discussion about the meaning of legacy before turning to Günter Grass and some important scholarly endeavors to preserve and deepen the Grimms' contribution to folklore.

The Legacy and Heritage of the Brothers Grimm

As I have already explained, the general meaning of "legacy" is associated with a bequest, generally money and property, handed down by an ancestor or predecessor. A bequest may be anything—land, houses, articles, jewelry, letters, documents, and so on. The bequest is generally recorded in a will or legally

determined by courts. It is frequently based on a conscious decision by the be-
queather before his or her death. Sometimes legacy is connected to a heritage or
inheritance, what the Germans call *Erbe*. During the existence of the two states,
East and West Germany from 1948 to 1990, there was a continual, sometimes
fierce debate about which nation-state was entitled to inherit the great cultural
tradition of the German humanities—the socialist East or the capitalist West. In
the case of the Brothers Grimm and their tales, there are no written testimonies
that indicate exactly what they wanted to bequeath or pass on as a heritage to
the German people. Yet their intentions are clear—that is, they were clear almost
from the beginning of their careers as scholars when they were still in their early
twenties, especially after they began studying with their mentor Carl von Savigny
at the University of Marburg at the beginning of the nineteenth century. As I have
already shown, the Grimms sought to collect and preserve all kinds of ancient
relics that consisted of tales, myths, songs, fables, legends, epics, documents, and
other artifacts as if they were sacred and precious gems. They intended to trace
and grasp the essence of cultural evolution and to demonstrate how natural language, stemming from the needs, customs, and rituals of the common people,
created authentic bonds and helped forge civilized communities. This is one of
the reasons why they called their collection of tales an educational primer (*Erziehungsbuch*), for the tales recalled the past foundation of the Germanic people
and also other European groups. Yet, the *Kinder- und Hausmärchen* is only a
small part of the Grimms' legacy, and to understand the role that the tales played
in their bequest to the Germans, we must bear in mind the following points:

1. Before they began collecting folk tales in 1806, the Grimms had begun gathering all kinds of sagas, epics, legends, songs, and manuscripts and writing
   about their historical significance. As Steffen Martus has demonstrated in
   his significant biography of the Grimms,[36] they were diligent workaholics,
   determined to prove themselves as the foremost scholars in the new fields of
   philology, ethnology, and folklore and bent on uncovering the mysteries of
   the origins of older texts. They were very competitive and ambitious.

2. Once they decided to publish the first two volumes of the *Kinder- und
   Hausmärchen* in 1812 and 1815, the framework of the corpus of their tales
   that kept changing formed one of the bequests that the Grimms made to the
   German people.

3. While they appreciated that their collected tales appealed to children, they
   intended that their seven collections of the large edition to be read by adults
   as an educational primer.

4. It was not until 1819, when Wilhelm took complete charge of editing all future editions of *Kinder- und Hausmärchen*, that there was a noticeable change in their consistent adaptation of their tales and publishing policy. Wilhelm expanded the bequest. Under the influence of Edgar Taylor's translation, *German Popular Stories* (1823), the Grimms decided to have their tales illustrated and to publish a small edition of fifty tales more dedicated to family reading and children, and not to publish footnotes or notes with the tales in the larger edition.

5. Though the Grimms focused on tales that seemed to have a clear Germanic lineage, they never called their tales German, as did Ludwig Bechstein, or label them Tyrolean, Austrian, Hessian, Swabian, Swiss, and so on, as other collectors of tales did. The more they collected, the more they realized that their tales were part and parcel of a large and extensive European oral and literary tradition.

6. By 1837—that is, with the publication of the third large edition—Jacob paid very little attention to the *Kinder- und Hausmärchen*, and even Wilhelm, who kept refining the tales to find the appropriate oral folk mode, did not devote much research or time to expand and revise the collection. By 1840 the Brothers turned their attention to collecting notes for the great project of their mature years, *The German Dictionary*, and other philological projects. The tales, if anything, were part of a huge body of the Grimms' philological works that formed a unique part of their legacy to the German people. The significance of the tales cannot be understood without grasping their relationship to the German language and culture—that is, to the German civilizing process.

Günter Grass and the Grimms

This last point is made significantly clear in Günter Grass's work, *Grimms Wörter: Eine Liebeserklärung* (*Grimms' Words: A Declaration of Love*, 2010),[37] part memoir and part testimony to the great legacy of the Grimms. In a 2010 interview with the German magazine, *Der Spiegel*, Grass reveals a deep gratitude to the Grimms: "My relationship with Wilhelm and Jacob Grimm reaches far back into my childhood. I grew up with the Grimms' fairy tales. I even saw a theater production of 'Tom Thumb' during Advent at the State Theater in Danzig, which my mother took me to see. Then later in my life, the brothers influenced my creative work. . . . This book is about the political and social side. The life of the Grimms, who lived through a period marked by radical change, just as I did, lends itself to this." [38] Indeed, Grass's sprawling declaration is a thought-provoking book with an unusual interpretation of the legacy of the Brothers Grimm that has little to do with fairy tales but more to do with politics and the usefulness of words. Indeed, what else could be expected from Günter Grass, the most famous, if not most notorious writer of postwar Germany? Despite the fact that he has written two fairy-tale novels, *Der Butt* (*The Flounder*, 1977) and *Die Rättin* (*The Rat*, 1986), as well as *Die Blechtrommel* (*The Tin Drum*, 1959), which has clear parallels with "Tom Thumb" tales, his book about the Brothers Grimm and their words does not focus much on their tales and their influence but on his own writing.

There are three strands of history that Grass weaves in this memoir: (1) a sociopolitical biography of the Brothers Grimm, Jacob (1785–1863) and Wilhelm (1786–1859); (2) a chronicle of the development of the *German Dictionary* (*Das deutsche Wörterbuch*, 1838–1961), first edited by the Brothers, who were only able to complete four volumes up to the letter F during their lifetime; and (3) pungent memories of Grass's political activities (from the 1930s to the present), which are linked to his two more recent memoirs.

The first strand deals with the sociopolitical conditions that shaped the Grimms' own declaration of love for the research of ancient words, tales, and documents. Grass's focus on the Göttingen period (1829–37) allows him to show how the Grimms, who were banished by the tyrannical King of Hannover, were swept up by the political struggles of the times and how their allegiance to the integrity of words such as their oath to the constitution of Hannover formed bonds that they refused to break. The Brothers developed a deep attachment to one another and to Germany through words, even though Germany was not unified at that time.

The second strand of Grass's book demonstrates that it is the *Dictionary* and the other philological works published by the Grimms that provide the basis of their legacy in Germany. He traces the remarkable and contradictory history of the *Dictionary* through the Nazi period to 1961, when all thirty-two volumes finally appeared together, and he explains how work on German words in a revised Grimms' *Dictionary* continues today.

The Grimms' legacy is, therefore, never-ending, just as Grass's interventions and play with words in his book are never-ending and form the third strand of his book. Grass inserts himself everywhere as he records the biography of the Grimms and their *Dictionary*. In fact, throughout the book, Grass tends to celebrate himself and his political actions more than the Grimms and their words. Yet, in many respects it is thanks to the provocative Grass that the Grimms' legacy receives the "proper" homage that it deserves. For most people in the world and in Germany itself, the Grimms are famous because of their tales. Yet more than ninety percent of their work involved profound philological research into the history and vitality of words and how and why we speak them. And so, Grass's verbosity and immodest celebration of his personal debt to the Grimms should help us alter our perspective as to why the words of their tales are so meaningful.

Scholarly Endeavors to Preserve the Grimms' Legacy to Folklore

This shift in perspective does not mean that we should spend more time analyzing the *Dictionary* and other philological works of the Brothers Grimm. It means that that we should be paying more attention to the interrelationship between philology and narratology in the Grimms collection of folk tales. Indeed, German scholars have been at the forefront of the historical and philological scholarship that deals with the Grimms' voluminous works. The Brüder Grimm-Gesellschaft in Kassel and the Europäische Märchengesellschaft have sponsored conferences and exhibits as well as the publication of annuals, magazines, and monographs for over fifty years. Some of their work is tedious and in need of critical revision, but for the most part, the scholarship is dependable and useful. It is also not by chance that the monumental *Enzyklopädie des Märchens*, the most significant and resourceful encyclopedia of folk and fairy tales in the western world, is housed in Göttingen and edited by some of the foremost scholars of folklore, who also contribute to *Fabula*, the leading European journal of folk and fairy tales.

Amid all the remarkable work of German folklorists, linguists, and literary critics, it is, in my opinion, Heinz Rölleke, who has been crucial for understanding the Grimms' legacy during the past fifty years. Rölleke began to make a name for himself as the most eminent scholar of the Grimms' tales when he published *Die älteste Märchensammlung der Brüder Grimm* (The Oldest Collection of the Tales of the Brothers Grimm) in 1975, the first and most thoroughly annotated edition of the Grimms' written manuscript of 1810, usually referred to as the Ölenberg manuscript.[39] This work enabled scholars to examine how the Grimms vastly changed the tales before they went into print in the first edition of 1812–15. Rölleke followed this book with *Märchen aus dem Nachlaß der Brüder Grimm* (Tales from the Unpublished Papers of the Brothers Grimm, 1977), selected tales from the Grimms' posthumous papers; *Wo das Wünschen noch geholfen hat* (When Wishing Still Helped, 1985), a collection of his shorter essays; and *Die Märchen der Brüder Grimm* (The Tales of the Brothers Grimm, 1985), an exceedingly informative introduction to the Grimms' tales that he revised in 2004.[40] Altogether he has published well over sixty books that deal with the

Grimms' tales, and he has also edited reprints of the first, third, and seventh editions of the *Kinder- und Hausmärchen* as well as the Grimms' correspondence. In short, Rölleke's careful philological work has laid the basis for most of the important scholarly work on the Grimms' tales in the late twentieth century and early twenty-first century.

His most recent book, whose title in English reads, *Once Upon a Time. . . The True Tales of the Brothers Grimm and Who Told Them to Them* (2011),[41] is a collaboration with the talented German illustrator, Albert Schindehütte, a notable Grimm specialist in his own right, who has provided highly unusual illustrations. The purpose of this edition—and to a certain extent Rölleke has come full circle in his research—is to uncover and pay tribute to the people who provided the Grimms with different kinds of tales in their earliest versions before they were changed and honed, largely by Wilhelm Grimm. It is commonly known that the Grimms did not provide detailed information about their informants and exactly when, where, and how they passed on the stories that they either told to the Grimms or wrote down for them. Even when the Grimms did indicate the sources of the tales, some of their information was misleading.

Rölleke has made it his "mission" during the past thirty-five years or so to trace the history of the informants. During the course of these years, his voluminous essays clarified how the Grimms obtained their tales and what their sources were. Finally, in *Es war einmal*, he has published selected tales from twenty-five informants that can be found either in the Ölenberg manuscript or in the 1812–15 edition. These tales are truer to the authentic storytelling tradition of their time and quite different from the same tales that the Grimms gradually edited until they reached their polished form in the seventh edition of 1857. Rölleke's plan is to let the informants speak for themselves, true to the present methods of modern folklorists, who generally take care to provide biographical information of the storytellers and the context in which the tales are recorded.

In *Es war einmal*, we now gain a more comprehensive understanding of the background of the tales and how the Grimms worked. Despite certain contradictions in their work, Rölleke maintains that the Grimms managed to uncover numerous mythological motifs, parallels, and explanations, important for the study of folklore and the German language. At the same time, they artfully reconstituted the tales they received in accordance with their philological concept and growing awareness that the tales were widespread in Europe. Moreover, as Rölleke stresses, these so-called Hessian or German tales owed more to a greater European literary and folklore tradition than most people realize. And perhaps this is the reason why the tales never belonged to the informants or to the Grimms and why they are so globally popular today. Whatever the truth may be, Rölleke's spadework adds luster to the accomplishment of the Grimms as great *European* folklorists, who bequeathed their tales to Europe and the world.

Rölleke is, of course, not the only major German scholar, who has added to our understanding of the multicultured legacy of the Brothers Grimm and their tales. For instance, after making a significant contribution to the field of international folklore by revising Antti Aarne and Stith Thompson's *The Types of the Folktales: A Classification and Bibliography* in 2004, Hans-Jörg Uther has performed another useful deed by producing *Handbuch zu den "Kinder- und Hausmärchen der Brüder Grimm. Entstehung—Wirkung—Interpretation (Companion to the Children's and Household Tales of the Brothers Grimm: Origin-Recpetion-Interpretation,* 2008),[42] the most thorough handbook of annotations to the Grimms' collection of folk tales to date, including all the tales that the Brothers had deleted or omitted in the course of publishing seven editions from 1812 to 1857. This is a major accomplishment, for Uther provides a plethora of references and sources to scholars and students who might be interested in the origins, impact, and criticism of the Grimms' tales, and he covers a wide range of scholarship (most of it German) with élan and perspicacity. Aside from this *Handbook*, Uther has written numerous essays about the Grimms' tales and has also edited reprints of the Grimms' second and seventh editions of the *Children's and Household Tales*.

In a much different and incisive theoretical study, *Das Buch, das wir sind: Zur Poetik der "Kinder- und Hausmärchen, gesammelt durch die Brüder Grimm,* [43] Jens Sennewald develops Rölleke's notion of the Grimms as modernist and romantic cultivators of folk tales, not just fairy tales. Following Jacob Grimm's debate about natural and artistic poetry and the meaning of fairy tales with Achim von Arnim, Sennewald makes clear what the Grimms' intentions were. It is to Sennewald's credit that he explores and explains the intentions and conceptions of the Grimms' as romantic writers and philologists. As I have remarked in previous chapters, Sennewald emphasizes that there was not just one edition of their tales, but seven, and that the narratives, consisting of fairy tales, animal tales, legends, religious stories, fables, and anecdotes, were constantly edited and changed over the course of forty-seven years. These seven editions were influenced by the Grimms' other linguistic and philological works. Sennewald maintains that the editions of the tales need to be considered as a collective whole, which, according to the Grimms, originated in antiquity and continued to be formed and reformed in a flowing process of remaking that sought to make words come alive, to resuscitate relics of the past and silenced words, so that they could speak for themselves in tone and structure.

Indeed, the Grimms paved the way for research—the collecting of tales and the gradual development of "romantic" precepts of folklore that numerous folklorists were to follow in the nineteenth century. This is not to say that the Grimms were idealistic visionaries who misrepresented the folk and folk tales by claiming they all emanated from a pristine past or mysterious divinity. The

German romantics such as Wackenroder, Tieck, Novalis, Friedrich and August Wilhelm von Schlegel, Brentano, Arnim, Eichendorff, and Hoffmann, were experimental, innovative, and highly educated. The Grimms intensely studied words, sayings, etymologies, themes, plots, and history and pieced together hundreds of versions and variants of folk and fairy tales to understand their core. This is why it is so difficult to talk about a single Grimm legacy, even if we limit ourselves to discussing just the tales that they collected. As Donald Haase has astutely pointed out:

> The problem has to do with the extraordinarily difficult nature of Grimms' text. Identifying Grimms' collection as a published text—as a book—is, perhaps surprisingly, a formidable task. While we speak without qualification and generously generalize about "Grimms' Fairy Tales," as if the referent of that phrase required no elaboration, the textual and editorial history of that title makes it impossible to speak definitively of a single text. In fact, Grimms' fairy tales constitute not simply a book but many books. As Grimm scholarship over the last twenty-five years has stressed, the *Kinder- und Hausmärchen* is a dynamic publishing phenomenon that existed in seventeen different authorized editions in the Grimms' lifetime alone.[44]

As pioneers who issued a call for more collecting of folk tales in the nineteenth century, the Grimms helped to open the dikes that had dammed the oral folk tales from being spread and had kept them from being known among the general population in Germany and European countries, and consequently, hundreds of unusual collections of folk tales appeared during their lifetime throughout Europe. By the 1870s, the great Sicilian folklorist Giuseppe Pitrè, who stemmed from a poor fisherman's family, collected fairy tales in dialect from illiterate lower-class women and men. They exhibited large repertoires of tales as did many of the peasant storytellers in France in the collections of François-Marie Luzel, Jean François Bladé, Paul Sébillot, Henry Carnoy and in other countries such as Russia in the collections of Alexander Afans'ev and Czechoslovakia in the collections of Karel Erben. The Grimms' "German" legacy of tales was always much more than German, and for the most part, they can sleep peacefully in their graves because the profound multicultural origins and essential historical meaning of their tales have been acknowledged, whether it be through popular kitsch and comics, artistic adaptations in literature, theater, opera, ballet, and film, or in thorough historical and philological research. Their "German" tales mean more in the world than words can articulate.

CHAPTER FIVE

How Superheroes Made Their Way into the World of Fairy Tales: The Appeal of Cooperation and Collective Action from the Greek Myths to the Grimms' Tales and Beyond

The attempts to distinguish myth from folktale in current usage are a methodological nightmare: this has only a limited bearing on the ancient usage of the Greek term mythos, *which tends to mean simply a tale, without any certain connotation of its truth. Partly, our perspectives have evolved historically, with nineteenth-century notions of folklore and folktale suggesting primitive survival and some twentieth-century notions of myth suggesting an element of genuine belief; this converges, up to a point, with the idea of myth as largely confined to creation and early etiological stories, but it is hardly practical to press such distinctions,. In this case, no definition at all is probably less misleading than one so loaded with qualification as to be practically useless.*

—Graham Anderson, *Greek and Roman Folklore*[1]

Several years ago I came across a book with the title *Snow White and the Seven Samurai* (2000), written by the popular British writer Tom Holt. Intrigued by the title, I bought the book and read it to the end, even though the novel is absurdly ridiculous, often boring, and always outrageous à la Monty Python. To demonstrate how preposterous this fairy-tale novel is, I shall summarize the complex plot, a pastiche of post-modern comic episodes, reminiscent of the American animated TV show *Family Guy*, to show how Holt makes a mockery of the heroic aspects of fairy tales, especially "Snow White" and other stories related to the Grimms' *Kinder- und Hausmärchen*.

Holt's fairy-tale novel, if one can call the book a novel, begins with three young hackers, two brothers and a sister, who break into fairyland's operating system controlled by the wicked queen's magic mirror. They accidentally cause the mirror's operations to crash; the sister is zapped into the fairy-tale domain; the brothers are turned into mice and seek to rescue their Sis; and everything in the system becomes so scrambled and confused that the wicked queen, who had been planning to kill Snow White, is prevented from carrying out her plans. Instead, she must take a backup memory bucket and find someone in the nearby forest to reload the liquid memory into the system to fix it. In the meantime all the fairy-tale characters and their stories have become meshed and messed up so that there are about ten different confusing plots occurring at the same time without rhyme or reason. The big bad wolf is transformed into a handsome prince named Fang and is supposed to rescue princesses. The Beast is persecuted by Beauty. Snow White becomes vicious, seeks to avenge herself on the queen, and hires the seven samurai to forget altruism and to murder the queen. In the meantime the dwarfs, led by Dumpy, Rumpelstiltskin, Tom Thumb, and an elf, go on a quest to protect the three pigs with anti-tank weapons and later do battle with the samurai. The Sis of the real world and the wicked queen, incapacitated ruler of the domain, become companions while trying to fix the operating system. At the same time the Brothers Grimm ruthlessly seek to gain control of the system so that they can have complete power over the anarchically transformed domain. All the crossed-plots, conflicts, and misunderstandings become so chaotic that Mr. Dawes, the owner of the domain in the real world, pulls the computer plug and causes the fairy-tale realm to be flooded. In the end the three young hackers return to the real world, and Mr. Dawes reveals how he controls the computer game, mixes reality with fantasy, and can arbitrarily start the fantasies again that lead to different stories.

Now, some of the novel's tangled plots may seem amusing if not intriguing, but as I said at the beginning, the more one reads this novel, the more one becomes bored and begins to think: Why am I reading this? And perhaps one might wonder why I kept reading and what I was perhaps hoping for. Well, I must confess that once I become engaged in reading anything dealing with fairy tales, it is difficult for me to stop even when the story may be banal, twisted, or dreary. I keep hoping I will find something unusual and generally read to the bitter end. After all, I am a fairy-tale junkie. In this case I was drawn to the novel because I thought it might shed some light on a unique connection between the samurai and dwarfs as well as on an important theme in the Grimms' fairy tales that few scholars have discussed—cooperation or superhuman cooperative efforts necessary to defeat evil. To say the least, the novel disappointed me, and yet it set off a string of associations about cooperation in fairy tales that I want to share before explaining why a tale such as "How Six Made Their Way in the World" and other similar tales in the Grimms' *Kinder- und Hausmärchen* significantly touch on a relevant memetic topic that we can find in myths and folk and fairy tales throughout the world.

Utopian Free Association: Samurai, Dwarfs, Helpful Animals, Superheroes, and Extraordinary Humans

I have always had an immense fondness for stories and artworks that involve collaboration and radical action to defeat tyranny. I don't know where it comes from. But all I can say is that when I hear or read the word "samurai," I immediately think of Akira Kurosawa's *Seven Samurai* (1954) and any film that depicts samurais who come to the rescue of oppressed people. I have watched Kurosawa's film numerous times as well as his *Yojimbo* (1961). I have marveled at Kenji Misumi's *The Tale of Zatoichi* (1962), which recounts the stunning deeds of an amazing blind samurai, and I have viewed many of the twenty-six other Zatoichi films that stir my soul because this superhuman warrior uses his skills and humor to help exploited people. Of course, not all samurai are noble protagonists; many are criminal. Nevertheless, even in their marginality, the samurai often raise the issue of collaboration, struggle of the oppressed, and social justice. And, the Japanese samurai films are not the only ones that have caught my imagination and interest. I have also been entranced by John Sturges' *The Magnificent Seven* (1960), Sergio Leone's *A Fistful of Dollars* (1964), and Phillip Noyce's *Blind Fury* (1989), all based on the samurai tradition.

To my playful mind, however, the samurai films and stories owe their appeal to the great tale of Japanese folklore, "Momatarō, the Peach Boy," which originated some time during the Edo period of the seventeenth century. Supposedly, Momatarō appeared on earth inside a giant peach that an elderly childless woman finds floating down a river. She takes the peach to her home, and when she and her husband pry open the peach to eat it, they discover the baby called Momatarō, which means peach and eldest son, and he tells them that he had been sent from the gods or heaven to be their son, for they had often lamented that they never had a child. As a baby Momatarō is already articulate and fantastically strong and intelligent. Moreover, he also has a gentle heart. When he is fully grown, he asks his parents for permission to depart because he wants to conquer the ferocious demons living on an island off the northern coast of Japan. They have caused great destruction among the Japanese. Knowing that he is divinely blessed, the elderly couple give their blessing. Along the way Momatarō meets a talking dog, monkey, and pheasant, wondrous helpful animals, who want to join him in his quest. They often squabble with one another, but Momatarō warns them: "If there is the slightest quarreling between you, I will send you back that very moment. In a war a good position is better than good luck, but union is better than either good luck or good position. However weak the enemy, we cannot be victorious unless we do not fight together."[2] Soon after they set sail for the demons' isle, they defeat the ferocious mauraders in a furious battle. In some versions of the tale the demon king is brought back to Japan and executed, and in others, he is pardoned by Momatarō, and the demon king is so grateful for this merciful act that he gives Momatarō all his vast treasures. Then Momatarō and his animal friends return home to share the treasures with the people of Japan.[3]

Like any folk tale, there are hundreds of oral and literary variants as well as films and plays about Momatarō. (Even the French director Michel Ocelot's recent films about a miraculous heroic baby, *Kirikou and the Sorceress* [1998], *Kirikou and the Wild Beasts* [2006], and *Kirikou and the Men and Women* [2012], owe a great debt, I think, to Momatarō, whether Ocelot knew the Japanese tale or not.) What has always thrilled me when I reread this tale is the way the extraordinary hero unites with some unusual companions to redress the wrongs done to weaker people. Moreover, they do not fight for personal gain but usually for social justice. As a child, I was always a sucker for stories like Momotarō. Perhaps "sucker" is the wrong word, but I was always instinctively drawn into and enraptured by stories and films that depicted strange, somewhat marginal characters joining together altruistically to resist exploitative and sinister upper-class rulers. Robin Hood and his merry men were my heroes in the early 1940s, and so were the camp-like seven dwarfs in Disney's "Snow White" film. Indeed, they work together to protect the dainty, helpless girl, and then they "accidentally" cause the wicked witch's death. During my comic-book phase (which has never totally ended) I wanted to join with Superman, Batman, Captain Marvel, the Green Hornet, Spiderman, and, despite my macho proclivities, even with Wonder Woman, Hawkgirl, and Batwoman to fight against evil and corruption and bring about justice. In some of the comic books these superhuman characters unite to do battle against the enormously sinister people and monsters bent on ruling the world. Again, it was this notion that cooperation and collective action were necessary to overcome wicked and monstrous criminals that appealed to me most. And even in my adult years, when I read about Howard the Duck and later the adventures of the Fantastic Four, the X-Men, and the Avengers, I continued to be entranced by the feats of these extraordinary heroes in comic books and films, generally portrayed as outsiders and even geeks, and how they were willing to come together to save humanity. I was particularly attracted to the X-Men (and Women) and the variety of their very unusual talents that stemmed from mutations. I was moved that Wolverine, Rogue, Storm, Colossus, Nightcrawler, Shadow Cat, Gambit, Psylocke, and other extraordinary mutants, outcasts, and marginal humans used their weird distortions collectively to benefit so-called normal people and stabilize moral order in the world.

But I don't want to privilege superheroes whose individual special talents must be collected for oppressed people to attain a goal or to be rescued from evil oppressors. I have also been very fond of the flawed protagonists and common people who need help to deal with their weaknesses and/or wounds and collaborate with others to fight for a just cause. For instance, one of my favorite books is J.R.R. Tolkien's *The Hobbit*, in which the petit bourgeois Bilbo Baggins, a nerdy hobbit, who has more talents than he realizes, must be awakened to confront a threat to moral order. Alone he is helpless, but in the right company, he becomes an accidental hero. It is through collective action, the joining and integration of forces, that creates the power necessary for social justice. Individual integrity depends on intentional collective action.

Although it was not obvious to me when I was young, it gradually became clear to me that all these superheroes, flawed heroes, and nerds in need were related to the Greek and Roman gods and also to other divinities conceived in the ancient pagan world thousands of years ago. I also became aware that many of the folk sagas and legends as well as popular heroes in dime novels and fiction such as Robin Hood, Zorro, the Scarlet Pimpernel, and Tarzan were part of this tradition of superheroes who used their skills and talents to benefit defenseless "normal" people. Deep down, very deep down, I identified with the superheroes and wished that I might someday become like them. And, I confess, I still have daydreams and wish that I might discover some extraordinary power in me that I could use to change the world. I see myself always working with other committed people who have extraordinary talents. When not caught up in my fantasies and when I am somewhat more rational, I realize that I shall never become a superhero, that I am a mere mortal commoner, if not a needy nerd, and that I am more like the discharged soldier in the Grimms' tale of "How Six Made Their Way in the World," and it is to this tale that I now want to turn to explore what draws me to it and to tales of superheroes and why we are all more or less attracted to superheroes who work together to help underdogs. I shall also continue my free association and focus on the theme of cooperation and how telling tales about the cooperation of superheroes has a relevant moral and memetic quality to it.

How Six and More Extraordinary Heroes Made Their Way in the World and into Our Minds

Another confession: "How Six Made Their Way in the World" is my favorite Grimms' fairy tale, and yet, to my dismay, it is barely known today, or it is known through hundreds of variants such as "The Fool of the World and the Flying

Ship," which has been published as a children's book, included in anthologies, and adapted as a film in the twentieth century.[4] However, the Grimms' "How Six Made Their Way in the World" has rarely been published separately as a picture book for young or older readers in any language.[5] Nor has it been made into a film. The Brothers Grimm obtained their version orally from the gifted story-teller Dorothea Viehmann and published it first in the second edition of *Children's and Household Tales* of 1819; and it was not altered very much by Wilhelm in the following years so that it remained essentially the same text in the final publication of the Grimms' tales in 1857. It begins this way:

> Once upon a time there was a man who had mastered all kinds of skills. He had fought in the war and had conducted himself correctly and courageously, but when the war was over, he was discharged and received three pennies for traveling expenses.
> "Just you wait!" he said. "I won't put up with that. If I find the right people, I'll force the king to turn over all the treasures of his kingdom to me."[6]

So he goes full of rage into the forest, and sure enough he finds five extraordinary humans who agree to serve him: a strong man, who can easily tear up trees and carry them; a sharpshooter, who can hit a fly on a branch two miles away; a blower, who can make the sails of windmills rotate two miles away; a runner, who flies faster than birds when he unbuckles one leg; and a man who can make the air freeze if he takes off his cap.

Once they are together, they travel to the city, where the king has proclaimed that anyone who can defeat his daughter in a foot race can have her for his wife. However, if he loses, he will be beheaded. The discharged soldier asks the king if he can use his servant the runner, and the king agrees saying that both will lose their heads if the runner is defeated. Of course, he doesn't lose thanks to the sharpshooter, who shoots a rock out from beneath his head when the runner decides to rest midway through the race and falls asleep with his head on a rock. However, the princess refuses to marry a common discharged soldier, and the king pretends to invite them to celebrate their victory with a feast in an iron room. Then the king locks the room and orders the cook to heat it to roast them to death. Little does the king know that the man with the cap can cool off the room, and in the morning the six heroes are well and alive. Once more, the king tries to prevent the discharged soldier from marrying his daughter, and instead of his daughter, he offers him all the gold he can carry from the castle. The soldier agrees but asks for two weeks to gather together all the tailors in the realm so that they can make the largest sack in the world for the strong man to carry away the gold. Indeed, not only does the strong man carry off all the gold but also the entire royal treasure. Infuriated, the king sends his cavalry after the six heroes, but the blower sends them dancing into the air and allows only a brave sergeant to return to the king to warn him that the blower will blast any regiment that the king sends. So the king gives up, and the six bring their treasure back home and divide it among themselves and live happily until they die.

Hans-Jörg Uther calls this tale a *Schwankmärchen* (a farce or tall tale) and cites similar types in the Grimms' collection such as "The Six Servants," "The Golden Goose," "The Gnome," "The Four Skillful Brothers," and "Strong Hans,"[7] but to label the tale a farce is to this miss the point of this serious story about co-operation to attain justice and its significance in the other tales that he cites as well. As we know, there are a number of ways that one can name, interpret, and classify tale types, and to my mind, "How Six Made Their Way in the World" is clearly a story of class warfare and revenge or, put more positively, a wish-fulfillment tale of social justice, probably first told by underdogs or exploited soldiers. It has its light side to it, as Uther astutely points out, but it is also revolutionarily comic, a daydream shared by commoners, a carnevalesque folk tale. In his most recent book about the informants of the Brothers Grimm, Heinz Rölleke writes that Viehmann suffered a good deal in her life and had a predilection for telling tales of social justice, generally tales in which young women manage to find happiness.[8] In this case it is a discharged soldier who needs extraordinary help.

There are ten tales about soldiers in the Grimms' *Kinder- und Hausmärchen* that reflect how common soldiers were exploited by their superiors and how the common soldiers, generally peasants, sought some kind of retribution. I have discussed the role of discharged soldiers briefly in my book *The Brothers Grimm: From Enchanted Forests to the Modern World* [9] and pointed out that they are fearless and virtuous and seek most of all to reintegrate themselves into society after serving in a war. A couple of these tales were contributed by an elderly ex-soldier Johann Friedrich Krause, who exchanged his stories with the Grimms for leggings. Krause was not an exception, for many ex-soldiers or soldiers could tell tales. Johann Wilhelm Wolf, a neglected German folklorist, systematically collected tales from soldiers in the region near Darmstadt in 1847 and published them as *Deutsche Hausmärchen* in 1851. They, too, reflect dreams and wishes of common soldiers for some kind of social justice.[10] Indeed, it is very import-ant to try to trace oral tales to their informants to understand their ideological perspective, especially since there has been relatively little study of soldier tales and wish-fulfillment in the Grimms' collection and other German collections of the nineteenth century. Here, however, I am more interested in the role that co-operation plays in tale types that celebrate collective action against tyranny and injustice, whether the oppressed protagonist is a soldier or not.

"How Six Made Their Way in the World" (ATU 513A) has been categorized as part of the cycle ATU 513, "The Extraordinary Companions," and some folklorists have also related it to ATU 313 "The Magic Flight," also called "The Obstacle Flight." The so-called heroes or protagonists of the numerous hybrid tales are not only soldiers but also wronged princes, third maltreated sons, bumbling dumblings, disguised princesses, maltreated daughters, simple peasants and craftsmen, and yes, discharged soldiers. Without the help of extraordinary human companions and some amazing talking animals or the intercession of a superhuman deity, they cannot succeed in their quest to gain respect for their integrity and to right wrongs done to them. In the Grimms' final notes to the 1857 edition of *Children's and Household Tales*, Wilhelm makes clear that he and Jacob knew several German variants as well as literary tales written by Giambattista Basile and Mme d'Aulnoy. It does not appear that they were familiar with the epic poem *Argonautica* by Apollonius of Rhodes written in the third century BCE. However, it is clear that this poem along with oral tales and legends played a major role in the formation of folk and fairy tales that gave rise to "How Six Made Their Way in the World" and hundreds if not thousands of tales about the cooperation of superheroes, and I want to briefly recall the interesting ways that authors like Apollonius, Giovanni Sercambi, Giambattista Basile, Mme d'Aulnoy, and Peter Christen Asbjørnsen varied the quests of their protagonists while always insisting that no hero can succeed without the cooperation of extraordinary companions. Then I shall conclude by exploring if not speculating why our disposition to cooperate has generated memetically a long tradition of similar tales and why the Grimms themselves were "driven" to emphasize cooperation throughout their lives.

Literary Variants

Written tales and printed stories are extremely valuable because they serve as concrete markers in cultural traditions of storytellers, who disseminated and disseminate their tales orally or in images, and it is for this reason I am turning to Apollonius, Sercambi, Basile, Mme d'Aulnoy, and Asbjørnsen, for they signal what tales were circulating in their cultural environments in changing times and also the possibilities for adapting them and addressing particular societal concerns. They make us alert that there are many ways to tell the same relevant story.

In his superb chapter on Apollonius's *Argonautica*, Graham Anderson paraphrases the paradigmatic plot of the tale complex that will be helpful to us in understanding how and why heroes continually need cooperation to succeed in their quests:

> A hero sets out on a quest with the help of a range of specialised companions with separate human skills, and/or a marvellous ship; or is tricked into the power of a mysterious other-worldly figure whose domain he must reach, sometimes with the help of aged informants and/or after viewing a battle of birds. He acquires a king's/ogre's daughter after the performance of three tasks with her help. On the return voyage the girl eludes her father's pursuit by creating a series of magic obstacles to the pursuers. But on return to her new husband's kingdom he forgets her, and she leaves him for a sequence of suitors whom she ingeniously prevents from spending the night with her; she finally returns to her husband.[11]

Apollonius's epic poem, written sometime during the third century BC, bears the markings of legends, oral tales, and literary works such as Homer's *Iliad* and *Odyssey*, and it is strange that the Grimms did not cite the Greco-pagan origins in the notes to "How Six Made Their Way in the World." This may be due to the fact that they were always looking for Nordic origins of the tales that they collected. Whatever the case may be, it is clear that the *Argonautica* became a foundational story for rip and roaring fairy tales about superheroes and collective action that flourish throughout the world as well as for chapbooks, dime novels, comics, cartoons, and films.

A short summary of the poem reveals just how pregnant it is with fairy-tale motifs: Once upon a time there was a nasty king named Pelias who had usurped the throne of Iolkos in Thessaly from his half-brother Aeson. Warned by an oracle that Aeson's baby son, Diomedes, would kill him one day, Pelias seeks to murder the baby. However, his mother smuggles him to Mount Pelion, where he is raised under the name of Jason by the centaur Chiron. When Jason turns twenty, an oracle sends him back to Iolkos in disguise. Along the way he loses a sandal because he kindly helps an old woman, the goddess Hera in disguise. In gratitude, Hera, who bears a grudge against Pelias, will assist Jason in the future. When Jason arrives in Iolkos, he attends a celebration and games to honor Poseidon, god of the sea, and is recognized by Pelias because an oracle had informed him that a young man with one sandal would kill him one day. Therefore, Pelias devises a plan to make sure Jason will die by sending him on a perilous mission to obtain the Golden Fleece in Colchis, guarded by a vicious dragon that never sleeps. To reach Colchis, Jason needs the help of the great shipmaker Argus, who builds the ship Argo. Then Jason recruits fifty of the most extraordinary superhuman and divine heroes to accompany him. Among this valiant group are Actor, Amphion, Heracles, Pollux, Nestor, Telamon, Atalanta, Lynceus, Phineas, Castor, Philias, Ihphitos, Peleus, Orpheus, and so on. They are all committed to this quest because they understand that they will be righting a wrong. They are champions of justice. They have numerous adventures in which Jason plays but a minor role, and they encounter all sorts of obstacles including the clashing rocks through which the Argo must sail. It is only thanks to his shipmates that Jason arrives in Colchis, where he faces another obstacle: King Aeetes of Colchis demands that Jason perform three impossible tasks if he is to obtain the golden fleece. Fortunately, Hera intercedes in his behalf and has Medea, the witch-daughter of Aeetes, fall in love with Jason. Consequently, Medea assists him in completing the tasks, and after he puts the ferocious dragon to sleep with a magic potion, Jason sails away in the Argo with Medea on board. However, King Aeetes pursues them, until Medea chops up her brother Apsyrtus and scatters his pieces in the sea, compelling Aeetes to stop and pick them up. So, Jason and Medea escape and eventually return to Iolkos, where Medea uses her sorcery again to trick Pelias's daughters to chop up their father and cook him in a cauldron. However, there is no happy end to this tale, for Medea and Jason must flee to Corinth, where Jason betrays her by becoming engaged to Creusa, the daughter of the King of Corinth. Medea, unlike the forgotten brides in later folk and fairy tales, takes her revenge by using her sorcery to burn Creusa and her father to death. Then she kills the two sons that she bore to Jason and flees to Athens. Jason later dies, a miserable and lonely flawed hero, when a piece of the rotting ship Argo falls upon him while he is sleeping.

There are hundreds if not thousands of versions of this tale that may have been a variant itself, and these tales have come down to us in the present; some even predate Apollonius's version. There have been two spectacular films with the same title, *Jason and the Argonauts* (1963), with special effects by Ray Harryhausen, and *Jason and the Argonauts* (2000), 180 minutes long, directed by Nick Willing, as well as an unusual animated variant, *The Fool of the World and the Flying Ship* (1990), narrated by David Suchet. Indeed, in modern times, Apollonius's tale has also been interpreted in manifold ways as an initiation voyage or a shamanistic exploration of the other world. But there is one consistent theme of shared intentionality and collaboration that is at the basis of all the stories and accounts for its appeal to us; it is why we retell it in so many different ways. As Richard Hunter remarks in his excellent introduction to Apollonius's *Jason and the Golden Fleece*: "Jason is not so dominant in his poem as Odysseus is in his, or even Achilles in his absence is in his. This is partly because of the extraordinary, in some cases . . . supra-natural crew which surrounds him, and partly because Apollonius chooses to be interested in other Argonauts as well as Jason (Herakles, Orpheus, Peleus). Guiding aesthetic principles of diversity and discontinuity are as visible in this facet of the poem as in all others."[12] Hunter adds that "the central Argonautic virtue is group solidarity and communality."[13]

Jason is significant, in my opinion, because he is a flawed and somewhat weak protagonist who seeks collective action even though his moral standing is questioned by the Argonauts. Moreover, his human and moral frailty, if you will, is central in many of the variants that owe their telling to the pool of stories surrounding the *Argonautica*: the hero lacks qualities that he needs to confront an injustice, and it is only through the solidarity of others that he can bring back order to the world, that is, regulate it according to norms of naïve morality. The tales that became known for fostering a sense of shared intentionality and community and that were told and published in the fifteenth and seventeenth centuries reveal how "flawed" protagonists compensate through supernatural heroes who modestly and altruistically use their talents for a cause they all support.

In Sercambi's *Novelle* (ca. 1400), there is a delightful tale "De Bon Facto di Pincaruolo" (About Pincaruolo's Good Deed),[14] which shows how the figure of Jason and his quest have been altered and adapted to be relevant in a different sociocultural context.[15] Sercambi's protagonist is a bumbling but clever peasant named Pincaruolo, who appears to be a child of fortune. In fact, many Italian Renaissance writers celebrated the role that Fortuna played in enabling flawed or humble protagonists to succeed in a kind of initiation into an outside world, often in humorous circumstances. Here Sercambi, who was influenced by Boccaccio, relates how a simple peasant boy of about fifteen makes his way in the world after his father dies. (See my translation of the tale in the appendix.) Left to support his mother, he cuts down trees in a village near Milan, loads them on the family ass, and sells the wood in the city. However, he inadvertently causes the death of the ass and compensates for his mistake by selling the ass's skin. Later, he decides to catch one of the ravens feeding upon the ass's corpse because ravens were supposed to have magical qualities. Once he accomplishes this feat, Pincaruolo forgets all about his mother and heads west to seek his fortune in the world.

Toward evening, when he is tired and hungry, he asks for lodging from a peasant woman who tells him to wait in the house until her husband returns home. While waiting he observes that she is hiding delicious food and drink from her husband that she intends to share with a priest the next day. The wife is unaware that Pincaruolo knows where she is hiding everything. When the husband returns home, Pincaruolo uses his wits and convinces the husband that the raven is a soothsayer and can prophesize where delicious food and drink are hidden. Consequently, Pincaruolo receives a great deal of money from him by revealing the wife's hiding places. As soon as he has this money, Pincaruolo changes his name to a more respectable one and calls himself Torre. Then he heads west again, and on his journey, he meets the swift runner Rondello, the grass-listener Sentimento, the sharpshooting archer Diritto, and the mighty blower Spazza, who agree to help him on his quest. When he hears King Philippe of France is offering his daughter Princess Drusiana to any suitor who can defeat her in a foot race, Torre agrees to race her with his helpers. However, if the suitor loses, he is to be beheaded. Torre is confident he will win, and thanks to his companions, he does. As usual, the princess tries to trick the runner Rondello during the race while Torre is imprisoned. But his friends alert Rondello to the princess's deception and Torre's life is saved, and he marries Drusiana. His companions are rewarded and depart to live long lives.

Sercambi was not a great stylist. He was a merchant and local politician in Lucca, who wrote chronicles about the city and aspired to mix with the elite. His language is dry, coarse, and terse. It is clear that he was influenced by oral storytelling in Lucca and intended his tales to be read aloud. It is also clear that he sympathized with marginal figures and simple souls and that there are some autobiographical elements that he weaves into this tale, which is one of the few fairy tales in his collection of 155 tales. While not emphasizing social justice, he does stress the necessity of cooperation and good fortune to attain success. What's more, it is evident that this tale stems from other tales that owe a debt to Greek tales about Jason and the Argonauts.

This is also the case with Basile's marvelous tale, "The Ignoramus" (ca. 1632), which is, however, much more humorous and artistic than Sercambi's story. Moscione, the protagonist, is described almost immediately as a jackass. He, too, is the son of a merchant, but he is called "wretched and worthless," and his rich father sends him off to the Orient because "he knew that seeing diverse countries and associating with different people awakens wits, sharpens reason, and makes a man clever."[16] On his way to Venice, where he intends to embark for Cairo, Moscione meets Flash, who runs as fast as lightning; Hare's-Ear, who can hear anything that's happening in the world; Sharpshooter, who can hit the smallest thing with his crossbow; Blowboy, who has the power of all four winds; and Strongback, who can carry a mountain on his back as if it were a feather. Once they are united with Moscione, they never make it to Venice. Instead, they come upon the realm of Bel Flower, where the king is offering his daughter in marriage to any man who can defeat her in a foot race. The tale then follows the traditional plot with the superheroes winning the race for Moscione and the king reneging on his promise. Here one can gain a flavor of Basile's unique Baroque carnevalesque style and how he depicted the flawed hero by reading the king's response to Moscione's triumph:

> Upon seeing that the victory had gone to a booby head, the palm to a featherbrain, and the triumph to a big sheep, the king thought long and hard about giving his daughter to Moscione. He called the wise men of his court to council, and they told him that Ciannetella was not a morsel for the teeth of a scoundrel

and a good-for-nothing birdbrain, and without the stain of going against his word he could commute the promise of his daughter into a monetary gift, which would satisfy this big ugly ragamuffin more than all the women in the world.[17]

Of course, Strongback empties the king's treasury, and Blowboy disperses the armed men who pursue the six companions. In the end they share the earnings, and Moscione returns to his father as a "gold-laden ass." If this was supposed to be an initiation tale in which the hero demonstrates how much he learns from his experiences to become a valiant hero, Basile denies expectations and turns it into a farce. And yet the comic diversion shows how important solidarity and cooperation is for success in societies in which fathers rule arbitrarily. Moscione is an anti-hero, while his companions are admirable, especially as they work to-gether to prevent a corrupt king from cheating them and possibly killing them. As a naïve bumpkin, who lacks great qualities, Moscione has a moral innocence that is celebrated through comedy. But other protagonists in tales of cooperation do tend to be more noble and mature.

For example, let us explore the adventures of Belle-belle in Mme d'Aulnoy's "Belle-belle, or the Chevalier Fortuné" (1698). Youngest daughter of an impover-ished nobleman, Belle-belle seeks to join the forces of her king who wants to re-gain his properties and power after having been vanquished by the evil Emperor Matapa. The king will only accept well-armed noblemen or sons of aristocrats in his army, and since Belle-belle's elderly father is too old to serve, and since he does not have sons, Belle-belle and her sisters dress up as men to join the king's army, but her two sisters fail to help a fairy in a forest and are sent home. Belle-belle is more generous and kind to the fairy disguised as an old woman so that the fairy rewards her noble actions with a magnificent talking horse named Comrade, who will provide her with advice, and a magic trunk that contains treasures and any kind of marvelous clothing that she needs. Then the fairy dubs her with the name Chevalier Fortuné and disappears. Disguised as a man, Belle-belle moves on, and after making a great impression on the people in a nearby city, she enters a forest, where she meets seven men with amazing talents, and her horse Comrade advises her to recruit them into her service: a woodcutter named Strongback, who has extraordinary strength; a runner named Swift, who can outrace deer; a hunter named Sharpshooter, who can spot and kill game more than four miles away; a man named Hear-all, who can listen to and under-stand the slightest sounds; another man named Boisterous, who can blow down anything; Tippler, who can swallow lakes when he is thirsty; and finally, Gorger, who has such a great appetite that he can eat sixty thousand loaves of bread at one time.

Despite their talents, these superhumans are all either poor or unfortunate, and Belle-belle promises to reward them and satisfy their needs if they help her and keep her identity secret. Soon they arrive at the king's ravished city, where he and his beautiful but arrogant sister are preparing to do battle with the enemy forces of Matapa. But there is some difficulty when brother and sister both fall in love with Belle-belle. Yes, even the king is enamored of Belle-belle dressed as a cavalier. To make a long complicated fairy tale short, the king's sister becomes infuriated when Belle-belle spurns her amorous advances. Consequently, she deceives her brother and manages to convince him that Belle-belle wants to kill a dragon and later wants to force the evil emperor Matapa to return all the treasures he had taken from the king. Of course, Belle-belle triumphs in all her battles with the aid of her seven champions and wise horse. One of the impossible tasks that Belle-belle is compelled to perform is to race against the emperor's daughter. If she wins—and of course, she wins thanks to her magnificent horse, the runner Swift, and the other extraordinary companions—he will be able to recover everything that her beloved king had lost. In the last melodramatic scene, after she returns victorious to the king's castle, the king's sister pretends that Belle-belle has violated her and demands that the cavalier be burned at the stake. When the guards rip off her blouse at the stake, everyone realizes that the Chevalier Fortuné is a woman and would not have violated the king's sister, who is poisoned to death. The seven extraordinary heroes are duly rewarded, and predictably, Belle-belle becomes queen.

Though naturally and socially noble, Belle-belle needs the help of a fairy and the cooperation of her horse and seven highly talented companions to succeed in her quest to serve the king and right a wrong. She has more dignity than Jason, Pincaruolo, and Moscione, but like them, she is interdependent, and the tale of her exploits celebrates collective action rather than individualism. Written in a totally different style than Basile's mock manneristic narrative, d'Aulnoy seeks to laud the precociousness of women. Indeed, she combines folk motifs through an elegant and sentimental style to depict a moral order that countered the decadence of Louis XIV's court. Belle-belle becomes exceptional, perhaps not because of superhuman talents, but because of her moral inclination and predisposition for shared intentionality.

Later, in the nineteenth century, most of the protagonists in similar tale types become just as exceptional, but they are mainly male—maltreated third sons, bumpkins, craftsmen, and peasants. In their 1857 notes, the Grimms cite Johann Wilhelm Wolf's "The Violinist and His Three Apprentices" ("Der Geiger und seine drei Gesellen," 1851), Ernst Meier's "The Ship That Runs on Water and Land" ("Das, Schiff, das zu Wasser und zu Lande geht," 1852), and Carl and Theodor Colshorn's "Peter Bear" ("Peter Bär," 1854), which involve a poor violin player, a merchant's third son, and a blacksmith, all who recruit unusually talented companions to help them. One of the more amusing Norwegian versions, "Ashiepattle and His Goodly Crew" (1887), collected by Asbjørnsen, was published posthumously later in the nineteenth century. The tale distinguishes itself, as do some other folk versions, because of a boat that recalls the Greek ship *Argo*. In this instance, however, it is a boat that sails on land. Asbjørnsen's tale is much more a *Schwankmärchen* than the Grimms' "How Six Made Their Way in the World." It concerns Espen Ashiepattle, the youngest of three sons, who received his name because he always sat in the hearth, raking ashes. One time, however, he goes to church with his brothers, where they learn that the king has proclaimed he would give half his kingdom and his daughter to anyone who could build a boat that sails just as fast by land as by water. The two elder brothers want to try and build such a boat but are dishonest with a decrepit old and mysterious man in the forest and fail in their quest. In contrast, the kind and generous Ashiepattle tells the wizard-like old man the truth and gives him something to eat. As a reward, the old man builds a magical boat while Ashiepattle is asleep, and afterward he instructs the naïve young lad to take everyone on board whom he meets as he sails to the king's palace over land. Then the old man disappears. Ashiepattle sails off and recruits a tramp eating stones because he cannot satisfy his appetite; a drinker sucking on the plug of a barrel of beer because he cannot get enough to drink; a man listening to the grass; a sharpshooter who can hit anything right to the end of the world; a runner who wears weights on his legs, otherwise he would zoom to the end of the world; a blower holding his mouth because he has seven summers and fifteen winters in his body. Soon they arrive at the king's palace on the boat, and Ashiepatttle expects to marry the king's daughter and receive half the kingdom. Of course, since Ashiepattle is black and sooty, the king refuses to give him his daughter unless he performs several tasks, the last of which is a race with the princess, which Ashiepattle wins thanks to his six companions. Reluctantly, the king gives him his daughter and kingdom, and the narrator closes the tale by remarking: "And so the wedding took place and they feasted and made merry and fired off guns and powder. While the people were running about searching for wadding for their guns, they took me instead, gave me some porridge in a bottle and some milk in a basket, and fired me right across here, so that I could tell you how it all happened."[18]

Given the mock tone of the narrator, we are not to believe this tall tale even though it is a serious daydream. Time and again these tales about cooperation and collective action rectify injustices and reinforce our urge to work with other talented people to bring about a new moral order. The sequence of events of most narratives from antiquity to the present that deal with a protagonist, who enlists the help of god-like X-Men and supernatural heroines, builds upon a proposition that social justice can be obtained only by people with a shared moral purpose or with a shared intention of improving their lot in the world. We instinctively rejoice in their actions, for they often succeed against the odds. We also know, however, that such cooperation among humans can be exploited for nefarious purposes; it can also lead to dictatorships and unjust societies. However, the strength and allure of fairy tales like "How Six Made Their Way in the World" are difficult to resist because the stories remind us of the virtues of cooperative action and almost always offer a more just counter world that contradicts the perversion of justice in real-existing societies. We seem to be driven to respond instinctively and memetically to these tales of cooperation, and I want to close by considering the significance of cooperation in these tales that offer us so much hope.

Why We Want Gods, Goddesses, Superhumans, Samurai, Dwarfs, Cowboys, Outlaws, X-Men and Women, and Other Extraordinary Mutants to Cooperate and Bring Justice to the World

We know we cannot depend on human kings, queens, presidents, prime ministers, generals, police chiefs, mayors, corporate executives, secretaries of education, university administrators, and religious leaders to bring justice to the world. They know it, too, but they like the aura of power to try their luck, and if they fail, which they always do, they will at least always have tasted power to dominate others and lead comfortable lives until they die or are killed. Power corrupts, and we know full well that we cannot depend upon these so-called normal humans to create and maintain social justice. We need the help of abnormal or supernormal creatures and/or, we need to cooperate more effectively among ourselves to reduce inequalities and create social and cultural conditions that benefit social democracy.

In his book *Why We Cooperate* (2009), Michael Tomasello, a rigorous developmental psychologist, maintains that

> whereas the "cultures" of other animal species are based almost exclusively on imitation and other exploitive processes, the cultures of human beings are based not only on exploitation, but on fundamentally cooperative processes as well. To an unprecedented degree, *homo sapiens* are adapted for acting and thinking cooperatively in cultural groups, and indeed all of humans' most impressive cognitive achievements—from complex technologies to linguistic

and mathematical symbols to intricate social institutions—are the products not of individuals acting alone, but of individuals inter-acting. As they grow, human children are equipped to participate in this cooperative groupthink through a special kind of cultural intelligence, comprising species-unique social-cognitive skills and motivations for collaboration, communication, social learning, and other forms of shared intentionality. These special skills arose from processes of cultural niche construction and gene-culture coevolution; that is to say, they arose as adaptations that enabled humans to function effectively in any one of their many different self-built cultural worlds.[19]

It is not the first time that Tomasello has written about the significance of co-operation for humans. He emphasized it in *The Cultural Origins of Human Cognition* (1999), when he wrote: "Individual human beings are able to create culturally significant artifacts only if they receive significant amounts of assis-tance from other human beings and social institutions."[20] And he also argued in *The Origins of Communication* (2008) that the evolution of a biological mech-anism in humans that enabled us to speak some two hundred to three hun-dred thousand years ago fostered linguistic and interpersonal communication and collaboration that allowed for greater learning and innovation in cultures throughout the world. In *Why We Cooperate* he introduces some new theses based on more than a decade of scientific work with apes, chimpanzees, and children that explain how children are instinctually predisposed to help victims and show empathetic concern in other human victims in laboratory experi-ments. He concludes that

> this suggests that infants' naturally occurring empathetic or sym-pathetic responses to the victim's plight affected their tendency to help. It is this "concern" then, we would argue, and not external rewards that motivates young children's helping. For these five reasons—early emergence, immunity from encouragement and undermining by rewards, deep evolutionary roots in great apes, cross-cultural robustness, and foundation in natural sympathetic emotions—we believe that children's early helping is not a be-havior created by culture and/or parental socialization practices. Rather, it is an outward expression of children's natural inclination to sympathize with others in strife. Research in other laboratories is consistent with this conclusion: even infants below one year of age distinguish helpful from unhelpful agents.[21]

In sum, Tomasello explains that humans develop social norms of altruism and cooperation that are derived from a natural instinct to cooperate. Such cooperation is based on shared intentionality that creates interdependence among us and also rational values that demand a certain conformity to be maintained. Those natural norms are transformed through social environments that affect the manner in which cooperation will be employed to benefit a culture. As Tomasello writes,

> The development of altruistic tendencies in young children is clearly shaped by socialization. They arrive at the process with a predisposition for helpfulness and cooperation. But then they learn to be selective about whom to help, inform, and share with, and they also learn to manage the impression they make on others—their public reputation and self—as a way of influencing the actions of those others toward themselves. In addition, they learn the social norms that characterize the cultural world in which they live, and they actively attempt to learn what these are and to follow them. They even begin to participate in the enforcement process by reminding others of the norms . . . and punishing themselves through guilt and shame when they cannot live up to them. All of this reflects not only humans' special sensitivity to social pressure of various kinds, but also a kind of group identity and social rationality that is inherent in all activities involving a shared, "we" intentionality.[22]

Tomasello is not alone in emphasizing the significance of cooperation in our daily lives no matter what our culture and society might be. For instance Richard Sennett has recently explored different aspects of cooperation in *Together: The Rituals, Pleasures and Politics of Cooperation* (2012). He maintains that "cooperation oils the machinery of getting things done, and sharing with others can make up for what we may individually lack. Cooperation is embedded in our genes, but cannot be stuck in routine behaviour; it needs to be developed and deepened. This is particularly true when we are dealing with people unlike ourselves; with them, cooperation becomes a demanding effort."[23] His book is a study of how cooperation has evolved and historically been shaped through sociocultural behaviors such as solidarity, commitment, responsiveness, and competition. Throughout his analysis he is concerned about how people have lost the skills and ability to strengthen cooperation through dialogue and ritual thus fostering great social and political inequalities. According to Sennett we are living in a critical period when cooperation has been perverted in the name of solidarity and individualism. Unfortunately, as Terry Eagleton has pointed out in a review of Sennett's study,[24] his proposal to counter the perversion of cooperation through ritual is fatalistic and is basically a piecemeal repair proposal that remains idealistic in light of the devastation of social relations caused by global capitalism.

This does not mean that cooperation has become totally perverted and useless as a positive force in contemporary society. It is at the basis of all that we undertake and make.[25] In another book, *Moral Origins: The Evolution of Virtue, Altruism, and Shame* (2012), Christopher Boehm, a notable evolutionary anthropologist, points out that we were, are, and shall always be cooperative and altruistic because we naturally benefit from such behavior in developing our relations and communities. Indeed, this behavior formed our social conscience, grounded our morals, and transcended families and clans thousands of years ago. Boehm focuses on the late Pleistocene foraging societies over 12,000 years ago to trace how bands of people forged morals from their interactions and cooperation. At the basis of morality is altruism, which Boehm equates with extrafamilial generosity that has become part of human nature: "The altruistic type of beneficence may refer either to acts of costly generosity toward specific unrelated individuals or to sacrifices of personal interests as the individual contributes to enterprises that benefit the community as a whole. Thus, altruism and the possibilities for human cooperation are intertwined, for altruistically generous individuals make for superior cooperation in groups that include nonkin."[26]

In the epilogue to his book, "Humanity's Moral Future," Boehm, like Sennett, provides a bleak prognostication of what might ensue from the international conflicts and wars that are presently causing havoc in the world. However, based on his anthropological and historical analysis of late Pleistocene foraging societies that brought about a sense of morality based on cooperation, he argues that that we all share a "basic, pro-socially-oriented moral capacity, which is inherent in being human," and that this capacity, a "sympathy for other human beings will always serve as a counterweight to conflict" that can be systematically amplified and used for the greater good."[27]

One of the cultural means that we have developed naturally to foster cooperation and shared moral intention is storytelling of all kinds that is sometimes studied by anthropologists as information, communication, gossip, and ritual in early history. Whatever the case may be, storytelling involves the transmission and dissemination of ideas and norms. From the ancient world to the present, storytelling, whether oral, printed, drawn, painted, or filmed, has involved group participation and dialogue that are predicated on social codes. Over thousands of years, certain tales, more relevant for the adaptation to social and natural environments than others, became similar to memes because they were remembered, stored in our brains, and passed on in various ways to reinforce naïve norms that enabled humans to benefit from cooperation and establish mutually beneficial rules of behavior.

In his book about the natural history of human cooperation, *Wired for Culture: The Natural History of Human Cooperation*, Mark Pagel notes:

> With the advent of culture, another sphere of evolving entities arose that does not share the same route into the future as our genes. The new sphere of evolution was the world of ideas. They are cultural replicators that exist by inhabiting our minds, and their purpose is to get us to transmit them to other minds. Richard Dawkins coined the term *memes* to describe these units of cultural evolution, which, like the biological brain parasites, will not necessarily evolve to have our interests in mind but *theirs*. . . . This is not to say that all elements of cultural evolution evolve to exploit us, or that all memes are viruses of our minds. Among the most common memes will be those that do us the most good.[28]

With the rise of language, memes as cultural replicators played a prominent and pertinent role to foster cooperation. Indeed, Pagel insists that language itself evolved because we would not have been able to undertake acts of cooperation without it: "Language evolved to solve the crisis that began when our species acquired social learning—probably some time around 160,000 to 200,000 years ago—and immediately had to confront the problem of 'visual theft.' Language solves this crisis by being the conduit that carries the information our species needs to reach agreements and share ideas, and as we saw earlier, it makes the 'marketplace of reputation' possible. It disarms our conflicts and turns them toward our advantage."[29]

All tales are conduits of information and ideas, and we tend to choose and remember those stories that enable us to live better lives or help us to adjust to difficult circumstances. Relevantly remembered tales arise in our minds in social contexts or when we are alone, and we tell them and pass them on when an incident calls for them. We do this consciously and unconsciously. These tales become viral and are spread because they benefit humankind and all cultures, particularly if they include notions of social justice that are natural to the species. Relevant and salient tales that enable us to grasp our abuses and contradictions and that propose naive moral principles to correct them become memetic for good reason,

As I have endeavored to explain in *Why Fairy Tales Stick* and as Michael Drout has so astutely elaborated in *How Tradition Works: A Meme-Based Cultural*

Poetics of the AngloSaxon Tenth Century and in *Tradition and Influence in Anglo-Saxon Literature*, similar relevant tales form memeplexes or pools of stories from which we draw to articulate our needs, wishes, values, and so on. They are never exactly alike, but they have similar plot structures, themes, characters, and motifs. We can call them "tale types" or use some other identifiable label that helps us order them, but they actually order themselves for us. They reach out to us, appeal to us, to be told. They are also within us.

From or before the times of Apollonius, through the Grimms' times, and up to the present, people have recounted tales that celebrate the exploits of super-humans who cooperate and come to the assistance of people in need and lacking qualities they need to resolve conflicts. These superhumans are almost always altruistic. Though there are also nefarious superhumans who work together to support tyranny or to exploit other humans for self-interests, the major relevant tales about superhumans throughout the world have radical seeds—that is, they are rooted in the human proclivity to cooperate in a shared intentionality to help one another and benefit a group. The tales by the Alexandrian Apollonius, the Lucchese Sercambi, the Neapolitan Basile, the Breton d'Aulnoy, the Hessian Grimms, and the Norwegian Asbjørnsen, as well as the anonymous Japanese peach-boy story and hundreds of samurai tales and films are part of a massive memeplex or ocean of specific tales with their own peculiar currents. They repeat the same plot of collective radical action in unusual and original ways, and they continue to be disseminated through every kind of media because they contain what we lack and wish for—pure social justice that will suffer no compromise.

CHAPTER SIX

The Grimmness of Contemporary Fairy Tales: Exploring the Legacy of the Brothers Grimm in the Twenty-First Century

The Grimms were especially pleased that their immortal collection of tales was soon translated into Dutch, Danish, English, French and eventually throughout the world and prompted similar endeavors everywhere. Their collection of tales, which they had first conceived as "genuinely Hessian," soon extended over and beyond the Hessian borders: contributions from Westphalia, Mecklenburg, and eventually from all over Germany were received and included. Nevertheless, the Grimms avoided using the title "German Tales" and rightfully so, for it had become clear to them through the background of some of their more important informants and their repertoires that tales know no borders, that they represent an entire European rich source of storytelling, and that their origins could rarely be traced and ordered according to a certain country. In the end the Brothers Grimm expanded their footnotes to the Kinder- und Hausmärchen *to include Indian, American, and even Japanese tales. Jacob and Wilhelm Grimm were and, to be sure, remained Hessians in their hearts and souls, but as their research increased, they felt themselves more and more to be Germans, Europeans, and citizens of the world. In this regard it was an excellent decision by UNESCO to declare the personal copy of the Grimms'* Kinder- und Hausmärchen *as the nucleus of the many great achievements made to the cultural heritage of the world.*

—Heinz Rölleke, "Ein literarischer Welterfolg: Grimms *Kinder- und Hausmärchen*"[1]

It is virtually and realistically impossible to escape the Brothers Grimm and their folk and fairy tales in the twenty-first century. Whether we like it or not, especially in the western world, their tales have penetrated our lives through all sorts of media, and they tend to stick with us. Of course, there are many other "classical" fairy tales that are also just as pervasive and were written by such well-known authors as Charles Perrault, Hans Christian Andersen, Lewis Carroll, and L. Frank Baum, not to mention the relevant memetic stories such as "Jack and the Beanstalk" by anonymous authors and storytellers. But just as the stories in the Bible and Koran have captured the minds and imaginations of millions of religious and even secular people, the Grimms' folk and fairy tales in all their different variants have become, more than any other group of classical tales, the most dominant in the cultural and commercial domains throughout the world and appeal to young and old. Here I think it is also important to bear in mind that the Bible and the Koran are compulsory ritual reading for millions of people, and their sacred tales have been institutionalized and are supported by wealthy hierarchical organizations. In contrast, the Grimms' folk and fairy tales are—despite some pinches of Christianity sprinkled by Wilhelm—generally pagan and secular, and nobody is compelled to read them. There is nothing holy about the Grimms' folk and fairy tales, and yet they have flourished the more the world has become secular and the more that people realize that their "verities" have become just as valuable for learning how to live as the Bible or the Koran.

Though there were parodies and unusual adaptations of the Grimms' tales in the nineteenth century and the first half of the twentieth century, the "deviations" of these works were not drastic nor memorable. For the most part, the Grimms' tales have been disseminated in the original German, in numerous translations and adaptations, and in various comic parodies that have validated the Grimms' stories as *the* "classical" fairy tales of the western world. This validation occurred mainly in the domain of children's literature, although folklorists always recognized the major role the Grimms tales played in the development of western folklore. In my opinion, it was not until Anne Sexton provocatively rewrote twenty-five Grimm tales in her book *Transformations* in 1971, however, that a new era, sparked in part by the feminist movement, signaled a change in the western world that led to a wave of new critical perspectives on the Grimms' tales and erupted into a tidal wave of experimenting with the tales in literature, theater, television, ballet, opera, film, storytelling, and other cultural fields of production by the end of the twentieth century.

The tidal wave became global by the beginning of the twenty-first century, as has been documented by the essays in Vanessa Joosen and Gillian Lathey's *Grimms' Tales around the Globe* (2014). Not only has the strong feminist strain in the adaptations and re-creations been maintained, but there have been numerous post-modern and post-post-modern experiments that are difficult to "label" and interpret. In the twenty-first century they have appeared not only in German- and English-speaking countries but throughout the world. There are literally thousands of diverse manifestations of and references to the Grimms' tales, but do we really know what the designator "Grimm" means? Do the Grimms' tales as source have a magic appeal? What is the cultural relevance of Grimm adaptations and remakes today?

Since it would take an enormous book or two to treat this vast topic, I want to limit myself to exploring some of the more salient contemporary Grimm variants primarily in the fields of literature and poetry that have appeared in North and South America, the United Kingdom, Ireland, and Australia during the twenty-first century. I shall endeavor to choose and discuss works that, in my opinion, represent significant artistic contributions to our understanding of the Grimms' folk and fairy tales and are innovations that seek to alter our viewpoints on how these tales relate to current sociopolitical conditions. But before I discuss the contemporary fairy tales, I want to explain what I mean when I use the terms "Grimmness" and "Grimm."

Grimm and Grimmness

Clearly, the name and word "Grimm" resonate among English- and German-speaking people strongly for two major reasons. First, the meaning of the word is older than the family name, and in the German language it can be traced back to old high and middle high German, when it generally meant a deeply repressed anger, restrained fury, or explosive rage. There are over twelve pages of definitions, quotations, and meanings in *The German Dictionary*, first edited by the Brothers Grimm until their deaths, and later developed and finished by German philologists in the twentieth century. The Grimms published the first volume in 1854, and the last one appeared thirty-two volumes later in 1961. As a noun, adjective, and adverb, "grimm" and "grimmig" have been used to indicate fury, anger, outrage, and terror.[2] In middle English the word "grim" tended to mean fierce or angry-looking as well as furious and hostile. It was sometimes used as a verb in other languages such as Icelandic and Dutch: to rage, to roar, to grunt, or to foam with rage. Today, most English speakers associate "grim" with something ghastly, forbidding, somber, and gloomy. In short, the word as adjective possesses its very own peculiar appeal.

Second, the family name Grimm, which may have derived somehow from the word meaning anger, gradually became a recognized and authoritative reference in the field of philology and folklore due to the accomplishments of the Grimms. This process began some time during the 1820s, and the fame of the family name spread throughout Europe and North America. By the end of the nineteenth century and beginning of the twentieth century, the name Grimm was associated more often with folklore and fairy tales, to be sure, with classical fairy tales, than with philological or linguistic laws. But it is important to bear in mind that one of the great linguistic laws of sound change is named after Jacob Grimm. In his book *Deutsche*

Grammatik (1822), he was among the first scholars to explain a nontrivial systematic sound change that was a turning point in the history of linguistics.

At first glance, linguistic distinctions about the word Grimm may seem somewhat incidental in efforts to identify the "grimmness" of contemporary fairy tales. However, they may help us understand part of the symbolical appeal of the word "Grimm" that harbors notions of rage, terror, forbidding gloom, and recognized authority. The popularity of the name Grimm in titles of all sorts of published materials grew in the twentieth century so that, in Germany, the book of the Grimms' tales is now second only to the Bible in popularity. Whether this is the case in English-speaking countries is difficult to say, but if one does a search either through Google, Amazon, Abebooks, and so on, one can easily see that book publications of the Grimms' fairy tales are by far more popular than those by any other classical or nonclassical author. Recently, the very popular British writer of fantasy works, Philip Pullman, rewrote fifty tales in a book titled *Fairy Tales from the Brothers Grimm: A New English Version* (2012), which derives its significance from the name Grimm. Pullman's name also lends the eloquent translations a certain celebrity status, but if it were not for the relevant and famous status of the Grimms, Pullman would not have engaged himself so seriously with the tales. Moreover, the Grimms' tales are cited in the mass media and the public spheres constantly, and motifs from their tales pervade our lives. For commercial and publicity reasons, as the two recent American television series *Grimm* (premiere October 28, 2011) and *Once Upon a Time* (October 23, 2011) have blatantly shown, the name Grimm has been ghastly and brazenly mined and exploited, or it has been associated with meaningless spectacles in films such as *Mirror, Mirror* (2012), *Snow White and the Huntsman* (2012), and *Hansel & Gretel: Witch Hunters* (2013).

Yet we must ask what's in the name Grimm other than gloom and authority that makes the tales of the Brothers Grimm so popular and what is it that draws so many writers and artists to them and compels them to want to rewrite and revisualize them? What nerve do they want to touch in us? What sensibility? What makes for the Grimmness of their tales?

In my opinion, the great accomplishment and attraction of the Grimms that accounts for the resilient Grimmness of their tales resides in the Brothers' profound philosophical, philological, and artistic approach to storytelling and all kinds of folk genres. As I have pointed out in other chapters, Jens Sennewald has amply demonstrated in one of the most significant studies of the Grimms' tales[3] that the Grimms were first and foremost philologists who artistically recreated tales they collected with the intention to trace their origins or preserve their origins, which they considered to be primeval if not somewhat divinely inspired. In fact, more than any of the other collectors of folk tales in Europe up to the beginning of the nineteenth century, they were interested in and fascinated by every single word, phrase, proverb, joke, allusion, motif, and reference that they gleaned from the tales they collected through listening to storytellers and through reading letters, manuscripts, and books. They began as curious neophytes in the study of law and philology and became experimental founders of folklore and internationally renowned philologists. Indeed, they stamped the manner in which the tales would be shaped and preserved in print throughout Europe and North America.

The Grimms were unique in the early part of the nineteenth century, and most Europeans interested in tales and storytellers recognized their pioneer efforts to conserve and restore folk tales to their rightful place in culture. They were especially unique because they did not believe that the narrative plots of their stories were absolute and definitive. Transformation and diversity were needed to disclose the truths that the tales conveyed. They worked hard to make their tales precise and striking. They rejoiced when they received different versions from friends and colleagues. They emphasized comparison of variants and historical research. They believed in the evolution of tales and in diversity. The Grimmness of their tales resides in their commitment to conserve tales of the people that stem from a great oral tradition that transcended Germany, and their commitment was their bequest to future writers, artists, storytellers, and artists to continue exploring words and truths that might form a moral compass for readers and viewers of the tales. To be sure, the Grimms were conservative in their conservation but tolerant of other voices and views implicit in the tales they collected. Ideologically speaking, they reinforced patriarchal and bourgeois notions of propriety. And yet a naïve or basic notion of social justice always weaves its thread through most of the narratives in the seven large editions of their tales. Sometimes they contradicted themselves and seemed to betray the standards they set for collecting tales faithfully from the lips of common people. The challenge for creators of fairy tales in the twenty-first century who call upon the Grimms is, nevertheless, to live up to the standards that the Grimms set despite or because of their contradictions. What can we build upon? What must we try to change?

In her book *Ghost Season* (*Temporadada fantasmas*), Ana María Shua, a fascinating Argentinean writer, who has written short, stunning stories and some critical adaptations of the Grimms' tales, produced an unusual version of a Grimm tale, which is not very popular and yet highly significant. Her microtale reads as follows:

The Stubborn Child

In the section of their work dedicated to children's legends, the Brothers Grimm refer to a popular German story that in its time was considered an appropriate cautionary tale for children. A stubborn boy was punished by God with illness and death, but after all that, he still didn't mend his ways. His pale little arm, with its hand like an open flower, would poke out of the grave time and time again. Only when his mother gave him a good swat with a hazelnut stick, did his little arm slip below the earth again, proof that the child had found peace.

Those of us who have passed by that cemetery know, however, that it still creeps out whenever he thinks no one's looking. Now it's the strong and hairy arm of an adult man, with fingers cracked and nails encrusted with dirt from struggling to force its way up and down. Sometimes the hand makes obscene gestures, surprisingly modern ones, which philologists assume are meant for the Brothers Grimm.[4]

Shua's other short, pungent adaptations, often told from a feminist perspective, indicate a serious, thoughtful, and critical Grimmness that I want to explore in the works of other contemporary authors and filmmakers. To tell the Grimms' tales again, no matter what form and no matter how critical, involves a serious engagement with their legacy within a storytelling tradition that the Grimms openly bequeathed to us. And yes, this engagement may sometimes involve making obscene gestures that include fingering the Grimms but also the culprits who have watered down and sanitized the Grimms' tales.

How and Why the Grimms and Grimmness Are Celebrated and Contested

Indeed, it is not so easy to explore Grimmness today because the pervasiveness of the Grimms' tales is so vast and unusual not to mention the enormous commercialization and banalization of their tales. Therefore, I shall primarily concentrate on a few examples that indicate how writers and filmmakers have grappled with Grimmness and banality. It should be noted that I shall exclude about ninety percent or more of the cultural and commercial merchandise that uses the name Grimm primarily to make a profit of some kind, and I shall avoid discussing parasitical writers and artists who try to make their name by living off the name of the Grimms with their trivial adaptations. Moreover, I shall not discuss the numerous reprinting of their tales and scholarly studies that have often been published in good faith with Grimmness. Nor shall I review the national, regional, and international celebrations that took place from 2012 through 2014 to commemorate the publication of the first edition of *Kinder- und Hausmärchen* (1812–15). There are always mixed motives behind the institutional honoring of celebrated cultural figures, and while the intentions may be good, these motives have relatively little to do with the motives of writers, artists, and intellectuals who want to engage themselves with the Grimmness of the Grimms.

The most salient aspect of the diverse works that have contended and contend with Grimmness can be seen in their ideological and aesthetic distinctness. What sets the more serious adaptations of the Grimms' tales apart from the trivial and commercial products of the culture industry is their careful and critical exploration of the social issues raised in the Grimms' tales. The most unusual adaptations of the Grimms' tales derive from writers and artists who share a feminist perspective, tend to be politically more secular and multicultural, are artistically experimental, and endeavor to address contemporary sociopolitical problems in light of the deleterious changes in the various national civilizing processes that have occurred throughout the world. Since it is impossible to analyze all the remarkable Grimm adaptations at the beginning of the twenty-first century, I shall limit myself to works that have personally struck me as meaningful efforts to question the Grimms' tales and yet continue their tradition of Grimmness. My examples are taken from recent North and South American, British, Irish, and Australian novels, short stories, poems, children's books, and graphic novels. And I shall begin with a novel that echoes the complaint aired in Shua's short story, "The Stubborn Child."

Diverse Novels of Grimmness for Young and Old

In a conversation with the Australian author Margo Lanagan, placed at the back of her book *Tender Morsels* (2008), she explains what it was that inspired her to write her novel:

> Seeing what the Brothers Grimm did when they took an old tale (Caroline Stahl's "The Ungrateful Dwarf") and rewrote it as "Snow-White and Rose-Red" was what started me thinking about this story. The changes they made transformed the fairy tale from an odd story about justice being done by luck into a moralistic tale for girls about putting up with men's behavior, no matter how beastly that behavior happens to be. I much preferred Stahl's lack of a message to the Grimms' urging girls to be passively accepting and reliably amiable, and it annoyed me that their version had survived rather than Stahl's. So in a way the story was an argument against their imposing their agenda on that story.[5]

While Lanagan is a bit harsh on the Brothers Grimm and also forgets that "Snow White and Rose Red" was entirely written by Wilhelm Grimm as a literary fairy tale, she rightfully focuses on a major flaw in the Grimms' conventional notions of gender and social justice. For them, as for most Europeans of the nineteenth century, principles of behavior and justice were to be determined by men whose moral duty was allegedly to protect and save helpless women, who were not capable of making decisions for themselves. Moreover, marriage and household sanctity were depicted as the major goals of most young women. Happiness was to be found either in a palace, a good clean home, or the arms of a noble hero. In Lanagan's challenging fairy-tale novel, the focus shifts to resilient women who learn to use their powers and cooperate among one another to counter the brutality of men and to gain retribution. Lanagan makes immense changes in Wilhelm Grimm's sentimental tale: instead of a sweet, mild mother who more or less guides her daughters to marry an enchanted bear/prince, she begins her tale, set in a medieval European country, by recounting how Liga, a fifteen-year-old girl, is brutally and continually violated by her father. At one point she dares to give birth to the daughter whom he sires, and the father accidentally dies. She names the blonde-haired baby girl Branza and begins to fend for herself. Soon thereafter, however, Liga is gang-raped and gives birth to another daughter, named Urdaa. Devastated, Liga wants to commit suicide but is magically saved by some natural force when she desperately wishes for another world and her wish becomes reality. She raises her daughters in this idyllic world, where the girls learn to trust bears and a wolf, who are men transported accidentally from a ritual in another world. One day, however, one of the daughters, Urdaa, wishes herself into this other world, which is actually the brutal true world that Liga had fled through magic. At one point Liga and the other daughter, Branza, join her, and all three fortunately learn to cope with injustice and inequality, thanks to the guidance of two witches. In the end Branza will marry one of the more decent men in this world; Urdaa will become a witch; Liga learns that her daughters must make their own way in an uncivil world and that her own struggle will never end.

This brief summary does not do justice to Lanagan's novel. For instance, she creates a unique language that has a quaint old Saxon and cockney flavor. The prominent male protagonists tell their own versions of the events in the first person so that readers have an array of colorful perspectives. Moreover, Flanagan does not mince words when describing scenes involving incest, rape, and violence. Her intent is clear: not only does she critique the Grimms' sexism, but she reflects upon the machismo and coarseness of men in contemporary Australia that is not unrelated to male aggressiveness and violence throughout the world.

Ironically, in critiquing the Grimms and retelling Wilhelm's fairy tale, Lanagan is following in their footsteps. As I have already mentioned, Wilhelm (and sometimes Jacob) continually reshaped their tales to bring out their deeply rooted truths and make them more effective. The difference between the Brothers and

Lanagan is that the Grimms held many patriarchal notions and customs to be truths and did not question the contradictions of the tales. Their major concern was conservation, and we must remember that the tales were not theirs. Lanagan's adaptation of "Snow White and Rose Red" is more an appropriation than conservation. That is, she makes Wilhelm's story her own and in doing this with great sincerity and commitment, she emphasizes innovation more than conservation because she does not believe that tradition holds venerable or absolute truths. Her process is dialectical, and it is important to remember that in the German concept of dialectics (*Aufhebung*), the thesis negated by the antithesis forms a new thesis. That is, what is old is not totally negated. The resilient and relevant qualities of the old are carried on in the new thesis. In Lanagan's case, she dialectically cancels elements of Wilhelm's tale while creating his tale anew with highly pertinent elements and motifs to address contemporary concerns related to social and human issues that we all share for better or worse. Without fully realizing it, Lanagan works within the Grimms' tradition of storytelling and writing while making it more viable and relevant for the present. This innovation constitutes the Grimmness of her novel.

Another Australian writer who has undertaken a provocative and innovative revision of the Grimms' tradition is Kate Forsyth. Her historical novel *The Wild Girl* (2013) focuses on Dortchen Wild (1793–1867), who provided the Brothers with numerous tales and also married Wilhelm Grimm in 1825. Daughter of a pharmacist and one of four sisters, she had known Wilhelm ever since she turned twelve. Why she and Wilhelm waited so long to marry is unclear, although Heinz Rölleke suggests that Dortchen, the last daughter in the Wild family to marry, had to wait until her parents died before assuming the task as "housekeeper" (*Hausfrau*) for the Grimms, who had lost their caretaker/sister through marriage.[6] Rölleke implies that one of the Brothers had to marry—Jacob refused to marry—so that some one would look after them. Whether that is true cannot be proven, and whether Forsyth's version is true cannot be proven either, but her narrative makes for a much more interesting story.

Forsyth has done exhaustive research and paints an intricate and colorful picture of life in Kassel from 1800 to 1825, tumultuous times when Kassel was occupied by the French, when the Grimm family suffered due to their impoverished condition, and when the Wild family also underwent great changes due to rebellion and marriage of the sisters, the death of their sick mother, and the wounded condition of their brother Rudolf, forced to fight for the French in the Napoleonic Wars. During this period, according to Forsyth, Dortchen fell in love with Wilhelm, and her love was reciprocated, but Wilhelm could not propose marriage to Dortchen because he was unemployed and could not support her nor neglect his own family. Moreover, Rudolf Wild, senior, the pharmacist, a cruel and hypocritical religious man, detested Wilhelm, and at a certain point began forcing Dortchen and one of the other sisters to have sex with him as punishment for their alleged sins. The shame felt by Dortchen drove her to separate from Wilhelm, and it was only through some of the tales that she told to him that she gave hints of the abuse she was suffering. After her father died, she works through the trauma of the incest, and by "confessing" to Wilhelm she was able to wed him. Though there is no historical evidence whatsoever that Dortchen's life was so tormented, Forsyth paints a convincing picture of daily life in the Wild family and the city of Kassel, and she also draws a convincing picture of Ferdinand Grimm, the ne'er-do-well brother, who becomes addicted to opium and tries to force himself on Dortchen. The imaginative sequences drawn by Forsyth brings readers closer to understanding the great difficulties that Dortchen and the Grimms endured as the Brothers began embarking on their great career as scholars. Most of all, her novel celebrates Dortchen and other women who made great contributions to the early collection of the Grimms that have been neglected. Thanks to Forsyth's serious and feminist reconstruction of history, the Grimms also become more "human" figures, and their humanity is revealed as well.

While not so historically based as Forsyth's narrative, the American Tom McNeal's unique fairy-tale novel, *far far away* (2013), delves into the "secret" life of Jacob Grimm and portrays him as more sensitive and fallible than most biographies about this famous "bachelor" that generally depict him as a supremely confident and unperturbed scholar. In fact, in his tour-de-force work, McNeal transforms Jacob Grimm into a very sympathetic ghost, who undertakes the task of protecting a young nerdy teenager named Jeremy Johnson Johnson living in a small town called Never Better, a microcosmic representation of American small-town life that bears the marks of petty minds and generous hearts at the same time. There are two strands to the plot of the first-person narrative told by Jacob Grimm: the mystery about the disappearance of a large number of young people from Never Better that the fifteen-year-old Jeremy and his friend Ginger, feisty and impetuous, endeavor to solve, and Jacob's revelations about the "failings" in his life that he tries to grasp and undo as a ghost in a world in between (*Zwischenraum*). Jacob has learned from a dead maiden "that only the troubled remain here in the *Zwischenraum*, those who are agitated and uneasy, still looking for what this maiden and others have called the thing undone. . . . It is unique to every ghost, tailored to his own failures, disenchantments, or regrets."[7] As a ghost, Jacob can see but cannot touch, smell but cannot taste, suffer but cannot weep, hasten but cannot fly, rest but cannot sleep, and speak but cannot be heard. That is, there are exceptional human beings who can hear ghosts, and Jeremy is one of those exceptions, probably because he grew up in a bookstore filled with fairy tales. Jacob learns that an evil Finder of Occasion is a threat to Jeremy and has probably been responsible for kidnapping and killing the youngsters who have disappeared from the town. To a certain extent, the novel's two mysteries are related: Jacob must learn who the kidnapper/killer is, and through his efforts to save Jeremy, he must try to understand the mystery of what he had left undone during his life and the desires that he had not realized while he had lived. If he is able to do this, he may be able to move beyond the *Zwischenraum* and find his brother Wilhelm.

As Jacob describes the events in Never Better, McNeal brilliantly weaves Jacob's inner monologues with dialogues that he holds with Jeremy often pushing Jeremy to speak in different languages and to utter surprising things that astonish his friends and townspeople—and himself. Often the dialogues between Jacob and Jeremy are comic and demonstrate Jacob's tender side. For instance, when Jeremy receives a notice of foreclosure that will drive him and his father from their house, Jacob writes:

> Jeremy touched his finger to his temple. "You here?" he whispered.
> *I am.*
> "Kind of a bad day," he said.
> *Yes, But things will turn out for the better. Often in the tales it is when circumstances seem most hopeless that good fortune intercedes.*
> "I thought you really didn't believe in the tales."
> *That does not mean I would not like to.*[8]

Jeremy restores Jacob's faith in the meaning of the different tales that are recalled in the course of events, and Jacob treats Jeremy with great care and concern as if he were his son. We learn from Jacob that he was once very much in love with Dortchen Wild, his brother Wilhelm's wife, but he never acted upon his deep desire to have a relationship with her because of his love for Wilhelm. After Dortchen married Wilhelm, they named their first son Jacob, and the child became very close to his uncle Jacob until he died at the age of four. His death devastated Jacob, and according to McNeal, Jacob threw himself even deeper into work that brought him success and fame. And it is one of the reasons that he keeps reiterating to Jeremy in a heavy German accent: *study, study, study.* Jeremy, who is steeped in the lore of the Grimms' tales and grew up in an attic filled with fairy tales, wants to please his talking ghost, but he also wants to fulfill his love for Ginger, who has drawn him from his shell. It is Ginger who encourages him to go far far away from Never Better, and who also wants to break away from the town. However, they trust the wrong person, the seemingly sincere and jovial Swedish baker Sten Blix. But eventually they discover that he is like the witch in

"Hansel and Gretel" and entices young people with his pastries and false kindness only to imprison them and kill them. It is Sten who is the Finder of Occasions, and Jacob must exert himself to save Jeremy and Ginger, who are captured and poisoned by the baker. It is through his dialogues and efforts that Jacob not only saves them but also realizes that there is more to life than just work and will probably be allowed to move beyond the *Zwischenraum* to find his brother.

McNeal writes very much in the spirit of the Grimms, whose tales were collected with the hope that they provide more than just entertainment for readers and listeners. Hope, as I shall discuss in the following chapter, is the "principle moral agent" that drives the Grimms' tales. In McNeal's novel, all three of the major protagonists are living hopeless lives when the ghost arrives in Never Better. Others too, like Jeremy's father and the mother of the kidnapped Possy, are miserable. But through resistance to perverse forces and by enlightening themselves, the protagonists learn what it means to live a "better" life, better than the lives they had led in Never Better. Throughout the novel, McNeal introduces relevant Grimm tales to guide them, and even Jacob learns to listen to tales that he never really appreciated. Reintroducing Jacob Grimm to the tales that he collected and that still maintain their deep value and power in contemporary times forms the unusual Grimmness of his exceptional novel.

There is no attempt in John Connolly's *The Book of Lost Things* (2006) to reconstitute the history of the Grimms by writing about the Brothers and their works. Yet his fantasy novel offers an intriguing view of the Grimms' tales. His narrative takes place in England at the outset of World War II. A twelve-year-old boy named David becomes extremely disturbed when his mother dies, and his father remarries and has a child with his new wife. Moreover, the bombing of London coincides with the traumatic events in David's life. The only things that enable David to cope with his shattered existence are the stories from books that his mother used to read him, and he comes to view himself as the caretaker of her books. Connolly writes.

> These stories were very old, as old as people, and they had survived because they were very powerful indeed. These were the tales that echoed in the head long after the books that contained them were set aside. They were both an escape from and an alternative reality themselves. They were so old, and so strange, that they found a kind of existence independent of the pages they occupied. The world of the old tales existed parallel to ours, as David's mother had once told him, but sometimes the wall separating the two became so thin and brittle that the two worlds started to blend together.[9]

In fact, when a German bomber plane crashes into the garden near his house, it creates a hole in a wall through which David enters into a strange world of stories. It seems that his mother's voice beckons him to undertake a quest to find her and be with her again. Yet he finds that the strange world is dangerous and filled with numerous obstacles, and the only way that he can find his way home is by seeking out the king of the realm and his book of lost things. As he learns, however, this is not an easy task because wolves and werewolves are gathering their forces to overthrow the king. He is also blinded by his resentment toward his stepmother and stepbrother. Fortunately, he encounters first the woodsman and then a soldier named Roland, who guide him on his quest so that David manages to elude the wolves, werewolves, and a trickster named the Crooked Man, who actually controls the realm and to a certain extent David's mind and imagination. In the end, after the Crooked Man kills the king, David resists the temptation to become the new king. He overcomes his fears and resentment toward his stepmother and finds his way back to the hole in the wall. Once he climbs through it, he finds himself in a hospital bed recuperating from the crash of the bomber.

The frame of the novel is formed around a conventional and contrived narrative of initiation. A disturbed young boy travels to another world to find himself. After he returns to the so-called real world, there is an epilogue that reveals David as the author of *The Book of Lost Things*, and his life after the bomb crash as a very unhappy one. His death is portrayed as a happy return to the other world of his imagination. Quite a trite ending. Nevertheless, this flawed novel has one major quality: it is a treatise about the capacity of fairy tales, in particular, about the capacity of the Grimms' tales, to make sense out of the conflicts in the real world and to enable us to come to terms with trauma and incomprehensible events. It is only through David's imaginative recall of fairy tales that he wakes up ready to confront and engage with a difficult real situation.

Within the frame narrative David has a series of difficult adventures that are marked by Connolly's unique retelling of Grimms' fairy tales such as "Little Red Riding Hood," "Hansel and Gretel," "Snow White," "The Goose Girl," "Rumpelstiltskin," and "The Water of Life." For the most part, they are startling and provocative adaptations and lead David to a new awareness of his situation. For example, in the terse retelling of "Little Red Riding Hood" by the Woodsman, we learn about a young girl who was always dressed in red and more clever than any man she met. Fearless, she frequently visited her grandmother in the woods. One day she encountered a wolf, fell in love with it, and seduced the animal. They had a werewolf offspring called a Loup, and since the girl in red wanted to help the wolves reproduce more Loups, she lured other girls into the woods to lie with the wolves. None of the girls were ever seen again, and the Loups eventually turned against humans. This story helps David understand the uprising of the Loups, as do other adaptations of the Grimms' tales, while familiar characters such as Snow White and Rumpelstiltskin actually appear in the main action as treacherous individuals. In a "Conversation with John Connolly" at the end of the novel, the author writes:

> I was always interested in something that the Brothers Grimm wrote in the introduction to one of their collections. They said that every society, and every age, produced its own version of the same tales. I think I saw some similarities between the earlier tales and elements of mystery and supernatural fiction, which was why they found their way into my earlier books too. In *The Book of Lost Things*, they become the building blocks for the creation of the world into which David retreats after the death of his mother. They are the first stories, the essence of later tales, and so he returns to them, and over the course of the book, learns from the variations upon them that he himself composes in his imagination.[10]

In the final analysis what is significant about Connolly's fairy-tale novel is his serious innovative endeavor to weave the Grimms' tales of the past to deal with personal and social trauma in the context of the dissolution of family. More recently, Catherynne Valente has demonstrated how a tale such as "Snow White" can be used not only to comment on the disintegration of family life in America but also to critique the barbarity of American imperialism and its devastating effects in the nineteenth century. Her unique novel, *Six-Gun Snow White* (2013), is narrated by Native Americans in a conversational unlettered English, first by Snow White and then by an anonymous storyteller familiar with the girl's history. The language is blunt, ungrammatical, and filled with metaphorical allusions to Indian folklore. It is the language of otherness told by a persecuted young girl and then by an unknown narrator who clearly sympathizes with the fate of the girl, representative of thousands of Native Americans in the nineteenth and twentieth centuries—and in this case, the focus is on Native American women.

But Valente's story of "Snow White" is not a documentary of American colonialism. Rather it is a pithy, somewhat poetic depiction of an unnamed girl whose name becomes symbolic of the racism in the American civilizing process. The young female narrator begins the novel by relating in a voice from below how she was born to a beautiful Crow maiden named Gun That Sings and to a brutal and an enormously rich Nevada miner named Mr. H. Her mother dies in childbirth, and her father neglects her and has her cared for by a series of governesses. However, the girl is never properly educated, although she becomes an expert with a six-gun. Allowed to roam free on a vast estate, her life changes at eleven when her Mr. H. comes home at one point with a new wife, beautiful and cruel, evidently a woman who has suffered abuse and fallen in social status. It is at this point that life changes for the young stepdaughter, as the new Mrs. H. proceeds to take control of her, and the girl utters comments such as:

> "Maybe it's not a lesson so much as it's a magic trick. You can make a little girl into anything if you say the right words. Take her apart until all that's left is her red, red heart thumping against the world."[11]

> "When Mrs. H. said I was not human she meant I was not white. She was wrong about the reason but not about the thing. I wasn't human. I was a small device who knew only how to shoot a gun, play the slots, and dress up in fancy clothes to please a rich man."[12]

> "She put me in her own corsets like nooses strangling my waist till I was sick, my breath gone and my stomach shoved up into my ribs—*there, now you're civilized,* she said, and I did not know if it was the corset or the sickness that did it."[13]

> "For myself I thought: this is how you make a human being. A human being is beautiful and sick. A human being glitters and starves."[14]

Mrs. H. fires all the help and compels her stepdaughter, whom she names "Snow White" sarcastically because the girl is dark and will never become white. No matter how much Snow White tries to please her "mother," she cannot succeed, and the "white" civilizing process becomes torture for the girl. Eventually, five years later when Mrs. H. gives birth to a son, Snow White decides to flee and search for her Crow relatives in Montana. It is at this point that the novel suddenly shifts narrators: "Girl deserves a rest, anyhow. You can tell a true story about your parents if you're a damn sight good at sorting lies like laundry, but no one can tell a true story about themselves."

The droll humor in the shifting narration conceals the desperate plight of Snow White. Mrs. H. hires a Pinkerton detective to track and capture her, but Snow White manages to evade him and eventually finds some comfort in a community of seven strange, outlaw women. This brief "happy" period in her life where she feels at one with nature and herself ends when she is tracked down by her witchlike stepmother, eats a poisoned apple, and falls into a deadly trance.

Instead of being rescued by a prince, however, she is put on display in a glass coffin in a traveling Wild West show:

> Alive and dead, alive and dead. Both happening so fast you can't see the blur. It doesn't matter which. The live girl carries around the deadness she worked on all those years. The dead girl holds on to that wick of living that's still green in there. It flips back and forth forever like a tick ace. *Thump, thump, thump* in the night as a girl sits up and lays down again.[15]

Though the novel ends on a tragic note, there is an exhilarating element to it. Perhaps exhilarating is the wrong word, but Valente, like Lanagan, has managed to appropriate the Grimms' version of "Snow White" in a manner that enables her to critique the Brothers' patriarchal bias while exploring the racist aspects of the American "civilizing" process. The clarity and poetry of the voices of under-dogs are actually what the Grimms also endeavored to mediate. As much as they expressed sympathy for persecuted heroines in the tales that they collected, how-ever, they lacked the profound understanding of female suffering that Valente and Lanagan clearly have, and it is because of their insights that their novels transform the Grimms' tales into strong and unusual indictments of contem-porary sexist and racist tendencies that expose contradictions in what we often proclaim to be civilized behavior.

There is no "civilized" behavior at the beginning of Helen Oyeyemi's un-flinching exploration of race and gender in *Boy, Snow, Bird* (2014), another remarkable adaptation of the Grimms' "Snow White," with its fantastic happy ending. Unlike the Grimms' optimistic story, however, this novel is highly realis-tic and told in the voices of a mother and a daughter, who become entangled in bitter struggles that appear to be endemic among women. In an interview with the British newspaper *Guardian/Observer* Oyeyemi has remarked:

For me *Boy, Snow, Bird* is very much a wicked stepmother story. Every wicked stepmother story is to do with the way women disappoint each other, and encourage each other, across generations. A lot of terrible things can come out of that disappointment. I also wanted to explore the feminine gaze, and how women handle beauty without it being to do with men, per se. The women all want approval from each other, and are trying to read each other. I also wanted to look at the aesthetics of beauty—who gets to be deemed the fairest of them all. And in *Snow White* that is very explicitly connected with whiteness. It had to be an American story because "passing" is an American phenomenon.[16]

Oyeyemi's novel begins in New York City during 1953 when a young blonde-haired woman named Boy, the narrator of the first part of the story, escapes her abusive father, a sadistic ratcatcher, and by chance, lands by bus in a small Massachusetts town called Flax Hills. After taking refuge in a boardinghouse and working odd jobs, she finds a pemanent position in a bookstore while dating a widowed history professor turned metal jewelry maker named Arturo Whitman. Eventually she marries Arturo, who has a beautiful seven-year-old daughter named Snow, and Boy is very much attracted to and fond of this poised black-haired girl with pale skin. However, when Boy has her own daughter, named Bird, with Whitman, the baby turns out to be black and reveals that the Whitman family had been passing for white for many years and had even sent Arturo's younger sister Clara to live in Mississippi with relatives because Clara had been born too "dark." Instead of following this pattern and sending her dark daughter, Bird, to Mississippi, however, Boy insists that Snow go to Mississippi because Snow is too beautiful and would cause her own daughter to suffer comparisons. This separation causes bitter tension among the sisters that they eventually resolve later in the 1960s.

Part two of the novel is told from the perspective of thirteen-year-old Bird suffering from racism and confusion, and part three, again from her blonde mother Boy, who tries to mend the hurt and misunderstandings that she has caused. There is no happy end to all the personal conflicts among the women from different generations, but there is a deeper awareness of the intricacies of race, gender, and beauty mirrored in the American landscape of the 1950s and 1960s. Throughout the novel there are references to "Snow White" and other fairy tales that set a framework for the different narrative perspectives, which never corraborate one another. What is unusual about Oyeyemi's book is that it reinvents and uses a fairy tale to intervene in a long discourse about how racism and notions of beauty define some of the more destructive aspects of American culture.

Other contemporary fairy-tale novels are also innovative and critical of gender bias and racism, but they tend to have more of a strong didactic feminist strain that streaks through the narratives. For instance, Carolyn Turgeon's *The Fairest of Them All* (2013) combines "Rapunzel" and "Snow White" to form an unusual tale that eventually pits the two famous fairy-tale characters against one another. Rapunzel, a witch's daughter, becomes pregnant after a passionate affair, but the prince marries another woman and has a child with her named Snow White. After seven years the wife dies, and the prince marries Rapunzel, who discovers from her magic mirror that Snow White is more beautiful than she is. From this point on, there are many twists and turns that include Rapunzel's desire for revenge, rape, rivalry, and incest. In the end, the conflict between Rapunzel and Snow White is resolved, for Turgeon is more interested in resolution between women than disagreement. As she states in the interview at the end of her novel: "I think all my fairy-tale books have a feminist undercurrent. I'm interested in looking at the roles of women in these stories, and especially the relationships these women have with each other. . . . There's a lot of rivalry and anger and unhappiness in these tales, and I like to explore that and then see if there's some way for these women to transcend their tales a bit and form alliances with each other. Female friendship is important to me, and there's typically not a lot of room for it in the original stories, and certainly not in the Disney movies."[17]

The significance of strong fairy-tale heroines can be seen in other contemporary novels. Marissa Meyer's *Cinder* (2012), which is the first volume of a science-fiction trilogy, transforms Cinderella into a cyborg living in a futuristic China. Treated poorly by her guardian mother, Cinder proves her worth as a mechanic, falls in love with the Emperor Kai and protects him from a wicked empress Levana, who wants to kill her because Cinder is actually a true princess named Selene. In another Cinderella-novel, *Bleeding through Kingdoms: Cinderella's Rebellion* (2005), Riley Lashea sets her story in the Black Forest several hundred years ago, and she blends several of the Grimms' tales in a narrative that depicts Cinderella fleeing from Prince Charming and causing havoc in different kingdoms by entering into the lives of Rapunzel, Snow White, Hansel and Gretel, and Red Riding Hood, who rebel against their author or the arbitrary authority of Grimm. In the end, Grimm is defeated by Cinderella and her allies, but their freedom from his pen/penis will not bring them eternal peace and harmony. What is important for Lashea is that women become free to write and live out their own destinies.

Two other novels, based mainly on "Little Red Riding Hood," display heroines with a feminist disposition. In Jackson Pearce's *Sisters Red* (2010), she employs two teenage sisters, Scarlett (eighteen) and Rosie (sixteen), to narrate their stories in alternating chapters and to explain why they seek to destroy werewolves called Fenris, who prey upon adolescent girls in the vicinity of Atlanta. In the end, Rosie leaves her sister for the love of a woodsman named Silas, while Scarlett continues to dedicate herself to hunting Fenris, indicating that the threat of rape and violence will continue until all werewolves are dead. In Vivian Vande Velde's *Cloaked in Red* (2010) she weaves eight different quirky versions of "Little Red Riding Hood," to mock the conservative and religious fundamentalists who believe that this tale is a strange and disturbing story and should not be shared with children. The difficulty is that Vande Velde actually yields to these critics by transforming the story of "Little Red Riding Hood" into harmless comic tales.

In other books such as Shanon Hale's *The Goose Girl* (2003) and Polly Shulman's *The Grimm Legacy* (2010), the authors tend to be more conventional in adapting the Grimms' tales. Yet, the feminist aspect remains strong. In Hale's reworking of "The Goose Girl," she endows a young princess named Ani, a misfit in the family, with the power to understand animals. When she is compelled to travel to a warlike kingdom to marry a prince whom she does not know, Ani is betrayed by her lady-in-waiting and flees into the forest, where her power to communicate with animals saves her. It is also in the forest where she tends geese that she comes into herself and ultimately finds her prince and becomes champion of the oppressed. In *The Grimm Legacy* (2010), we have another misfit or outcast as heroine. This time it is Elizabeth Rew, a teenager, mistreated by her stepmother and schoolmates. Fortunately, she finds a job at the New York Circulating Material Repository, where she works in a room with the special Grimm Collection, which contains objects such as dancing shoes, the seven-league boots, a mermaid's comb, a magic mirror, and so on. Soon after she begins working, she discovers that some of the magic objects have gone missing, and she organizes her coworkers to track down the culprit, and in the process she also comes to terms with her family and school mates.

All the novels that I have discussed thus far, with the exception of Lanagan's *Tender Morsels*, Forsyth's *The Wild Girl*, Connolly's *The Book of Lost Things*, Valente's *Six-Gun Snow White*, and Oyeyemi's *Boy, Snow, Bird*, have been written expressly for the YA market and reveal the limits of innovation when the authors adhere to the conventions of this market. Their tales have either been self-censored or censored by their editors to maintain propriety and good taste, not to mention happy endings. The writing is competent, but there is more dedication to convention than to Grimmness. The most obvious artificial adaptations of the Grimms' tales for young readers are the series manufactured for profit such as *The Sisters Grimm* by Michael Buckley and the Simon and Schuster "Once Upon a Time Series" for teenagers. Buckley's books depict two orphaned sisters who flee foster families and a social worker to become detectives in the town of Everafter, while the Simon and Schuster books written largely by Suzanne Weyn, Tracy Lynn, and Debbie Viguié are kitschy retellings of classical Grimms' tales intended to appeal to the sentimental interests of female readers. There are of course exceptions. For instance Adam Gidwitz's *A Tale Dark and Grimm* (2010), intended for young readers, is a novelistic pastiche of several tales told with provocative humor. The introduction by the fictitious narrator reveals his style and also purpose:

> Once upon a time, fairy tales were awesome.
>
> I know, I know. You don't believe me. I don't blame you. A little while ago, I wouldn't have believed it myself. Little girls in red caps skipping around the forest? Awesome? I don't think so.
>
> But then I started to read them. The real, Grimm ones. Very few little girls in red caps in those.

Well, there's one. But she gets eaten.

"Okay," you're probably saying, "if fairy tales are awesome, why are all the ones I've heard so unbelievably, mind-numbingly boring?" You know how it is with stories. Someone tells a story. Then somebody repeats it, and it changes again. Then somebody's telling it to their kid and taking out all the scary, bloody scenes—in other words, the awesome parts—and the next thing you know the about an adorable little girl in a red cap, skipping through the forest to take cookies to her granny. And you're so bored you've passed out on the floor.

The real Grimm stories are not like that.[18]

And the narrator concludes his introduction by stating:

Before I go on, a word of warning: Grimms' stories—the ones that weren't changed for little kids—are violent and bloody. And what you're going to hear now, the one true tale in *The Tales of Grimm*, is as violent and bloody as you can imagine.

Really.

So if such things bother you, we should probably stop right now.

You see, the land of Grimm can be a harrowing place. But it is worth exploring. For, in life, it is in the darkest zones one finds the brightest beauty and the most luminous wisdom.

And, of course, the most blood.[19]

What is stunning about the book is not the blood but the serious defense of children's rights and interrogation of the Grimms' tales that underlie the comic style. Gidwitz employs a frame narrative based on the Grimms' "Faithful Johannes" and "Hansel and Gretel" with the narrator providing an estrangement effect by constantly interrupting the narrative flow with ironic and caustic comments. The plot is initially determined by the action of the young king in the realm of Grimm who cuts the throats of his two children, Hansel and Gretel, because he is beholden to his loyal servant Johannes, who had been turned into a statue to save the king's life. Similar to the biblical story of Abraham and Isaac, the king sacrifices his children for the sake of a high principle that will save Johannes, and of course, Johannes rewards the king by restoring the twins Hansel and Gretel to life. This would seem to be a happy ending, but it isn't, for the children realize that they cannot trust their parents or Johannes, who are essentially murderers. So they run away from the palace and seek a home where they will be loved and protected. Their adventures are meshed with other Grimms' tales: "The Seven Ravens," "The Seven Swallows," "Brother and Sister," "The Robber Bridegroom," and "The Three Golden Hairs." In each case, they are threatened with death by brutal adults who either want to devour them or exploit them. Eventually, they meet Faithful Johannes, who persuades them to return to the Kingdom of Grimm because a dragon is destroying the realm, and their parents need their help. When they return, they participate in a bloody battle against the dragon only to discover that their father, the king, is the dragon. That is, there is a malevolent worm within him, and his head must be cut off to destroy the worm. When this is accomplished, Hansel and Gretel bind his head back on his body with magic twine. The king and queen abandon the throne in recognition that Hansel and Gretel can take better care of the subjects of the Grimm Kingdom, whom they call their children, than they have.

This ending may seem somewhat sentimental and didactic, but it is really not an ending but a beginning, and in light of the comic, terse style of the narration and its structure, it gives pause for thought more than a lesson. This is also the case in his second fairy-tale novel, *In a Glass Grimmly*, which Gidwitz bases on the story of "Jack and Jill," while interweaving other Grimms' tales such as "The Frog King" and tales by other authors such as Hans Christian Andersen and Jacobs. As he explains, "For hundreds of generations, writers and storytellers have taken the threads of older tales and have rewoven them into new garments— new garments that reflect our hands and our visions, and that fit the children we know and care for. All writers do this, even today. We who write in folk traditions are just a little more transparent about it."[20] This is evident in Gidwitz's third novel, *The Grimm Conclusion* (2013), in which he relies heavily on the Grimms' tale "Jorinda and Joringel," and sends the brother/sister pair on all kinds of perilous adventures that reveal how children must learn to fend for themselves and conceive their own world. He concludes this novel by stating: "There is no king, no queen in the Jungeich. Children are allowed to live their lives there—to run, to play, to tell their tales. At night, they go home to their parents in the Kingdom of Grimm. Mostly. And they go to school and do their chores. Mostly. But they venture into the woods whenever they want—to tell their tales and face their fears and let whatever is inside out."[21]

In all three of his novels, Gidwitz touches on some very problematic aspects of the Grimms' tales, expressed already by Ana María Shua—namely, the abuse of children that is often rationalized or repressed in the tales. More than seventy-five percent of the Grimms' tales involve the manipulation and exploitation of young people whose lives are put at risk because of their parents or other adults. In Gidwitz's dedication to Grimmness, he demonstrates how children are maltreated not only in the tales but in contemporary society, and he echoes the sociopsychological critique of the great Swiss psychoanalyst Alice Miller, who wrote:

> The tradition of sacrificing children is deeply oriented in most cultures and religions. For this reason it is also tolerated, and indeed commended, in our western civilization. Naturally, we no longer sacrifice our sons and daughters on the altar of God, as in the biblical story of Abraham and Isaac. But at birth and throughout their later upbringing, we instill in them the necessity to love, honor, and respect us, to do their best for us, to satisfy our ambitions—in short to give us everything our parents denied us. We call this decency and morality. Children rarely have any choice in the matter. All their lives, they will force themselves to offer parents something that they neither possess nor have any knowledge of, quite simply because they have never been given it: genuine, unconditional love that does not merely serve to gratify the needs of the recipient.[22]

Gidwitz is not the only writer who innovatively transforms the Grimms' tales in defense of children. Liesl Shurtliff's recent novel YA novel, *Rump: The True Story of Rumpelstiltskin* (2013), is a unique defense of the little fellow who is always chastised for exploiting a miller's daughter through his unique gift of spinning straw into gold and demanding her first-born child. In Shurtliff's version of the "true" story of Rumpelstiltskin, we learn that an orphan named Rump, raised by his Granny, discovers that he has inherited the talent of spinning straw into gold from his mother, who was originally from a region called Yonder and had unique powers that she abused. As Rump grows, he is constantly picked on by the miller, his sons, and daughter Opal. Despite the bad treatment that he receives, Rump enables Opal to wed a pompous king interested in money by spinning straw into gold for Opal. But he does not really want to have her first-born child as a reward. Instead, Rump goes on a quest to discover the complete meaning of his name Rumpelstiltskin, and it is by learning the meaning of his name, his magic powers, and how to control them that he frees himself of any obligation that he has to the miller's family and the king.

While Shurtliff's novel is filled with gnomes, pixies, and other magical characters often found in fairy tales, and while the redemption of Rumpelstiltskin is commendable, her work is not as provocative and innovative as some other adaptations of the Grimms' tales for young readers. For instance, Linda Lee began a remarkable series of cartoon books about angry little girls with different ethnic backgrounds, all furious about the way they are perceived and treated. In her fourth book, *Fairy Tales for Angry Little Girls* (2011), she depicts the antic dilemmas of five of them: Kim, the Angry Little Asian Girl; Maria, the Crazy Little Latina; Wanda, the Dresh Little Soul Sistah; Xyla, the Gloomy Arabic Girl; and Deborah, the White Disenchanted Princess. All the girls are feisty and complicated, and two of the tales are based on similar complaints aired in Gidwitz's novel: child abuse. In Lee's hilarious version of "Rapunzel," which she titles "RapPunsWell," Wanda is angry because her parents abandon her to an old white lady, who wants to make her into a clever little rapper who will make money for her. The first song she must learn as a baby is "I am black but my mom is not. But that's okay cuz I love her a lot!" Eventually, RapPunsWell does make a fortune but is locked up in a tower as punishment for disobeying the old white lady. Then she is thrown from the tower by the lady and is reunited with her blinded prince, who cannot find his way back to his own kingdom. In "Little Miss Wears-a-Hood," Xyla plays a guilt-tripped daughter who questions her mother when asked to bring the sick grandmother baked bread.

"Why do I have to go? What if I catch her germs and die?"

The mother responds: "I have chores to do. Besides, I'm your mother, so you must do as I say and be helpful and dutiful to me."

Xyla thinks: "There she goes using duty to guilt me into doing stuff for her!"

The mother declares: "And you know I never go outside. It's too scary."

Xyla thinks: "Why is the world so scary?"

"You must wear your hood so strange men can't see how pretty you are. Walk quickly and don't talk to any strangers!!!"

"Can I pick flowers along the way?"

"No! They might be poisonous! Don't touch anything and do not talk to anyone! Just walk straight to Grandmother's!"

Xyla thinks: "Why must my mother speak of so much doom and gloom? She makes me think everyone is out to get me."

So Xyla turns away from a woodsman in favor of an animal, the wolf, only to be saved by the woodsman, who also learns that Little Miss-Wears-A-Hood demands that he also save her from her own thoughts.

The irony of Lee's tales raises important questions concerning the use of Grimms' tales to socialize children. Long before Bruno Bettelheim falsely explained how fairy tales could therapeutically help children, as if that were the purpose of tales told and written for adults, the Grimms' tales had been sanitized to convey proper morals and manners and a notion of happiness and rewards for good behavior. Lee's adaptations like the best of fractured fairy tales explodes these ideas while addressing contemporary issues of racism and stereotyping. Like Gidwitz, Lee shows her dedication to Grimmness through provocation and innovation that deepen and expand the quality of storytelling that the Grimms themselves sought. Clearly, they lacked the humor of contemporary writers. But one can't expect everything from those diligent philologists, whose lives were marred by the loss of their father at a young age, social prejudices, war, needy brothers and a sister to support, and political battles at German libraries and universities!

Short Stories and Poetry

In contrast to the Grimms, contemporary authors in Europe and North and South America tend to be more humorous and ironic than the Grimms. In addition, they often alter the dynamics of the Grimms tales in highly complex narratives that probe the darker side of the stories. The list of remarkably talented American and British writers of the late twentieth and early twenty-first centuries who have experimented with the Grimms' tales is enormous, and I cannot include all of their works in a discussion of their Grimmness. For example, here is a very short list of prominent talented writers who have taken the Grimms' tales seriously to task: Angela Carter, Donald Barthelme, Peter Redford, A. S. Byatt, Margaret Atwood, Robert Coover, Jane Yolen, Donna Jo Napoli, Francesca Lia Block, Emma Donoghue, Terri Windling, Tanith Lee, Steven Millhauser, Kelly Link, Neil Gaiman, Robin McKinley, Kate Bernheimer, Sara Maitland, Philip Pullman, Gregory Maguire, Luisa Valenzuela, and so on. Many other writers and their fairy tales can be found in my anthology *Spells of Enchantment*, as well as in the numerous fairy-tale anthologies edited by Terri Windling and Ellen Datlow and in several other anthologies published in the 1990s and beginning of the twenty-first century. The radical aesthetics and themes of contemporary stories based on the Grimms' fairy tales are so great that it is impossible to summarize the extraordinary appropriation of the Grimms' tales that began in the 1970s. What is significant is that most of these writers have contested the Grimms' authoritative versions while simultaneously exploiting them and carrying on the Grimms' tradition of editing, reshaping, and retelling tales that have deep roots in folk traditions throughout the world. In fact, educated writers and artists have always played an enormous role in registering, marking, and changing stories that might have evaporated if it were not for the invention of writing and printing. And once again, let me state that the Grimms were part of this tradition and broke new ground for a greater exchange between the oral and literary traditions. And yet, within this discursive tradition, it is important to question and contest their authority and forbidding dominance and at the same time to provide elaboration and validation of the tales they conserved.

As I have already mentioned, the depiction of gender and gender roles in the Grimms' tales leaves a lot to be desired, and beginning with Anne Sexton and Olga Broumas in poetry and followed by Tanith Lee, Angela Carter, and Margaret Atwood in prose, contemporary writers have revealed a great disposition to turn the Grimms' tales literally inside out, often in carnevalesque and postmodern fashion. For instance, Rikki Ducornet published two tales, "Electric Rose" and "Sleeping Beauty," which drastically change the Grimms' "Briar Rose" and Charles Perrault's "Sleeping Beauty." Her version of "Sleeping Beauty" begins this way:

> It is written in the Sacred Books: at puberty she will be pricked and bleed and sleep one hundred years. Then a frog will tumble down the chimney and, leaving a rope of slime across the counter-pane, kiss her. Or, depending on this and that, a wolf reeking of the shit of slain deer will leap into her bed and eat her. Beauty's destiny hangs from the fitful runes that totter and dance upon the face of the moon.[23]

Ducornet's disturbing short tale, which is filled with images of red, blood, shoes, and dancing, turns the princess's dark destiny at the side of a king into a flight of liberation. Her awakening is a rupture with a binding tradition.

In "Rapunzel Revisited," Sara Maitland also emphasizes the need to come to terms with a tradition that has held her captive. She begins her retelling of the Grimms' tale by presenting an elderly Rapunzel who returns to her tower after her husband has died and her twins have grown. It is there that she reminisces, and her poetic revelry raises questions about whether her parents had loved her, whether she hated the witch, and whether she loved the prince. In her solitude she comes to a new awareness in old age, and the narrator remarks:

> It is, and you were fairly warned, not a story, only the ghost, the legend of a story. There is no plot, no narrative. Nothing happens. But still the wind swings in from the sea and the birds sing before the day's dawn; and still she listens to the sounds of silence which she had missed, despite the delights of the Court. Still she finds witches and whimbrels to enchant her days and still she looks through the refracting lens of all the stories to try and find her own truth, her own story: the story of the woman who has been child and beloved and queen and has finished with all those tasks and must now try to learn to be herself.[24]

Maitland is clearly concerned in rewriting fairy tales to comprehend the identity formation of young and elderly women and in voicing those concerns from a personal and critical perspective. In another one of her tales, "The Wicked Stepmother's Lament," she surprisingly paints a picture of a vindictive stepmother who rationalizes her abuse of Cinderella because she is too sweet, kind, and passive. The story, told in the first person by the stepmother, is not really a lament but an ironic accusation that charges Cinderella with masochism, questioning the traditional stereotype of the good persecuted heroine.

Maitland's unique dedication to maintaining the Grimmness of the Grimms' tales through adaptation can best be ascertained in her latest book, *Gossip from the Forest: The Tangled Roots of Our Forests and Fairytales* (2012), which is a highly original and poetical rendition of twelve Grimms' fairy tales interwoven with stunning essays about their relationship to British forests. Reading her book is like taking a stroll with one of the wise women of the woods who has a profound knowledge of folk tales, their underlying meanings, and how they emanated from forests. Her observations of places, plants, trees, and animals are subtly embedded in her stories, which lend a new vitality to the Grimms' nineteenth-century tales. Moreover, Maitland does not shy away from a political critique of deforestation and other "inhumane" ways that we regard and treat our natural environment. There is also a strong feminist current in her essays and tales. On the page that follows the dedication of her book, she already strikes a challenge to the mindless definitions of the *Oxford English Dictionary*, which equates gossip with women's idle talk: "This is one of my favorite examples of how the trivialising of women's concerns distorts language. The Gossip of my title is the encouraging, private spiritual talk that we all want in times of trouble. Stories that are not idle; tales that are not trifling."[25]

One example will suffice to demonstrate the unusual quality of her essays and tales. In her chapter about Epping Forest and "Hansel and Gretel" she links her observations about forest preservation with the resilience of children. Her marvel at the public spaces in this serene environment leads her to think about free spaces in which children can play and find themselves. As she meditates about children, she comments that we are failing to nourish the quality of resilience in children that enables them to cope even when horrible and dangerous things happen. Maitland maintains that forests and fairy stories are antidotes to the lack of nourishment in contemporary society:

> Forests offer infinite possibilities for creative play—especially I think because they often provide a choice of physical levels; climbing up a tree is different from hiding inside one. A long view through or over woodland is radically other from hiding behind or within a thicket. And, where stores are still told, everyone knows that forests are magical. The fairy stores themselves are also training grounds for resilience. Terrible, terrible dangers threaten the

children in fairy stories—from cruel and abusive parents to giants, wolves and witches. But in every single case, not through special skills or miraculous interventions but through the application of good sense (and interestingly good manners) the children do not merely survive they return home wiser, richer and happier.[26]

Maitland's ruminations lead her to retell "Hansel and Gretel," but it is the post-history of the brother and sister, when they have become older and prosperous. Hansel is head forester to the king, married to a miller's daughter, and they have five children. Gretel lives alone in the forest by choice, a woman of the woods, who cultivates herbs, flowers, and vegetables. Her sturdy house resembles a bright gingerbread house. Occasionally, Hansel visits her as he tours the forest. They live two miles away from each other. One time, when he visits her in her idyllic spot, they talk about what happened many years ago, and Gretel bursts into tears and confesses that she feels terribly guilty for having pushed the witch into the oven. She wonders whether what they tell themselves is a true story. Then Hansel responds: "Sometimes they are true. . . . Here is a true story. Once upon a time there was a brave little girl; she had a foolish brother, a weak and pathetic father, and an evil cruel stepmother who certainly wanted to kill her. But in terrible fear, in the raging danger and sadness and terror, she kept her head. She rescued them both. That is a true story."

And Maitland's revised "Hansel and Gretel" tale probes the trauma more deeply than the Brothers Grimm. Gone is a father who profits from abandoning his children, and gone is a silly duck. What is left is a learning experience transformed into a tale that grown-ups tell to one another because, as Maitland stresses, the tale has allowed them to come back into sunshine.

Whereas Maitland's revisions of the Grimms' tales are striking because of their poetic quality, Michael Cadnum prefers humor and sarcasm. In "Ella and the Canary Prince" (2006), he uses the first person to tell a droll story. Here the narrator is one of the beautiful stepsisters who insults the fairy godmother described as a "chewed-looking thing," while Ella—that is, Cinderella—is a simpleminded klutz. However, the fairy godmother brings about her marriage with a prince who is gay, while the stepsister narrator reveals that she has been sleeping with the king, the prince's father, and will eventually become Ella's mother. In this slight amusing tale all stereotypical roles are reversed to mock the Grimms' fairy-tale tradition.

Most of Cadnum's amusing tales in his collection *Can't Catch Me and Other Twice-Told Tales* (2006) are based on motifs from the Grimms' tales and tend to be modernized. In fact, this is the tendency in two recent anthologies, *Grimm & Grimmer: Dark Tales for Dark Times* (2009), edited by Adrienne Jones and Pete

Allen, and in Kate Bernheimer's *My Mother She Killed Me, My Father He Ate Me* (2010), a title taken from the Grimms' disturbing tale "The Juniper Tree." There is a problem, however, in these anthologies because most of the writers were recruited and commissioned to produce "modernized" tales, and it is clear from their endeavors to be original that their stories are often contrived and artificial and lack a certain integrity of purpose. That is, most of the tales did not emanate from the writers' own desires to engage the Grimms, and their tales often reveal more a desire to be original and spectacular than a desire to grasp the nature of storytelling. Nevertheless, all the authors are compelled to question why the Grimms' tales continue to be relevant in our post-modern times.

In *Grimm & Grimmer*, there are two tales that point in the direction of horror to shock and warn readers about the implications of the Grimms' tales. Adrienne Jones's "Rapugnant" is a Gothic rendition of the Grimms' "Rapunzel" that shows how wary one must be of stories and storytellers. She sets her tale in Yorkshire and depicts two elderly men in a pub, quarreling about the truth of a tale. They debate whether there really is a beautiful lass who does strange things with her hair in a tower up north in Goathland, otherwise called witchland. To settle the argument they set out for the tower only to be horrified. When they are pulled up into the tower by the golden lass, she turns into a monster and eats one of the men. The other escapes, returns to the tavern, where he has a dispute with a young farmer and decides to tell a tale to this farmer so he will be curious to find out more about the golden lass. Another "horror" tale in this anthology, Chris Cox's "Snow White" takes place in contemporary London, where Snow is a heroin addict and has hallucinations with small Boonyars that haunt her. They are likened to the dwarfs, and her stepmother, an ex-model, who has lost her beauty, wants her killed, but the Hunter lets her go. Consequently, the witch stepmother has him executed. After Snow is almost killed and recovers in a hospital, she is saved by the Hunter's brother, who kills the stepmother. In the end Snow escapes with him with the goal of cleaning up her life. In contrast to Jones's tale, Cox's "Snow White" is a good example of predictable clichéd writing that is more like a soap opera than a fairy tale that needs more than window dressing to be taken seriously.

Some more serious modernized fairy tales can be found in Bernheimer's anthology. For example Francine Prose's "Hansel and Gretel" is a subtle reminiscence of an incident that took place twenty years ago in the countryside of Vermont when a young woman named Polly is taken on a spontaneous honeymoon by her husband to visit his ex-mother-in-law, an eccentric elderly woman named Lucia de Medici. As Polly recounts the story, we become aware that she is Gretel betrayed by her callous husband, who puts her through hell by introducing her to the witchlike Lucia and siding with the witch. Instead of a happy ending, Polly must endure cruelty that she understands only some twenty years later through the lens of the Grimms' original "Hansel and Gretel." In another contemporary fairy tale in Bernheimer's collection, this time, "Snow White, Rose Red" by Lydia Millet, the narrator is the bear—that is, a homeless man suffering a midlife crisis when his wife leaves him for another man. He flees to the Adirondack Mountains in upstate New York, where he befriends two girls, eleven and twelve, spending the summer at their rich father's mansion. He lives in an abandoned airport hangar and develops a close friendship with the girls and observes how they are treated badly by their anorexic mother and aloof father. At one point, mother and father have a brutal argument, and as the father begins to strangle the mother, the bear/narrator steps in and almost kills the father in front of the girls, Snow and Rose. However, he actually saves the family, for the mother and father reform themselves, and the bear/narrator draws deep satisfaction in having prevented the breakup of a family. Unfortunately, this adaption of "Snow White and Rose Red" is another soap opera indicating that melodramatic versions of the Grimms' tales with modern characters and settings do not suffice to make up for a lack of artistic storytelling.

Perhaps the most prolific adapter of Grimms's tales with Grimmness is the American writer Jane Yolen, who collected all her tales, poems, and essays in *Once Upon a Time (She Said)* in 2005. The majority of these works were written from the early 1970s to 2000, and not all of them are based on the Grimms' tales. Yet this book reveals just how immersed in the Grimm tradition Yolen has been and how she has struggled to address urgent contemporary issues as she did in her remarkable fairy-tale novel, *Briar Rose* (1992), which concerned the Holocaust. Two of her more remarkable tales in this collection are "The Fisherman's Wife" (1986) and "Allerleihrauh" (1995), both terse critical commentaries on the Grimms' versions. In "The Fisherman's Wife" Yolen depicts a fisherman named John Merton who lives with his deaf wife, Mair. He is lonely because of the silence between the two of them, and after he rescues a mermaid on the beach and throws her back into the sea, he longs to be with her. In fact, he is lured by her to his death in the sea. Mair does not accept his death and manages to bring him back from the undersea palace, knowing full well that she will never fully break the spell that the mermaid had cast on him. There is no explicit reference to the Grimms' misogynous tale, "The Fisherman's Wife." There is no need because the title is so well-known, and Yolen subtly provides another portrait of a wife, not avaricious but rather dedicated, courageous, and more understanding of her husband than he realizes. In "Allerleirauh," her tale cuts through the happy-ending Grimm narrative about incest by realistically depicting how incest is continued by kings in power. Yolen's princess marries her father, becomes pregnant, and dies in childbirth. And the king will wait again for another daughter to grow until he can continue to cycle of incest. In most of Yolen's prose and poetic adaptations of the

Grimms' tales, there are unexpected acts and denouements that, while critical of the Grimms tales, make them more pertinent, vital, and personal.

Poetic Adaptations

As we know, prose can be just as poetic as actual poetry, and before I analyze the Grimmness of contemporary poetry, I want to discuss Eva Figes's unusual book, *Tales of Experience: An Exploration* (2003), because it resists definition. Neither novel nor poem, neither fiction nor nonfiction, this poetical memoir is a stunning dialogue between a grandmother and her granddaughter as they await the birth of the girl's sibling. Here it is important to know that Figes escaped the Nazis in 1939, when she was seven years old, and she spent the rest of her life in London. As the grandmother babysits her granddaughter by reading and telling stories, questions arise that animate Figes as narrator to explore her past through the Grimms' tales. Taking care to tell tales to her granddaughter that will not evoke the terror that she herself experienced, Figes explores their personal meanings and relives her past and the discovery of how her own grandparents were murdered. Each short chapter in her memoir is a surrealistic interlude in which she dwells on incidents and comes to terms with irresolution and death. As she writes in one of the final segments:

> In my end is my beginning. I have come through the forest, faced its terrors, real and imaginary, and reached the fringe, where sunlight glows on the meadows. I want to put it behind me, go back to my starting point, as children do in fairy tales. Unscathed, obviously not. My life is not a fairy tale, and the child who escapes the forest cannot possibly be the unknowing child who was sent into it. But perhaps the beloved dead do watch over us, as they so often do in Grimms' stories. If only because early loss will never dwindle into forgetfulness. Those taken from us too soon refuse to die, go with us, wherever we go.[27]

The poems derived from the Grimm tradition of storytelling are also very personal, introspective, and deal forthrightly with salient aspects of the Grimms' tales. The most significant contemporary poems have been gathered in the prodigious anthology *The Poets Grimm: 20th Century Poems from Grimm Fairy Tales*, edited by Jeanne Marie Beaumont and Claudia Carlson. There are over 150 poems organized according to themes such as "Mapping the Way," "Desire and Its Discontents," "The Grimm Sisterhood," and "Living the Tales." Unlike many of the prose adaptations, these poems, whether trite or meaningful, critical or complimentary, tend to be deeply felt expressions of attachment to the Grimms. The poets all seem to embark on a quest to capture the essence of storytelling and the significance of the Grimms' tales. The last two poems of the comprehensive anthology that appear in the section, "Living the Tales" express many of the sentiments in the other poems that deal with the differences between dream and reality, pessimism and optimism. In Lisa Mueller's poem "Reading the Brothers Grimm to Jenny," the narrator asks why she bothers to read the Grimms' fairy tales to the innocent Jenny when her own world is filled with corruption and she feels that she is lying:

> Why do I read you tales
> in which birds speak the truth
> and pity cures the blind, and beauty reaches deep
> to prove a royal mind?
> Death is a small mistake
> there, where the kiss revives;
> Jenny, we must make just dreams out of our unjust lives.
> Still, when your truthful eyes,
> your keen, attentive stare,
> endow the vacuous slut
> with royalty, when you match
> her soul to her shimmering hair,
> what can she do but rise
> to your imagined throne?
> And what can I, but see
> beyond the world that is
> when, faithful, you insist
> I have the golden key—
> and learn from you once more
> the terror and the bliss,
> the world as it might be?[28]

Mueller clearly values the dialogic impact of the tales as projecting other more just worlds that are absorbed by listeners and readers. And in the very next poem "Kinder- und Hausmärchen," by Diane Thiele, there is an affirmation in the quotation from Friedrich Schiller that begins the poem:

> deeper meaning
> lies in the fairy tales of my childhood
> than in the truth that life teaches.[29]

She begins by citing unbelievable tales that reveal nothing is what it seems to be, and she implies that it is the unbelievable quality of the stories that give her hope and optimism.

Rotkäppchen's wolf was someone that she knew,
who wooed her with a man's words in the woods.
But she escaped. It always struck me most
How Grandmother, whose world was swallowed whole,
leapt fully formed out of the wolf alive.
Her will came down the decades to survive
in mine—my heart still desperately believes
the stories where somebody reconceives
herself, emerges from the hidden belly, the warring home dug deep
    inside the city.
We live today those stories we were told.
Once upon a time in the deep deep wood."[30]

Five more recent books of fairy-tale poems bear out Thiele's assertion. Poets are continuing to live the Grimms' tales. For instance, Ron Koertge begins his unusual collection of fairy tales, *Lies, Knives, and Girls in Red Dresses*, told in free verse with stunning, black-and-white cut-paper illustrations by Andrea Dezsö, this way:

Do you want to sleep? Find another storyteller. Do you
want to think about the world in a new way?
Come closer. Closer, please.
I want to whisper in your ear.[31]

Koertge retells twenty-three tales mainly from the works of the Grimms, Perrault, and Andersen, and he addresses contemporary social problems in a frank offsetting manner. So Rapunzel's mother sees a therapist to hold her marriage together after the witch takes away her child. Hansel and Gretel are not so happy after they return home to their father even though their sadistic mother is dead.

Not so fast. Regularly the siblings slip out from under
their 4000-thread-count sheets and pad into their father's
plush bedroom. They watch him sleep. They fondle
the lockets that carry the witch's ashes. They like
being together, just the two of them. They like revenge.

So they'll go on a picnic. Dad and the kids.
back into the forest. Deep, deep. So deep
nobody will ever find him.[32]

In Koertge's revision of "The Robber Bridegroom," the miller's daughter who had a near-death experience at the robber's house and survived to see the robber dismembered, does not want to marry any of the men who killed him.

But she finds men untrustworthy now. She prefers
to live alone and teach Feminist Theory & Practice
at the local community college.[33]

All Koertge's prose poems have a cutting edge to them as do Jane Yolen's terse retellings in her collection, *The Last Selchie Child* (2012), which contains several poems dedicated to critically reviewing the Grimms' tales. In one poem, "Märchen," she accuses Wilhelm Grimm of loving words more than stories, while she notes:

I, on the other hand,
drink in tales,
giving them out again
in mouth-to-ear
resuscitation.[34]

Indeed, Yolen has written many novels and stories based on the Grimms' tales. In this poetry collection. There are several poems that make an interesting use of their tales. In particular, in "Ridinghood" she suggests that she publishes so that her soul does not perish while her wolf-like agent sleeps with editors. Ironically, she feels at one point, she will have to follow the old story and kill her agent.

Interestingly, there are a series of Grimms' fairy-tale poems about agents, publishers, and editors in Lawrence Schimel's *Fairy Tales for Writers* (2007). In his version of "Little Red Riding Hood," the little girl and her grandmother are naive amateur poets and fall into a trap by a wolf publisher, who awards them a prize to have their poems published in a volume that they must agree to buy. A professor from a community college warns them about the scam, but they refuse to believe him and accuse him of jealousy. The poem ends on a note of irony:

And even though, in their disillusionment,
they deride him and give him no thanks

for his disturbing their sleep in the belly of the wolf,
he cannot regret what he's done. [35]

Many poems referring to the Grimms' version of "Little Red Riding Hood" have played with different motifs from this tale, but the most significant revision of the story in poetry is Cornelia Hoogland's *Woods Wolf Girl* (2011), a tour-de-force retelling of the tale from the perspective of the mother, Red, and the woodsman. Short poems recount what happens to Red when she enters the forest. The first poem begins succinctly:

A girl walks into the woods.
Little Red Riding Hood.
Nothing in her life has prepared her.
She's speechless.[36]

What follows are a series of short poems about the initiation of the girl and the trials and tribulations that she faces: child abuse, lack of protection, violation, religious indoctrination. Some of the poems are dialogues between mother and daughter, or Red and the woodsman. Some are confessions. For instance, at one point, Red states:

It was my stoical self who made me
endure a life
that had to betray me, shock me
to my senses.
O Grandmother, what big eyes you have![37]

Hoogland traces Red's life from puberty to old age and shows, often with references to contemporary events in America and Canada, that mother, grandmother, wolf, and woodsman will always be inside her and with her. Red will be marked and her mark throughout her life.

The Grimms' "Little Red Riding Hood" is, of course, not the only tale that poets have dwelled upon at length. Another superb collection of poems, which focus on "Hansel and Gretel," is Avell Leavell Haymon's *Why the House Is Made of Gingerbread*. Haymon's major concern is the plight of Gretel, and she divides her poems into four sections: "Every Girl Hungry," "Smell of Baking," "Every Girl Sings Herself an Old Lullaby," and "Every Story Makes Its Way Home." Like Hoogland, Haymon uses the Grimms' tale to recount the initiation of Gretel as an every girl into a difficult life that entails murdering a witch to survive abandonment in the forest. Gretel, too, will carry this experience as tale throughout her life, her hands scarred by burns from the oven. In one of the last poems in the collection that traces Gretel's maturation as a wife and mother, she looks down at herself after freeing Hansel and notes how skinny and sore she is:

> Sees she is
> the last woman in the story, as her mother
> was the first, many adventures ago.
> Shoves Hansel in the direction of home
> and father, takes nothing in her hands,
> no stones, no crumbs, shoves him toward
> the ending, where there is no happiness
> ever after, not in any version.[38]

Haymon's somber revision of "Hansel and Gretel," somewhat in the tradition of Anne Sexton, may not be characteristic of all the poems based on the Grimms' tales, but it does reflect just how seriously poets have sought to engage with the Grimms' tales. Like the writers of novels and stories and artists of paintings and illustrations, they have appropriated the Grimms tales to make them meaningful for the present. The Grimmness of their works can, in my opinion, be clearly determined, felt, and evaluated by the manner in which they take themselves and the Grimms seriously and not bow to the commodification of the Grimms' tales that, as Schiller long ago suggested, have deeper meaning than the truths that life teaches us.

As I have argued earlier and in previous chapters, there are manifold legacies of the Grimms' tales in different cultural fields. Consequently, it is difficult to determine which writers and artists are following in their footsteps, whether their endeavors to go beyond the Grimms is authentic, and what determines authenticity. What is significant for me is that the Grimms challenge us to deal with their tales, to confront them, and to question why we think it is still so important to retell them and reinterpret them. It is as though we have inherited the golden key to the casket buried in the forest and are charged with preserving a magical heritage of tales that we are about to discover and will compel us to reconsider whether we want to retain and revise them to speak to issues in our present lives.

A Curious Legacy: Ernst Bloch's Enlightened View of the Fairy Tale and Utopian Longing, or Why the Grimms' Tales Will Always Be Relevant

Certainly good dreams can go too far. On the other hand, don't the simple fairy-tale dreams remain too far behind? Of course, the fairy-tale world, especially as a magical one, no longer belongs to the present. How can it mirror our wish projections against a background that has long since disappeared? Or, to put it a better way: How can the fairy tale mirror our wish-projections other than in a totally obsolete way? Real kings no longer even exist. The atavistic and simultaneously feudal-transcendental world from which the fairy tale stems and to which it seems to be tied has most certainly vanished. However, the mirror of the fairy tale has not become opaque, and the manner of wish-fulfillment that peers forth from it is not entirely without a home. It all adds up to this: the fairy tale narrates a wish-fulfillment that is not bound by its own time and the apparel of its contents. In contrast to the legend, which is always tied to a particular locale, the fairy tale remains unbound.[1]

—Ernst Bloch, "The Fairy Tale Moves on Its Own in Time"

It is significant that two of the greatest minds in German intellectual history, Ernst Bloch (1885–1977), the great philosopher of hope, and Theodor Adorno (1903–69), the foremost critical thinker of the Frankfurt School, contributed to the Grimms' cultural legacy by exploring the profound ramifications of the fairy tale.[2] Both were amply familiar with the Grimms' tales. Both had escaped the Nazi nightmare by fleeing to America in the early 1940s and then had returned to East and West Germany respectively in the late 1940s with the intention of helping rebuild two different kinds of Germanies, which laid claims to represent the genuine cultural heritage of Germany. Bloch and Adorno had not met while in America. It was only in 1964 that they encountered each other in Frankfurt am Main, and their views on politics and literature were very different. Nevertheless, in this one encounter, late in their lives, they came together to discuss the nature of utopian longing with surprising results.

In fact, it was not long after Bloch escaped the dystopian realm of East Germany in 1961 that he held a fascinating radio discussion with Adorno about the contradictions of utopian longing. Bloch had been somewhat disappointed by the socialist experiment in East Germany that he had experienced from 1949 to 1961, and Adorno had become a major critic of the culture industry in postwar western societies and was disappointed by the commercialization of art and literature. Their conversation was intriguing because, at times, Adorno sounded more like a utopian thinker than Bloch. Moreover, both displayed an unusual interest in fairy tales and were very familiar with the Grimms' tales, which they considered to be utopian. To be sure, Adorno questioned the concept of utopia in his usual incisive manner, but he seemed to share Bloch's faith in utopia and yet to be very disillusioned about genuine possibilities for the realization of utopian longings, while Bloch continued to be more hopeful about the future of utopia, despite the fact that his own hope had been disappointed by East Germany and the Soviet bloc.

In his opening statement Adorno, very much in keeping with his critique of the culture industry,[3] asserted that utopian dreams had been fulfilled in a way that leads to deception and monotony:

> The fulfillment of the wishes takes something away from the substance of the wishes, as in the fairy tale where the farmer is granted three wishes, and, I believe, he wishes his wife to have a sausage on her nose and then must use the second wish to have the sausage removed from her nose.[4] In other words, I mean that one can watch television (*fernsehen*) today, look at the things that are far away, but instead of the wish-image providing access to the erotic utopia, one sees in the best of circumstances some kind of more or less pretty pop singer, who continues to deceive the spectator in regard to her prettiness insofar as she sings some kind of nonsense instead of showing it, and this song generally consists in bringing together "roses" with "moonlight" in harmony. Above and beyond this, one could perhaps say in general that the fulfillment of utopia consists largely only in a repetition of the continually same "today."[5]

Bloch was not entirely in agreement with Adorno and maintained that the wish-images of utopia had not been entirely emptied or banalized. "There is still a much older level of utopias that we should not forget," he responded, that *we least of all* should not forget—the fairy tale. The fairy tale is not only filled with social utopia, in other words, with the utopia of a better life and justice, but it is also filled with technological utopia, most of all in the oriental fairy tales. In the fairy tale "The Magic Horse," from the *Arabian Nights*, there is a "helicopter." One can read the *Arabian Nights* in many places as a manual for inventions. Bacon addresses this and then sets himself off from the fairy tale by saying that what *he* means, the real magic, relates to the oldest wish-images of the fairy tale as the deeds of Alexander relate to the deeds of King Arthur's Round Table. Thus, the content of the utopian images change according to the social situation.[6]

Indeed, Bloch insisted that the content always changes over time, but the longing for a better life and justice would always remain and indicate what is missing in life. Utopian longing keeps generating wish-images that must be examined and judged critically and individually as to whether they allow for the possibility of realization. The formation of utopias that stem from longing not only offers a critique of reality, but it also opens up possible alternatives. It is because possibility challenges and subverts the status quo of society that it is treated poorly and neglected by ruling elites. Yet, possibility as a philosophical category must be regarded seriously, and both Bloch and Adorno agreed that the utopian wish-image, even when it is false, conveys a critique of what is present and points at the same time to what could and should be.

At the end of their conversation, Bloch discussed the principle of hope and its relationship to perfection. "But what is valid is that each and every criticism of perfection, incompleteness, intolerance, and impatience already without a doubt presupposes the conception of, and longing for, a possible perfection."[7] This hope for perfection, however, does not provide confidence or security. "Hope is critical and can be disappointed. However, hope still nails a flag on the mast, even in decline, in that the decline is not accepted, even when this decline is still very strong. Hope is not confidence. Hope is surrounded by dangers, and it is the consciousness of danger and at the same time the determined negation of that which continually makes the opposite of the hoped-for object possible."[8]

Even though Adorno appeared to agree with Bloch by the end of the radio conversation, we cannot really consider him a "hopeful" philosopher, and he certainly did not embrace the hope of the student and anti-authoritarian movement at the end of the 1960s, when he unfortunately died from a heart attack. On the other hand, Bloch supported this movement and never abandoned the principle of hope throughout his life; he sought traces of it everywhere—in high and low culture, in mass movements of protest, in technology, music, art, and daily customs and habits. More than any genre, however, it was in the fairy tale that he most often found wishful-images of hope. He frequently used it to illustrate the utopian longing and creativity of human beings and the possibilities to change the world that it represented. This is undoubtedly why Adorno had brought up the topic of the fairy tale early in their conversation, and it is also why Bloch almost immediately referred to it as representative of utopia. But what was it exactly about the fairy tale that induced Bloch to use it constantly as a utopian example? After all, the fairy tale is often associated with escapist fantasies, irrelevant in philosophy and politics, and a genre of writing and telling primarily intended for children. In fact, the traditional fairy tales of Charles Perrault, the Brothers Grimm, and Hans Christian Andersen are filled with tendencies that can be considered elitist, sexist, and racist. Did Bloch, who was born into the land of the Grimms, really understand what a fairy tale was? Did he have a misconception of this genre and place too much value on its utopian potential?

Bloch wrote two complete essays dedicated to the fairy tale that are worthwhile examining for an understanding of why the fairy tale was so vital for his philosophy of hope: "The Fairy Tale Moves on Its Own in Time" ("Das Märchen geht selber in der Zeit," 1930) and "Better Castles in the Sky at the Country Fairy and Circus, in Fairy Tales and Colportage" ("Bessere Luftschlösser in Jahrmarkt und Zirkus, in Märchen und Kolportage," 1959, included in *Prinzip Hoffnung*). In each case Bloch was not concerned with the literary or literary historical meaning of the fairy tale, but its philosophical and social implications and relationship to his principle of hope.

In "The Fairy Tale Moves on Its Own in Time," he immediately points to the unique quality of the fairy tale, often citing the Grimms' tales. Though the wish-fulfillment of the fairy tale may appear to be obsolete and depict feudal kingdoms with kings and queens, it transcends time and place. " Not only does the fairy tale remain as fresh as longing and love, but the demonically evil, which is abundant in the fairy tale, is still seen at work here in the present, and the happiness of 'once upon a time,' which is even more abundant, still affects our visions of the future."[9]

For Bloch, the fairy tale in all its forms, ancient and modern, remains vibrant and touches the dreams and wishes of common people who want to overcome the dreariness of their daily lives. The appeal of the fairy tale, no matter what its form may be, is boundless because its tendency or tendentiousness indicates the possibility for change and the fulfillment of dreams. Bloch discusses works by Jean Cocteau, Ferenc Molnár, and Jules Verne that are not exactly fairy tales but represent the modernization of fairy tales in Bloch's own time—that is, the time of 1930, a year after the Great Depression had erupted:

What is significant about such kinds of modern fairy tales is that it is reason itself that leads to the wish projections of the old fairy tales and serves them. Again what proves itself is a harmony with courage and cunning, as that earliest kind of enlightenment which already characterizes "Hansel and Gretel": consider yourself as born free and entitled to be totally happy, dare to make use of your power of reasoning, look upon the outcome of things as friendly. These are the genuine maxims of fairy tales, and fortunately for us they appear not only in the past but in the now. Unfortunately we must equally contend with the smoke of witches and the blows of ogres habitually faced by the fairy-tale hero in the now.[10]

About thirty years later, in 1959, Bloch picked up the theme of cunning and courage in his second essay and continued to write about it: "Despite the fantastic side of the fairy tale, it is always cunning in the way it overcomes difficulties. Moreover, courage and cunning in fairy tales succeed in an entirely different way than in life, and not only that: it is, as Lenin says, always the existing revolutionary elements that tie the given strings of the story together here." [11] Bloch uses many of the fairy tales collected and edited by the Brothers Grimm as examples in which we can find heroes such as peasants, tailors, soldiers, simpletons, who become "enlightened" and knowingly overcome oppressive tyrants such as kings, ogres, witches, and so on. At one point he states:

But the fairy tale does not allow itself to be fooled by the present owners of paradise. Thus, it is a rebellious, burned child and alert. One can climb a beanstalk up into heaven and then see how angels made gold. In the fairy tale "Godfather Death," the Lord God himself offers to be the godfather in a poor man's family, but the poor man responds, "I don't want you as a godfather because you give to the rich and let the poor starve." Here and everywhere, in the courage, the sobriety and hope, there is a piece of the Enlightenment that emerged long before there was such a thing as the Enlightenment. The brave little tailor in the Grimms' fairy tale kills flies in his home and goes out into the world because he feels that his workshop is too small for his bravery. He meets a giant who takes a rock in his hand and squeezes it with such strength that water drips from it. Then he throws another rock so high that into the air that one can barely see it. However, the tailor outsmarts the giant by squeezing a piece of cheese into pulp instead of a rock, and next he throws a bird so high into the air that it never returns.

Finally, at the end of the fairy tale, the clever tailor overcomes all obstacles and wins the king's daughter and half the kingdom. This is the way a tailor is made into a king in the fairy tale, a king without taboos, who has gotten rid of all the hostile maliciousness of the great people.[12]

Fairy-tale heroes perceive how to take advantage of all kinds of magical or wish instruments that benefit their struggles. In this essay, which is much longer than "The Fairy Tales Moves On in Its Own Time," Bloch refers to a broad array of fairy tales written by Edgar Allen Poe, Wilhelm Hauff, E.T.A. Hoffmann, Gottfried Keller, Selma Lagerlöff, and Rudyard Kipling to demonstrate how they open up wondrous views and send their protagonists on adventures that break down boundaries and reveal how possible the impossible can be. Rarely do the dreams of the adventurers go unfulfilled in these literary fairy tales that stem from a profound oral tradition based on how adults viewed the world.

For Bloch, who always made unusual if not startling associations in his thinking, there is a connection between the wish-images of the fairy tales and the sideshows at country fairs and the performances at the circus. The sensational images in the sideshow or the circus tent, like the miraculous events in the fairy tale, cannot be replicated. Yet they leave behind an indelible impression in the imagination of spectators. Though the scenes and tales may seem to be nonsense, there is a deep sense to our attraction to an unusual attraction that is too easily dismissed by people who putatively possess culture and consider the circus, sideshows at the country fair, and even fairy tales as trivial, vulgar, and decadent. Bloch thinks differently:

The age-old pleasure of people, in no way simple and no way decadent, is preserved in the fair, wanders within it and outside. There is a piece of frontier here, set at reduced admission, but with preserved meanings, with strange utopian meanings, conserved in a brutal show, in vulgar crypticness. It is a world that has not been sufficiently investigated for its specific wish areas. In particular, it is that "oddity," the kind that was last called such during the Baroque period, that keeps itself above water here, above land.[13]

By bringing together the fairy tale with sideshows of the country fair and the performances in circus rings, Bloch intended to demonstrate how all popular culture has traces and remnants of utopian longing. This is why he concludes this essay by discussing colportage, the cheap adventure novels and stories, that became popular in the latter part of the nineteenth century and prepared the way for all kinds of "low-brow" romances, adventure stories, criminal novels, science fiction, fantasy and so on in the twentieth and twenty-first centuries. "The dream of colportage is: never again to be trapped by the routine of daily life. And at the end there is: happiness, love, victory. The splendor toward which the adventure story heads is not won through a rich marriage and the like as in the magazine story but rather through an active journey to the Orient of the dream."[14]

Bloch draws comparisons between Schiller's *The Robbers* and Beethoven's *Fidelio* to demonstrate how they were liberating fairy-tale plays about rescue and liberation that formed a strong current in all kinds of colportage literature up to the present:

> Dark dungeons, pistols, signals, rescue—things in the more re-fined literature of the new kind never appear by themselves. These things produce one of the strongest possible tensions available: that between night and light. Accordingly, a reevaluation of this genre is especially evident on the strength of its highly legitimate wish-image in its mirror. Here, missing meanings are fresh every-where, and those that are not missing are waiting, as in the fairy tale. . . . The fairy-tale like colportage is a castle in the sky par ex-cellence, but one in good air, and insofar as this can at all be true about plain wish work: the castle in the sky is right. In the final analysis, it derives from the Golden Age and would like to stand in such an age again, in happiness, which pushes forward from night to light.[15]

For Bloch, the fairy tale was not a genre of escape literature but rather one of enlightenment. It is interesting to note that his own writing was metaphori-cal, aphoristic, and elliptical often bordering on the mystical, and the process of reading *Das Prinzip Hoffnung* can be metaphysically compared to an abstract adventure and experiment that sheds light on human struggles for revelation. The writing and telling of fairy tales depend very much the same way on sym-bol, allegory, surrealism, and magic realism to dispel clouds of deception and reveal enlightening ways in which oppressed and disadvantaged protagonists might triumph against cruel foes. To be sure, from a literary or folkloristic view-point, Bloch had a somewhat naïve and indiscriminate understanding of the fairy tale and did not distinguish between oral and literary tales or grasp them in their sociohistorical contexts. Nor did he offer careful readings of tales to study gender and racial stereotypes or how they reinforced feudal notions of power. Not every swineherd who becomes a king will use his newly achieved power to benefit other disadvantaged people. Not every peasant maiden who becomes a queen and begins bearing children will be autonomous and live happily ever after. Not every fairy tale possesses a utopian tendency. Bloch often simplifies how fairy tales are received by the reading and viewing public. For instance, many fairy tales divert audiences and "blind" them so that they do not gain enlightenment. Fairy tales are made for fun and profit. One could argue that the manner in which Disney appropriated and adapted fairy tales for the cinema and also for book publishing, tales that stem from the seventeenth, eighteenth, and nineteenth centuries, did not shed light on liberating possibilities for common people but perverted their utopian longings and channeled them so they have become better consumers. Louis Marin has written a scintillating and scathing study of how Disney manipulated fairy-tale elements and motifs to create a utopic degeneration[16] that exploits genuine utopian longings. There is no light in the Disneylands spread across the globe, only darkness and banality. Bloch, in contrast to Adorno, placed much too much faith in the fairy tale as a beacon of light that contained an anticipatory illumination (*Vor-Schein*) of utopia, just as he placed much too much faith in much of commodified art to offer a glow of possible change.

Nevertheless, Bloch did have a profound insight about the genre of the fairy tale, which is one of the most unique forms of storytelling that pervades almost all art forms today—including TV sitcoms, advertisements, toys, garments, fantasy literature, films, paintings, sculptures, poetry, Internet sites, and so on. Whether a fairy tale is progressive—illuminates contradictions in a fictitious realm and tendentiously sides with the oppressed—or regressive—reinforces conservative notions of the status quo by furthering elitist ideas of hegemony even if disadvantaged people rise to the top—the genre continually brings out what is missing in most people's lives. The constant repetition of the fairy-tale maxims is not always and necessarily what Adorno asserted it to be, a banalization of utopia or homogenization of daily life, but rather represents a persistent refusal to accept life as it is and a demand that utopian longings be fulfilled. There is indeed something still missing, deeply missing even when people buy into deception. The emptiness of life is projected through the flaccid happy fulfillments of the fairy tale in all art forms, high and low, and these banal happy fulfillments show paradoxically that people deeply feel how much is still missing and that the temporary "plug of happiness" will not stop the longing. I believe that the Grimms felt this as well and turned to the ancient folk and fairy tales in an endeavor to fill something that was missing in their lives and keeps missing.

In this sense Bloch and Adorno are strange heirs to the Grimms' legacy of folk and fairy tales. Both Bloch and Adorno agreed that something was missing in contemporary society—had always been missing—that engendered utopian longing. Adorno tried to elaborate a theory of negative dialectics in his *Aesthetic*

Theory toward the end of his life, and it is clearly why he proposed to Bloch that "at any rate utopia is essentially in the determined negation, in the determined negation of that which merely is, and by concretizing itself as something false, it always points at the same time to what should be."[17] Though Bloch felt that the world had become completely devoid of a utopian conscience and utopian pre-sentiment, he believed that "utopia cannot be removed from the world in spite of everything, and even the technological, which must definitely emerge and will be in the great realm of the utopian, will form only small sectors." In other words, utopia was not only in the determined negation but in the anticipatory illumination. Glimmers of hope for this utopia were projected and are projected through the fairy tale, but the conditions for its realization must be adequate. As Bloch wryly stated toward the end of his conversation with Adorno, "People must first fill their stomachs, and then they can dance. That is a *condition sine qua non* for being able to talk earnestly about the other without it being used for deception. Only when all the guests have sat down at the table can the Messiah, can Christ come. Thus, Marxism in its entirety, even when conveyed in its most illuminating form and anticipated in its entire realization, is only a *condition* for life in freedom, life in happiness, life in possible fulfillment, life with content."[18]

APPENDIX: "ABOUT PINCARUOLO'S GOOD FEAT," BY GIOVANNI SERCAMBI

In a village near Milan there was a peasant who was quite well-off and had a good-looking son named Pincaruolo. Upon his death, Pincaruolo's father left behind him his wife named Buona, who was to be the mistress of the house and his son. Indeed, his widow remained in charge of the fifteen-year-old boy, and one day this woman said: "Pincaruolo, my son, your father is dead, and it would be advisable for us to live within our means, that is, with what your father's left us. For this reason, my son, I think you should cut wood every now and then and bring it to Milan on our ass. This way we'll be able to manage like our neighbors."

"Mother," Pincaruolo said, "I'll do as you wish."

And he began to cut wood, which he would carry to Milan and then bring the money that he earned back to his mother. And this is how things went for some time.

One foggy day full of fumes, Pincaruolo cut down a little elder tree, but the ass was loaded too much and couldn't carry the wood from the forest. Despite the blows it received and because of the mud and also because of what it ate, the ass happened to die. When Pincaruolo saw the ass was dead, he thought of skinning it and taking the skin to Milan to sell. No sooner thought than done. When Pincaruolo received the money for the skin, he returned to his mother and said: "Here's the money I got for our ass's skin."

His mother wanted to know how the ass had died, and Pincaruolo told her everything.

"My son," his mother said, "don't become depressed. We'll get another ass."

When evening arrived, his mother went to bed thinking about the ass they had lost, as did Pincaruolo.

The next morning Pincaruolo said: "Mother, I want to go and see what has happened to our ass."

"Don't bother," his mother replied. "We have the money."

"I just want to go and see," Pincaruolo answered his mother, and so he went to the place where he had left the dead ass and saw that there were many ravens around it.

"Well," he said to himself, "if I could get one of those birds, I'd be rich." And he immediately took some stones and traps, went to the ass with the intention of putting them into the ass's dead body, and when the ravens approached, he would catch one of them by their claws.

This was the plan that he put into effect. He chased the ravens so that they flew into the ass's skinned body, and then Pincaruolo grabbed hold of one of them, joyously took it from the ass's body, and then tied its claws with some cord. He was so overjoyed that he didn't bother to think of returning to his mother. Instead, he started walking toward the west.

By evening Pincaruolo arrived in a village fifteen miles from Milan, and when it became dark, he stopped at a peasant's house. The peasant's wife was there, and he asked her whether he and his bird might have lodging for the night.

"My husband isn't here," the woman said. "But wait, and he'll give you a place to stay."

Pincaruolo waited. He was very hungry and sat down to rest at the entrance to the house. As he was resting there, the woman immediately took out a cooked capon from a pot and wrapped it in a tablecloth and put it into a chest. Then she carried two clay containers with chicken pies and put them into a cupboard. After putting the containers away, she opened the oven and took out some buns sprinkled with cheese, and she also put them into the chest. Pincaruolo pretended not to see anything, and the woman thought that the boy hadn't noticed a thing.

Soon thereafter the woman's husband, whose name was Bartolo, called out to his wife, Sofia: "Who's this boy?"

"Seems to be somebody who wants to spend the night here," she replied. "If it's all right with you, please let him stay."

"All right," Bartolo said and took the boy into the house. Then he closed the door and turned on the lamp. When he sat down at the table to eat, he told Pincaruolo to eat with him. Pincaruolo, who was still very hungry and had thought he would be eating those things that the woman had put away, was content and sat down at the table. He held the raven in his arm. The woman brought Bartolo and his companion a simple loaf of bread and some cold beans and two plates with food that was not particularly nutritious. Bartolo, who had dug up a field near the house the entire day, was hungry and began to eat and so did the boy, and it seemed to them that they were eating ham. The woman had poured them some wine, and they gulped down every mouthful together. Then Bartolo said to the boy, "Go and lay down in that little bed, " and he and this wife went to sleep in their bed.

Pincaruolo, who had seen the things that the woman had put away, and that they hadn't received, was completely convinced that she was bad-natured. So he began thinking of some ways to arouse Bartolo so that they could eat better than they had eaten. After some time had passed, the boy squeezed the raven's claws so tightly that the raven began to caw. Pincaruolo cried out to the raven to be quiet and said: "Stop behaving so badly! Don't you wake this good man and his wife after they have showed us such great hospitality this evening!"

When Bartolo heard the boy scolding the raven, he asked what was happening, and the boy replied: "My bird said to me that he wanted some of the capon that was in the chest."

Bartolo got up at once and went to the chest where he found the capon. Then he called to the boy and got him up. Together they ate the capon along with some bread. As Bartolo was giving some to the raven, he said, "Sofia treats me this way. She gives me simple bread and beans, and she keeps the capon to enjoy with some priest."

When the wife heard all this, she cursed the arrival of the boy in their house. After everything had been eaten, Bartolo returned to the bed and said nothing to his wife. After two more hours had passed, Pincaruolo once more made the raven caw and began reprimanding the bird in a loud voice. Upon hearing the cries, Bartolo said he wanted to know what the bird was saying. The boy replied that the bird didn't want to say anything except that he wanted some of the chicken pies and buns with cheese in the cupboard. Upon hearing this, Bartolo got out of the bed and went to the cupboard where he found the chicken pies and some good buns. So Bartolo called the boy, poured the wine, and together they ate the chicken pies and the buns. Of course, the raven was given some of this meal.

Now, even though his wife could hear him, Bartolo began whispering to Pincaruolo and said, "Eh, tell me please, what kind of a bird is this?"

"This bird's a soothsayer and can predict anything that anyone will do during the day or night," Pincaruolo said.

"Now that I've seen this," Bartolo said, "I believe you. So, tell me, will you sell this bird to me?"

"It's worth a treasure," said the boy.

"I'll give you 500 florins and a pair of my oxen in exchange for your soothsayer," Bartolo replied.

"Well, since you gave me a place to stay and some food this evening, I'm satisfied, but I must tell you that if by chance someone pisses on its head, the bird will immediately die. Otherwise, it's immortal."

Bartolo answered, "I'll make such a very high pole with a long string attached to its legs that nobody will be able to piss on its head."

The boy told him it was a good idea. Meanwhile, Sofia, who had heard everything, remained quiet until dawn.

When morning came, Pincaruolo departed with the money and two oxen and traveled westward. Meanwhile, Bartolo set up the pole, placed the soothsayer on top, and then went off with his spade to work in the field near his house. His wife remained sad and miserable at home. Suddenly Rustico, the village priest, arrived and said, "Sofia, how are you doing?"

"Badly," Sofia replied.

"Why?" asked the priest.

Sofia told him about all that happened to the chicken pies, the capon, and the buns and all about the boy and his soothsayer. She also told him that Bartolo had bought the raven for 500 florins and a pair of oxen and that she would no longer be able to make love with the priest.

"Why not?" asked the priest.

"The bird's a soothsayer."

"But can't we bring about the soothsayer's death?"

"Yes, if someone pisses on its head."

"I can certainly do this," the priest said.

"How?" Sofia asked.

"I'll climb on top of the roof of the house. You hit the soothsayer's head, on top and on the bottom, and I'll take out my trusty companion to piss on the bird and kill it."

"Oh, my father! May your companion expand and get larger since you have thought of such a clever idea!"

So the priest climbed on top of the roof while Sofia started hitting the pole. The priest felt his way along the top of the roof and advanced, and once he was on the beams, he took out his flourishing companion and pissed on the soothsayer. Now the raven behaved according to its nature as soon as it smelled the odor of flesh. The bird raised its eyes toward the roof and saw the priest Rustico's companion, convinced that it was flesh, which it was, and so the raven flew straight to Rustico and took some of his flesh in its claws and beak. Feeling attacked from the rear, the priest immediately screamed. Now, Bartolo, who was in the field working, looked up and heard the screams. Then he spotted the priest Rustico on top of the roof. So he ran off to his house and saw his soothsayer holding on tightly to a piece of the priest's flesh.

"Hold on with all your might, soothsayer!" Bartolo yelled.

When the priest Rustico heard Bartolo, he uttered out of pain and afraid of dying, "I implore you, Bartolo. Pity me!"

Once again Bartolo yelled at the soothsayer, "Hold on with all your might!"

The priest who was in great pain said, "Oh, Bartolo, I promise you, if you get the soothsayer to let go of me, I'll never enter your house again. Moreover, I'll give you 300 florins and a horse and a new cloak. Just let me go!"

Once Bartolo heard what the priest Rustico had offered, he was content and took the string attached to the raven and pulled it down with such force that the priest's flesh was ripped from the bird, something that the priest had very much needed.

Now the priest Rustico went into the house and gave Bartolo 300 florins and the horse and the cloak. Then, nearly dead, he departed. Meanwhile, Bartolo mounted the horse and took with him the 300 florins and the cloak and set out on the road that Pincaruolo had taken. When he found the boy, he said: "Your soothsayer is worth ten of them," and he told him the entire story of what had happened to the priest. Then he said: "My boy, I didn't pay you well enough. Now I'm going to give you this horse and another 300 florins, but I ask you to give me back my oxen, and I want to keep this cloak."

"I'm satisfied," said Pincaruolo, and he took the money and the horse and returned the oxen to Bartolo. Then he said his farewell with blessings from God.

Once Pincaruolo was mounted on a horse with his 800 florins, he said to himself: "I can be a fine gentleman now that I'm on horseback and have so much money. From now on I shall call myself Torre, no longer Pincaruolo." And he headed in the direction of Troyes in the region of Champagne. This road took him past the Alps and into the Valley of Briga and the plain of Champagne in France.

As he was riding over the plain, he saw a man who was standing in a position as though he wanted to run. So Torre stopped, and since he didn't see any one else with this man, he said to himself: "What's he doing?" Then he asked him what he was doing.

"I'm trying to catch a deer."

"But you don't have any dogs or nets. So how do you think you're going to do something like that?" Torre asked.

"I'll do it by running," he responded.

Torre was amazed and said: "How's that possible?"

"If you wait, you will see."

Soon thereafter a deer came out of the woods, and the man went straight after the deer and in a few strides he got hold of it and presented the deer to Torre.

"Did you see how fast I run?" he asked.

And Torre responded, "Truly, you run very well, and I want to say to you that if you come with me, I'll pay you 100 florins and expenses, and if I earn something, you'll get your share in each case. But please, tell me, what's your name?"

"I'm called Rondello," the man responded, "and I'll be glad to come along with you, and I also accept the 100 florins."

So, Torre opened his purse of florins and gave him 100. Soon after, Rondello began traveling with him.

Along the way Torre saw a man lying on the ground and said to Rondello, "That man seems to be dead."

"I'll go and see," responded Rondello.

He was immediately at the side of the man and saw that he was alive. Torre went over to the man and saw that he was holding his ear to the ground.

"What are you doing?" Torre asked.

"I'm listening to the grass grow," he replied.

Torre was amazed by this skill, and the man said, "I heard you when you said 'That man is dead.'"

Torre asked him whether he wanted to come along with him and what his name was.

"My name is Sentimento," the man said, "and I'd be glad to come along, providing that I have a salary."

Torre offered him 100 florins. Sentimento took them, and they set out together.

After journeying for some time Torre saw a man with a bow and arrow and asked him what he was doing.

"I'm waiting to shoot a bird for my dinner," he responded.

"But how can you shoot and hit one when there are no trees here where the birds can land?" Torre asked.

"If you wait, you'll see what I can do," the man said.

Shortly thereafter a swallow flew in the air, and the man shot an arrow and hit the bird, which fell dead at Torre's feet. When Torre saw the man's skill as an archer, Torre thought he'd be a good companion with the others and asked him his name and offered him 100 florins if he would come along. The man said his name was Diritto and that he would be glad to travel with him. He took the 100 florins and set out with Torre and the others.

When they were within a day's journey of Paris, Torre saw a man who had a mill without water and wind in front of him.

"What is that man doing?" Torre said, and he went over to him and asked what he was doing.

"I'm grinding grain with my breath," the man responded.

"You certainly have a great breath if you can grind grain," Torre remarked.

"You'll have proof right away when you see what I can do," the man responded, and he began to stir up three bushels of grain, then blew the windmills and didn't stop blowing until the three bushels of grain were ground. When Torre saw the result, he asked the man whether he would like to come along with him. He said he'd give the man 100 florins like he gave the others, and then he asked him his name,

"My name's Spazza," the man replied, "and I'd be glad to have the 100 florins."

Torre immediately gave him the 100 florins, and they set out together. Torre now had four companions, and as they were approaching Paris, he heard that King Philippe had a young daughter named Drusiana, his only daughter, ready to wed, but according to custom, the suitor had to defeat her in a race, and if he lost, he was put to death. There had already been many men who had raced her, and all of them had lost their lives because she had been victorious.

Upon hearing this, Torre consulted with the runner Rondello and asked him to be the man to run against Drusiana and whether he would be willing to put his head at stake.

"Master," Rondello replied, "you needn't have any doubts. If you want, I'll win the race, and you will get to marry the princess."

Torre was pleased by Rondello's good words and pledge. Then he turned to the other three companions and asked, "What's your opinion?"

"Signor Torre," said Spazza, "since you desire to have King Philippe's daughter, who will run the race and is beautiful, please permit me to help you fulfill your wishes. If Rondello doesn't run faster than the princess, I shall hold her back with my breath so that Rondello can reach the finish line before she does. In this way you'll be able to gain Drusiana for your wife."

Torre was pleased by this, and he responded: "You others, what do you say?"

Sentimento and Diritto gave their individual opinions and said that they would do everything necessary for him to win. Torre was glad to have their pledge as well.

When they arrived in Paris, they stopped at an inn, where Torre dressed himself in a dignified way and rested for a few days. Then Torre went to King Philippe's court and told him that he was there to become his son-in-law and would fulfill all the customary conditions. The king said that he'd make all the arrangements and set the day and date of the race. Meanwhile, he had Torre imprisoned. In the event that the man named to run the race with Drusiana were to lose, Torre was to be beheaded right away.

On the Sunday scheduled for the race, each participant in the race had to get dressed in the appropriate clothes and those assisting them also had to wear the appropriate clothes. Rondello stood ready before the king and asked which path he was to take, and the king responded: "Both of you are to run with a leather bottle until Saint Denis, and the first to return with the bottle full of water from the fountain of Saint Denis will be the winner. The one who remains behind will be the loser."

As soon as Rondello heard this, he replied at once: "Now it's time for the signal to begin."

Spazza took a place along the path with Sentimento and Diritto waiting for the signal to be given, and as soon as it was time, the princess began running, while Rondello, who could easily outrun any animal, reached Saint Denis right away and filled the bottle with water from the fountain. As he was returning, he encountered Drusiana midway, and she stopped and said to Rondello: "My boy, alas, I see that you've won. You've certainly served your lord and mine very well. So you might as well rest a little without much worry."

Upon hearing these sweet words, Rondello sat down and rested with Drusiana, and the songs she sang to him were also so sweet that he fell asleep. As soon as she saw he was asleep, Drusiana emptied his bottle of water into her bottle and put the empty one by his side. Then she turned around and started running back to Paris.

Spazza saw Drusiana coming and said, "It's going badly for us!"

So he took a position to block her and to blow her backward, and as soon as she came, Spazza turned her around ten times, and by doing this he held her back for some time. However, since Rondello still didn't show his face, he said, "Rondello's dead for sure."

"I'll soon know his condition," Sentimento responded.

He put his ear to the ground and heard Rondello sleeping.

"He's sleeping!"

"Tell me how far we are from where he is and on what part of the path he's sleeping," Diritto said.

"He's three miles from here and right in the middle of the path," Sentimento replied.

Diritto took his bow and aimed an arrow in the direction of the bottle beneath Rondello's head. As soon as the arrow hit the bottle, Rondello awoke and thought: "I've been tricked." However, he hoped that Spazza was holding back the princess, and he immediately took the bottle, returned to Saint Denis, and filled it with water. Once that was done, he turned, and in very little time he arrived in Paris before the princess reached the city. This was the way that Torre escaped with his life.

When Torre was freed from the prison, King Philippe allowed him to marry the princess, and he held a grand celebration for a long time. All ordinary activities were suspended at the court and other parts of the realm of France, such as Milan, where Torre had come from. Later his companions, Spazza, Rondello, Diritto, and Sentimento gave accounts of themselves in some other countries and lived for a long time.

NOTES

Introduction. The Vibrant Body of the Grimms' Folk and Fairy Tales, Which Do Not Belong to the Grimms

1. Y. M. Sokolov, *Russian Folklore* (Hatboro, PA: Folklore Associates, 1966): 52.
2. Timothy Baycroft and David Hopkin, eds. *Folklore and Nationalism in Europe during the Long Nineteenth Century* (Leiden: Brill, 2012): 409.
3. Onions, C. T., ed. *The Oxford University Dictionary on Historical Principles*. 3rd. rev. ed. Oxford, UK: Oxford University Press, 1944.
4. Jacob und Wilhlem Grimm, *Kinder- und Hausmärchen gesammelt durch die Brüder Grimm* [1812/1815, Erstausgabe], ed. Ulrike Marquardt and Heinz Rölleke, vol. 1 (Göttingen: Vandenhoeck & Ruprecht, 1986): xviii–xxi. (My translation.)
5. Ibid., vol. 2, vii–x. (My translation.)
6. See Jacob and Wilhelm Grimm, *The Original Folk and Fairy Tales of the Brothers Grimm: The First Edition* (Princeton, NJ: Princeton University Press, 2014).
7. André Jolles, *Einfache Formen: Legende/Sage/Mythe/Spruch Kasus/Memorabile,Märchen/Witz* (Darmstadt: Wissenschaftliche Buchgesellschaft, 1958): 243. Reprint of the 1930 edition.
8. Jeffrey Peck, "'In the Beginning Was the Word': Germany and the Origins of German Studies." In *Medievalism and the Modernist Temper*, ed. R. Howard Bloch and Stephen Nichols (Baltimore: Johns Hopkins University Press, 1996): 129.
9. For a full account of the exchange with Achim von Arnim, see chapters 5 and 8 in Reinhold Steig and Hermann Grimm, eds., *Achim von Arnim und die ihm nahe standen*, vol. 3 (Stuttgart: J. G. Cotta'schen Buchhandlung, 1904): 115–44 and 213–73.
10. Jens Sennewald, *Das Buch, das wird sind: Zur Poetik der "Kinder- und Hausmärchen" gesammelt durch die Brüder Grimm* (Würzburg: Königshausen & Neumann, 2004): 346.
11. Seven years after the discovery of the manuscript, it was published as a book. See Joseph Lefftz, ed., *Märchen der Brüder Grimm. Urfassung nach der Originalhandschrift der Abtei Ölenberg im Elsaß* (Heidelberg: C. Winter, 1927). This edition is somewhat faulty. The most thorough scholarly edition is Heinz Rölleke, *Die älteste Märchensammlung der Brüder Grimm. Synopse der handschriftlichen Urfassung von 1810 und der Erstdrucke von 1812* (Cologny Geneva: Fondation Martin Bodmer, 1975).
12. Vanessa Joosen, "Back to Ölenberg: An Intertextual Dialogue between Fairy-Tale Retellings and the Sociohistorical Study of the Grimm Tales," *Marvels & Tales* 24.1 (2010): 99–115.
13. Heinz Rölleke, *Märchen aus dem Nachlaß der Brüder Grimm*, 3rd rev. ed. (Bonn: Bouvier, 1983).
14. See Wilhelm Stapel, ed., *Fünfundfünfzig vergessene Grimmsche Märchen* (Hamburg: Hanseatische Verlagsanstalt, 1922); Ruth Michaelis-Jena and Arthur Ratcliffe, eds. *Grimms' Other Tales: A New Selection*, illustr. Gwenda Morgan (London: Golden Cockerel Press, 1956); Heinz Rölleke, ed. *Die wahren Märchen der Brüder Grimm* (Frankfurt am Main: Fischer Taschenbuch, 1989); Heinz Rölleke, *Grimms Märchen wie sie nicht im Buch stehen* (Frankfurt am Main: Insel Taschenbuch, 1993). Some omitted and posthumous tales can be found in the appendix of my translation of the 1857 edition. See Jacob and Wilhelm Grimm, *The Complete Fairy Tales of the Brothers Grimm*, ed. and trans. Jack Zipes, 3rd rev. and enlarged ed. (New York: Bantam, 2003).
15. Reprinted in Heinz Rölleke, *Die Märchen der Brüder Grimm* (Munich: Artemis, 1987): 63–69.

16. All these quotations are taken from Jacob Grimm's letter to Brentano, which can be found in Reinhold Steig, *Clemens Bretano und die Brüder Grimm* (Stuttgart: J. G. Cotta'sche Buchhandlung, 1914): 164–71.

17. Jacob Grimm, *Circular wegen Aufsammlung der Volkspoesie*, ed. Ludwig Denecke, afterword Kurt Ranke (Kassel: Brüder Grimm-Museum, 1968): 3–4.

18. Pierre Bourdieu, *The Field of Cultural Production: Essays on Art and Literature*, ed. Randal Johnson (New York: Columbia University Press, 1993): 30.

19. Jeep Leerssen, "From Bökendorf to Berlin: Private Careers, Public Sphere, and How the Past Changed in Jacob Grimm's Lifetime," in *Free Access to the Past: Romanticism, Cultural Heritage and the Nation*, ed. Lotte Jensen, Joep Leerssen, and Marita Mathijsen (Leiden, Netherlands: Brill Academic Publishers, 2009): 69.

20. See Albert Schindehütte, ed., *Krauses Grimm'sche Märchen* (Kassel: Johannes Staude, 1985).

21. For complete information about Viehmann, see the excellent collection of essays edited by Holger Ehrhardt, *Dorothea Viehmann* (Kassel: Euregioverlag, 2012).

22. Edgar Taylor, who published two volumes of the Grimms' tales under the title *German Popular Stories* in 1823 and 1826, went on to publish a third volume in 1839: *Gammer Grethel; or German Fairy Tales Popular Stories, From the Collection of MM. Grimm, and Other Sources; with illustrative notes.* (London: John Green, 1839). The frontispiece to this edition was the drawing of Dorothea Viehmann, who in Taylor's hands was made into the ideal storyteller.

23. Grimm, *Kinder- und Hausmärchen gesammelt durch die Brüder Grimm* [1812/1815, Erstausgabe], vol. 2, iv–vi.

24. See Albert Schindehütte, *Die Grimm'schen Märchen der jungen Marie* (Marburg: Hitzeroth, 1991).

25. See Heinz Rölleke, *"Wo das Wünschen noch geholfen hat." Gesammelte Aufsätze zu den "Kinder- und Hausmärchen" der Brüder Grimm* (Bonn: Bouvier, 1985); *Die Märchen der Brüder Grimm: Quellen und Studien* (Trier:Wissenschaftlicher Verlag Trier, 2000); *Es war einmal . . . Die wahren Märchen der Brüder Grimm und wer sie ihnen erzählte*, illustr. Albert Schindehütte (Frankfurt am Main: Eichorn, 2011).

26. Heinz Rölleke, ed. *Die älteste Märchensammlung der Brüder Grimm. Synopse der handschriftlichen Urfassung von 1810 und der Erstdrucke von 1812* (Cologny-Geneva: Fondation Martin Bodmer, 1975): 144.

27. Ibid., 145.

28. Jacob and Wilhelm Grimm, *The Complete Fairy Tales of the Brothers Grimm*, ed. and trans. Jack Zipes, 3rd rev. ed. (New York: Bantam, 2003): 2.

29. For a thorough study of this tale type, see Lutz Röhrich, *Wage es, den Frosch zu küssen: Das Grimmsche Märchen Nummer Eins in seinen Wandlungen* (Cologne: Eugen Diederichs Verlag, 1987).

30. Siegfried Neumann, "The Brothers Grimm as Collectors and Editors of German Folktales," in *The Reception of Grimms' Fairy Tales: Response, Reactions, Revisions*, ed. Donald Haase (Detroit: Wayne State University Press, 1993): 30.

31. See Karoline Stahl, *Fabeln und Erzählungen für Kinder* (Nürnberg, 1818).

32. Ibid., 33–34. In his remarks, Neumann cites Hermann Strobach, ed., *Geschichte der deutschen Volksdichtung* (Berlin: Akademie-Verlag, 1981): 90.

33. For more information about Wolf, see Ludwig Fränkel, "Wolf, Johann Wilhelm," in *Allgemeine Deutsche Biographie (ADB)*, vol. 43 (Leipzig: Duncker & Humboldt, 1898): 765–77.

34. For a full account of his life, see Ines Köhler-Zölch, "Heinrich Pröhle: A Successor to the Brothers Grimm," in *The Reception of Grimms' Fairy Tales: Responses, Reactions, Revisions*, ed. Donald Haase (Detroit: Wayne State University Press, 1993): 41–58.

35. Heinrich Pröhle, *Märchen für die Jugend* (Halle: Verlag des Waisenhauses, 1854): x.

36. Köhler-Zülch, "Heinrich Pröhle," 51–52.

37. See the bibliography for a complete list of their works.

38. See Luisa Del Giudice and Gerald Porter, eds., *Imagined States: Nationalism, Utopia and Longing in Oral Cultures* (Logan: Utah State University Press, 2001); Jennifer Schacker, *National Dreams: The*

Remaking of Fairy Tales in Nineteenth-Century England (Philadelphia: University of Pennsylvania Press, 2003); Joep Leerssen, *National Thought in Europe: A Cultural History* (Amsterdam: Amsterdam University Press, 2006); and Baycroft and Hopkin, eds., *Folklore and Nationalism in Europe During the Long Nineteenth Century* (2012).

39. See Marte Hvam Hult, *Framing a National Narrative: The Legend Collections of Peter Christen Asbjørnsen* (Detroit: Wayne State University Press, 2003).

40. See Reimund Kvideland, "The Collecting and Study of Tales in Scandinavia," in *A Companion to the Fairy Tale*, ed. Hilda Ellis Davidson and Anna Chaudhri (Cambridge, UK: D. S. Brewer, 2003): 159–68.

41. Ibid., 160.

42. See Timothy Tangherlini, ed. and trans., *Danish Folktales, Legends and Other Stories* (Seattle: University of Washington Press, 2013), and the excellent book review, Paul Binding, "Respect the Goblin," *Times Literary Supplement* (October 4, 2013): 5.

43. See James Riordan, "Russian Fairy Tales and Their Collectors," in *A Companion to the Fairy Tale*, ed. Hilda Ellis Davidson and Anna Chaudhri (Cambridge, UK: D. S. Brewer, 2003): 217–26.

44. See David Hopkin, *Voices of the People in Nineteenth-Century France* (Cambridge, UK: Cambridge University Press, 2012).

45. Randal Allison, "Tradition," in *Folklore: An Encyclopedia of Beliefs, Customs, Tales, Music, and Art*, ed. Thomas Green (Santa Barbara, CA: ABC-CLIO, 1997): 799–800.

46. Eric Hobsbawm and Terrence Ranger, eds., *The Invention of Tradition* (Cambridge, UK: Cambridge University Press, 1983), 1. See also Tad Tuleja, "Invented Tradition," in *Folklore: An Encyclopedia of Beliefs, Customs, Tales, Music, and Art*, ed. Thomas Green (Santa Barbara, CA: ABC-CLIO, 1997), 466–68.

47. Ibid., 9.

48. Elliott Oring, "Thinking through Tradition," in *Tradition in the Twenty-First Century: Locating the Role of the Present in the Past*, ed. Trevor Blank and Robert Glenn Howard (Logan: Utah State University Press, 2013):25.

49. Simon Bronner, "The 'Handiness' of Tradition," in *Tradition in the Twenty-First Century: Locating the Role of the Present in the Past*, ed. Trevor Blank and Robert Glenn Howard (Logan: Utah State University Press, 2013), 189. This essay also appears in Bronner's thought-provoking and comprehensive study, *Explaining Traditions: Folk Behavior in Modern Culture* (Lexington: The University Press of Kentucky, 2011).

50. Ibid., 197.

51. See Jan Assmann, Cultural Memory and Early Civilization: Writing, Remembrance, and Political Imagination (Cambridge, UK. Cambridge University Press, 2011); and Aleida Assmann, *Cultural Memory and Western Civilization: Functions, Media, Archives* (Cambridge, UK: Cambridge University Press, 2011). See also Tristan Landry, *La mémoire du conte folklorique de l'oral à l'écrit· Les freres Grimm et Afanas'ev* (Laval, Canada: Les Presses de l'Université Laval, 2005), which is based on Jan Assmann's work.

52. Jan Assmann, *Cultural Memory and Early Civilization*, 2–3.

Chapter One. *German Popular Stories* as Revolutionary Book

First appeared as the introduction to Brothers Grimm, *German Popular Stories*, edited by Jack Zipes. Kent, UK: Crescent Moon, 2012. It is printed here in a longer version with permission of Crescent Moon Publishing.

1. Albert, Leitzmann, ed., *Briefwechsel der Brüder Jacob und Wilhelm Grimm mit Karl Lachmann*, vol. 1 (Jena: Verlag der Frommannschen Buchhandlung, 1927): 390. Lachmann was one of the

foremost German philologists of the nineteenth century and became a professor at the Humboldt University in Berlin.

2. David Blamires, "The Early Reception of the Grimms' *Kinder- und Hausmärchen* in England," *Bulletin of the John Rylands University Library of Manchester* 71.3 (1989): 69.

3. Brian Alderson, "The Spoken and the Read: *German Popular Stories* and English Popular Diction," in Donald Haase, ed., *The Reception of Grimms' Fairy Tales: Responses, Reactions, Revisions* (Detroit: Wayne State University Press, 1993): 67.

4. Ibid., 66–67. Alderson perceptively notes: "One can argue that the Grimms—as they themselves recognized—were well served by this translation. For although it is deeply conservative in its response to the originalities of the *Kinder- und Hausmärchen*, and although it is cavalier over the precise matching of words—which the Grimms also recognized—it is nevertheless a version with a proper feeling for the rhythms of English prose. If the Grimms could not finally follow the ideals of a 'pure' recording of the storyteller's voice, we can hardly expect their translator—embattled in the 'fastidious' climate of 1823—to exceed them. What he did do, over many pages of his book was to respond naturally to the language of the stories and make them sound as though they originated in English rather than in German."

5. In 1948, Puffin Classics (Penguin) published an edition with the title *Grimms' Fairy Tales*, which does not indicate who the translator is, but it does highlight Cruikshank's illustrations. The cover is a colored rendition of "Hans in Luck."

6. *Fairy Tales from the Brothers Grimm*, intro. by Cornelia Funke, illustr. by George Cruikshank (London: Puffin, 2012). To spruce up this anniversary edition, there are six color illustrations by well-known illustrators: Oliver Jeffers, Quentin Blake, Raymond Briggs, Emma Chichester Clark, Axel Scheffler, and Helen Oxenbury. Little did these illustrators know that they weren't illustrating the Grimms' tales, but Taylor's adaptations.

7. For information about Cruikshank's work, see Robert Patten, "George Cruikshank's Grimm Humor," in Joachim Müller, ed., *Imagination on a Long Rein: English Literature Illustrated* (Marburg: Jonas, 1988): 3–28; and *George Cruikshank: Life, Times, and Art*, 2 vols. (New Brunswick, NJ: Rutgers University Press, 1992).

8. The dates of the Large Edition are 1812/1815, 1819, 1837, 1840, 1843, 1850, 1857. The last edition contained 210 tales. The dates of the Small Edition are 1825, 1833, 1836, 1839, 1841, 1844, 1847, 1850, 1853, 1858. They always contained 50 tales that were generally revised in accordance with the same tales in the Large Edition, though there were some small differences. The Small Edition began with "The Frog King" and ended with the "The Star Coins," two tales clearly adapted for young readers. The illustrations by Ludwig Pietsch tend to be realistic and somewhat sanctimonious. See Heinz Rölleke's "Nachwort" in *Kinder- und Hausmärchen gesammelt durch die Brüder Grimm: Kleine Ausgabe von 1858* (Frankfurt am Main: Insel, 1985): 291–95; and Ruth Bottigheimer, "The Publishing History of Grimms' Tales: Reception at the Cash Register" in Donald Haase, ed., *The Reception of the Grimms' Fairy Tales: Responses, Reactions, Revisions* (Detroit: Wayne State University Press, 1993): 78–101.

9. Most of the recent scholarship on Taylor's "revolutionary" transformation of the Grimms' tales are in agreement on this point, with slight differences of emphasis. See David Blamires, "The Early Reception of the Grimms' *Kinder- und Hausmärchen* in England," (1989); Brian Alderson, "The Spoken and the Read: *German Popular Stories* and English Popular Diction" (1993); Martin Sutton, *The Sin-Complex: A Critical Study of English Versions of the Grimms' Kinder- und Hausmärchen in the Nineteenth Century* (Kassel: Schriften der Brüder Grimm-Gesellschaft, 1996); Jennifer Schacker, *National Dreams: The Remaking of Fairy Tales in Nineteenth Century England* (Philadelphia: University of Pennsylvania Press, 2003); Gillian Lathey, *The Role of Translators in Children's Literature: Invisible Storyteller* (New York: Routledge, 2010).

10. See Molly Clark Hillard, *Spellbound: The Fairy Tale and the Victorians* (Columbus: Ohio State University Press, 2014).

11. See Heinz Rölleke, ed., *Die älteste Märchensammlung der Brüder Grimm. Synopse der handschriftlichen Urfassung von 1810 und der Erstdrucke von 1812* (Cologny-Geneva: Fondation Martin Bodmer, 1975).

12. Jens Sennewald, *Das Buch, das Wir Sind: Zur Poetik der "Kinder- und Hausmärchen, gesammelt durch die Brüder Grimm"* (Würzbrug: Königshausen & Neumann, 2004): 14–18.

13. Ibid., 42–47.

14. Reinhold Steig and Herman Grimm, eds., *Achim von Arnim und die ihm nahe standen*, vol. 3 (Stuttgart: J. G. Cotta'schen Buchhandlung, 1904): 237.

15. Ibid., 269.

16. Ibid., 271.

17. *Kinder- und Hausmärchen gesammelt durch die Brüder Grimm* [1812/1815, Erstausgabe], ed. Ulrike Marquardt and Heinz Rölleke, vol. 2. (Göttingen: Vandenhoeck & Ruprecht, 1986): vii–x.

18. Some more biographical information about Taylor can be found in Ruth Michaelis-Jena,"Edgar and John Edward Taylor, die ersten englischen Übersetzer der Kinder- und Hausmärchen," in *Brüder Grimm Gedenken*, ed. Ludwig Denecke, vol. 2. (Marburg: N. G. Elwert, 1975): 183–202; Sutton, *The Sin-Complex: A Critical Study of English Versions of the Grimms' Kinder- und Hausmärchen in the Nineteenth Century*; and Schacker, *National Dreams: The Remaking of Fairy Tales in Nineteenth Century England*.

19. Francis Cohen, "Antiquities of Nursery Literature: Review of *Fairy Tales, or the Lilliputian Cabinet, Containing Twenty-Four Choice Pieces of Fancy and Fiction, collected by Benjamin Tabart*," *Quarterly Review* 21.41 (January 1819): 92–93.

20. For the most thorough account of Cohen's life and his correspondence with the Grimms, see Lothar Bluhm, "Sir Francis Cohen/Palgrave. Zur frühen Rezeption der *Kinder- und Hausmärchen* in England," in *Brüder Grimm Gedenken*, ed. Ludwig Denecke, vol. 7 (Marburg: N. G. Elwert, 1987): 224–42.

21. See Edgar Taylor, "German Popular and Traditional Literature," *New Monthly Magazine and Literary Journal* 2 (1821): 146–52, 329–36, 537–44; and 4 (1822): 289–96.

22. Ibid., 2: 146–47.

23. Robert Patten, "George Cruikshank's Grimm Humor," in Joachim Müller, ed., *Imagination on a Long Rein: English Literature Illustrated* (Marburg: Jonas, 1988): 14.

24. Sir Walter Scott, "Letter to Edgar Taylor, January 16 1823," in *The Letters of Sir Walter Scott*, ed. Herbert Grierson, vol. 7 (London: Constable, 1934): 310.

25. Cohen also has an interest in this work.

26. *Grimm's Goblins. Grimm's Household Stories, Translated from the Kinder und Haus Marchen*, illustr. George Cruikshank (London: R. Meek, 1876): viii.

27. F. J. Harvey Darton, *Children's Books in England: Five Centuries of Social Life*, 3rd rev. ed. by Brian Alderson (Cambridge, UK: Cambridge University Press, 1982): 99.

28. See Sutton, *The Sin-Complex: A Critical Study of English Versions of the Grimms' Kinder- und Hausmärchen in the Nineteenth Century*; Schacker, *National Dreams: The Remaking of Fairy Tales in Nineteenth Century England*; and Matthew Grenby, "Tame Fairies Make Good Teachers: The Popularity of Early British Fairy Tales," *The Lion and the Unicorn* 30 (2006): 1–24.

29. See Sutton, 22–47.

30. Taylor, Edgar, ed., *German Popular Stories*, illustr. George Cruikshank (London: John Camden Hotten, 1869): 122.

31. *Gammer Grethel or German Fairy Tales, and Popular Stories*, from the collection of MM. Grimm, and other sources, with illustrative notes (London: John Green, 1839): 1.

Chapter Two. Hyping the Grimms' Fairy Tales

Appeared in a slightly modified version as "Hyping the Grimms' Fairy Tales," by Jack Zipes, in *The Cambridge Companion to Fairy Tales*, edited by Maria Tatar. Cambridge, UK: Cambridge University Press, 2014. Copyright © 2014 Cambridge University Press. Reprinted with permission.

1. Donald Haase, "Framing the Brothers Grimm: Paratexts and Intercultural Transmission in Postwar English-Language Editions of the *Kinder- und Hausmärchen*," *Fabula* 44.1/2 (2003): 66.

2. Jonathan Gray, *Show Sold Separately: Promos, Spoilers, and Other Media Paratexts* (New York: New York University Press, 2010): 5.

3. Ibid., 5.

4. Gérard Genette, *Paratexts: Thresholds of Interpretation*, trans. Jane Lewin (Cambridge, UK: Cambridge University Press, 1997): 2.

5. Ibid., 6.

6. See Roland Barthes, "The Death of the Author" [1967], in *Image-Music-Text*, ed. and trans. Stephen Heath (New York: Hill and Wang, 1977): 142–48; and Michel Foucault, "What Is an Author?"[1969], in *Language, Counter Memory, Practice*, ed. and trans. Donald Bouchard and Sherry Simon (Ithaca, NY: Cornell University Press, 1977): 124–27.

7. Haase, "Framing the Brothers Grimm," 56–57.

8. Ibid., 57.

9. In Maria Tatar, *The Hard Facts of the Grimms' Tales* (Princeton, NJ: Princeton University Press, 1987): 216–17.

10. See Hermann Gerstner, ed., *Grimms Märchen: Die kleine Ausgabe aus dem Jahr 1825* (Dortmund: Harenberg, 1982).

11. E-mail letter with Michael Drout on July 1, 2011. See his book for a further discussion of memes: *How Tradition Works: A Meme-Based Cultural Poetics of the AngloSaxon Tenth Century* (Tempe: Arizona Center for Medieval and Renaissance Studies, 2006).

12. Available at http://adisney.go.com/disneypictures/tangled/.

13. See Yvonne Verdier, "Grand-mères, si vous saviez: le Petit Chaperon Rouge dans la tradition orale," *Cahiers de Littérature Orale* 4 (1978): 17–55; and Jan Ziolkowski, *Fairy Tales from before Fairy Tales: The Medieval Latin Past of Wonderful Lies* (Ann Arbor: University of Michigan Press, 2006).

14. For a translation, see Paul Delarue, ed., *The Borzoi Book of French Folk Tales*, trans. Austin Fife. Illustr. Warren Chappell (New York: Knopf, 1956).

15. Available at http://herocomplex.latimes.com/2010/11/16/red-riding-hood-director-catherine -hardwicke-explains-the-big-bad-sexy-secret/.

16. Susan Carpenter, "'Red Riding Hood' Movie Is Already Hot as a Novel and E-book," *Los Angeles Times* (March 8, 2011). http://articles.latimes.com/2011/mar/08/entertainment/la-et-red-riding -novel-20110308.

17. "Hoodwinked Too! HOOD VS. EVIL," April 28, 2009. http://www.hollywoodgo.com/movie/hood winked-too-hood-vs-evil-3396/.

18. Jake Coyle, "'Hoodwinked Too!'—More Polished, Less Funny," Associated Press (April 29, 2011). http://www.mercurynews.com/movies-dvd/ci_17949919.

19. For a thorough analysis of how blockbusters operate, see Anita Elberse, *Blockbusters: Hit-Making, Risk-Taking, and the Big Business of Entertainment* (New York: Henry Holt, 2013).

20. Guy Debord, *The Society of the Spectacle*, trans. Donald Nicholson-Smith (New York: Zone Books, 1995): 19. First published as *La Societé du spectacle* (Paris: Buchet-Chastel, 1967).

21. Available at http://en.wikipedia.org/wiki/Hansel_%26_Gretel:_Witch_Hunters.

22. Ibid.

23. Claudia Puig, "'Hansel and Gretel': No Happily Ever After, or During." http://usatoday.com/story /life/movies/2013/01/25/hansel-and-gretel-review/1864211/Usatoday.com.

24. Greg Gilman, "Paramount Planning 'Hansel & Gretel: Witch Hunters' sequel, http:// movies.yahoo .com/news/paramount-planning-hansel-gretel-witch-hunters-sequel-003927815.html, Reuters, March 19, 2013.

Chapter Three. Americanization of the Grimms' Folk and Fairy Tales: Twists and Turns of History

1. Simon Bronner, "The Americanization of the Brothers Grimm," *Following Tradition: Folklore in the Discourse of American Culture* (Logan: Utah State University Press, 1998): 236.

2. Erik Bergstrom, *Grimmer Tales: A Wicked Collection of Happily Never After Stories* (New York: Penguin, 2010).

3. *The Wonderful World of the Brothers Grimm* (1962), directed by Henry Levin and George Pal; *Once Upon a Brothers Grimm* (1977), directed by Norman Campbell; and *The Brothers Grimm* (2005), directed by Terry Gilliam.

4. See the excellent comprehensive article by Kendra Magnus-Johnston, "'Reeling In' Grimm Masculinities," *Marvels and Tales* 27.1 (2013): 65–88.

5. For the most thorough study of this process, see Bronner, "The Americanization of the Brothers Grimm," in *Following Tradition*.

6. See Wayland Hand, "Die Märchen der Brüder Grimm in den Vereinigten Staaten," in Ludwig Denecke and Ina-Maria Greverus, eds., *Brüder Grimm Gedenken*, vol. 1 (Marburg: N. G. Elwert, 1963): 525–44; Simon Bronner, "The Americanization of the Brothers Grimm," in *Following Tradition*, 184–236; and William Bernard McCarthy, ed. *Cinderella in America* (Jackson: University of Mississippi Press, 2007).

7. Bronner, 186–87.

8. Ibid., 236.

9. See Henry Pochmann, *German Culture in America: Philosophical and Literary Influences, 1600–1900* (Madison: University of Wisconsin Press, 1957).

10. McCarthy, *Cinderella in America*, 8.

11. Ibid., 15.

12. Orrin Robinson, *Grimm Language: Grammar, Gender and Genuiness in the Fairy Tales* (Amsterdam: John Benjamins, 2010): 32.

13. Thomas Frederick Crane, "The External History of the *Kinder- und Hausmärchen* of the Brothers Grimm: I," *Modern Philology* 14.10 (February 1910): 599.

14. Horace E. Scudder, *Fables and Folk Stories* (Boston: Houghton Mifflin, 1906): vii–viii.

15. See David Blamires, "The Early Reception of the Grimms' *Kinder- und Hausmärchen* in England," *Bulletin of the John Rylands University Library of Manchester* 71.3 (1989): 69–77; and M. O. Grenby, "Tame Fairies Make Good Teachers: The Popularity of Early British Films," *The Lion and the Unicorn* 30 (2006): 1–24.

16. See Andrea Immel, "Tabart, Benjamin," in Jack Zipes, ed., *The Oxford Encyclopedia of Children's Literature*, vol. 4 (Oxford, UK: Oxford University Press, 2006): 69; and Matthew Grenby, "Tame Fairies Make Good Teachers: The Popularity of Early British Fairy Tales," *The Lion and the Unicorn* 30 (2006): 1–24.

17. See G. Richard, *Contes Bleus et Roses pour l'amusement des grands et des petits enfants* (Paris: Librairie du Petit Journal, 1865).

18. Martin Sutton, *The Sin-Complex: A Critical Study of English Versions of the Grimms' Kinder- und Hausmärchen in the Nineteenth Century* (Kassel: Schriften der Brüder Grimm-Gesellschaft, 1996). For a discussion of the Margaret Hunt translation, see pp. 261–304.

19. Laura Kready, *A Study of Fairy Tales* (Boston: Houghton Mifflin, 1916): viii–ix.

20. *Grimm's Fairy Tales*, trans. Margaret Hunt, illustr. John Gruelle (New York: Cupples and Leon, 1914).

21. The trend to adapting "Cinderella" for the cinema began even earlier in America, as Kristian Moen points out in his important study, *Film and Fairy Tales: The Birth of Modern Fantasy* (London: I. B. Tauris, 2013): 115: "Along with numerous versions in other media and the prominence of the general narrative arc, several film versions of 'Cinderella' had appeared in the early 1910s, making it one of the most frequently adapted film subjects of the time."

22. See Anthony Manna. "The Americanization of the Brothers Grimm: Or, Tom Davenport's Film Adaptation of German Folktales," *Children's Literature Association Quarterly* 13 (1998): 142–45; and Elizabeth Rose Gruner, "Saving 'Cinderella': History and Story in *Ashpet* and *Ever After*," *Children's Literature* 31 (2003): 142–54.

23. See Thomas Frederick Crane, "The Diffusion of Popular Tales," *Journal of American Folk-Lore*, 1 (1888): 8–15; and "The External History of the *Kinder- und Hausmärchen* of the Brothers Grimm," *Modern Philology* 14.10 (1917): 577–610; 15.2 (June 1917): 65–77; and 15.6 (October 1917): 355–83.

24. David Singh Grewal, *Network Power: The Social Dynamics of Globalization* (New Haven, CT: Yale University Press, 2008): 3.

Chapter Four. Two Hundred Years after Once Upon a Time: The Legacy of the Brothers Grimm and Their Tales in Germany

Expanded from "Two Hundred Years after Once Upon a Time: The Legacy of the Brothers Grimm and Their Tales in Germany," by Jack Zipes. *Marvels & Tales: Journal of Fairy-Tale Studies*, Volume 28, Number 1 (Spring 2014). Copyright © 2014 Wayne State University Press. Used with permission of Wayne State University Press.

1. Aleida Assmann, *Cultural Memory and Western Civilization: Functions, Media, Archives* (Cambridge, UK: Cambridge University Press, 2011): 22
2. Jeffrey Peck, "'In the Beginning Was the Word': Germany and the Origins of German Studies," in R. Howard Bloch and Stephen Nichols, eds., *Medievalism and the Modernist Temper* (Baltimore, MD: Johns Hopkins University Press, 1996): 129.
3. See Ludwig Denecke and Ina-Maria Greverus, eds., *Brüder Grimm Gedenken: 1963* (Marburg: N. G. Elwert, 1963); and Donald Haase, ed. *The Reception of Grimms' Fairy Tales: Reponses, Reactions, Revisions* (Detroit: Wayne State University Press, 1993).
4. Julia Franke and Harm-Peer Zimmermann, eds. *Grimmskrams & Märchendising.* (Marburg: Panama Verlag, 2008).
5. Harm-Peer Zimmermann, "Grimm in Massen," in Julia Franke and Harm-Peer Zimmermann, eds., *Grimmskrams & Märchendising* (Berlin: Panama Verlag, 2009): 16.
6. Klaus Kaindl and Berthold Friemel, *Die Brüder Grimm in Berlin* (Stuttgart: Hirzel Verlag, 2004).
7. Harm-Peer Zimmermann, ed., *Zwischen Identität und Image: Die Popularität der Brüder Grimm in Hessen* (Marburg: Jonas Verlag, 2009).
8. Holger Ehrhardt, *Dorothea Viehmann* (Kassel: Euregio Verlag, 2012).
9. Andreas Hedwig, ed., *Die Brüder Grimm in Marburg* (Marburg: Schriften des Hessischen Staatsarchivs, 2013).
10. Thorsten Smidt, ed., *Expedition Grimm* (Leipzig: Sandstein Verlag, 2013).
11. See Ulrike Marquardt and Heinz Rölleke, eds., *Kinder- und Hausmärchen gesammelt durch die Brüder Grimm* [1812/1815, Erstausgabe], 2 vols. (Göttingen: Vandenhoeck & Ruprecht, 1986); Hans-Jörg Uther, *Kinder- und Hausmärchen gesammelt durch die Brüder Grimm* [1819, zweite Ausgabe], 2 vols. (Cologne: Diederichs, 1982); Heinz Rölleke, ed., *Kinder- und Hausmärchen gesammelt durch die Brüder Grimm* [1837, dritte Aufgabe] (Frankfurt am Main: Deutscher Klassiker Verlag, 1985); Heinz Rölleke, ed., *Kinder- und Hausmärchen gesammelt durch die Brüder Grimm letzter Hand mit Originalenanmerkungen* [1857, siebte Ausgabe], 3 vols. (Stuttgart: Reclam, 1980); Hans-Jörg Uther, ed., *Kinder- und Hausmärchen. Nach der Großen Ausgabe von 1857, textkritisch revidiert, kommentiert und durch Register erschlossen*, 7th ed. (Darmstadt: Wissenschaftliche Buchgesellschaft, 1996).
12. See Heinz Rölleke, ed., *Märchen aus dem Nachlaß der Brüder Grimm*, 3rd rev. ed. (Bonn: Bouvier, 1983); *Grimms Märchen wie sie nicht im Buche stehen* (Frankfurt am Main: Insel, 1993); *Die wahren Märchen der Brüder Grimm* (Frankfurt am Main: Fischer Taschenbuch Verlag, 1995).
13. Dagmar Kammerer, illustr., *Mein großes Märchenbuch* (Cologne: Schwager und Steinlein, 2009).
14. Claudia Blei-Hoch, *Das große Märchen Bilderbuch der Brüder Grimm* (Stuttgart: Thienemann, 2006).
15. Rotraut Susanne Berner, *Märchen-Stunde* (Weinheim: Beltz & Gelberg, 1998), and *Märchen-Comics* (Berlin: Jacoby & Stuart, 2008).
16. Armin Abmeier and Rotraut Susanne Berner, *Grimmige Märchen: 13 kurze Märchen aus der Sammlung der Brüder Grimm* (Augsburg: Maro Verlag, 1999).
17. Linda Knoch, *Praxisbuch Märchen: Verstehen-Deuten-Umsetzen* (Gütersloh: Gütersloher Verlagshaus, 2001); Cordula and Reinhold Pertler, *Kinder in der Märchenwerkstatt: Kreative Spiel- und*

Projektideen (Munich: Don Bosco Medien, 2009); and Ute Hoffmann, *Die kreative Märchen-Werkstatt* (Hamburg: Persen im Aap Lehererfachverlag, 2010).

18. Nikolaus Heidelbach, *Märchen der Brüder Grimm* (Weinheim: Beltz & Gelberg, 1995).

19. Nikolaus Heidelbach, *Hans Christian Andersens Märchen* (Weinheim: Beltz & Gelberg, 2004), and *Märchen aus aller Welt* (Weinheim: Beltz & Gelberg, 2010).

20. Susanne Janssen, *Rotkäppchen* (Rostock: Hintsorff, 2007), and *Hänsel und Gretel* (Rostock: Hintsorff, 2009).

21. Květa Pacovská, *Rotkäppchen* (Bargtheide: Michael Neugebauer Edition, 2007), and *Hänsel und Gretel* (Bartgheide: Michael Neugebauer Edition, 2007).

22. Ulrike Persch, *Rotkäppchens List* (Bad Soden: Kinderbuchverlag Wolff, 2005).

23. Peter Hellinger, *Wenn das die Grimms wüssten! Neue Märchen zum Grimm-Jahr 2012* (Nürnberg:Art & Words, 2012).

24. See Mart Klein, *Rotkäppchen* (Mainz: Unfug-Verlag, 2009).

25. Theodor Ruf, *Die Schöne aus dem Glassarg: Schneewittchens märchenhaftes und wirkliches Leben* (Würzburg: Königshausen und Neumann, 1995); and Anna Kühne, *Der goldene Mörser* (Frankfurt am Main: Fouqué Literaturverlag, 2000; rev. ed., Berlin: Jutribog Verlag, 2008).

26. René Hemmerling, *Total versaute Märchen: Die Brüder Grimm finden das schlimm* (Norderstedt: Books on Demand, 2006); and René Hemmerling and Sebastian Grosser, *Das Semi-Comic-Märchenbuch*, vol. 1 (Nordstedt: Books on Demand, 2007).

27. Cornelia Funke, *Reckless*, trans. Oliver Latsch (Boston: Little, Brown, 2010); published in German as *Reckless. Steineres Fleisch* (Fearless: Stony Flesh) (Hamburg: Cecilia Dressler Verlag, 2010). Funke, *Fearless*, trans. Oliver Latsch (Boston: Little Brown, 2012); published in German as *Fearless: Lebendige Schatten* (Fearless: Live Shadows) (Hamburg: Cecilia Dressler Verlag, 2012).

28. Karen Duve, *Grrrimm* (Berlin: Galiani, 2012).

29. Florian Weber, *Grimms Erben* (Berlin: Metrolit Verlag, 2012).

30. See Freund, "Cornelia Funke knöft sich reaktionäre Märchen vor," *Die Welt* (September 18, 2010), http://www.welt.de/kultur/article9613379/Cornelia-Funke-knoepft-sich reaktionaere-Maerchen-vor. Accessed May 14, 2013.

31. *Grimms Erben*, 411.

32. Sebastian Heiduschke, "GDR Cinema as Commodity: Marketing DEFA Films since Unification," *German Studies Review* 36.1 (2013): 65.

33. See Quinna Shen, "Barometers of GDR Cultural Politics: Contextualizing the DEFA Grimm Adaptations," *Marvels & Tales* 25.1 (2011): 70–95; and Jack Zipes, "Between Slave Language and Utopian Optimism: Neglected Fairy-Tale Films of Central and Eastern Europe," in *The Enchanted Screen: The Unknown History of Fairy-Tale Films* (New York: Routledge, 2011): 321–48.

34. Daniel Drascek, "'SimsalaGrimm': Zur Adaption und Modernisierung der Märchenwelt," *Schweizerisches Archiv für Volkskunde* 97 (2001): 79–89.

35. Kurt Franz and Walter Kahn, eds., *Märchen—Kinder—Medien:Beiträge zur medialen Adaptation von Märchen und zum didaktischen Umgang* (Hohengehren: Schneider, 2000). See also the book review by Emer O'Sullivan in *Perspicuitas. Internet-Periodicum für mediävistische Sprach-, Literatur-und Kulturwissenschaft*, http://www.perspicuitas.uni-essen.de.

36. Steffen Martus, *Die Brüder Grimm: Eine Biografie* (Berlin: Rowohlt, 2009).

37. Günter Grass, *Grimms Wörter: Eine Liebeserklärung* (Göttingen: Steidl, 2010).

38. Günter Grass, "Spiegel Interview with Günter Grass: 'The Nobel Prize Doesn't Inhibit Me in My Writing,'" (August 20, 2010). Interview conducted by Volker Hage and Katja Thimm, http://www.spiegel.de/international/zeitgeist/spiegel-interview-with-guenter-grass-the-nobel-prize-doesn-t-inhibit-me-in-my writing-a-712715.html. Accessed July 2, 2013.

39. Heinz Rölleke, ed., *Die älteste Märchensammlung der Brüder Grimm. Synopse der handschriftlichen Urfassung von 1810 und der Erstdrucke von 1812* (Cologny-Geneva: Fondation Martin Bodmer, 1975).

40. See Heinz Rölleke, ed., *Märchen aus dem Nachlaß der Brüder Grimm*, 3rd rev.ed. (Bonn: Bouvier, 1983); *Die Märchen der Brüder Grimm* (Munich: Artemis, 1985); *"Wo das Wünschen noch geholfen*

hat." *Gesammelte Aufsätze zu den "Kinder- und Hausmärchen" der Brüder Grimm* (Bonn: Bouvier, 1985); *Die Märchen der Brüder Grimm: Quellen und Studien* (Trier: Wissenschaftlicher Verlag Trier, 2000); and *Die Märchen der Brüder Grimm: Eine Einführung* (Stuttgart: Philipp Reclam, 2004).

41. Heinz Rölleke, ed., *Es war einmal . . . Die wahren Märchen der Brüder Grimm und wer sie ihnen erzählte*, illustr. Albert Schindehütte (Frankfurt am Main: Eichorn, 2011).

42. Hans-Jörg Uther, *Handbuch zu den "Kinder- und Hausmärchen der Brüder Grimm: Entstehung— Wirkung—Interpretation* (Berlin: Walter de Gruyter, 2008).

43. Jens Sennewald, *Das Buch, das Wir Sind: Zur Poetik der "Kinder- und Hausmärchen, gesammelt durch die Brüder Grimm*" (Würzbrug: Königshausen & Neumann, 2004).

44. Donald Haase, "Framing the Brothers Grimm: Paratexts and Intercultural Transmission in Postwar English-Language Editions of the *Kinder- und Hausmärchen*," *Fabula* 44.1/2 (2003): 59.

Chapter Five. How Superheroes Made Their Way into the World of Fairy Tales: The Appeal of Cooperation and Collective Action from the Greek Myths to the Grimms' Tales and Beyond

1. Graham Anderson, *Greek and Roman Folklore: A Handbook* (Westport, CT: Greenwood Press, 2006): 68.

2. Susan Ballard, ed. and trans., *Fairy Tales from Far Japan* (London: The Religious Tract Society, 1899): 50.

3. For an informative historical account of the tale, see Klaus Antoni, "Momotarō (The Peach Boy) and the Spirit of Japan: Concerning the Function of a Fairy Tale in Japanese Nationalism of the Early Shōwa Age," *Asian Folklore Studies* 50.1 (1991): 155–88.

4. See Arthur Ransome. *The Fool of the World and the Flying Ship*, illustr. Uri Shukevitz (New York: Farrar, Straus and Giroux, 1968); and Valeri Gorbachev, *The Fool of the World and the Flying Ship: A Ukrainian Folk Tale*, illustr. Valeri Gorbachev (New York: Starbright Books, 1998). See also the remarkable film, *The Fool of the World and the Flying Ship* (1989), directed by Francis Vose, written by John Hambley, and produced by Chris Taylor. The film was narrated by David Suchet.

5. For some of the more interesting books for young readers, see *Sechse kommen durch die ganze Welt: Ein Märchen der Gebrüder Grimm*, illustr. Jürg Obrist (Zurich: Schweizerische Bibliothek für die Blinden, 1960); Arthur Ransome, *The Fool of the World and the Flying Ship*, illustr. Uri Shu-levitz (New York: Farrar, Straus, and Giroux, 1968); Pat O'Shea, *Finn MacCool and the Small Men of Deeds*, illustr. Stephen Lavis (New York: Holiday House, 1987); and Valeri Gorbachev, *The Fool of the World: A Ukrainian Folk Tale*, illustr. Valeri Lavis (Long Island City, NY: Star Bright Books, 1998).

6. Jacob and Wilhelm Grimm. *The Complete Fairy Tales of the Brothers Grimm*, ed. and trans. Jack Zipes, illustr. John B. Gruelle, 3rd rev. ed. (New York: Bantam, 2003): 253.

7. Hans-Jörg Uther, *Handbuch zu den "Kinder- und Hausmärchen der Brüder Grimm: Entstehung— Wirkung—Interpretation* (Berlin: Walter de Gruyter, 2008): 169–71.

8. Heinz Rölleke, ed., *Es war einmal . . . Die wahren Märchen der Brüder Grimm und wer sie ihnen erzählte*, illustr. Albert Schindehütte (Frankfurt am Main: Eichorn, 2011): 115–52.

9. Jack Zipes, *The Brothers Grimm: From Enchanted Forests to the Modern World*, 2nd rev. ed. (New York: Palgrave, 2002): 80–84.

10. See the modern edition Johann Wilhelm Wolf, *Verschollene Märchen* (Nordlingen: Franz Greno, 1988), first published as *Deutsche Hausmärchen* (Göttingen: Dieterich'sche Buchhandlung, 1851).

11. Graham Anderson, *Fairytale in the Ancient World* (London: Routledge, 2000): 72.

12. Apollonius of Rhodes, *Jason and the Golden Fleece*, ed. and trans. Richard Hunter (Oxford, UK: Oxford University Press, 1993): xxviii.

13. Ibid., xxix.

14. See Giovanni Sercambi, *Novelle*, vol. 1, ed. Giovanni Sinicropi (Bari: Laterza, 1972): 195–210.
15. See the appendix for the translation of this tale.
16. Giambattista Basile, *The Tale of Tales, or Entertainment for Little Ones*, ed. and trans. Nancy Canepa, illustr. Carmelo Lettere (Detroit: Wayne State University Press, 2007): 267.
17. Ibid., 271.
18. Peter Christen Asbjørnsen, *Fairy Tales from the Far North*, trans. H. L. Bræstad (London: D. Nutt, 1897): 148.
19. Michael Tomasello, *Why We Cooperate* (Cambridge, MA: MIT Press, 2008): xv–xvi.
20. Michael Tomasello, *The Cultural Origins of Human Cognition* (Cambridge, MA: Harvard University Press, 1999).
21. *Why We Cooperate*, 13.
22. Ibid., 43–44.
23. Richard Sennett, *Together: The Rituals, Pleasures and Politics of Cooperation* (New Haven, CT: Yale University Press, 2012): ix.
24. See Terry Eagleton, "On Meaning Well," book review of Richard Sennett's *Together*, in *Times Literary Supplement* (April 20, 1012): 8–9.
25. Edward O. Wilson also emphasizes the significance of cooperation in his book, *The Social Conquest of Earth* (New York: Norton, 2012).
26. Christopher Boehm, *Moral Origins: The Evolution of Virtue, Altruism, and Shame* (New York: Basic Books, 2012): 9.
27. Ibid., 352.
28. Mark Pagel, *Wired for Culture: The Natural History of Human Cooperation* (London: Penguin, 2012): 21
29. Ibid., 280.

Chapter Six. The Grimmness of Contemporary Fairy Tales: Exploring the Legacy of the Brothers Grimm in the Twenty-First Century

1. Heinz Rölleke, "Ein literarischer Welterfolg: Grimms *Kinder- und Hausmärchen*," in *Expedition Grimm*, ed. Thorsten Smidt (Kassel: Sandstein Verlag, 2013): 75.
2. See *Deutsches Wörterbuch von Jacob und Wilhelm Grimm*, eds. Arthur Hübner and Hans Neumann, vol. 4 (Leipzig: S. Hirzel, 1937): 340–63.
3. Jens Sennewald, *Das Buch, das Wir Sind: Zur Poetik der "Kinder- und Hausmärchen, gesammelt durch die Brüder Grimm"* (Würzbrug: Königshausen & Neumann, 2004).
4. Ana María Shua, *Quick Fix: Sudden Fiction*, trans. Rhonda Dahl Buchanan, illustr. Luci Mistratov (Buffalo, NY: White Pine Press, 2008): 164.
5. Margo Lanagan, *Tender Morsels*. (New York: Alfred Knopf, 2008): 6.
6. See Heinz Rölleke, *Es war einmal . . . Die wahren Märchen der Brüder Grimm und wer sie ihnen erzählte*, illustr. Albert Schindhütte (Frankfurt am Main: Eichborn, 2011): 347–51. In *Clever Maids: The Secret History of the Grimm Fairy Tales* (New York: Basic Books, 2005), Paradiž, too, suggests that Wilhelm married Dortchen for her merits as caregiver and house cleaner. "Wilhelm Grimm witnessed Dortchen's sacrifice for her family with respect and admiration. Her ability to keep her equilibrium in the face of extreme hardship resonated deeply with the Grimms' own familial values" (114).
7. Tom McNeal, *far far away* (New York: Alfred Knopf, 2013): 9.
8. Ibid., 112.
9. John Connolly, *The Book of Lost Things* (New York: Atria Books, 2006): 10.
10. Ibid., 543–44.
11. Catherynne Valente, *Six-Gun Snow White* (Burton, MI: Subterranean Press, 2013): 41.

12. Ibid., 41–42.
13. Ibid., 42.
14. Ibid., 43.
15. Ibid., 164.
16. Liz Hoggard, "Helen Oyeyemi: 'I'm Interested in the Way Women Disappoint One Another,'" interview in the Saturday edition of *The Guardian/Observer*, March 1, 2014. http://www.the guardian.com/books/2014/mar/02/helen-oyeyemi-women-disappoint-one-another.
17. Carolyn Turgeon, "A Conversation with Carolyn Turgeon," *The Fairest of Them All* (New York: Simon and Schuster, 2013): unpaginated at the end of the book.
18. Adam Gidwitz, *A Tale Dark & Grimm* (New York: Dutton, 2010): 2.
19. Ibid., 3.
20. Adam Gidwitz, *In a Glass Grimmly* (New York: Dutton, 2012): 316.
21. Adam Gidwitz, *The Grimm Conclusion* (New York: Dutton, 2013): 341.
22. Alice Miller, *The Body Never Lies: The Lingering Effects of Cruel Parenting*, trans. Andrew Jenkins (New York: W. W. Norton, 2005).
23. Rikki Ducornet, *The Complete Butcher's Tales* (Normal, IL: Dalkey Archive Press, 1994): 139.
24. Sara Maitland, *Far North and Other Dark Tales* (London: Maia Press, 2008).
25. Sara Maitland, *Gossip from the Forest: The Tangled Roots of Our Forests and Fairytales* (London: Granta, 2012). The American edition published in 2012 by Counterpoint in Berkeley, California, has a different title: *From the Forest: A Search for the Hidden Roots of Our Fairy Tales*. I am not certain why Maitland made this change, but I prefer the original title.
26. Ibid., 100–101.
27. Eva Figes, *Tales of Innocence and Experience: An Exploration* (London: Bloomsbury, 2003): 182.
28. Jeanne Marie Beaumont and Claudia Carlson, *The Poets' Grimm: 20th Century Poems from Grimm Fairy Tales* (Ashland, OR: Story Line Press, 2003): 258–59.
29. Ibid., 260.
30. Ibid., 260.
31. Ron Koertge, *Lies, Knives, and Girls in Red Dresses*, illustr. Andrea Deszö (Somerville, MA: Candle-wick Press, 2012): i.
32. Ibid., 33.
33. Ibid., 54.
34. Jane Yolen, *The Last Selchie Child* (New York: A Midsummer Night's Press, 2012): 9.
35. Lawrence Schimmel, *Fairy Tales for Writers* (New York: A Midsummer Night's Press, 2007): 8.
36. Cornelia Hoogland, *Woods Wolf Girl* (Hamilton, Ontario: Wolsak and Wynn, 2011): 7.
37. Ibid., 76.
38. Ava Leavell Haymon, *Why the House Is Made of Gingerbread* (Baton Rouge: Louisiana State University Press, 2010): 52.

Epilogue. A Curious Legacy: Ernst Bloch's Enlightened View of the Fairy Tale and Utopian Longing, or Why the Grimms' Tales Will Always Be Relevant

1. "The Fairy Tale Moves on Its Own Time," in Ernst Bloch, *The Utopian Function of Art and Literature: Selected Essays*, trans. Jack Zipes and Frank Mecklenburg (Cambridge, MA: MIT Press, 1988): 163.
2. Bloch is famous for his three-volume work, *Das Prinzip Hoffnung* (Berlin: Aufbau-Verlag, 1954–59); *The Principle of Hope*, trans. Neville Plaice, Stephen Plaice, and Paul Knight (Cambridge, MA: MIT Press, 1986). Among Adorno's notable works are *Dialektik der Aufklärung*, written with Max Horkheimer (Amsterdam: Querido, 1947); *Dialectic of Enlightenment*, trans. John Cumming (New York: Herder and Herder, 1972); *Negative Dialektik* (Frankfurt am Main: Suhrkamp, 1966);

Negative Dialectics, trans. E. B. Ashton (New York: Seabury, 1966); *Ästhetische Theorie*, ed. Gretel Adorno and Rolf Tiedemann (Frankfurt am Main: Suhrkamp, 1970); *Aesthetic Theory*, ed. Gretel Adorno and Rolf Tiedemann, trans. Robert Hubert-Kentor (Minneapolis: University of Minnesota Press, 1997)

3. For an excellent collection of Adorno's various essays on the culture industry, see Theodor Adorno, *The Culture Industry*, ed. J. M. Bernstein (London: Routledge, 1991).

4. Actually, Adorno is mistaken about the incidents in this tale. He is referring to Charles Perrault's "The Foolish Wishes" ("Les souhaits ridicules," 1694), in which a poor woodcutter is given three wishes by Jupiter. He stupidly wastes the first one by wishing for a sausage. After his wife berates him, he wishes for a sausage on her nose. Finally, as his third wish, he asks that the sausage be removed from his wife's nose.

5. "Something's Missing: A Discussion between Ernst Bloch and Theodor W. Adorno on the Contradictions of Utopian Longing (1964)," in Ernst Bloch, *The Utopian Function of Art and Literature: Selected Essays*, trans. Jack Zipes and Frank Mecklenburg (Cambridge, MA: MIT Press, 1988): 1–2. See "Etwas fehlt . . . Über die Widersprüche der utopischen Sehnsucht. Ein Gespräch mit Theodor W. Adorno (1964)," in *Gespräche mit Ernst Bloch*, eds. Rainer Traub and Harald Wieser (Frankfurt am Main: Suhrkamp, 1975): 58–59.

6. Ibid., 5.

7. Ibid., 16.

8. Ibid, 16–17.

9. Bloch, "The Fairy Tale Moves on Its Own in Time," 163.

10. Ibid., 165–66.

11. Ibid., 168–69.

12. Ibid., 169.

13. Ibid., 182.

14. Ibid., 183.

15. Ibid., 184.

16. Louis Marin, *Utopics: Spatial Play*, trans. Robert A. Vollrath (Atlantic Highlands, NJ: Humanities Press, 1984). See especially, "Utopic Degeneration: Disneyland," 239–258.

17. Ibid., 12.

18. Ibid., 15.

BIBLIOGRAPHY

Texts

All texts are listed in chronological order by date of original publication, unless noted otherwise.

Jacob and Wilhelm Grimm Editions

ÖLENBERG MANUSCRIPT

Lefftz, Joseph, ed. *Märchen der Brüder Grimm. Urfassung nach der Originalhandschrift der Abtei Ölenberg im Elsaß*. Heidelberg: C. Winter, 1927.

Rölleke, Heinz, ed. *Die älteste Märchensammlung der Brüder Grimm. Synopse der handschriftlichen Urfassung von 1810 und der Erstdrucke von 1812*. Cologny-Geneva: Fondation Martin Bodmer, 1975.

Derungs, Kurt, ed. *Die ursprünglichen Märchen der Brüder Grimm: Handschriften, Urfassung und Texte zur Kulturgeschichte*. Bern: Edition Amalia, 1999.

LARGE EDITION

Grimm, Jacob and Wilhelm. *Kinder- und Hausmärchen der Brüder Grimm: Vollständige Ausgabe in der Urfassung*. Wiesbaden: Emil Vollmer, 1955.

———. *Kinder- und Hausmärchen gesammelt durch die Brüder Grimm* [1812/1815, Erstausgabe]. Ed. Ulrike Marquardt and Heinz Rölleke. 2 vols. Göttingen: Vandenhoeck & Ruprecht, 1986.

———. *Kinder- und Hausmärchen der Gebrüder Grimm: Erstdruckfassung 1812–1815*. Frankfurt am Main: Dietmar Klotz, 1997.

———. *Kinder- und Hausmärchen gesammelt durch die Brüder Grimm* [1819, zweite Ausgabe]. Ed. Hans-Jörg Uther. 2 vols. Cologne: Diederichs, 1982.

———. *Kinder- und Hausmärchen gesammelt durch die Brüder Grimm* [1837, dritte Aufgabe]. Ed. Heinz Rölleke. Frankfurt am Main: Deutscher Klassiker Verlag, 1985.

———. *Kinder- und Hausmärchen gesammelt durch die Brüder Grimm* [vierte Ausgabe]. 2 vols. Göttingen: Verlag der Dieterichschen Buchhandlung, 1840.

———. *Kinder- und Hausmärchen gesammelt durch die Brüder Grimm* [fünfte Ausgabe]. 2 vols. Göttingen: Verlag der Dieterichschen Buchhandlung, 1843.

———. *Kinder- und Hausmärchen gesammelt durch die Brüder Grimm* [sechste Ausgabe]. 2 vols. Göttingen: Verlag der Dieterichschen Buchhandlung, 1850.

————. *Kinder- und Hausmärchen gesammelt durch die Brüder Grimm letzter Hand mit Originalenanmerkungen* [1857, siebte Ausgabe]. Ed. Heinz Rölleke. 3 vols. Stuttgart: Reclam, 1980.

————. *Kinder- und Hausmärchen. Nach der Großen Ausgabe von 1857, textkritischrevidiert, kommentiert und durch Register erschlossen.* Ed. Hans-Jörg Uther. 7th ed. Darmstadt: Wissenschaftliche Buchgesellschaft, 1996.

SMALL EDITION

Grimm, Jacob and Wilhelm. *Grimms Märchen: Die kleine Ausgabe aus dem Jahr 1825.* Ed. Hermann Gerstner. Dortmund: Harenberg, 1982.

————. *Kinder- und Hausmärchen gesammelt durch die Brüder Grimm* [Kleine Ausgabe, 1825]. Ed. Peter Rühmkorf. Zurich: Haffmans Verlag bei Zweitausendeins, 2007.

————. *Kinder- und Hausmärchen gesammelt durch die Brüder Grimm: Kleine Ausgabe von 1858.* Ed. Heinz Rölleke. Illustr. Ludwig Pietsch. Frankfurt am Main: Insel, 1985.

Tales from the Posthumous Papers, Notes, and Early Editions of the Brothers Grimm

Stapel, Wilhelm, ed. *Fünfundfünfzig vergessene Grimmsche Märchen.* Hamburg: Hanseatische Verlagsanstalt, 1922.

Michaelis-Jena, Ruth, and Arthur Ratcliff, eds. *Grimms' Other Tales: A New Selection.* Illustr. Gwenda Morgan. London: Cockerel Press, 1956.

Rölleke, Heinz, ed. *Märchen aus dem Nachlaß der Brüder Grimm.* 3rd rev. ed. Bonn: Bouvier, 1983.

————. *Grimms Märchen wie sie nicht im Buche stehen.* Frankfurt am Main: Insel, 1993.

————. *Die wahren Märchen der Brüder Grimm.* Frankfurt am Main: Fischer Taschenbuch Verlag, 1995.

Schindehütte, Albert, ed. *Krauses Grimm'sche Märchen.* Kassel: Johannes Stauda Verlag, 1985.

————. *Die Grimm'schen Märchen der jungen Marie.* Marburg: Hitzeroth, 1991.

Edgar Taylor Editions

GERMAN POPULAR STORIES

Taylor, Edgar. *German Popular Stories. Translated from the Kinder und Haus Marchen, collected by M.M. Grimm, from Oral Tradition.* London: C. Baldwyn, 1823.

————. *German Popular Stories. Translated from the Kinder und Haus Marchen, collected by M.M. Grimm, from Oral Tradition.* London: James Robins & Co., 1825.

———. *German Popular Stories. With Illustrations, after the original designs of George Cruikshank.* Ed. Edgar Taylor. A New Edition, with Introduction by John Ruskin, M.A. London: John Camden Hotten, 1869.

———. *Grimms' Fairy Tales. With Twenty-one Illustrations by George Cruikshank.* London: Puffin Books, 1948. (Reissued 1971.)

———. *German Popular Stories.* Ed. Jack Zipes. Maidstone, Kent, UK: Crescent Moon Publishing, 2012. A reprint of the 1869 edition with John Ruskin's introduction, Sir Walter Scott's letter, and Edgar Taylor's correspondence with the Brothers Grimm.

GAMMER GRETHEL

Taylor, Edgar. *Gammer Grethel or German Fairy Tales, and Popular Stories.* From the collection of MM. Grimm, and other sources; with illustrative notes. London: John Green, 1839.

———. *Gammer Grethel; or, German Fairy Tales and Popular Stories.* From the collection of MM. Grimm, and other sources. Ed. Mrs. Follen. Boston: J. Munroe & Co., 1840.

———. *German Fairy Tales and Popular Stories as Told by Gammer Grethel.* Translated from the Collection of M.M. Grimm, by Edgar Taylor. With illustrations from designs by George Cruikshank and Ludwig Grimm. London: Joseph Cundall, 1846.

———. *Gammer Grethel's Fairy Tales.* Illustrated by George Cruikshank and others with an introduction by Laurence Housman. London: Alexander Moring, 1905.

John Edward Taylor Editions

The Fairy Ring: A New Collection of Popular Tales. Translated from the German of Jacob and Wilhelm Grimm with twelve illustrations by Richard Doyle. London: John Murray, 1846.

Stray Leaves from Fairy Land, for Boys and Girls. New Translation from the German of Jacob and Wilhelm Grimm, by J. Edward Taylor. 5th ed. Philadelphia: G. Collins, 1855.

Other Editions of Complete Tales of the Brothers Grimm

Paull, Mrs. H. B. *Grimms' Fairy Tales.* Illustr. W. J. Weigand. London: Frederick Warne, and New York: Scribner, Welford and Armstrong, 1872.

Crane, Lucy, trans. *Household Stories from the Collection of the Bros. Grimm.* Illustr. Walter Crane. London: Macmillan, 1882.

Hunt, Margaret, ed. and trans. *Grimm's Household Tales.* Intro. Andrew Lang. 2 vols. London: George Bell and Sons, 1884.

Magoun, Francis, and Alexander Krappe, eds. and trans. *The Grimms' German Folk Tales.* Carbondale: Southern Illinois University Press, 1960.

Manheim, Ralph, trans. *Grimms Tales for Young and Old: The Complete Stories*. London: Victor Gollancz, 1978.

Zipes, Jack, ed. and trans. *The Complete Fairy Tales of the Brothers Grimm* [1988]. 3rd rev. and enlarged ed. New York: Bantam, 2003.

Folk and Fairy Tales (in alphabetical order)

Aal, Katharyn Machan. *Rapunzel, Rapunzel: Poems, Prose, and Photographs by Women on the Subject of Hair*. Ithaca, NY: McBooks Press, 1980.

Abmeier, Armin, and Rotraut Susanne Berner, eds. *Grimmige Märchen: 15 kurze Märchen aus der Sammlung der Brüder Grimm*. Augsburg: Maro Verlag, 1999.

Apollonius of Rhodes. *Jason and the Golden Fleece*. Ed. and trans. Richard Hunter. Oxford, UK: Oxford University Press, 1993.

Apollonius Rhodios. *The Agonautika: The Story of Jason and the Quest for the Golden Fleece*. Ed. and trans. Peter Green. Berkeley: University of California Press, 1997.

Asbjørnsen, Peter Christen. *Fairy Tales from the Far North*. Trans. H. L. Bræstad. London: D. Nutt, 1897.

Ash, Jutta. *Rapunzel*. New York: Holt, Rinehart, and Winston, 1982.

Atwood, Margaret. *The Robber Bride*. New York: Doubleday, 1993.

Bail, Murray. *Eucalyptus*. London: Harvill, 1998.

Basile, Giambattista. *The Tale of Tales, or Entertainment for Little Ones*. Ed. and trans. Nancy Canepa. Illustr. Carmelo Lettere. Detroit: Wayne State University Press, 2007.

Barthelme, Donald. *Forty Stories*. New York: Putnam, 1987, 92–97.

Beaumont, Jeanne Marie, and Claudia Carlson. *The Poets' Grimm: 20th Century Poems from Grimm Fairy Tales*. Ashland, OR: Story Line Press, 2003.

Bechstein, Ludwig. *Deutsches Märchenbuch*. Leipzig: Wigand, 1845.

——. *Ludwig Bechsteins Märchenbuch*. Leipzig: Wigand, 1853.

——. *Neues Deutsches Märchenbuch*. Vienna: Hartleben, 1856.

Beck, Ian. *Hansel and Gretl*. London: Doubleday, 1999.

Beckett, Sandra. *Revisioning Red Riding Hood around the World: An Anthology of International Retellings*. Detroit: Wayne State Univesity Press, 2014.

Bergstrom, Erik. *Grimmer Tales: A Wicked Collection of Happily Never After Stories*. New York: Penguin, 2010.

Bender, Aimee. *The Color Master*. New York: Doubleday, 2013.

Berner, Rotraut Susanne. *Märchen-Comics*. Berlin: Jacoby & Stuart. 2008.

——. *Märchen-Stunde*. Weinheim: Beltz & Gelberg, 1998.

Bernheimer, Kate. *The Complete Tales of Ketzia Gold*. Tallahassee: Florida State University Press, 2001.

——. *The Complete Tales of Merry Gold*. Tuscaloosa: University of Alabama Press, 2006.

——. *Horse, Flower, Bird*. Minneapolis: Coffee House, 2010.

———, ed. *My Mother She Killed Me, My Father He Ate Me: Forty New Fairy Tales.*
New York: Penguin, 2010.

Biro, Val. *Hansel and Gretel.* Oxford, UK: Oxford University Press, 1997.

Black, Holly. *The Poison Eaters and Other Stories.* New York: Margaret McElderry
Books, 2011.

Blackwell, Su, and Wendy Jones. *The Fairy-Tale Princess: Seven Classic Stories from
the Enchanted Forest.* London: Thames & Hudson, 2012.

Blakely-Cartwright, Sarah. *Red Riding Hood.* New York: Poppy, 2011.

Blei-Hoch, Claudia. *Das große Märchen Bilderbuch der Brüder Grimm.* Stuttgart:
Thienemann 2006.

Block, Francesca Lia. *Dangerous Angels: The Weetzie Bat Books.* New York: Harper-
Collins, 1998.

———. *Fairy Tales in Electri-City.* New York: A Midsummer Night's Press, 2011.

———. *I Was a Teenage Fairy.* New York: HarperCollins, 1998.

———. *The Rose and the Beast: Fairy Tales Retold.* New York: HarperCollins, 2000.

Border, Rosemary. *Hansel and Gretel.* Illustr. Maxun Tang. Oxford, UK: Oxford
University Press,1995.

Browne, Anthony. *Hansel and Gretel.* London: Julia MacRae, 1981.

———. *Into the Forest.* London: Walker Books, 2003.

Buckley, Michael. *The Sisters Grimm: The Fairy-Tale Detectives.* New York: Abrams,
2004.

———. *The Sisters Grimm: The Problem Child—Book #2.* New York: Abrams, 2005.

———. *The Sisters Grimm: The Usual Suspects—Book #3.* New York: Abrams, 2006.

Büsching, Johann Gustav, ed. *Volksagen, Märchen und Legenden* [1813].
Hildesheim: Georg Olms, 1969.

Busk, Rachel. *The Folk-Lore of Rome: Collected by Word of Mouth from the People.*
London: Longmans, Green, 1874.

Byatt, A. S. *Little Black Book of Stories.* London: Chatto and Windus, 2003.

Cadnum, Michael. *Can't Catch Me and Other Twice-Told Tales.* San Francisco:
Tachyon Publications, 2006.

Carter, Angela. *The Bloody Chamber and Other Stories.* New York: Penguin, 1979.

Child, Lauren. *Beware of the Storybook Wolves.* New York: Scholastic, 2000.

Claverie, Jean. *Le Petit Chaperon Rouge.* Paris: Albin Michel Jeunesse, 1997.

Colshorn, Carl and Theodor. *Märchen und Sagen aus Hannover.* Hannover: Carl
Rümpler, 1854.

Connolly, John. *The Book of Lost Things.* New York: Washington Square Press, 2006.

Coover, Robert. *Briar Rose.* New York: Grove Press, 1996.

———. *A Child Again.* San Francisco: McSweeney's Books, 2005.

———. *Hansel and Gretel: The Traditional Tale.* Ed. Alison Hedger. London: Golden
Apple Productions, 2000.

———. *Stepmother.* Illustr. Michael Kupperman. San Francisco: McSweeney's
Books, 2004.

———. "The Frog Prince." *New Yorker* (January 27, 2014): 62–63.

Coronedi-Berti, Carolina. *Favole Bolognesi*. Bologna: Forni, 1883.

———. *Novelle popolari bolognesi*. Bologna: Tipi Fava e Garagnani, 1873.

Cosquin, Emmanuel. *Contes populaires de Lorraine*. Paris: Vieweg, 1886.

———. *Contes populaires de Lorraine*. Ed. Nicole Belmont. Arles: Philippe Picquier, 2003.

———. *Les Contes populaires européens et leur origine*. Paris: C. Douniol, 1873.

Crane, Thomas Frederick, ed. *Italian Popular Tales*. Boston: Houghton, Mifflin & Co., 1885.

Croker, Thomas Croften. *Fairy Legends and Traditions of the South of Ireland*. 3 vols. London: J. Murray, 1825–28.

Csipkay, Nicolette. *Black Umbrella Stories*. Buffalo, NY: Starcherone Books, 2003.

Curtin, Jeremiah. *Myths and Folk-Lore of Ireland*. Boston: Little, Brown and Company, 1890.

———. *Myths and Folk Tales of the Russians, Western Slavs, and Magyars*. London: Sampson Low, Marston, Searle, and Livington, 1890.

Daily, Audry. *Hansel and Gretel: A Traditional Tale*. Illustr. Isabella Misso. London: Ladybird, 1999.

Datlow, Ellen, and Terri Windling, eds. *The Beastly Bride: Tales of the Animal People*. Illustr. Charles Vess. New York: Viking, 2010.

———. *Black Heart, Ivory Bones*. New York: Avon, 2000.

———. *Black Thorn, White Rose*. New York: Avon, 1993.

———. *Faery Reel: Tales from the Twilight Realm*. New York: Viking, 2004.

———. *Ruby Slippers, Golden Tears*. New York: Avon, 1995.

———. *Silver Birch, Blood Moon*. New York: Avon, 1999.

———. *Snow White, Blood Red*. New York: Avon, 1994.

———. *Swan Sister: Fairy Tales Retold*. New York: Simon & Schuster, 2003.

———. *Troll's Eye View: A Book of Villainous Tales*. New York: Viking, 2009.

———. *A Wolf at the Door and Other Retold Fairy Tales*. New York: Simon & Schuster, 2000.

Destefano, Merrie. *How to Draw Grimm's Dark Tales, Fables & Folklore*. Illustr. Rachel Marks. Irvine, CA: Walter Foster, 2013.

Doherty, Berlie. *Classic Fairy Tales*. Illustr. Jane Ray. Somerville, MA: Candlewick Press, 2000.

Dokey, Cameron. *Beauty Sleep: A Retelling of "Sleeping Beauty."* New York: Simon and Schuster, 2006.

———. *Before Midnight: A Retelling of "Cinderella."* New York: Simon and Schuster, 2007.

———. *Golden: A Retelling of "Rapunzel."* New York: Simon and Schuster, 2007.

Donoghue, Emma. *Kissing the Witch: Old Tales in New Skins*. New York: Harper-Collins, 1997.

Ducornet, Rikki. *The Complete Butcher's Tales*. Normal, IL: Dalkey Archive Press, 1994.

———. *The One Marvelous Thing*. Champaign, IL: Dalkey Archive Press, 2008.

Duffy, Carol Ann. *Grimm Tales*. Dramatized by Tim Supple. London: Faber & Faber, 1996.

———. *More Grimm Tales*. Dramatized by Tim Supple. London: Faber and Faber, 1997.

———. *Rumpelstiltskin and Other Grimm Tales*. Illustr. Markéta Prachatická. London: Faber and Faber, 1999.

———. *Stolen Childhood and Other Dark Fairy Tales*. Illustr. Jane Ray. London: Puffin, 2003.

Duffy, Chris, ed. *Fairy Tale Comics*. New York: Roaring Book Press, 2013.

Duve, Karen. *Die entführte Prinzessin*. Frankfurt am Main: Eichborn, 2005.

———. *Grrrimm*. Berlin: Galiani, 2012.

Eisner, Will. *The Princess and the Frog*. New York: Nantier, Beall, Minoustchine, 1999.

Fairy Tales from Grimm (Christmas Stocking Series). Intro. by L. Frank Baum. Chicago: Reilly & Britton, 1905.

Fairy Tales from the Brothers Grimm. Intro. by Cornelia Funke. Illustr. George Cruikshank. London: Puffin, 2012.

Figes, Eva. *Tales of Innocence and Experience: An Exploration*. London: Bloomsbury, 2003.

Flinn, Alex. *Beastly*. New York: HarperTeen, 2007.

———. *Cloaked*. New York: HarperTeen, 2011.

———. *A Kiss in Time*. New York: HarperTeen, 2009.

Forsyth, Kate. *The Wild Girl*. Sydney: Random House, 2013.

Fox, Cameron. *Hansel and Gretel*. Harlow: Pearson Education, 2000.

Frost, Gregory. *Fitcher's Brides*. New York: Tom Doherty, 2002.

Funke, Cornelia. *Fearless*. Trans. Oliver Latsch. Boston: Little Brown, 2012. Published in German as *Fearless: Lebendige Schatten* (Fearless: Live Shadows).

———. *Reckless*. Trans. Oliver Latsch. Boston: Little, Brown, 2010. Published in German as *Reckless. Steineres Fleisch* (Reckless: Stony Flesh) by Cecilia Dressler Verlag in Hamburg, 2010.

Gaarder, Jostein. *The Orange Girl*. Trans. James Anderson. London: Weidenfeld & Nicolson, 2003.

Gág, Wanda. *More Tales from Grimm*. New York: Coward-McCann, 1947.

———. *Snow White and the Seven Dwarfs*. New York: Coward-McCann, 1938.

———. *Tales from Grimm*. New York: Coward-McCann, 1936.

———. *Three Gay Tales*. New York: Coward-McCann, 1943.

Gaiman, Neil. "Snow, Glass, Apples" [1994]. In *Smoke and Mirrors: Short Fictions and Illusions*. New York: Avon, 1998, 325–39.

Galloway, Priscilla. *Truly Grim Tales*. New York: Bantam, 1995.

Garcia, Camille Rose. *Snow White by the Brothers Grimm*. New York: HarperCollins Publishers, 2012.

Gelberg, Hans-Joachim, ed. *Daumesdick. Neuer Märchenschatz mit vielen Bildern*. Weinheim: Beltz & Gelberg, 1990.

Gidwitz, Adam. *In a Glass Grimmly*. New York: Dutton, 2012.

———. *The Grimm Conclusion*. New York: Dutton, 2013.

———. *A Tale Dark & Grimm*. New York: Dutton, 2010.

Gonzenbach, Laura. *Sicilianische Märchen*. 2 vols. Leipzig: W. Engelmann, 1870.

Gorbachev, Valeri. *The Fool of the World and the Flying Ship: A Ukrainian Folk Tale*. Illustr. Valeri Gorbachev. New York: Starbright Books, 1998.

Gregory, Raven, Joe Brusha, and Ralph Tedesco. *Grimm Fairy Tales: The Dream Eater Saga*. Vols. I and II. Horsham, PA: Zenescope, 2011–12.

———. *Grimm Fairy Tales: Myths and Legends*. Vols. I and II. Horsham, PA: Zenescope, 2011–12.

Grimm—Aunt Marie's Book of Lore. London: Titan Books, 2013.

Grimm, The Brothers. *Hansel and Gretel*. Illustr. Arnold Lobel. New York: Delacorte, 1971.

———. *Hansel and Gretel*. Illustr. Susan Jeffers. Trans. Mrs. Edgar Lucas. New York: Dial, 1980.

———. *Hansel and Gretel*. Illustr. Anthony Browne. Adapt. from the trans. by Eleanor Quarrie. London: Julia MacRae, 1981.

Grimm, Gebrüder. *Hänsel and Gretel*. Illustr. Lisbeth Zwerger. Basel, Switzerland: Neugebauer, 1978.

Grimm, Jacob. *Hansel and Gretel*. Illustr. Antonella Bolliger-Savelli. New York: Oxford University Press, 1981.

Grimm, Jacob and Wilhelm. *The Brave Little Tailor*. Trans. Anthea Bell. Illustr. Sergei Goloshapov. New York: North-South Books, 1997.

———. *The Six Servants*. Trans. Anthea Bell. Illustr. Sergei Goloshapov. New York: North-South Books, 1996.

Grimm, Jakob and Wilhelm. *Hansel & Grettel*. Illustr. Monique Felix. Mankato, MN: Creative Education, 1983.

Gubernatis, Angelo. *Le novelline di Santo Stephano*. Turin: A. F. Nego, 1869.

———. *Zoological Mythology or the Legends of Animals, 2 vols*. London: Trübner & Co., 1872.

Hahn, Johann Georg von. *Griechische und albanesische Märchen*. Leipzig: W. Engelmann, 1864.

Hale, Dean, and Hale, Shannon. *Calamity Jack*. New York: Bloomsbury, 2010.

———. *Rapunzel's Revenge*. New York: Bloomsbury, 2008.

Hale, Shannon. *Book of a Thousand Days*. New York: Bloomsbury, 2007.

———. *The Goose Girl: Books of Bayern*. New York: Bloomsbury, 2003.

Hargreaves, Georgina. *Hansel and Gretel*. London: Dean, 1976.

Harris, Stephen, and Gloria Platzner, eds. *Classical Mythology: Images and Insights*. 2nd ed. Mountain View, CA: Mayfield Publishing Company, 1998.

Hay, Sara Henderson. *Story Hour*. Illustr. Jim McMullan. Garden City, NY: Doubleday, 1963.

Hayes, Sarah. *Hansel and Gretel*. London: Walker, 1985.

Haymon, Ava Leavell. *Why the House Is Made of Gingerbread*. Baton Rouge: Louisiana State University Press, 2010.

Healy, Christopher. *The Hero's Guide to Saving Your Kingdom*. New York: Walden Pond Press, 2012.

Heidelbach, Nikolaus. Nikolaus. *Hans Christian Andersens Märchen*. Weinheim: Beltz & Gelberg, 2004.

———. *Märchen aus aller Welt*. Weinheim: Beltz & Gelberg, 2010.

———. *Märchen der Brüder Grimm*. Weinheim: Beltz & Gelberg, 1995.

Hellinger, Peter, ed. *Wenn das die Grimms wüssten!* Nürnberg: Art & Words, 2012.

Hemmerling, René. *Total versaute Märchen: Die Brüder Grimm finden das schlimm*. Norderstedt: Books on Demand, 2006.

Hemmerling, René, and Sebastian Grosser. *Das Semi-Comic-Märchenbuch*. Vol. 1. Nordstedt: Books on Demand, 2007.

Hines, Jim. *Mermaid's Madness*. New York: DAW Books, 2009.

———. *Red Hood's Revenge*. New York: DAW Books, 2010.

———. *The Snow Queen's Shadow*. New York: DAW Books, 2011.

———. *The Stepsister Scheme*. New York: DAW Books, 2009.

Hoffman, Wim. *Klein Däumchen*. Tabu Verlag, 1995.

———. *König Wikkepok*. Munich: Middelhauve, 1998.

———. *Schwarz wie Tinte*. Munich: Middlehauve, 1999.

Holmes, Sara Lewis. *Letters from Rapunzel*. New York: HarperCollins, 2007.

Holt, Tom. *Snow White and the Seven Samurai*. London: Orbit, 1999.

Hoppe, Felicitas. *Iwein Löwenritter*. Frankfurt am Main: S. Fischer Verlag, 2011.

———. *Picknick der Friseure: Geschichten*. Frankfurt am Main: S. Fischer Verlag, 1996.

———. *Pigafetta*. Frankfurt am Main: S. Fischer Verlag, 2006.

———. *Verbrecher und Versager: Fünf Poträts*. Hamburg: Marebuchverlag, 2004.

Hoogland, Cornelia. *Woods Wolf Girl*. Hamilton, Ontario: Wolsak and Wynn, 2011.

Imbriani, Vittorio. *La Novellaja fiorentina*. Livorno: F. Vigo, 1871.

———. *La Novellaja Milanese*. Livorno: F. Vigo, 1877.

Jacobs, A. J. *Fractured Fairy Tales*. New York: Bantam, 1997.

Janssen, Susanne. *Hänsel und Gretel*. Rostock: Hintsorff, 2009.

———. *Rotkäppchen*. Rostock: Hintsorff, 2007

Jarvis, Shawn, ed. *Im Reich der Wünsche. Die schönsten Märchen deutscher Dichterinnen*. Munich: C. H. Beck, 2012.

Jones, Adrienne, and Peter Allen, eds. *Grimm & Grimmer: Dark Tales for Dark Times*. Cincinnati, OH: Mundania Press, 2009.

Jones, Christine, and Jennifer Schacker, eds. *Marvelous Transformations: An Anthology of Fairy Tales and Contemporary Critical Perspectives*. Toronto: Broadview Press, 2013.

Joyce, Graham. *Some Kind of Fairy Tale*. New York: Doubleday, 2012.

Jukes, Mavis. *Cinderella 2000: Looking Back*. New York: Dell Yearling, 1999.

Junko, Mizuno. *Hansel and Gretel*. San Francisco: Viz Communications, 2003.

Kammerer, Dagmar, illustr. *Mein großes Märchenbuch*. Cologne: Schwager und Steinlein, 2009.

Kazimer, J. A. *Curses! A F***ed-Up Fairy Tale*. New York: Kensington, 2012.

Kerr, Peg. *The Wild Swans*. New York: Warner, 1999.

Klein, Mart. *Rotkäppchen*. Mainz: Unfug-Verlag, 2009.

Knipfel, Jim. *These Children Who Come at You with Knives*. New York: Simon & Schuster, 2010.

Koertge, Ron. *Lies Knives and Girls in Red Dresses*. Illustr. Andrea Dezsö. Somerville, MA: Candlewick Press, 2012.

———. *The Ogre's Wife*. Pasedena, CA: Red Hen Press, 2013.

Kouf, Jin, and David Greenwalt. *Grimm: The Coins of Zakynthos*. Vol. 1. Mt. Laurel, NJ: Dynamite Entertainment, 2013.

Kühne, Anna. *Der goldene Mörser*. Frankfurt am Main: Fouqué Literaturverlag, 2000. Rev. ed. Berlin: Jutribog Verlag, 2008.

Lackey, Mercedes. *The Black Swan*. New York: DAW Books, 1999.

———. *The Fairy Godmother*. New York: Luna, 2004.

———. *The Sleeping Beauty*. New York: Luna, 2010.

———. *The Snow Queen*. New York: Luna, 2009.

Lanagan, Margo. *Black Juice*. New York: HarperCollins, 2004.

———. *Red Spikes*. New York: Alfred Knopf, 2006.

———. *Tender Morsels*. New York: Alfred Knopf, 2008.

———. *White Time*. New York: HarperCollins, 2006.

———. *Yellow Cake*. Crows Nest, Australia: Allen & Unwin, 2011.

Larbalestier, Justine. *How to Ditch Your Fairy*. New York; Bloomsbury, 2008.

———. *Magic Lessons*. New York: Razorbill, 2006.

———. *Magic or Madness*. New York: Razorbill, 2005.

Lashea, Riley. *Bleeding through Kingdoms: Cinderella's Rebellion*. Nashville, TN: Tattered Essence Publishing, 2005.

Lee, Lela. *Fairy Tales for Angry Little Girls*. New York: Abrams ComicArts, 2011.

Lee, Tanith. *Red as Blood or Tales from the Sisters Grimmer*. New York: Avon, 1983.

———. "Snow Drop," In *Snow White, Blood Red*, ed. Ellen Datlow and Terri Windling. New York: William Morrow, 1993, 106–29.

———. *White as Snow*. New York: TOR, 2000.

Levine, Gail Carson. *Cinderellis and the Glass Hill*. Illustr. Mark Elliott. New York: Harper Collins, 2000.

———. *Ella Enchanted*. New York: HarperCollins, 1997.

———. *The Fairy's Test*. Illustr. Mark Elliott. New York: HarperCollins, 1999.

———. *Princess Sonora and the Long Sleep*. Illustr. Mark Elliott. New York: Harper Collins, 1999.

———. *The Princess Test*. Illustr. Mark Elliott. New York: HarperCollins, 1999.

Link, Kelly. *Magic for Beginners*. New York: Harcourt, 2005.

———. *Pretty Monsters*. New York; Viking, 2008.

———. *Stranger Things Happen*. Brooklyn: Small Beer Press, 2000.

Lo, Malinda. *Huntress*. Boston: Little, Brown and Company, 2011.

Luzel, F. M. *Contes Bretons. Les Contes de Luzel.* Ed. Françoise Morvan. Rennes: Presses Universitaires de Rennes, 1994.

———. *Contes Bretons recueillis et traduits.* Quimperlé: Clairet, 1870.

———. *Contes de Basse-Bretagne.* Ed. Françoise Morvan. Rennes: Éditions Ouest-France, 2007.

———. *Contes populaires de la Basse-Bretagne.* 3 vols. Paris: Maisonneuve et Leclerc, 1887.

———. *Contes populaires de la Basse-Bretagne. Les Contes de Luzel.* Ed. Françoise Morvan. Rennes: Presses Universitaires de Rennes, 1996.

Lynn, Tracy. *Snow: A Retelling of "Snow White and the Seven Dwarfs."* New York: Simon and Schuster, 2006.

Maguire, Gregory. *Confessions of an Ugly Stepsister.* Illustr. Bill Sanderson. New York: Regan Books, 1999.

———. *Mirror Mirror.* New York: Regan Books, 2003.

Maitland, Sara. *On Becoming a Fairy Godmother.* London: Maia Press, 2003.

———. *Far North and Other Dark Tales.* London: Maia Press, 2008.

———. *Gossip from the Forest: The Tangled Roots of Our Forests and Fairytales.* London: Granta, 2012.

Mayer, Mercer. *Favorite Tales from Grimm.* Retold by Nancy Garden. Illustr. Mercer Mayer. New York: Four Winds Press, 1982.

Mayo, Margaret. *Hansel and Gretel.* Illustr. Philip Norman. London: Orchard, 2002.

McCarthy, William Bernard, ed. *Cinderella in America: A Book of Folk and Fairy Tales.* Jackson, MS: University Press of Mississippi, 2007.

McKinley, Robin, and Peter Dickinson. *Fire: Tales of Elemental Spirits.* New York: Putnam, 2009.

———. *Rose Daughter.* New York: Ace, 1990.

———. *Spindle's End.* New York: G. P. Putnam's Sons, 2008.

———. *Sunshine: Tales of Elemental Spirits.* New York, Jove, 2004.

McNeal, Tom. *far far away.* New York: Alfred Knopf, 2013.

Meier, Ernst. *Deutsche Volksmärchen aus Schwaben.* Stuttgart: E. B. Scheitlin's Verlagshandlung, 1852.

Meyer, Marissa. *Cinder.* New York: Feiwel and Friends, 2012.

Mieder, Wolfgang, ed. *Disenchantments. An Anthology of Modern Fairy Tale Poetry.* Hanover, NH: University Press of New England, 1985.

Millhauser, Steven. *Enchanted Night.* New York: Crown, 1999.

Millien, Achille. *Contes de Bourgogne.* Ed. Françoise Morvan. Rennes: Éditions Ouest- France, 2008.

Mongredien, Sue. *Master Hansel and Miss Gretel.* Oxford, UK: Oxford University Press, 2001.

Morgan, Amy Leigh, ed. *Six Short Fairy Tales, Some with Unhappy Endings.* Illustr. Diana Sudyka. Seattle: Fairy Tale Factory, 2011.

Morpurgo, Michael. *Hansel and Gretel.* Illustr. Emma Chichester Clark. Cambridge, MA: Candlewick Press, 2008.

Murphy, Louise. *The True Story of Hansel and Gretel*. New York: Penguin, 2003.

Napoli, Donna Jo. *Crazy Jack*. New York: Delacorte, 1999.

——. *Jimmy, The Pickpocket of the Palace*. New York: Dutton, 1995.

——. *The Magic Circle*. New York: Dutton, 1993.

——. *The Prince of the Pond*. Illustr. Judith Byron Schachner. New York: Dutton, 1992.

——. *Sirena*. New York: Scholastic, 1998.

——. *Zel*. New York: Dutton, 1998.

Napoli, Donna Jo, and Richard Tchen. *Spinners*. New York: Dutton, 1999.

——. *The Wager*. New York: Henry Holt, 2010.

Oyeyemi, Helen. *Boy, Snow Bird*. New York: Riverhead Books, 2014.

——. *Mr. Fox*. New York: Riverhead Books, 2011.

——. *White Is for Witching*. New York: Doubleday, 2009.

Pacovská, Kvĕta. *Hänsel und Gretel*. Bartgheide: Michael Neugebauer Edition, 2007.

——. *Rotkäppchen*. Bargtheide: Michael Neugebauer Edition, 2007.

——. Pearce, Jackson. *Sisters Red*. New York: Little, Brown, 2010.

Philip, Neil, ed. *American Fairy Tales: From Rip Van Winkle to the Rootabaga Stories*. Illustr. Michael McCurdy. New York: Hyperion, 1996.

Pitrè, Giuseppe. *The Collected Sicilian Folk and Fairy Tales of Giuseppe Pitrè*. 2 vols. Ed. and trans. Jack Zipes and Joseph Russo. New York: Routledge, 2008.

——. *Fiabe, novelle e racconti popolari siciliani*. 4 vols. Palermo: Lauriel, 1875.

——. *Novelle Popolari Toscane*. Florence: G. Babèra, 1885.

Pröhle, Heinrich. *Kinder- und Hausmärchen*. Leipzig: Avenarius und Mendelsohn, 1853.

——. *Märchen fir die Jugend*. Halle: Verlag des Waisenhauses, 1854.

Pullman, Philip. *Fairy Tales from the Brothers Grimm: A New English Version*. New York: Viking, 2012.

——. *I Was a Rat!* New York: Knopf, 1999.

Ragan, Kathleen, ed. *Fearless Girls, Wise Women and Beloved Sisters: Heroines in Folktales from around the World*. New York: Norton, 1998.

Ralston, William R. S. *Russian Folk-Tales*. London: Smith, Elder & Co., 1873.

Ransome, Arthur. *The Fool of the World and the Flying Ship*. Illustr. Uri Shukevitz. New York: Farrar, Straus and Giroux, 1968.

Richard, G. *Contes Bleus et Roses pour l'amusement des grands et des petits enfants*. Paris: Librairie du Petit Journal, 1865.

Rowe, Louise. *Hansel and Gretel*. London: Tango Books, 2010.

Rowland, Claire. *Piroska: Three Short Fairy Tales for Adults*. Pawleys Island, SC: Naked Snake Press, 2011.

Ruf, Theodor. *Die Schöne aus dem Glassarg: Schneewittchens märchenhaftes und wirkliches Leben*. Würzburg: Königshausen und Neumann, 1995.

Rushforth, Peter. *Kindergarten*. New York: Alfred Knopf, 1980.

Schimmel, Lawrence. *Fairy Tales for Writers*. New York: A Midsummer Night's Press, 2007.

Schindehütte, Albert, ed. *Die Grimm'schen Märchen der jungen Marie*. Marburg: Hitzeroth, 1991.

———. *Krauses Grimm'sche Märchen*. Kassel: Johannes Stauda Verlag, 1985.

Schlepp, Wayne. "Cinderella in Tibet," *Asian Folklore Studies* 61 (2002): 123–47.

Schmidt, Bernhard. *Griechische Märchen, Sagen und Volkslieder*. Leipzig: Teubner, 1877.

Scudder, Horace. *The Book of Fables and Folk Stories*. Boston: Houghton Mifflin, 1906.

———. *The Book of Folk Stories Rewritten by H. E. Scudder*. Boston: Houghton Mifflin, 1887.

———. *The Book of Legends*. Boston: Houghton Mifflin, 1899.

Sercambi, Giovanni. *Novelle*. 2 vols. Ed. Giovanni Sinicropi. Bari: Laterza, 1972.

Shirley, John. *Grimm: The Icy Touch*. London: Titan Books, 2013.

Shua, Ana María. *Quick Fix: Sudden Fiction*. Trans. Rhonda Dahl Buchanan. Illustr. Luci Mistratov. Buffalo, NY: White Pine Press, 2008.

———. *Microfictions*. Trans. Steven Stewart. Lincoln: University of Nebraska Press, 2009.

Shulman, Polly. *The Grimm Legacy*. New York: G. P. Putnam's Sons, 2010.

Shurtliff, Liesl. *Rump: The True Story of Rumpelstiltskin*. New York: Alfred Knopf, 2013.

Sierra, Judy, ed. *Cinderella*. Phoenix: Oryx, 1992.

Slater, Lauren. *Blue beyond Blue: Extraordinary Tales for Ordinary Dilemmas*. Illustr. Stephanie Knowles. New York: W. W. Norton, 2005.

Smarr, Janet Levarie, ed. and trans. *Italian Renaissance Tales*. Rochester, MI: Solaris Press, 1983.

Snider, Jesse Blaze, and Patrick Storck. *Muppet Snow White*. Illustr. Shelli Paroline. Los Angeles: Broom Kids, 2010.

Spiegelman, Art, and Françoise Mouly, eds. *Little Lit: Folklore and Fairy Tale Funnies*. New York: HarperCollins, 2000.

Springer, Nancy. *Fair Peril*. New York: Avon, 1997.

Stahl, Karoline. *Fabeln und Erzählungen für Kinder*. Nürnberg, 1818.

Stanley, Diane. *Rumpelstiltskin's Daughter*. New York: William Morrow, 1997.

Stapel, Wilhelm, ed. *Fünfundfünfzig vergessene Grimmsche Märchen*. Hamburg: Hanseatische Verlagsanstalt, 1922.

Steig, William. *Shrek!* New York: Farrar, Straus, and Giroux, 1990.

Tangherlini, Timothy, ed. and trans. *Danish Folktales, Legends and Other Stories*. Seattle: University of Washington Press, 2013.

Tchana, Katrin. *The Serpent Slayer and Other Stories of Strong Women*. Illustr. Trina Schart Hyman. Boston: Little Brown, 2000.

Tepper, Sheri. *Beauty: A Novel*. New York: Doubleday, 1991.

Turgeon, Carolyn. *The Fairest of Them All*. New York: Touchstone, 2013.

———. *Godmother*. New York: Three Rivers Press, 2009.

———. *Mermaid: A Twist on the Classic Tale*. New York: Crown, 2011.

Valente, Catherynne M. *The Girl Who Circumnavigated Fairyland in a Ship of Her Own Making*. New York: Feiwel and Friends, 2011.

———. *The Orphan's Tales: In the Cities of Coin and Spice*. New York, Spectra, 2007.

———. *The Orphan's Tales: In the Night Garden*. New York: Spectra, 2006.

———. *Six Gun Snow White*. Burton, MI: Subterranean, 2013.

Valenzuela, Luisa. *Open Door*. Trans. Hortense Carpentier, et al. San Francisco: North Point Press, 1988.

———. *Symmetries*. Trans. Margaret Jull Costa. London: Serpent's Tale, 1998.

Vankin, Jonathan, ed. *The Big Book of Grimm by the Brothers Grimm*. New York: Paradox Press, 1999.

Velde, Vivian Vande. *Cloaked in Red*. Tarrytown, NY: Marshall Cavendish, 2010.

———. *The Rumpelstiltskin Problem*. New York: Houghton Mifflin, 2000.

———. *Tales from the Brothers Grimm and the Sisters Weird*. New York: Sandpiper, 2005.

Walker, Nancy G. *Feminist Fairy Tales*. San Francisco: Harper, 1996.

Weber, Florian. *Grimms Erben*. Berlin: Metrolit Verlag, 2012.

Webster, Rev. Wentworth. *Basque Legends*. Collected chiefly in the Labourd. With an essay on the Basque Language by M. Julien Vinson. London: Griffith and Farran, 1877.

Wenzel, David, and Douglas Wheeler. *Fairy Tales of the Brothers Grimm*. New York: Nantier, Beall, and Minoustchine, 1995.

Weyn, Suzanne. *The Night Dance: A Retelling of "The Twelve Dancing Princesses."* New York: Simon and Schuster, 2008.

———. *Water Song: A Retelling of "The Frog Prince."* New York: Simon & Schuster, 2006.

Wilson, David Henry. *The Coachman Rat*. New York: Carroll and Graf, 1989.

Windling, Terri, ed. *The Armless Maiden and Other Tales for Childhood's Survivors*. New York: TOR, 1995.

Wolf, Johann Wilhelm. *Deutsche Hausmärchen*. Göttingen: Dieterich'sche Buchhandlung, 1851. (Republished as *Verschollene Märchen*. Nordlingen: Franz Greno, 1988.)

———. *Deutsche Märchen und Sagen*. Leipzig: Brockhaus, 1845.

———. *Märchen, Sagen und Lieder aus Hessen*. Darmstadt, 1851.

———. *Niederländische Sagen*. Leipzig: Brockhaus, 1843.

Wood, Lucy. *Diving Belles and Other Stories*. Boston: Houghton Mifflin Harcourt, 2012.

Wortsman, Peter, ed. and trans. *Selected Tales of the Brothers Grimm*. Brooklyn: Archipelago Books, 2013.

Wratislaw, Albert Henry. *Sixty Folk-Tales from Exclusively Slavonic Sources*. Boston: Houghton, Mifflin and Company, 1890.

Wrede, Patricia. *Book of Enchantments*. New York: Harcourt Brace, 1996.

Yolen, Jane. *Briar Rose*. New York: TOR, 1992.

———. *The Last Selchie Child*. New York: A Midsummer Night's Press, 2012.

————. *Not One Damsel in Distress: World Folktales for Strong Girls*. Illustr. Susan Guevara. San Diego: Silver Whistle/Harcourt, 2000.

————. *Once Upon a Time (She Said)*. Ed. Priscilla Olson. Framingham, MA: NESFA Press, 2005.

Yolen, Jane, and Heidi Stemple. *Mirror, Mirror: Forty Folktales for Mothers and Daughters to Share*. New York: Viking, 2000.

Zelinsky, Paul O. *Rapunzel*. New York: Dutton, 1997.

Zipes, Jack, ed. and trans. *Beauties, Beasts and Enchantment: Classic French Fairy Tales*. New York: New American Library, 1989.

BRITISH SCHOLASTIC SERIES (IN ALPHABETICAL ORDER)

Branford, Henrietta. *Hansel and Gretel*. Illustr. Lesley Harker. London: Scholastic, 1998.

Doherty, Berlie. *The Snow Queen*. Illustr. Sin Bailey. London: Scholastic, 1998.

Fine, Anne. *The Twelve Dancing Princesses*. Illustr. Debbi Gliori. London: Scholastic, 1998.

Garner, Alan. *Grey Wolf, Prince Jack and the Firebird*. Illustr. James Mayhew. London: Scholastic, 1998.

Gates, Susan. *The Three Heads in the Well*. Illustr. Sue Heap. London: Scholastic, 1998.

Geras, Adèle. *The Six Swan Brothers*. Illustr. Ian Beck. London: Scholastic, 1998.

Morporgo, Michael. *Cockadoodle-doo, Mr. Sultana!* London: Scholastic, 1998.

Pullman, Philip. *Mossycoat*. Illustr. Peter Bailey. London: Scholastic, 1998.

Temperley, Alan. *The Simple Giant*. Illustr. Mark Edwards. London: Scholastic, 1999.

Wilson, Jacqueline. *Rapunzel*. Illustr. Nick Sharratt. London: Scholastic, 1998.

Wilson, Susan. *Beauty*. New York: Simon and Schuster, 1996.

Wright, Kit. *Rumpelstiltskin*. Illustr. Ted Dewan. London: Scholastic, 1998.

Wynne Jones, Diana. *Puss in Boots*. Illustr. Fanghorn. London: Scholastic, 1999.

Websites (in alphabetical order)

Ashliman, D. L. "Folklore and Mythology Electronic Texts." http://www.pitt.edu /~dash/folktexts.html.

Blais, Joline, Keith Frank, and Jon Ippolito. "Fair e-Tales." http://www.three.org /fairetales/.

Brown, David K. "Cinderella Stories." http://ucalgary.ca/~dkbrown/cinderella.html.

"The Cinderella Project." http://www-dept.usm.edu/~engdept/cinderella/cinderella .html.

Journal of Memetics. http://www.jom-emit.org/.

Memetics. http://pespmc1.vub.ac.bc/Memes.html.

"Once Upon a Blog." fairytalenewsblog.blogspot.com.

"SurLaLune Fairy Tale Pages." http://members.aol.com/surlalune/frytales/index.htm.

Vandergrift, Kay. "Kay Vandergrift's Snow White Page." http://www/scils.rutgers
    .edu/special/Kay/snow white.html.
Windling, Terri. "The Endicott Studio of Mythic Arts." http://www.endicott-studio
    .com/.

References

Adorno, Theodor. *Aesthetic Theory*. Eds. Gretel Adorno and Rolf Tiedemann. Trans,
    Robert Hubert-Kentor. Minneapolis: University of Minnesota Press, 1997.
——. *The Culture Industry*. Ed. J. M. Bernstein. London: Routledge, 1991.
——. *Negative Dialectics*. Trans. E. B. Ashton. New York: Seabury, 1966.
Adorno, Theodor, and Max Horkheimer. *Dialectic of Enlightenment*. Trans. John
    Cumming. New York: Herder and Herder, 1972.
Agamben, Giorgio. *Potentialities: Collected Essays in Philosophy*. Ed. and trans.
    Daniel Heller-Roazan. Stanford, CA: Stanford University press, 2000.
Alderson, Brian. "The Spoken and the Read: *German Popular Stories* and English
    Popular Diction." In *The Reception of Grimms' Fairy Tales: Reponses, Reactions,
    Revisions*, ed. Donald Haase. Detroit: Wayne State University Press, 1993,
    59–77.
Allison, Randal. "Tradition." In *Folklore: An Encyclopedia of Beliefs, Customs, Tales,
    Music, and Art*, ed. Thomas Green. Santa Barbara, CA: ABC-CLIO, 1997,
    799–802.
Anderson, Graham. *Fairytale in the Ancient World*. London: Routledge, 2000.
——. *Greek and Roman Folklore: A Handbook*. Westport, CT: Greenwood Press,
    2006.
Antoni, Klaus. "Momotarō (the Peach Boy) and the Spirit of Japan: Concerning
    the Function of a Fairy Tale in Japanese Nationalism of the Early Shōwa Age."
    Asian Folklore Studies 50.1 (1991): 155–88.
Ashliman, D. L. *Folk and Fairy Tales: A Handbook*. Westport, CT: Greenwood Press,
    2004.
Assmann, Aelida. *Cultural Memory and Western Civilization: Functions, Media,
    Archives*. Cambridge, UK: Cambridge University Press, 2011.
Assmann, Jan. *Cultural Memory and Early Civilization: Writing, Remembrance, and
    Political Imagination*. Cambridge, UK: Cambridge University Press, 2011.
Bacchilega, Cristina. *Fairy Tales Transformed? Twenty-First Century Adaptations
    and the Politics of Wonder*. Detroit: Wayne State University Press, 2013.
Baycroft, Timothy, and David Hopkin. *Folklore and Nationalism in Europe during
    the Long Nineteenth Century*. Leiden: Brill, 2012.
Barthes, Roland. "The Death of the Author" [1967]. In *Image-Music-Text*, ed. and
    trans. Stephen Heath. New York: Hill and Wang, 1971, 142–48.
——. *Image-Music-Text*. New York: Hill and Wang: 1971.
——. *Mythologies*. Trans. Annette Lavers. London: Granada, 1973.

Bauman, Zygmunt. *Culture in a Liquid World*. London: Polity, 2011.

Baycroft, Timothy, and David Hopkin, eds. *Folklore and Nationalism in Europe during the Long Nineteenth Century*. Leiden: Brill, 2012.

Bendix, Regina, and Galit Hasan-Rokem. *A Companion to Folklore*. Oxford, UK: Wiley- Blackwell, 2012.

Bendix, Regina, and Ulrich Marzolph, eds. *Hören, Lesen, Sehen, Spüren: Märchenrezeption im europäischen Vergleich*. Hohengehren: Schneider, 2008.

Berghahn, Volker. "Debate on 'Americanization' among Economic and Cultural Historians." *Cold War History* 10.1 (February 2010): 107–30.

Binding, Paul. "Respect the Goblin." *Times Literary Supplement* (October 4, 2013): 5.

Blamires, David. "The Early Reception of the Grimms' Kinder- und Hausmärchen in England." *Bulletin of the John Rylands University Library of Manchester* 71.3 (1989): 63–77.

———. "From Madame d'Aulnoy to Mother Bunch: Popularity and the Fairy Tale." In *Popular Children's Literature in Britain*, ed. Julia Briggs, Dennis Butts, and M. O. Grenby. Aldershot, Hampshire, UK: Ashgate, 2008, 69–86.

Blank, Trevor, and Robert Glenn Howard, eds. *Tradition in the Twenty-First Century: Locating the Role of the Past in the Present*. Logan: Utah State University Press, 2013.

Bloch, Ernst. "Etwas fehlt . . . Über die Widersprüche der utopischen Sehnsucht. Ein Gespräch mit Theodor W. Adorno" [1964]. In *Gespräche mit Ernst Bloch*, eds. Rainer Traub and Harald Wieser. Frankfurt am Main: Suhrkamp, 1975, 52–60.

———. *The Principle of Hope*. Trans. Neville Plaice, Stephen Plaice, and Paul Knight. Cambridge, MA: MIT Press, 1986.

———. *The Utopian Function of Art and Literature: Selected Essays*. Trans. Jack Zipes and Frank Mecklenburg. Cambridge, MA: MIT Press, 1988.

Bloch, R. Howard, and Setphen Nichols, eds. *Medievalism and the Modernist Temper*. Baltimore: Johns Hopkins University Press, 1996.

Bluhm, Lothar. "Sir Francis Cohen/Palgrave. Zur frühen Rezeption der Kinder- und Hausmärchen in England." In *Brüder Grimm Gedenken*, ed. Ludwig Denecke, vol. 7. Marburg: N. G. Elwert, 1987, 224–42.

Bluhm, Lothar, and Achim Hölter, eds. *"Daß gepflegt werde der feste Buchstab": Festschrift für Heinz Rölleke zum 65. Geburtstag am 6. November 2001*. Trier: Wissenschaftlicher Verlag Trier, 2001.

Boehm, Christopher. *Moral Origins: The Evolution of Virtue, Altruism, and Shame*. New York: Basic Books, 2012.

Bottigheimer, Ruth. "The Publishing History of Grimms' Tales: Reception at the Cash Register." In *The Reception of the Grimms' Fairy Tales: Responses, Reactions, Revisions*, ed. Donald Haase. Detroit: Wayne State University Press, 1993, 78–101.

Bourdieu, Pierre. *The Field of Cultural Production*. Trans. Randal Johnson. New York: Columbia University Press, 1993.

Briggs, Katharine. "The Influence of the Brothers Grimm in England." In *Brüder Grimm Gedenken*, ed. Ludwig Denecke and Ina-Maria Greverus, vol. 1. Marburg: N. G. Elwert, 1963, 511–24.

Brill, Edward. "The Correspondence between Jacob Grimm and Walter Scott." In *Brüder Grimm Gedenken*, ed. Ludwig Denecke and Ina-Maria Greverus, vol. 1. Marburg: N. G. Elwert, 1963, 489–510.

Bronner, Simon. "The Americanization of the Brothers Grimm." In *Following Tradition: Folklore in the Discourse of American Culture*. Logan, UT: Utah State University Press, 1998, 184–236.

——. *Explaining Traditions: Folk Behavior in Modern Culture*. Lexington: University Press of Kentucky, 2011.

Brown, Nicola. *Fairies in Nineteenth-century Art and Literature*. Cambridge, UK: Cambridge University Press, 2001.

Calaresu, Melissa, Filippo de Vivo, and Joan-Paul Rubés, eds. *Exploring Cultural History: Essays in Honor of Peter Burke*. Farnham, Surrey, UK: Ashgate, 2010.

Cohen, Avner. "Myth and Myth Criticism Following the Dialectic of the Enlightenment." *European Legacy* 15.5 (2010): 583–98.

Cohen, Francis. "Antiquities of Nursery Literature: Review of Fairy Tales, or the Lilliputian Cabinet, Containing Twenty-Four Choice Pieces of Fancy and Fiction, collected by Benjamin Tabart." *Quarterly Review* 21.41 (January 1819): 91–112.

Comfort, N. "Cultural Darwinism." *European Legacy* 12.6 (2007): 695–713.

Crane, Thomas Frederick. "The Diffusion of Popular Tales." *Journal of American Folk- Lore* 1 (1888): 8–15.

——. "The External History of the *Kinder- und Hausmärchen* of the Brothers Grimm." *Modern Philology* 14.10 (February 1917): 577–610; 15.2 (June 1917): 65–77; and 15.6 (October 1917): 355–83.

Darton, F. J. Harvey. *Children's Books in England: Five Centuries of Social Life*. 3rd rev. ed. by Brian Alderson. Cambridge, UK: Cambridge University Press, 1982.

Davidson, Hilda Ellis, and Anna Chaudhri, eds. *A Companion to the Fairy Tale*. Cambridge, UK: D. S. Brewer, 2003.

Debord, Guy. *The Society of the Spectacle*. Trans. Donald Nicholson-Smith. New York: Zone Books, 1995. (First published as *La Societé du spectacle*, Paris: Buchet- Chastel, 1967.)

Dehane, Stanislas. *Reading in the Brain: The New Science of How We Read*. New York: Viking Penguin, 2009.

Denecke, Ludwig, and Ina-Maria Greverus. *Brüder Grimm Gedenken: 1963*. Marburg: N. G. Elwert, 1963.

Dhubhne, Éilis Ní. "The Name of the Helper: *Kinder- und Hausmärchen* and Ireland." *Béaloideas* 80 (2012): 1–22.

Dollerup, Cay. "Translation as a Creative Force in Literature: The Birth of the Bourgeois Fairy Tale." *The Modern Language Review* 90.1 (1995): 94–102.

——. *The Grimm Tales from Pan-Germanic Narratives to Shared International Fairytales*. Amsterdam: John Benjamins, 1999.

Drascek, Daniel. "'SimsalaGrimm': Zur Adaption und Modernisierung der Märchenwelt." *Schweizerisches Archiv für Volkskunde* 97 (2001): 79–89.

Drout, Michael. *How Tradition Works: A Meme-Based Cultural Poetics of the Anglo-Saxon Tenth Century*. Tempe: Arizona Center for Medieval and Renaissance Studies, 2006.

———. *Tradition & Influence in Anglo-Saxon Literature: An Evolutionary, Cognitivist Approach*. New York; Palgrave Macmillan, 2013.

Eagleton, Terry. "On Meaning Well." Book review of Richard Sennett's *Together* in *Times Literary Supplement* (April 20, 1012): 8–9.

Ehrhardt, Holger. *Dorothea Viehmann*. Kassel: Euregio Verlag, 2012.

Elberse, Anita. *Blockbusters: Hit-Making, Risk-Taking, and the Big Business of Entertainment*. New York: Holt, 2010.

Erll, Astrid. *Memory in Culture*. Trans. Sara Young. Basingstoke, Hampshire, UK: Palgrave, 2011.

Feldmann, Christian. *Von Aschenputtel bis Rotkäppchen: Das Märchen-Entwirrbuch*. Munich: Gütersloher Verlagshaus, 2009.

Forsdyke, Sara. *Slaves Tell Tales and Other Episodes in the Politics of Popular Culture in Ancient Greece*. Princeton, NJ: Princeton University Press, 2012.

Foucault, Michel. "What Is an Author?" [1969]. In *Language, Counter Memory, Practice*, ed. and trans. Donald Bouchard and Sherry Simon. Ithaca, NY: Cornell University Press, 1977, 124–127.

Frank, Arthur. *The Wounded Storyteller: Body, Illness, and Ethics*. Chicago: University of Chicago Press, 1995.

Franke, Julia, and Harm-Peer Zimmermann, eds. *Grimmskrams & Märchendising*. Marburg: Panama Verlag, 2008.

Fränkel, Ludwig. "Wolf, Johann Wilhelm." In *Allgemeine Deutsche Biographie (ADB)*, vol. 43. Leipzig: Duncker und Humboldt, 1898, 765–77.

Franklin, Nancy. "Another World: 'Pan Am' and 'The Playboy Club.'" *The New Yorker* (October 3, 2011): 72–74.

Franz, Kurt, and Claudia Maria Percher. *Kennst du die Brüder Grimm?* Weimar: Bertuch Verlag, 2012.

Franz, Kurt, and Walter Kahn, eds. *Märchen—Kinder—Medien: Beiträge zur medialen Adaptation von Märchen und zum didaktischen Umgang*. Hohengehren: Schneider, 2000.

Freund, Wieland. "Cornelia Funke knöpft sich reaktionäre Märchen vor." *Die Welt* (September 9, 2010). *Welt Online*, available at http://www.welt.de/kultur /article9613379/Cornelia-Funke-knöpft-sich- reaktionäre- Märchen-vor. Accessed May 14, 2013.

Genette, Gérard. *Paratexts: Thresholds of Interpretation*. Trans. Jane Lewin. Cambridge, UK: Cambridge University Press, 1997.

Giudice, Luisa Del, and Gerald Porter, eds. *Imagined States: Nationalism, Utopia, and Longing in Oral Cultures*. Logan: Utah State University Press, 2001.

Gombrecht, Hans Ulrich, and Jeffrey Schnapp, eds. and trans. "Preface to *Kinder- und Hausmärchen gesammelt durch die Brüder Grimm* (1819)." In *Medievalism and the Modernist Temper*, ed. R. Howard Bloch and Stephen Nichols. Baltimore: Johns Hopkins University Press, 1996, 340–65.

Graf, Fritz. *Magic in the Ancient Word*. Trans. Franklin Philip. Cambridge, MA: Harvard University Press, 1997.

Gray, Jonathan. *Show Sold Separately: Promos, Spoilers, and Other Media Paratexts*. New York: New York University Press, 2010.

Grass, Günter. *Grimms Wörter: Eine Liebeserklärung*. Göttingen, Steidl, 2010.

———. "Spiegel Interview with Günter Grass: 'The Nobel Prize Doesn't Inhibit Me in My Writing'" (August 20, 2010). Interview conducted by Volker Hage and Katja Thimm. http://www.spiegel.de/international/zeitgeist/spiegel-interview-with- guenter-grass-the-nobel-prize-doesn-t-inhibit me-in-my writing-a-712715.html. Accessed July 2, 2013.

Greene, Thomas, ed. *Folklore: An Encyclopedia of Beliefs, Customs, Tales, Music, and Art*. 2 vols. Santa Barbara: CA: ABC-CLIO, 1997.

Greenhill, Pauline, and Sidney-Eve Matrix, eds. *Fairy Tale Film and Cinematic Folklore: Visions of Ambiguity*. Logan, UT: Utah State University Press, 2012.

Greenhill, Pauline, and Kay Turner, eds. *Transgressive Tales: Queering the Grimms*. Detroit: Wayne State University Press, 2012.

Grenby, Matthew. "Tame Fairies Make Good Teachers: The Popularity of Early British Fairy Tales." *The Lion and the Unicorn* 30 (2006): 1–24.

Grewal, David Singh. *Network Power: The Social Dynamics of Globalization*. New Haven, CT: Yale University Press, 2008.

Grierson, Herbert. *The Letters of Sir Walter Scott*. 12 vols. London: Constable, 1932–37.

Grimm, Jacob. *Kleinere Schriften*. Vol. 1. Berlin: F. Dümmler, 1864.

———. *Reden und Aufsätze: Eine Auswahl*. Ed. Wilhelm Schoof. Munich: Winkler, 1966.

———. *Über den Ursprung der Sprache* [1851]. Frankfurt am Main: Insel, 1958.

Gruner, Elizabeth Rose. "Saving 'Cinderella': History and Story in *Ashpet* and *Ever After*." *Children's Literature* 31 (2003): 142–54.

Haase, Donald, ed. "Framing the Brothers Grimm: Paratexts and Intercultural Transmission in Postwar English-Language Editions of the *Kinder- und Hausmärchen*." *Fabula* 44.1/2 (2003): 55–69.

———. "Kiss and Tell: Orality, Narrative, and the Power of Words in 'Sleeping Beauty.'" In *Des* Fata *aux fées: regards croisés de l'Antiquité à nos jours*, ed. Martine Hennard Dutheil de Rochère and Véronique Dasen, special issue of *Études de Lettres* 289 (2009): 279–96.

———. *The Reception of Grimms' Fairy Tales: Reponses, Reactions, Revisions*. Detroit: Wayne State University Press, 1993.

———. "Re-Viewing the Grimm Corpus: Grimm Scholarship in an Era of Celebrations." *Monatshefte* 91 (1999): 121–31.

Hand, Wayland. "Die Märchen der Brüder Grimm in den Vereinigten Staaten." In *Brüder Grimm Gedenken*, ed. Ludwig Denecke and Ina-Maria Greverus, vol. 1. Marburg: N. G. Elwert, 1963, 525–44.

Hansen, William. *Ariadne's Thread: A Guide to International Tales Found in Classical Literature.* Ithaca, NY: Cornell University Press, 2002.

Harris, Jason. *Folklore and the Fantastic in Nineteenth-Century British Fiction.* Aldershot, Hampshire, UK: Ashgate, 2008.

Harrison, Rodney, ed. *Heritage: Critical Approaches.* London: Routledge, 2013.

———. *Understanding the Politics of Heritage.* Manchester, UK: Manchester University Press, 2010.

Hartwig, Otto. "Zur ersten englischen Übersetzung der Kinder- und Hausmärchen der Brüder Grimm." *Centralblatt der Bibliothekswesen* 15.1/2 (January–February, 1898): 1–16.

Hedwig, Andreas, ed. *Die Brüder Grimm in Marburg.* Marburg: Schriften des Hessischen Staatsarchivs, 2013.

Heidenreich, Bernd, and Ewald Grothe, eds. *Die Grimms—Kultur und Politik.* 2nd rev. ed. Frankfurt am Main: Societäts-Verlag, 2008.

Heiduschke, Sebastian. "GDR Cinema as Commodity: Marketing DEFA Films since Unification." *German Studies Review* 36.1 (2013): 61–78.

Heyer, Siegfried. "Der Briefwechsel Thomas Crofton Crokers und Thomas Keightleys mit Wilhelm Grimm über die 'Fairy Legends.'" In *Brüder Grimm Gedenken*, ed. Ludwig Denecke, vol. 7. Marburg: N. G. Elwert, 1987, 110–39.

Hillard, Molly Clark. *Spellbound: The Fairy Tale and the Victorians.* Columbus: Ohio State University Press, 2014.

Hobsbawm, Eric, and Terrence Ranger, eds. *The Invention of Tradition.* Cambridge, UK: Cambridge University Press, 1983.

Höck, Alfred. *Die Brüder Grimm als Studenten in Marburg.* Marburg: Elwert, 1978.

Hoffmann, Ute. *Die kreative Märchen-Werkstatt.* Hamburg: Persen im Aap Lehererfachverlag, 2010.

Hoggard, Liz. "Helen Oyeyemi: 'I'm Interested in the Way Women Disappoint One Another.'" Interview in the Saturday edition of *The Guardian/Observer*, March 1, 2014. http://www.the guardian.com/books/2014/mar/02/helen-oyeyemi-women-disappoint-one-another. Accessed April 15, 2014.

Hopkin, David. "The Ecotype, or a Modest Proposal to Reconnect Cultural and Social History." In *Exploring Cultural History: Essays in Honor of Peter Burke*, ed. Melissa Calaresu, Filippo de Vivo, and Joan-Paul Rubés. Farnham, Surrey, UK: Ashgate, 2010, 31–54.

———. *Voices of the People in Nineteenth-Century France.* Cambridge, UK: Cambridge University Press, 2012.

Hübner, Arthur, and Hans Neumann, eds. *Deutsches Wörterbuch von Jacob und Wilhelm Grimm.* Vol. 4. Leipzig: S. Hirzel, 1937.

Hult, Marte Hvam. *Framing a National Narrative: The Legend Collections of Peter Christian Asbjørnsen.* Detroit: Wayne State University Press, 2003.

Hunter, Allan. *Princes, Frogs & Ugly Sisters: The Healing Power of the Grimm Brothers' Tales.* Forres, Scotland: Findhorn Press, 2010.

Jolles, André. *Einfache Formen: Legende/Sage/Mythe/Spruch Kasus/Memorabile Märchen/Witz.* Darmstadt: Wissenschaftliche Buchgesellschaft, 1958. (Reprint of the 1930 edition.)

Jones, Christine. "Mother Goose's French Birth (1697) and British Afterlife (1729)." *Public Domain Review.* http://publicdomainreview.org/2013/05/29/mother-gooses-french-birth-1697-and-british-afterlife-1729. Accessed June 7, 2013.

Joosen, Vanessa. "Back to Olenberg: An Intertextual Dialogue between Fairy-tale Retellings and the Sociohistorical Study of the Grimm Tales." *Marvels & Tales* 24.1 (2010): 99–115.

Joosen, Vanessa, and Gillian Lathey, eds. *Grimms' Tales around the Globe: The Dynamics of Their International Reception.* Detroit: Wayne State University Press, 2014.

Kaindl, Klaus, and Berthold Friemel. *Die Brüder Grimm in Berlin.* Stuttgart: Hirzel Verlag, 2004.

Kamenetsky, Christa. *The Brothers Grimm and Their Critics: Folktales and the Quest for Meaning.* Athens: Ohio University Press, 1992.

Kérchy, Anna, ed. *Postmodern Reinterpretations of Fairy Tales: How Applying New Methods Generates New Beginnings.* Lewiston, NY: Edwin Mellen Press, 2011.

Knoch, Linda. *Praxisbuch Märchen: Verstehen-Deuten-Umsetzen.* Gütersloh: Gütersloher Verlagshaus, 2001.

Köhler-Zulch, Ines. "Der Diskurs über den Ton: Zur Präsentation von Märchen und Sagen in Sammlungen des 19. Jahrhunderts." In *Homo narrans: Studien zur populären Erzählkultur,* ed. Christoph Schmitt. Münster: 1999, 25–50.

———. "Heinrich Pröhle: A Successor to the Brothers Grimm." In *The Reception of Grimms' Fairy Tales: Responses, Reactions, Revisions,* ed. Donald Haase. Detroit: Wayne State University Press, 1993, 41–58.

Kosok, Heinz. "Thomas Croker, die Brüder Grimm und die irische Erzählliteratur." In *"Daß gepflegt werde der feste Buchstab": Festschrift für Heinz Rölleke zum 65. Geburtstag am 6. November 2001,* ed. Lothar Bluhm and Achim Hölter. Trier: Wissenschaftlicher Verlag Trier, 2001, 288–302.

Kready, Laura. *A Study of Fairy Tales.* Boston: Houghton Mifflin, 1916.

Kujundžić, Nada. "Didactic Tales, Formula Tales, and Tall Tales in Grimms' *Kinder- und Hausmärchen.*" *Libri & Liberi* 1.2 (2012): 179–96.

Kukkonen, Karin. "Popular Cultural Memory: Comics, Communities and Context Knowledge." *Nordcom Review* 29 (2008): 261–73.

Kvideland, Reimund. "The Collecting and Study of Tales in Scandinavia." In *A Companion to the Fairy Tale,* ed. Hilda Ellis Davidson and Anna Chaudhri. Cambridge: D. S. Brewer, 2003, 159–68.

Kyritsi, Maria-Venetia. "The Untranslated Grimms' *Kinder- und Hausmärchen.* Tales of Violence and Terror." *New Review of Children's Literature and Librarianship* 10/1 (2004): 27–40.

Landry, Tristan. *La mémoire du conte folklorique de l'oral à l'écrit: Les freres Grimm et Afanas̓ev.* Laval, Canada: Les Presses de l'Université Laval, 2005.

Lathey, Gillian. *The Role of Translators in Children's Literature: Invisible Storytellers.* New York: Routledge, 2010.

Leerssen, Joep. "From Bökendorf to Berlin: Private Careers, Public Sphere, and How the Past Changed in Jacob Grimm's Lifetime." In *Free Access to the Past: Romanticism, Cultural Heritage and the Nation,* ed. Lotte Jensen, Joep Leerssen, and Marita Mathijsen. Leiden, Netherlands: Brill Academic Publishers, 2009. 55–70.

———. *National Thought in Europe: A Cultural History.* Amsterdam: Amsterdam University Press, 2006.

Lefftz, Joseph, ed. *Märchen der Brüder Grimm: Urfassung nach der Originalhandschrift der Abtei Ölenberg im Elsass.* Heidelberg: C. Winter, 1927.

Leitzmann, Albert, ed. *Briefwechsel der Brüder Jacob und Wilhelm Grimm mit Karl Lachmann.* Vol. 1. Jena: Verlag der Frommannschen Buchhandlung, 1927.

Lysaght, Patricia. "The Wonder Tale in Ireland." In *A Companion to the Fairy Tale,* ed. Hilda Ellis Davidson and Anna Chaudhri. Cambridge, UK: D. S. Brewer, 2003, 169–90.

Magnus-Johnston, Kendra. "'Reeling In' Grimm Masculinities: Hucksters, Cross-Dressers, and Ninnies." *Marvels & Tales* 27.1 (2013): 65–88.

Manna, Anthony. "The Americanization of the Brothers Grimm: Or, Tom Davenport's Film Adaptation of German Folktales." *Children's Literature Association Quarterly* 13 (1998): 142–45.

Martus, Steffen. *Die Brüder Grimm: Eine Biografie.* Berlin: Rowohlt, 2009.

Mazenauer, Beat, and Severin Perrig. *Wie Dornröschen seine Unschuld gewann: Archäologie der Märchen.* Leipzig: Gustav Kiepeneuer, 1995.

McGrady, Donald. "Were Sercambi's Novelle Known from the Middle Ages On?" *Italica* 57.1 (Spring, 1980): 3–18.

Michaelis-Jena, Ruth. "Edgar and John Edward Taylor, die ersten englischen Übersetzer der Kinder- und Hausmärchen." In *Brüder Grimm Gedenken,* ed. Ludwig Denecke, vol. 2. Marburg: N. G. Elwert, 1975, 183–202.

———. "Oral Tradition and the Brothers Grimm." *Folklore* 82.4 (1971): 265–75.

Mieder, Wolfgang. *Tradition and Innovation in Folk Literature.* Hanover, NH: University Press of New England, 1987.

Miller, Alice. *The Body Never Lies: The Lingering Effects of Cruel Parenting.* Trans. Andrew Jenkins. New York: W. W. Norton, 2005.

Moen, Kristian. *Film and Fairy Tales: The Birth of Modern Fantasy.* London: I. B. Tauris, 2013.

Motzkin, Gabriel. "Memory and Cultural Translation." In *The Translatability of Cultures: Figurations of the Space Between,* ed. Sanford Budick and Wolfgang Iser. Stanford, CA: Stanford University Press, 1996, 265–81.

Naithani, Sadhana. *Relocating Folklore in Postwar Germany: The Contribution of Lutz Röhrich.* Jackson: University Press of Mississippi, 2013.

Neumann, Siegfried. "The Brothers Grimm as Collectors and Editors of German Folktales." In *The Reception of Grimms' Fairy Tales: Response, Reactions, Revisions*, ed. Donald Haase. Detroit: Wayne State University Press, 1993, 4–40.

———. "Volksmärchen und Erzählerpersönlichkeit." In *Sichtweisen in der Märchenforschung*, ed. Siegfried Neumann and Christoph Schmitt. Baltmannsweiler: Schneider Verlag Hohengehren, 2013, 69–93.

Neumann, Siegfried, and Christoph Schmitt, eds. *Sichtweisen in der Märchenforschung*. Baltmannsweiler: Schneider Verlag Hohengehren, 2013.

Nicholson, Peter. "The Two Versions of Sercambi's Novelle." *Italica* 53.2 (summer 1976): 201–13.

Onions, C. T., ed. *The Oxford Universal Dictionary on Historical Principles*. 3rd. rev. ed. Oxford, UK: Oxford University Press, 1944.

Pagel, Mark. *Wired for Culture: The Natural History of Human Cooperation*. London: Penguin, 2012.

Paradiž, Valerie. *Clever Maids: The Secret History of the Grimm Fairy Tales*. New York: Basic Books, 2005.

Patten, Robert. "George Cruikshank's Grimm Humor." In *Imagination on a Long Rein: English Literature Illustrated*, ed. Joachim Müller. Marburg: Jonas, 1988, 13–28.

———. *George Cruikshank: Life, Times, and Art*. 2 vols. New Brunswick, NJ: Rutgers University Press, 1992.

Peck, Jeffrey. "'In the Beginning Was the Word': Germany and the Origins of German Studies." In *Medievalism and the Modernist Temper*, ed. R. Howard Bloch and Stephen Nichols. Baltimore: Johns Hopkins University Press, 1996, 127–47.

Pertler, Cordula, and Pertler, Reinhold. *Kinder in der Märchenwerkstatt: Kreative Spiel- und Projektideen*. Munich: Don Bosco Medien, 2009.

Pochmann, Henry. *German Culture in America: Philosophical and Literary Influences, 1600–1900*. Madison: University of Wisconsin Press, 1957.

Pöge-Alder, Katrin. *Märchenforschung: Theorien, Methoden, Interpretationen: Eine Einführung*. 2nd rev. ed. Tübingen: Günter Narr Verlag, 2011.

Rearick, Charles. *Beyond the Enlightenment: Historians and Folklore in Nineteenth Century France*. Bloomington: Indiana University Press, 1974.

Rebel, Hermann. *When Women Held the Dragon's Tongue and Other Essays in Historical Anthropology*. New York: Berghahn Books, 2010.

Rigney, Anne. *Imperfect Histories: The Elusive Past and the Legacy of Romantic Historicism*. Ithaca, NY: Cornell University Press, 2001.

Riordan, James. "Russian Fairy Tales and Their Collectors." In *A Companion to the Fairy Tale*, ed. Hilda Ellis Davidson and Anna Chaudhri. Cambridge, UK: D. S. Brewer, 2003, 217–26.

Robinson, Orrin. *Grimm Language: Grammar, Gender, and Genuineness in the Fairy Tales*. Amsterdam: John Benjamins, 2010.

Rochère, Martine Hennard Dutheil de, and Véronique Dasen, eds. *Des* Fata *aux* fées: regards croisés de l'Antiquité à nos jours. Special issue of *Études de Lettres*, 289–; Lausanne: Université de Lausanne, 2009.

Röhrich, Lutz. *Folktales and Reality*. Trans. Peter Tokofsky. Bloomington: Indiana University Press, 1991.

———. *Wage es, den Frosch zu küssen: Das Grimmsche Märchen Nummer Eins in seinen Wandlungen*. Cologne: Eugen Diederichs Verlag, 1987.

Rölleke, Heinz, ed. *Die Märchen der Brüder Grimm*. Munich: Artemis, 1985.

———. *Die Märchen der Brüder Grimm: Eine Einfürhung*. Stuttgart: Philipp Reclam, 2004.

———. *Die Märchen der Brüder Grimm: Quellen und Studien*. Trier: Wissenschaftlicher Verlag Trier, 2000.

———. *Es war einmal . . . Die wahren Märchen der Brüder Grimm und wer sie ihnen erzählte*. Illustr. Albert Schindehütte. Frankfurt am Main: Eichorn, 2011.

———. *Märchen aus dem Nachlaß der Brüder Grimm*. 3rd rev. ed. Bonn: Bouvier, 1983.

———. *"Wo das Wünschen noch geholfen hat." Gesammelte Aufsätze zu den "Kinder- und Hausmärchen" der Brüder Grimm*. Bonn: Bouvier, 1985.

Ruf, Theodor. *Die Schöne aus dem Glassarg: Schneewittchens märchenhaftes und wirkliches Leben*. Würzburg: Königshausen und Neumann, 1995.

Schacker, Jennifer. *National Dreams: The Remaking of Fairy Tales in Nineteenth Century England*. Philadelphia: University of Pennsylvania Press, 2003.

Schede, Hans-Georg. *Die Brüder Grimm*. Rev. ed. Hanau: CoCon-Verlag, 2009.

Schmitt, Christoph, ed. *Erzählkulturen im Medienwandel*. Münster: Waxmann, 2008.

Schuller, Wolfgang, and D. M. Erwin Wittstock. "Zu den Quellenangaben bei Herodot und den Brüdern Grimm." *Studia Antiqua et Archaeologica* 9 (2003): 173–85.

Schultz, Franz, ed. *Die Märchen der Brüder Grimm in der Urform*. Offenbach: Klingspor, 1924.

Scott, Sir Walter. *The Letters of Sir Walter Scott*. Ed. Herbert Grierson. Vol. 7. London: Constable, 1934.

Sennett, Richard. *Together: The Rituals, Pleasures and Politics of Cooperation*. New Haven, CT: Yale University Press, 2012.

Sennewald, Jens. *Das Buch, das Wir Sind: Zur Poetik der "Kinder- und Hausmärchen, gesammelt durch die Brüder Grimm."* Würzbrug: Königshausen & Neumann, 2004.

Shen, Quinna. "Barometers of GDR Cultural Politics: Contextualizing the DEFA Grimm Adaptations." *Marvels & Tales* 25.1 (2011): 70–95.

Smidt, Thorsten, ed. *Expedition Grimm*. Leipzig: Sandstein Verlag, 2013.

Sokolov, Y. M. *Russian Folklore*. Hatboro, PA: Folklore Associates, 1966.

Steig, Reinhold. *Clemens Brentatno und die Brüder Grimm*. Stuttgart: J. G. Cotta'sche Buchhandlung, 1914.

———. *Goethe und die Brüder Grimm*. Berlin: Hertz, 1892.

Steig, Reinhold, and Herman Grimm, eds. *Achim von Arnim und die ihm nahe standen*. Vol. 3. Stuttgart: J. G. Cotta'schen Buchhandlung, 1904.

Strohbach, Hermann, ed. *Geschichte der deutschen Volksdichtung*. Berlin: Akademie-Verlag, 1981.

Sumpter, Caroline. "Fairy Tale and Folklore in the Nineteenth Century." *Literature Compass* 6.3 (2009): 785–98.

Sutton, Martin. *The Sin-Complex: A Critical Study of English Versions of the Grimms' Kinder- und Hausmärchen in the Nineteenth Century*. Kassel: Schriften der Brüder Grimm-Gesellschaft, 1996.

Tatar, Maria. *The Hard Facts of the Grimms' Fairy Tales*. Princeton, NJ: Princeton University Press, 1987.

Taylor, Edgar. "German Popular and Traditionary Literature." *New Monthly Magazine and Literary Journal* 2 (1821): 146–52, 329–36, 537–44; and 4 (1822): 289–96.

Thesz, Nicole. "Nature Romanticism and the Grimms' Tales: An Ecocritical Approach to Günter Grass's *The Flounder* and *The Rat*." *Marvels & Tales* 25.1 (2011): 96–116.

Tomasello, Michael. *The Cultural Origins of Human Cognition*. Cambridge, MA: Harvard University Press, 1999.

———. *A Natural History of Human Thinking*. Cambridge, MA: Harvard University Press, 2014.

———. *The Origins of Communication*. Cambridge, MA: MIT Press, 2008.

———. *Why We Cooperate*. Cambridge, MA: MIT Press, 2009.

Tuleja, Tad. "Invented Tradition." In *Folklore: An Encyclopedia of Beliefs, Customs, Tales, Music, and Art*, ed. Thomas Green. Santa Barbara, CA: ABC-CLIO, 1997, 466–68.

Turner, Kay, and Pauline Greenhill, eds. *Transgressive Tales: Queering the Grimms*. Detroit: Wayne State University Press, 2012.

Uther, Hans-Jörg. "Die Brüder Grimm als Sammler von Märchen und Sagen." In *Die Grimms—Kultur und Politik*, ed. Bernd Heidenreich and Ewald Grothe. 2nd rev. ed. Frankfurt am Main: Societäts-Verlag, 2008, 81–137.

———. *Handbuch zu den "Kinder- und Hausmärchen der Brüder Grimm: Entstehung—Wirkung—Interpretation*. Berlin: Walter de Gruyter, 2008.

———. *The Types of International Folktales: A Classification and Bibliography*. 3 vols. Ff Communications No. 284. Helsinki: Suomalainen Tiedeakatemia, 2004.

Velay-Vallantin, Catherine. "Charles Perrault, la conteuse et la fabuliste: L'image dans le tapis." *Féeries* 7 (2010): 95–121.

Venzke, Andreas. *Die Brüder Grimm und das Rätsel des Froschkönigs*. Würzburg: Arena Verlag, 2012.

Vivarelli, Ann West. "Giovanni Sercambi's *Novelle* and the Legacy of Boccaccio." *MLN* 90 (1975): 109–26.

Wilson, Edward O. *The Social Conquest of Earth*. New York: W. W. Norton, 2012.

Wojcik-Andrews, Ian. *Children's Films: History, Ideology, Pedagogy, Theory*. New York: Routledge, 2000.

Zimmermann, Harm-Peer, ed. *Zwischen Identität und Image: Die Popularität der Brüder Grimm in Hessen*. Marburg: Jonas Verlag, 2009.

Ziolkowski, Jan. "A Fairy Tale before Fairy Tales: Egbert of Liège's 'De puellis a lupellis seruata' and the Medieval Background of 'Little Red Riding Hood.'" *Speculum* (1992): 549–75.

———. *Fairy Tales from Before Fairy Tales: The Medieval Latin Past of Wonderful Lies*. Ann Arbor: University of Michigan Press, 2006.

———. "Old Wives' Tales: Classicism and Anticlassicism from Apuleius to Chaucer." *Journal of Medieval Latin* 12 (2002): 90–113.

Zipes, Jack. *The Brothers Grimm: From Enchanted Forests to the Modern World* [1988]. Rev. and expanded 2nd ed. New York: Palgrave, 2002.

———. *The Enchanted Screen: The Unknown History of Fairy-Tale Films*. New York: Routledge, 2010.

Zirnbauer, Heinz. "Grimms Märchen mit englischen Augen. Eine Studie zur Entwicklung der Illustration von Grimms Märchen in englischer Übersetzung von 1823 bis 1970." In *Brüder Grimm Gedenken*, ed. Ludwig Denecke, vol. 2. Marburg: N. G. Elwert, 1975. 203–41.

Zuk, Marlene. *Paleofantasy: What Evolution Really Tells Us about Sex, Diet, and How We Live*. New York: Norton, 2013.

FILMOGRAPHY

All films are listed chronologically in each section.

General List

THE WONDERFUL WORLD OF THE BROTHERS GRIMM (1962)

USA, color, 135 minutes
Director: Henry Levin and George Pal
Screenplay: David Harmon, Charles Beamont
Music: Leigh Harline
Camera: Paul Vogel
Producer: George Pal
Cast: Laurence Harvey, Karlheinz Böhm, Claire Bloom, Walter Slezak, Barbara Eden

JASON AND THE ARGONAUTS (1963)

USA, color, 104 minutes
Director: Don Chaffey
Screenplay: Jan Read, Beverley Cross
Music: Bernard Hermann
Camera: Wilkie Cooper
Producers: Charles Schneer, Ray Harryhausen
Cast: Todd Armstrong, Nancy Kovack, Laurence Naismith, Michael Gwynn,
    Douglas Wilmer, Nigel Green

ONCE UPON A BROTHERS GRIMM (1977)

USA, color, 120 minutes
Director: Norman Campbell
Screenplay: Jean Holloway
Music: Mitch Leigh
Camera: Jerry Greene
Producers: Bernard Rothman, Jack Wohl
Cast: Dean Jones, Paul Sand, Betsy Beard, Sorrell Brooke, Arte Johnson, Ruth Buzzi

THE FOOL OF THE WORLD AND THE FLYING SHIP (1990)

UK, animation, color, 60 minutes
Director: Francis Vose
Screenplay: John Hambley
Music: Mike Harding
Camera: Mark Stewart

Producer: Bruce Taylor
Voiceover: David Suchet, Robin Bailey, Maurice Denham, Jimmy Hibbert

JASON AND THE ARGONAUTS (2000)

USA, color, 180 minutes
Director: Nick Willing
Screenplay: Matthew Faulk, Mark Skeet
Music: Simon Boswell
Camera: Sergey Koslov
Producers: Robert Halm, Sr., Dyson Lowell
Cast: Jason London, Frank Langella, Natasha HenstridgJason London, Frank Langella, Natasha Henstridg

IN THIS VERY MOMENT (*MILCHWALD*, 2003)

Germany, color, 87 minutes
Director: Christoph Hochhäusler
Screenplay: Benjamin Heisenberg, Christoph Hochhäusler
Music: Benedikt Schiefer
Camera: Ali Olay Gözkaya
Producers: Clarens Grollmann, Mario Stefan
Cast: Sophie Charlotte Conrad, Leo Bruckmann, Judith Engel, Horst-Günter Marx, Miroslaw Baka

THE BROTHERS GRIMM (2005)

USA, color, 118 minutes
Director: Terry Gilliam
Screenplay: Ehren Kruger
Music: Dario Marianelli
Camera: Newton Thomas Sigel
Producers: Daniel Bobker, Charles Roven
Cast: Petr Ratimec, Matt Damon, Heath Ledger

THE FISHERMAN AND HIS WIFE (*DER FISCHER UND SEINE FRAU*, 2005)

Germany, color, 87 minutes
Director: Doris Dörrie
Screenplay: Doris Dörrie
Camera: Rainer Klausmann
Producers: Bernd Eichinger, Franx X. Gerstl
Cast: Alexandra Maria Lara, Christian Ulmen, Simon Verhoeven. Young-Shin Kim

SEVEN DWARFS—MEN ALONE IN THE FOREST (*7 ZWERGE—MÄNNER ALLEIN IM WALD*, 2004)

Germany, color, 95 minutes
Director: Sven Unterwaldt

Screenplay: Bernd Eilert, Otto Walkes, Sven Unterwaldt
Music: Joja Wendt
Camera: Jo Heim
Producers: Bernd Eilert, Otto Walkes, Douglas Welbat
Cast: Otto Waalkes, Mirco Nontschew, Boris Aljinovic, Heinz Hoenig, Marcus Majowski, Martin Schneider, Ralf Schmitz, Cosma Shiva Hagen, Nina Hagen

SEVEN DWARFS—THE FOREST IS NOT ENOUGH (*7 ZWERGE—DER WALD IST NICHT GENUG*, 2006)

Germany, color, 95 minutes
Director: Sven Unterwaldt
Screenplay: Bernd Eilert, Otto Walkes, Sven Unterwaldt
Music: Joja Wendt
Camera: Peter von Haller
Producers: Bernd Eilert, Otto Walkes, Douglas Welbat
Cast: Otto Waalkes, Mirco Nontschew, Boris Aljinovic, Heinz Hoenig, Marcus Majowski, Martin Schneider, Ralf Schmitz, Cosma Shiva Hagen, Nina Hagen

HOODWINKED TOO! HOOD VS. EVIL (2011)

USA, color, animation, 86 minutes
Director: Mike Disa
Screenplay: Cory Edwards, Tom Edwards, Mike Disa, Tom Leech
Music: Murray Gold, Tom Keane, Dean landon
Art Direction: Ryan Carlson
Producers: Joan Collins Carey, Maurice Kanbar
Voiceover: Glenn Close, Hayden Panettiere, Cheech Mann, Patrick Warburton, Joan Cusick, Bill Haden, Amy Poehler

BRAVE (2012)

USA, color, 93 minutes
Director: Mark Andrews, Brenda Chapman
Screenplay: Brenda Chapman, Mark Andrews, Steve Purcell, Ireven Mecchi
Music: Patrick Doyle
Producer: Katherine Sarafian
Voiceover: Kelly Macdonald, Billy Connolly, Emma Thompson

Hansel and Gretel

BREAD CRUMBS (2011)

USA, color, 88 minutes
Director: Mike Nichols
Screenplay: Anthony Masi, Sam Freeman
Music: Matt Sorensen
Camera: Ian Dudley

Producers: Pamela DeRanieri, Ronald DeRanieri
Cast: Jim Barnes, Steve Cary, Amy Crowdis. Alana Curry. Michael Goodin, Mari-
    anne Hagan, Rex Irons, Kristina Klebe, Mike Nichols, Douglas Nyback, Dan
    Shaked, Zoe Sloane, Shira Weitz, Jonathan Whitcup, Darbi Worley

WITCHSLAYER GRETEL (2012)

USA, color
Director: Mario Azzopardi
Screenplay: Angela Mancuso, Brook Durham
Music: Stacy Hersh
Camera: Russ Goozee
Producer: Robert Vaughn
Cast: Paul McGillion, Emilie Ullerup, Shannen Doherty

HANSEL & GRETEL: WITCH HUNTERS (2013)

USA, color, 88 minutes
Director: Tommy Wirkola
Screenplay: Tommy Wirkola
Music: Atli Örvarsson
Camera: Michael Bonvillain
Producers: Will Ferrell, Beau Flynn, Chris Henchy
Cast: Jeremy Renner, Gemma Arterton, Famke Janssen

HANSEL AND GRETEL (2013)

USA, color, 90 minutes
Director: Anthony Ferrante
Screenplay: Jose Prendes
Music: Alan Howarth
Camera: Ben Demaree
Producer: Dan Michael Latt
Cast: Dee Wallace, Stephanie Greco, Brent Lydic

HANSEL & GRETEL: WARRIORS OF WITCHCRAFT (2013)

USA, color, 83 minutes
Director: David DeCoteau
Screenplay: Larson Tretter
Music: Harry Manfredini
Camera: David De Couteau
Producers: Jeffrey Schenck, John Schouweiler
Cast: Fivel Stewart, Booboo Stewart, Eric Roberts

H AND G (2013)

Canada, color, 95 minutes
Director: Danishka Esterhazy

Screenplay: Danishka Esterhazy, Rebecca Gibson
Music: Joe Silva
Camera: Andrew Luczenczyn
Producers: Rebecca Gibson, Ashley Hirt, Rebecca Sandulak
Cast: Breazy Diduck-Wilson, Annika Elyse Irving

Jack and the Beanstalk

JACK AND THE BEANSTALK: THE REAL STORY (2001)

USA, color, 180 minutes
Director: Brian Henson
Screenplay: James Hart, Brian Henson
Music: Rupert Gregson-Williams
Camera: John Fenner
Producers: Martim Baker, Thomas Smith
Cast: Matthew Modine, Vanessa Redgrave, Mia Sara

JACK AND THE BEANSTALK (2010)

USA, color, 94 minutes
Director: Gary Tunnicliffe
Screenplay: Flip Kobler, Cindy Marcus
Music: Randy Miller
Camera: Brian Baugh
Producers: Gary DePew, Gary Tunnicliffe
Cast: Paul McGillion, Emilie Ullerup, Shannen Doherty

JACK THE GIANT SLAYER (2013)

USA, color, 114 minutes
Director: Bryan Singer
Screenplay: Darren Lemke, Christopher McQuarrie , Dan Studney
Music: John Ottman
Camera: Newton Thomas Sigel
Producers: Bryan Singer, Richard Brener, Michael Disco, David Dobkin
Cast: Nicholas Hoult, Ewan McGregor, Stanley Tucci , Eleanor Tomlinson

Little Red Riding Hood

HANNA (2011)

USA, color, 111 minutes
Director: Joe Wright
Screenplay: Seth Lochhead, David Farr
Music: Tom Rowlands, Ed Simmons
Camera: Alwin Küchler
Producers: Marty Edelstein, Leslie Holleran, Scott Nemes

Cast: Saoirse Ronan, Eric Bana, Vicky Krieps, Cate Blanchett, Paris Arrowsmith, John Macmillan, Tim Beckmann

RED RIDING HOOD (2011)

USA, color, 100 minutes
Director: Catherine Hardwicke
Screenplay: David Johnson
Music: Alex Heffes, Brian Reitzell
Camera: Mandy Walker
Producer: Leonard DiCaprio, Jennifer Killoran, Julie Yom
Cast: Amanda Seyfried, Gary Oldman, Billy Burke, Julie Christie, Shiloh Fernandez, Max Irons

Sleeping Beauty

SLEEPING BETTY (2007)

Canada, animation, 9 minutes
Director: Claude Cloutier
Screenplay: Claude Cloutier
Music: Pierre Yves Drapeau
Producer: Marcel Jean

THE SLEEPING BEAUTY (*LA BELLE ENDORMIE*, 2010)

France, color, 82 minutes
Director: Catherine Breillat
Screenplay: Catherine Breillat
Camera: Denis Lenoir
Producers: Sylvette Frydman, Jean-François Lepetit
Cast: Carla Besnaïnou, Julia Artamonov, Kerian Mayan, David Chausse , Luna Charpentier, Rhizlaine El Cohen, Delia Bouglione-Romanès, Diana Rudychenko

SLEEPING BEAUTY (2011)

Australia, color, 102 minutes
Director: Julia Leigh
Screenplay: Julia Leigh
Music: Ben Frost
Camera: Geoffrey Simpson
Producers: Jessica Brentnall, Timothy White, Sasha Burrows, Jamie Hilton
Cast: Emily Browning, Rachel Blake, Ewen Leslie, Michael Dorman, Mirrah Foulkes, Henry Nixon

Snow White

SNOW WHITE: A DEADLY SUMMER (2012)

USA, color, 85 minutes

Director: David DeCoteau
Screenplay: Barbara Kymlicka
Music: Harry Fredini
Camera: David DeCoteau
Cast: Maureen McCormick, Eric Roberts, Tim Abell

GRIMM'S SNOW WHITE (2012)

USA, color, 90 minutes
Director: Rachel Goldenberg
Screenplay: Naomi L. Selfman
Music: Chris Ridenhour
Camera: Alexander Yellen
Cast: Jane March, Eliza Bennett, Jamie Thomas King

BLANCANIEVES (2012)

Spain, black and white, 104 minutes
Director: Pablo Berger
Screenplay: Pablo Berger
Music: Alfonso de Vilallonga
Camera: Kiko de la Rica
Producers: Pablo Berger, Jérome Vidal
Cast: Maribel Verdú, Daniel Giménez Cacho, Ángela Molina

MIRROR, MIRROR (2012)

USA, color, 103 minutes
Director: Tarsem Singh
Screenplay: Jason Keller, Marc Klein, Melisa, Wallack
Music: Alan Menken
Camera: Brendan Galvin
Producers: Bernie Goldmann, Ryan Kavanaugh
Cast: Julia Roberts, Lily Collins, Armie Hammer, Nathan Lane

SNOW WHITE AND THE HUNTSMAN (2012)

USA, color, 127 minutes
Director: Rupert Sanders
Screenplay: Evan Daugherty, John Lee Hancock, Hossein Amini
Music: James Newton Howard
Camera: Greig Fraser
Producer: Joe Roth
Cast: Kristen Stewart, Charlize Theron, Chris Hemsworth, Sam Claflin, Ian
    McShane

INDEX

Note: Page numbers in italics indicate illustrations.